Rust for the IoT

Building Internet of Things Apps with Rust and Raspberry Pi

Joseph Faisal Nusairat

Apress®

Rust for the IoT: Building Internet of Things Apps with Rust and Raspberry Pi

Joseph Faisal Nusairat
Scottsdale, AZ, USA

ISBN-13 (pbk): 978-1-4842-5859-0   ISBN-13 (electronic): 978-1-4842-5860-6
https://doi.org/10.1007/978-1-4842-5860-6

Managing Director, Apress Media LLC: Welmoed Spahr
Acquisitions Editor: Steve Anglin
Development Editor: Matthew Moodie
Coordinating Editor: Mark Powers

Cover designed by eStudioCalamar

Cover image by Maarten van den Heuvel on Unsplash (www.unsplash.com)

Distributed to the book trade worldwide by Apress Media, LLC, 1 New York Plaza, New York, NY 10004, U.S.A. Phone 1-800-SPRINGER, fax (201) 348-4505, e-mail orders-ny@springer-sbm.com, or visit www.springeronline.com. Apress Media, LLC is a California LLC and the sole member (owner) is Springer Science + Business Media Finance Inc (SSBM Finance Inc). SSBM Finance Inc is a **Delaware** corporation.

For information on translations, please e-mail booktranslations@springernature.com; for reprint, paperback, or audio rights, please e-mail bookpermissions@springernature.com.

Apress titles may be purchased in bulk for academic, corporate, or promotional use. eBook versions and licenses are also available for most titles. For more information, reference our Print and eBook Bulk Sales web page at http://www.apress.com/bulk-sales.

Any source code or other supplementary material referenced by the author in this book is available to readers on GitHub via the book's product page, located at www.apress.com/9781484258590. For more detailed information, please visit http://www.apress.com/source-code.

Printed on acid-free paper

To my beautiful, wonderful, wife Heba Fayed, your patience and support is what got this book finished. Thank you for everything you do.

Table of Contents

About the Author

Joseph Faisal Nusairat, author of three Apress books, is currently a Senior Staff Engineer at Tesla, developing the next generation of products for the Platform Engineering team. He has experience in a full range of the development life cycle from requirements gathering, to full stack development, to production support of applications, in addition to speaking, coaching, and training of software. Joseph started his career in 1997 doing primarily Java/JVM full stack applications. In the Java realm, he became proficient and gave talks on Java, Groovy, Scala, Kotlin, and Clojure. In the last few years, other languages like Rust, Go, and Elixir have caught not only his interest but his dedication. Over the years, he's learned to create code that not only is readable but maintainable all while trying to minimize its memory footprint and maximizing performance. His career has led through a variety of industries from banking, insurance, fraud, retailers, defense, and now electric cars. Joseph is a graduate of Ohio University with dual degrees in Computer Science and Microbiology with a minor in Chemistry.

Joseph is a published author, speaker, and trainer. He can be found on twitter, github, and gitlab as @nusairat.

About the Technical Reviewer

 **Kan-Ru Chen** is a Software Engineer at Amazon who builds cloud services for millions of customers. Before that, Kan-Ru worked six years at Mozilla, tuning Firefox performance. He was exposed to the Rust programming language while at Mozilla and fell in love with it.

At his free time, he enjoys contributing to free and open source projects, like Rust. He is also a long-time Debian Developer. His main areas of interest include programming languages, parser, compiler, performance, and security.

You can reach him at kanru.rust [at] kanru.info or on Twitter at @kanru.

Acknowledgments

Technical books are one of the biggest labors of love for those who write. They most often don't make much money for the amount of time we spent working on them and are mostly written to fulfill a dream of writing something we are passionate about and a desire to communicate with you that information. This dream is not fulfilled by just the author, there are many people along the way that help both directly and indirectly, and I would be remiss if I did not thank them for getting me there.

First, the love of my life, Heba. You met me when I first started writing this book and have supported me every step of the way. This included many weekends we couldn't go out because I was working on the book, many vacations I had my laptop open, and many late nights I didn't go to bed till late because of it. Not only did you support me but you helped me with some of the diagrams, as well as proofreading the book to tell me when my explanations made no sense. You are amazing!

Mac Liaw, you've been not only a great friend but an awesome mentor as well. You've given me opportunities for not only new jobs, but you were there responding to texts at 1 a.m. when I was getting stuck on topics for the book. Your help was greatly appreciated. Also thank you for the excellent advice on where to propose to Heba; it made that day unforgettable.

Next my technical reviewer Kan-Ru Chen, I can't thank you enough; you did cause my author reviews to run longer, but you saved my butt by pointing out in detail sections that were convoluted, incorrect, or could have been written better. Often we are pushed to get things done in a timely fashion and one ends up rushing. I'm grateful to have had you help fix those errors and provide great feedback. And Mark Powers, my editor, who I initially told this book will be done in September or late fall, thank you for your patience in letting me put together an enormous set of information even though it meant missing quite a few deadlines.

Joseph Swager, the man who dragged me out to the bay and gave me a shot in some new directions in my work life and also whose idea it was to write this book in the first place and was initially my coauthor, you unfortunately had to bail a few chapters in due to work, but hopefully our shared vision is what this book ended up being. Next book we'll do!

ACKNOWLEDGMENTS

Additionally, my past work experience has been littered with many people who've helped not only make me a better developer but helped me in my career and world advice. You all have been there to help guide and give feedback and support when needed. Brian Sam-Bodden, founder of Integrallis Software, you got me into writing my first book, giving my first presentation, never would I have gotten this far without you. Jason Warner, you gave me my first job in Arizona, and continue to give great advice to this day. (Incidentally, he has a GitHub page where you can get great advice/perspective too; I say we force him to keep answering questions for years to come (github.com/jasoncwarner/ama).)

And a final few folks: Jeff Hart, thanks for all your technical wisdom on cloud systems and for helping me to debug my Rust code at random times. Aaron Kark, we worked together 18 years ago, and 1 year ago, hopefully it doesn't take 17 more to work together again. Kelli Alexander and Veronica Martinez, thanks for being very supportive friends. I also want to give a final praise to my current team: Sheen, Ilia, Kouri, Konstantin, Clark, Ross, Issac, Crystal, and Nick, you are of the best groups of people I've ever had the pleasure of working with.

Lastly, thank you, the reader, for picking up and selecting this book. I really hope it helps you despite what errors may have snuck into the code. This book has taken more time than I initially had planned and has been one of the biggest labors of love in my professional career. I hope I've delivered something you can really learn from.

Very last, thank you mum, you're the best mother, grandma, person I know.

Preface

This book is for anyone with programming experience who wants to jump into the Internet of Things space. This book covers the set from cloud application building and deploying to creation of the Raspberry Pi application and communication between. While there are many crates in the Rust world to write applications, this book shows you which crates you will need and how to combine them together to create a working IoT cloud and device application. This book while not an advanced Rust language book does cover a few more advanced features. It is best to have at least some understanding before starting.

Chapter Listing

The book is composed of the following chapters:

- Chapter 1 – This covers what this book is going to solve; we tackle the issues and problems surrounding IoT applications and their architecture. We also go over the hardware that is needed for this book, and the chapter ends with some simple Rust examples.

- Chapter 2 – This starts with setting up and creating our first microservice, the `retrieval_svc`; this will set up simple calls to it and integrate and set up the database for it.

- Chapter 3 – This chapter is more heavily focused on the `upload_svc`, and in here we learn how to upload images and video files to store locally. We then parse the metadata out of the files and call the `retrieval_svc` to store their metadata.

- Chapter 4 – Back to the `retrieval_svc`, we add GraphQL to use on top of the web tier instead of pure RESTful endpoints. We also create the `mqtt_service` that will serve as our bridge to communicate between the back end and the Pi using MQTT.

- Chapter 5 – Enhancing both the `retrieval_svc` and the `mqtt_service` by using serialized binary data via Cap'n Proto to talk, instead of having the communication between the two be REST calls. Also on the `retrieval_svc` side, we add CQRS and eventual consistency to our graph mutations for comments.

- Chapter 6 – This adds using Auth0 to authenticate the user so that our database can identify a device to a user. We also add self-signed certificates to secure the communication of the MQTT.

- Chapter 7 – In this chapter, we learn how to create Docker images of all our microservices, combining them with Kubernetes and deploying to a cloud provider with Helm charts.

- Chapter 8 – This is our first hands-on chapter with the Raspberry Pi in which we will set up the heartbeat to communicate to the MQTT backend we created earlier.

- Chapter 9 – This incorporates the Sense HAT device to gather data about our environment to the Pi. The Sense HAT provides us a visual LED display, temperature sensors, and a joystick for interactions.

- Chapter 10 – In this chapter, we add a camera to the device which will allow us to do facial tracking and recording.

- Chapter 11 – This is one of the last chapters in which we incorporate the video camera to send data back to the cloud as well as allowing the Pi to receive recording commands from the cloud, and finally we allow the Pi to be used as a HomeKit device to show temperature and motion.

- Chapter 12 – This final short chapter discusses how we would build an ISO image for our given application and other bundling issues.

CHAPTER 1

Introduction

The Internet of Things (IoT) is a highly encompassing term that covers everything from your home network-connected camera to the oven that is Wi-Fi connected, all the way to your modern electric cars like the Tesla that are always connected to the network and almost always on. The most basic premise of IoT is a hardware device that is a connected network appliance. In modern days, that usually means Internet and almost always connected to a cloud service, but it can just as easily be a local area network.

Only in the last 10 years have we truly embraced the IoT model for not only offices and factories but for everyday living. The most common consumer IoT systems are the ones from or supported by Apple, Google, and Amazon that provide cameras, thermostats, doorbell, and lights. All of those devices can then be used in conjunction with each other and for home automation and control. While many of these devices are used for fun in a home, they have beneficial application for elderly care and for medical monitoring and even can be used in industrial and manufacturing components. Devices in factories can report on the status of how many components are rolling off the assembly line, if there is a failure at a point, or even throughput of a factory. Used in conjunction with machine learning, the possibilities are endless.

And while IoT as a term didn't make our way officially in the lexicon till 1999 by Kevin Ashton of Procter & Gamble, the concept has been around since well before that. What gave birth to IoT dates back to 1959 with the Egyptian-born Inventor Mohamed M. Atalla and Korean-born Dawon Kahng while working at Bell Labs in 1959. They created the MOSFET (metal-oxide-semiconductor field-effect transmitter) which is the basis for the semiconductor, which revolutionized electronics from huge tubes to the microchip components we have in our smart watches, phones, cameras, cars, and even your ovens. It would still take another 23 years though till someone at Carnegie Mellon decided to hook up monitoring a Coca-Cola machine for its inventory that would mark the first true IoT device, before anyone even thought of what IoT was, and then another 10 years before companies like Microsoft and Novell really proposed usable solutions. However, even then chips were expensive and relatively big. Today Raspberry Pi packs way more punch than the desktops of the 1990s, especially in the GPU department.

© Joseph Faisal Nusairat 2020

J. F. Nusairat, *Rust for the IoT*, https://doi.org/10.1007/978-1-4842-5860-6_1

Who Is This Book For?

This book is for anyone from your hobbyist to someone trying to create their own commercial IoT products. I guess for your hobbyist, there is the question of why. Purchasing IoT applications has become inexpensive, fairly customizable, and routine; why bother to create your own? And while one answer is simply for fun, another is that you want to create a fully customizable solution. And finally another answer that became even more apparent this year was ownership, that you are the sole owner. This importance became obvious to me in two cases this year. This first was with the Amazon-owned company Ring. They had had to let go of four employees due to privacy concerns that they had spied on customers snooping in on their feeds. And while this is likely the exception and not the rule, it still lends to the idea of wanting to create pipes that are 100% solely owned by you.[1] The second was Sonos, who after customers spent years buying components found out the older products will no longer be backward compatible, leaving many in the dark to use new software updates.[2] And while it would be hard to replicate the amount of code they write, the open source community that integrates with custom Pi components is growing and will help to live on even if it means you have to code it yourself.

This book is titled *Rust for the IoT*. Before we discuss what we are going to build, let's break out those two words further.

What Is IoT?

Internet of Things, or IoT, which will be used to reference it for the rest of the book, has become a new and ever-growing marketplace in the last few years, even though it's been around for decades. At its core, it's a network of devices that communicate with each other and often with the cloud.

The most common IoT systems are the ones from or supported by Apple, Google, and Amazon that provide cameras, thermostats, doorbell, and lights that all interact with each other. These devices in conjunction can be used in home automation and control.

---

[1] www.usatoday.com/story/tech/2020/01/10/amazons-ring-fired-employees-snooping-customers-camera-feeds/4429399002/

[2] https://nakedsecurity.sophos.com/2020/01/23/sonoss-tone-deaf-legacy-product-policy-angers-customers/

While many of these devices are used for fun in a home, they have beneficial application for elderly care and for medical monitoring and even can be used in industrial and manufacturing components.

In addition, IoT does not stop there; it's gained dominance in all realms of device use. Car companies have started adopting IoT to have a more fully connected car. Tesla started the trend, and others have really picked it up full speed and use the same concepts and features as your smart device. Incidentally, this is something I know quite a bit about because I was in charge of architecting and coding Over-The-Air (OTA) updates for one such car company.

For this book though, I am sticking to personal use in the home, since most people into IoT are home enthusiasts and because creating one for a car is a tad more expensive since you would need a car. But the same principles can be applied everywhere.

I have had an interest in IoT since the rudimentary RF devices you could purchase in the 1980s from RadioShack. Quite a bit has changed since then. We are now in an age where home automation is actually pretty good. We have cameras, devices, cloud, and voice integration, but there are still many improvements to be made. We feel this book could start you on your way as a hobbyist or even in a professional setting. Why Rust? When reviewing what languages we could use for both embedded board development and was extremely fast cloud throughput computing at a low cost, Rust kept coming up.

IoT 10K Foot Picture

IoT at its core is the concept of connectivity, having everything interconnected with each other; executing that is often not the most simple concept. In Figure 1-1, I have diagramed your basic IoT interactive diagram.

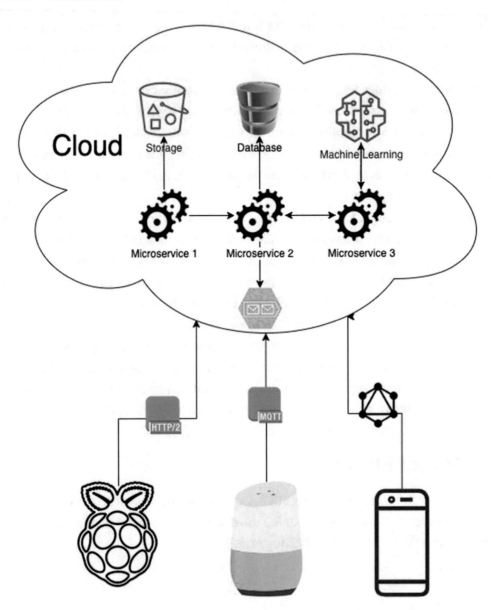

Figure 1-1. *Showing your standard IoT diagram*

Let's get a few takeaways from this diagram. You will notice at the bottom there are a few hardware devices and a mobile application. Hardware devices in our case will be a Raspberry Pi, but they could just as easily be your Google Home Hub, Alexa, or a car. These are all devices you are familiar with. The Raspberry Pi and Google Home Hub in the picture serve as endpoints that can play music, capture video, or record other information about their surroundings. The mobile devices then serve a role in communicating with those devices (in the case of the Google Home Hub, it serves a dual role, one in communicating and the other in capturing the world around it).

The end goal as we said is to have a fully connected system, so not only do these devices communicate with the cloud, but they receive communications back from the cloud. The communication back from the cloud can be due to input from your mobile application or could be a scheduled call. The pipes between represent this communication, but you will notice we have a variety of communication paths listed.

HTTPS

This is your standard HTTPS path. These paths exist often from the device to the cloud. Remember the endpoint in your cloud will have a static domain name like `rustfortheiot.xyz`. This domain name allows a constant path for the IoT device to talk to. The device can upload video or other large data and can download video, music, and other media content. And it's also available for anything that would require an immediate request/response, for example, if we wanted to know what the forecast was for today.

The downside to HTTPS connections is that if the server endpoints are down, if they are overloaded, they may be slow or not responsive at all. In addition, there is data that the device will send back that doesn't require a response.

The hardware is the core feature the reason we even have the rest of the diagram. These will give life to our commands. A car every time you drive is generating data on your speed, distance, and so on. Your home devices know when you turn on the lights and when you walk by a camera even if it's not recording; it's detecting the motion. For that data, HTTP may not even work or is overkill.

Message Queue

Message queues (MQs) you have often used with any publication/subscriber system and that in many ways are a few of the use cases we just described. If you are sending health data of your device, periodical temperature readings, this is all pub/sub type systems. The device wants to send the data to the cloud, but it doesn't care where the data eventually ends. MQs are battle tested to handle high loads and are not as often updated as your microservice updates. This means you can easily update your microservices without worrying about downtime of the application. In addition, if you need to take the microservice down for an extended time, you won't lose the data; it will receive it once it reconnects to the message queue.

We will use the message queue as the intermediary for sending messages back and then the HTTPS call from the hardware for retrieving videos. Also remember that the calls you will be making for HTTPS will be secure connections, and the MQ calls should be via Transport Layer Security (TLS). Now let's jump to the cloud. You will notice a fairly standard application layer with microservices, a database, and a bucket to store files in. In our case, we will used a local store for saving image and video files. Two other interesting items are the message queue (MQ) and machine learning. Machine learning (ML) is growing and really helps with IoT devices since often they generate so much data. We just mentioned all the data that the MQ can retrieve. This data is invaluable in being able to use ML to generate guides, suggestions, and adaptive feedback. We won't dive into machine learning in this book, that will be a book in of itself. If you are interested, you can read *Practical Machine Learning with Rust* (`www.apress.com/us/book/9781484251201`). The microservice architecture in the backend allows you to create a variety of small services you can scale independently of each other but can also communicate as if they are on one endpoint (we will discuss how to do this when we get to Chapter 7). These microservices can then talk to database, bucket stores (like S3), or the message queue. All of that backend will process data, serve as endpoints to route data from mobile to the device, and even send notifications either to the device or the mobile application.

Why Rust?

The next question that may come to mind is why did we pick Rust? If you look at most web applications, they aren't written in Rust; if you look at most board development, it isn't in Rust either. So why Rust? Rust is a multi-paradigm programming language that focuses on performance and safety. Rust, by what it allows you to do, has quite a bit more performance and safety implemented than other languages. The biggest way this is shown is in Rust's borrowing and ownership checks. Rust makes it so that there are specific rules around when a variable is borrowed, who owns it, and for how long they own it for. This has been the main attraction of Rust for many. The code becomes faster, less memory intensive, and less like to have two variables access each other at the same time. We will get into this more in the borrowing section. Stylistically, Rust is similar to languages like Go and has C-like syntax with pointers and references. And while some of the Rust crates lack the maturity of other languages, the language itself is continuously enhancing and added to.

Pre-requisites

While we are covering some Rust syntax at the end of this chapter, this is not an introduction to Rust. And while I don't think you need an advanced understanding of Rust, if you are familiar with other functional or imperative languages, then you should be able to get away with a basic understanding. However, if you don't have that background and have already purchased this book or are thinking of doing so not to fret, I'd suggest one of two options:

1. *Learn Rust* (`www.rust-lang.org/learn`) – Between reading the online book and the examples, you can gain quite a good understanding of book. The book is often updated and usually up to date. It's how I initially learned Rust.

2. *Beginning Rust* book (`www.apress.com/gp/book/9781484234679`) – Often it's easier to learn through longer books that will go into greater detail, and if that's what you need, *Beginning Rust* is for you.

In addition, throughout the book we are going to cover a number of topics from microservices, GraphQL, CQRS, Kubernetes, Docker, and more. And while I will provide some explanations and backgrounds for each technology we introduce, there are entire books devoted to each of those tools. If you ever feel you need to learn more, I would suggest looking online; we will give resource links during those chapters.

Components to Purchase

In the first half of this book, we will create a cloud application, and while we will be deploying that application to DigitalOcean cloud services, that isn't actually a requirement in building everything. Even then, we are picking DigitalOcean over services like AWS to mitigate the cost.

However, the second half of the book does deal with creating a Raspberry Pi–based application with a few add-ons. And while you will be able to follow along with this book without any cloud or hardware, to make the most of it, we will recommend a few cloud pieces and hardware that is designed to integrate with the software in this book. In the following section, I've given a list of hardware that you will need to purchase to fully follow along with the book. I've also provided the links on Amazon, but you can get the actual hardware from anywhere, and after some time the links may change:

1. Raspberry Pi 4 4 GB Starter Kit (`https://amzn.com/B07V5JTMV9`) – This kit will run about $100 but will include everything we need to get the basic Raspberry Pi up and running: from cables to connect it to your monitor, to power cables, and even a 32 GB SD card to be used for application and video storage. There are cheaper kits you can buy, but the all-in-ones will be a great starting point. Note: I selected and used the 4 for development, but if you used a 3, it should work as well; you will just have to adjust some endpoints when downloading OS software. The full Pi 4 kit will cost roughly $100.

2. Raspberry Pi Debug Cable (`https://amzn.com/B00QT7LQ88`) – This is a less than $10 cable that you can use to serially connect your Pi to your laptop without having to have a monitor, keyboard, or SSH ready. We will use this for initial setup, but if you are willing to hook your keyboard and monitor directly, it's not necessary.

3. Sense HAT (`https://amzn.com/B014HDG74S`) – The Sense HAT is an all-in-one unit that sits on all the Pi's GPIO pins that provides an 8 x 8 LED matrix display as well as numerous accelerometer, gyroscope, pressure, humidity, temperature sensors, and a joystick. We will be making use of the temperature, LED, and joystick later in this book. But this HAT provides quite a bit for $35.

4. Raspberry Pi Camera Module with 15 Pin Ribbon (`https://amzn.com/B07JPLV5K1`) – The camera we will be using is a $10 simple camera that is connected by ribbon to the Raspberry Pi. Since we are using this for simple video and face detection, the camera can be fairly basic, but it's up to you how much you want to spend on it.

While I have given you Amazon links to purchase everything, you are free to purchase from any supplier; it's all the same. This was just for ease of use.

We will cover and use all these components throughout the book.

Goals

The main goal of this book is to create a complete IoT application from the device all the way to the backend and all the parts in between. Without taking too many shortcuts, we will be using practices and techniques that are used for larger-scale applications. The goal is to give you all the lessons needed should you wish to expand your IoT application.

What we will actually be building is a HomeKit-enabled video recording device that stores and parses for metadata video and image files to the cloud and allow downloading and commenting on those videos. Here are the details:

Raspberry Pi – Allow a user to authenticate so that we know which Pi the files originate from. Allow the user to click a button on the Pi to see the temperature. Record video with facial recognition storing the video and image captures and sending the data to the cloud.

Cloud – Allow downloading and uploading of video and image files. Parse video and image files for metadata content. Create endpoints in the backend for users to create comments and query comments for the video files.

To perform all these features, we will use dozens of rust crates all working together to create a seamless system. We will create an application using a variety of tools like GraphQL, OpenCV, and eventual consistency (EC), all words that will become more clear as we go on. I will say what I am writing is not anything you couldn't figure out yourself if you know what to look for. Most of this information is available online, if you dig far enough, but it's sometimes hard to pick the right crates and get them to work together, and we've spent countless hours researching for our own work and for the book to bring it together. And in many instances, I've forked crates to either upgrade them for our use or to provide customizations we need. The code for the book will cover in more detail the following techniques:

1. Server side

    a. Creating a deployable set of microservices

    b. Server application that exposes GraphQL endpoints

    c. Server application that uploads and downloads files

    d. Communicating with hardware securely via MQTT

    e. Creating and using certificates

    f. Creating Docker, Helm, and Kubernetes scripts to deploy the application

2. Hardware side

   a. Setting up a Raspberry Pi

   b. Adding peripherals to the development board/Raspberry Pi

   c. Interacting with HomeKit

   d. Capturing video data

      i. Performing OpenCV on the video

      ii. Recording and uploading video content

      iii. Using SQLite to have a resilient store of data

Before we start coding, we are going to discuss the server and hardware side more.

Source Code

All of the source code for this book will be located on my GitHub page at `http://github.com/nusairat/rustfortheiot`.

This will include the services for the cloud, the applications for the Raspberry Pi, and the necessary build-and-deploy docker files. While I do step you through most of the code in the book, some of the more repetitive items like arguments for variables I only show you once to apply to your other services/applications. If you have any issues, please create an issue or you can tweet me at @nusairat. Now of course be aware that as the years go on, there could be compilation issues due to the version of Rust that is the current version. As of the time of finishing this book, the version of Rust is 1.43.1.

Web Application

The first half of the book will be on the server side. On that side, we will create a multitude of endpoints and tools that work with each other. The following is what we are going to make:

1. Microservices

   a. Upload/download service

   b. Retrieval service

   c. MQ service

2. Postgres database

3. Eventstore database

4. Message queue

All of those services will become more clear later. The first backend server we are going to design is going to serve a multitude of purposes, but essentially act as a bridge between your IoT device and the cloud. This will allow us a multiple of flexible options that you may not get with having a stand-alone IoT application and certainly is the way that most home devices work these days:

1. Act as a remote storage. When recording video or images from your IoT device, we will store it locally on the IoT device initially. However, this is not ideal if we want to retrieve the data from a remote client device; the round trip would be extremely slow. In that case, the application would have to call a server, and the server would then have to call the IoT device and start the transfer of data. While this is fine for real-time live video, if you are trying to view lots of historical archives, the slow download speed would become uncomfortably noticeable. In addition, it's great to have offsite storage of the data to serve as backup for your application. Most cloud providers will provide fairly cheap storage for large data; they just charge you for access to the data. As long as you aren't constantly accessing the data, you are fine moneywise. Our cloud application will be able to store to the local file store of the server it's on as well as to cloud storage services like S3. The reason for this will become apparent later, but this will allow us to run one of the upload services locally from a Raspberry Pi (or other server) co-located in your house and to the cloud. This can help lower costs for storage and servers and is common in any do-it-yourself system.

2. Another issue we want to tackle is sending commands to the IoT device. Mobile devices allow you to send commands to your home units through the backend. In our application, we are going to allow recording start and stop commands to be sent via a RESTful endpoint to the backend that will control whether the Pi records or not.

3. Querying of data. As you store more and more files, images, and
   video, you are going to want to add tags to these uploads but also
   search for them, not only custom tags but the metadata associated
   with the files. Images and video often have metadata created and
   stored with them. These can include things like location, time,
   aperture and other settings (for video/camera), quality rate, and so
   on. These are all services the user will want to search for. We will
   parse the video and image files and store their metadata for use later.

Board Application

When we first started thinking of what we wanted to use with Rust, the board is what
attracted us the most. With the board, there are many options from your Raspberry Pi
to a more advanced iMX.8 board, which we initially thought of going for, but then the
Raspberry Pi 4 came out. The 4 is an extremely powerful and advanced board, and it is
not only a hobbyist board of choice but is often used in the real world. In the real world,
before you've created your custom chipset, design, and others for your hardware piece,
the Pi can serve a short-term prototyping tool that your engineers can work on while
waiting for revisions of the production board. Raspberry Pis are the hobbyist choice
because of their cost, size, and ability. There are a few ways of creating IoT solutions,
and companies employ a variety of solutions. You have anywhere that range from
relatively dumb devices that do one thing like take record temperature and send it back
to a common device (think of Ecobee's thermostat sensors) to a more encompassing
device that has speakers and cameras like a a smart doorbell, or even more advance
that has monitors, sensors, and so on. With the Pi, our options are a bit more limitless
since we can attach whatever sensors we want to the Pi. In addition for something that
is just recording temperature, you could go down to a cheaper Pi Zero. All of this will be
future options for your components; for now, we are sticking with one Pi that has all the
components attached to itself.

With this setup, we are going to be able to record video via attached camera, have
display interactions, and show the temperature. The purpose is to give you a powerful
starting point for creating your own applications. You will interact with the GPIO and
the camera port and learn how to build and deploy applications to the board. One of
the biggest hurdles will be how to run multiple processes at once in Rust on the board to
perform heartbeats, face monitoring, and receive input.

The set of applications we will build for the board are as follows:

1. Face recognition video recording

    a. Background uploading of video

2. Communicate with MQTT

    a. Send heartbeat

    b. Receive recording commands

3. LED display

    a. Display pictures for holidays

    b. Display device code for authentication

    c. Display temperature

4. Homekit integration

    a. Display temperature

    b. Display motion detection

Basic Rust

While I mentioned a few other resources for learning Rust, I feel I'd be remiss if I did not at least cover a basic introduction and touched on topics and language syntax that you will see throughout the book. As software developers, and especially modern-day software developers, switching languages is part of our everyday job; as a community, we keep evolving to solve new problems. In this final section of Chapter 1, we are going to discuss the Rust language, its syntax, and its features and go over some code samples which will help you understand the language. If you already are comfortable with Rust, you can skip this section and start Chapter 2; if not, read on.

Rust Origins

Rust is not a new language but rather has been around since 2008 but until recently got popular in the main stream. It was started by and still the biggest contributors to it are Mozilla. It was mainly used as a language for the Mozilla browser engine. Rust syntactically is like C/C++ with the standard curly brackets and language syntax.

However, it is not the class-based inheritance-type language you find with C/C++ or Java; instead, it's a very functional language. The main focus of rust was speed and memory safety. And it exceeds in both; it is extremely fast beating, even Golang in many tests as well as C and C++. Memory management like we discussed earlier is very competent without you having to micromanage the application. So what are the places to use Rust? Well, here are four significant areas for Rust.

Command Line

Rust has great support for command-line tools and can run quickly and start up fast. There are tools to make it easily distributable as a binary to others (we will be creating these later). You can also create a robust set of configurations to make it work in multiple environments, have first world logging, and can talk to about any set of data points. The final item, the data points, makes it very good as a cloud-based middleman service. If you need a service that monitors webhooks, databases, and message queues, it can serve in a low CPU/memory pod funneling and processing data between other systems all the while not exposing NodePorts or easily attack vectors into the pod.

Modules

For existing or even for more full-featured applications, there are often slow components or performance critical components for it. Rust can be used in many languages to perform high-throughput processing of data, JSON, and so on. WebAssembly is a commonly used for this to create performance critical JavaScript and wrapped in a module.

Microservices

While not traditionally designed for web applications, microservice architecture is a great use of Rust. This often fills the same space that Golang and other languages try to create. Rust's speed and memory management lends it well to microservices that are accessed repeatedly but where you may fear memory growing out of control. Much like Golang, Rust can use Docker scratch containers (more on this later) that will allow you to deploy an application with low memory footprint. This, for anyone deploying to the cloud, will save money in the long run; this is one of the biggest reasons shops are switching from the traditional JVM model to the scratch container model.

Embedded

Embedded is where the biggest need for a next-generation language really relies. For decades now, C and C++ have been the language of choice for embedded designs. Because of this, there are already many libraries written in C for working with embedded systems. To help this, there is some shared interoperability between the languages, including Rust containing C-type data structures that can be used in your code. We will go over these later in the chapter. The two biggest reasons is that it's compiled down, so it can be run without an interpreter, and its memory-safe by writing your own memory allocation and deallocation. However, Rust really helps to solve both problems; it's compiled to byte code, and the memory management has rules that it forces you to live by making the memory allocation predictable and repeatable. Rust also makes it impossible to perform accidental concurrency.

So of those four areas, we will cover in this book the command line, microservices, and embedded.

Learning Rust

This book at its heart is not a "learning rust" book; it is more a book on systems engineering of an IoT system with Rust. You will need to know at least some Rust to understand the examples. If you haven't learned it yet, there are many great resources to learn the Rust language. Probably the easiest and best is the *Rust Programming Language* written by Nicholas Matsakis and Aaron Turon; it's an online book you can download and use (https://doc.rust-lang.org/book/index.html). Or if you want more details, Carlo Milanesi has *Beginning Rust: From Novice to Professional* that is also useful. I've also read the *Rust in Action MEAP*, and that book goes into some very deep concepts and base coding that can be fascinating as well, but I don't think it's necessarily a book for beginners.

Now this being said, if you are like us, picked up the book and wanted to dive in as fast as you can, then this next part is for you. We will go over many of the basic concepts of Rust and the syntax and rules for the language including many of the features we are going to use in the book. This section is obviously much shorter than a book or a site dedicated but should help you at least get your feet wet enough to be able to read many of these examples of the book. This is far from comprehensive but should get you going enough to be dangerous.

Let us dive in with what the most basic Rust application looks like, and we can build up the application from there. So let's start with the traditional `Hello World` application.

Installing Rust

First up in order to use Rust, you will have to install rust. While this seems straightforward, my experience has been it is not as straightforward as it usually is. Often when I am installing a new application (and note I am on a Mac), I just go to Homebrew and install the new tool set, be it Clojure, Python, Golang, or Elixir. With Rust, you don't necessarily want to go that route.

Do not use Homebrew to install `Rust` directly.

What you want to install is `rustup`; this is the system installer for `Rust`. Part of the reason for this is you do not want to install just `Rust`, you are going to want to install a few other items that will make your life easier:

> Cargo – This is the package manager for `Rust` we will be using throughout the book and our examples to run `Rust` applications.
>
> RLS (Rust Language Server) – While you can run Rust from the command line without RLS, you will want RLS if you plan to use `VS Code` and other editors. RLS will allow rust to compile and run from your editors.

There are two ways to install `rustup`; there is a Homebrew script you can install called `rustup-init` that then runs the `rustup` initializer. I do NOT recommend this way. It really doesn't buy you anything. Most direct is in Listing 1-1 where we run the curl command at `https://rustup.rs/`: `curl https://sh.rustup.rs -sSf | sh`. This will install `Rust` and `Cargo` for you. Once installed, you can run `rustup -V` to make sure you have it properly installed; it should have a version of at least 1.16 or higher.

Listing 1-1. Installing rustup

```
➜ curl https://sh.rustup.rs -sSf | sh
➜ rustup-V
rustup 1.16.0 (beab5ac2b 2018-12-06)
➜ cargo -V
cargo 1.34.0-nightly (4e74e2fc0 2019-02-02)
```

Now that you have Rust installed, we can move on and start coding in Rust.

Hello World

We shall start our tutorial with the quintessential example that every software book will have (or at least some variation of it). Listing 1-2 shows the `Hello World` example.

Listing 1-2. main.rs, the most basic application

```rust
fn main() {
    println!("Hello, world!");
}
```

The first thing you may notice is the file extension; we use an `.rs` extension for our Rust language files. The next thing you notice is the function definition `fn main()`; every application you create will start with a `main` function in a file called `main.rs`. In addition, you will notice the semicolon at the end; this is required (kind of, but we will get into that later). Also what is called the `println!` is actually a call to a macro, not a function. This is your most basic method that you can create and run, printing out `Hello World`. For most of our applications, we will compile via cargo since we will be relying on dependencies and multiple file interactions. However, for one file, we can use `rustc`, the rust compiler to build and execute the application. When you compile with `rustc`, it will create a binary file that can be then run without any interpreter or other system files.

Listing 1-3. Commands to compile and run the application

```
➜ rustc main.rs
➜ ./main
Hello, world!
```

OK, so now that we have the customary introduction to every language, let's start diving into doing things more than `println`.

Writing in Rust

A theme you will see in this book and in general talking about Rust is that it has C/C++-like syntax and the memory management, so consequently those are the two major things we will be discussing and showing. Much of this chapter is showing you the syntax and the features; for those of you who want to dive all in to Rust, let's get to it.

Variables and Data Types

We showed the most basic Hello World example; now let's in Listing 1-4 show the basics of programming: creating variables and setting them to particular data types. Creating a variable in Rust is extremely simple; all you need to do is use the keyword `let` followed by the variable name set equal to a value.

Listing 1-4. Setting values three different ways

```
let a = 3;
let b = 'J';
let c = "Joseph";
```

This is about as simple declaration as you can get. Each line creates a variable, setting it to a different type:

1. The first line is setting a to the number 3; by default, this will be set to a medium size number type of `u32` (more about that in a bit).

2. The second line should be familiar to most; the single line denotes setting a char.

3. Finally, the third line is setting what looks to be a String, like we have in most languages. This however is not; it is what's called a string slice. And in fact, it has a static lifetime, which when you think about, makes sense since we have hard-coded the string on the right; it isn't a variable that will get changed.

Tip   It will be important to understand the difference between string slices and Strings and when to use each.

While this is an acceptable way of creating variables, the preferred way is to define the type when creating the variable like we have in Listing 1-5. This is more readable for anyone coming into the application; in addition, it will help your IDE in performing code completion. Rust and many dynamic languages are interesting in their ability to allow optionals, but generally it's best to define it. Also with types, you can define your variables without initializing them (you can't do that without a type since it would have no clue what type to create).

Listing 1-5. Setting values three different ways with types

```
let v :u32 = 3;
let x :char = 'J';
let y :&str = "Joseph";
let z :i64;
```

The previous listings all follow with the corresponding types; I added a fourth one showing how you could create a blank variable. However, the way it's currently written is rather useless since you can't set any of these values once initialized. If you are familiar with other languages like Java, they wrap various number types in things like integer, double, and float which require you to then remember their size. In Rust, as you can see, it's more upfront so that you have an idea of the amount of bits you are allocating for the data type. One other difference is every type can have a signed and unsigned version; this lets you allocate smaller sizes for bigger numbers if you do not need the negative versions. I've marked here the various types you can use as well as a C++ and Java equivalent to help if you are coming from either language.

Type	Signed	Unsigned	C++ Equivalent	Java Equivalent
8-bit	i8	u8	int8_t/unit8_t	byte
16-bit	i16	u16	short int	short
32-bit	i32	u32	int/float	int
64-bit	i64	u64	double/long double	long/double
128-bit	i128	u128	custom	BigInteger
arch	N/A	N/A	isize	usize

Note: The 8-bit one in C++ is an unsigned char.

Changing the Variable

In order to mark a variable that we want to change, in Listing 1-6 we have to apply the mut before the variable and then we can set it.

Listing 1-6. Mutation example

```
let mut x = 3; ①
x = 5;
let mut y :i32; ②
y = 25;
let mut z :i32 = 3; ③
z = 2;
println!("X : {} / Y: {} / Z: {}",x ,y, z);
```

① Changing a value of a variable you have set.

② Changing a value of a variable you have not set; in this case, you HAVE to set the type.

③ Changing a value of a variable whose type has also been set.

Changing Value That You Have Passed In

There are also other types you can define and use. In Listing 1-7 we have examples of those types.

Other types are as follows:

Type	Sample
bool	true/false
char	'a'/'🐱','U+10FFFF'
array	
slice	
str	
tuple	(i32, f64)

Listing 1-7. Example of using a variety of types

```
let x :bool = true;
let y: char = '\u{00e9}';
let z: char = 'a';
let a: char = '🐱';
println!("Extra Chars: {} , {}, {}, {} ", x, y, z, a);
```

Borrowing and Ownership

We mentioned the borrowing and ownership earlier, and this is one of the keys to the Rust language. And honestly, this will be the hardest part to wrap your head around when coming from other languages that have very loose borrowing rules. When you first start writing Rust code, you will probably get quite a bit of borrow checker errors on compilation; this is normal, and the more advance of a feature, the better it will be. I still get the same problems, albeit it's usually due to the library I am using.

But let's go over two quick examples, one where we reassign a variable and one that doesn't work. In Listing 1-8, we set a variable and then reset it to another variable.

Listing 1-8. Setting a variable and then changing the contents to another variable

```
let zed = "4";
let me = zed;
println!("Zed : {}", zed);
```

This will compile and run and print "Zed : 4". Let's try this again, but this time in Listing 1-9, we will use a struct.

Listing 1-9. Setting a variable and then changing the contents to another variable but with a struct

```
#[derive(Debug)]
struct Number {
    num: i32
}

fn run() {
    let n = Number { num : 25i32};
    let mv = n;
    println!("Number : {:?}", n);
}
```

This is basically doing the same thing as the previous, but this one will fail with a "value borrowed here after move" for the println. Why is this? Let's break down what's happening. On the first line of the method, n is initialing the Number to a section of memory. On the second line, that memory is now pointed to mv instead of n. Since only one section of memory has a variable pointed to it, n now has nothing pointed. This makes sense but begs the question why did the first set of code work, but this code fail. That is because in the first set it was actually performing a copy of the memory instead. Thus, zed and me were both pointing to different memory both holding "4". We can actually do the same with the second example by adding Copy and Clone to the derive; this will allow the compiler to automatically have in the second reference to perform a copy task instead. You will see that the borrowing and reference are all done via compiler optimization as well, making it much faster.

In addition, the same concepts apply when passing a variable to a method. When passing a variable to a method, we let the method borrow the variable, and won't be able to use is it after the method returns, since the method has taken ownership of the variable and is now considered the final owner. In Listing 1-10, we borrow passing a u32; as you can see, this works because it performs a copy.

Listing 1-10. Passing a u32 to a method

```
fn create() {
    let x :u32 = 3;
    copy_var_to_method(x);

    println!("X :: {}", x);
}

fn copy_var_to_method(x :u32) {
    println!("x: {}", x);
}
```

However, much like the previous example in Listing 1-11, a String which does not implement Copy tries to perform the same sequence, but it would fail (hence, why I have the println commented out).

Listing 1-11. Passing a String to a method

```
fn create_str() {
    let x :String = String::from("Joseph");
    take_ownership_str(x);

    //println!("This would fail : {} ", x);
}
```

```
fn take_ownership_str(y :String) {
    println!("x: {}", y);
}
```

However, just because we pass the ownership to a function, it doesn't mean we can't pass the ownership back to the calling function. In Listing 1-12, we pass the ownership to the function and then return it back to the same variable.

Listing 1-12. Passing ownership to a method and then returning it

```
fn create_str_and_move() {
    let mut x :String = String::from("Joseph");
    x = take_ownership_str_and_return(x);

    println!("End of method : {} ", x);
}

fn take_ownership_str_and_return(y :String) -> String {
    println!("x: {}", y);
    y
}
```

Note you do have to make the variable mutable to set it; if not, you would have received a "cannot assign twice to immutable variable" had you tried to reassign x.

Memory

When talking about borrowing, it's also useful to talk about the lifetime of the memory associated with it. Memory in any system is finite, and if you've ever worked with a large or heavy use application, you've probably run into some memory issues. Much of this is simply because the way other systems handle memory isn't optimal. When we talk about C, we would use alloc and dealloc to allocate and deallocate the memory accordingly. This is a manual process, but gives the developer great flexibility in controlling memory usage. However, I've seen quite a few times this also leads to memory leaks due to programmer error. Java decided to take this out of the programmer's hand and used garbage collection to clean up memory. Periodically, Java will run a garbage collector to free up what it considers memory no longer in use. This works great most of the time; however, this gives the developer no ability to control memory cleanup and in heavy use or an application creating quite a bit of objects no ability to control its cleanup.

Rust, as we said, uses borrowing to know when the memory is being created and also when it no longer has owner to it (like when you pass a variable to a method and then return from the method). Therefore, Rust at compile time can control when memory is allocated and when it's deallocated by using the rules of its borrowing and ownership to know when a variable is no longer have an active pointer to it. To that avail, you can see this happen if you implement the destructor on a struct. Destructors work by implementing the Drop trait. In Listing 1-13, I implement the Drop trait for a person.

Listing 1-13. Implementing the Drop trait for Person

```
#[derive(Debug)]
struct Person {
    name: String
}

fn run_outofscope() {
    let p = Person { name: "Joseph".to_string()}; ②
    move_memory(p);
    println!("Finished");
}

fn move_memory(p: Person) {
    println!("Person: {:?}", p); ③
}

impl Drop for Person { ①
    fn drop(&mut self) {
        println!("Dropping!"); ④
    }
}
```

    ①   Implement Drop trait on Person.

    ②   Instantiate a Person and create the memory for it.

    ③   At this point, the variable will go out of memory.

    ④   Destructor is called.

If you run this set of code, you will get this:

```
Person: Person { name: "Joseph" }
Dropping!
Finished
```

As you can see, the destructor gets called once we return from the function. Since most of Rust's memory is by default allocated to the stack as well, the memory space is now free to be used by any other item initialized down the chain.

Reference and Dereferencing

Instead of passing variables for complete ownership transfer, we can send references of the variable to the function. This allows us to still use the variable when the method is complete. When you do pass a variable though and want to alter it, you will have to dereference the variable to set the memory. In Listing 1-14, we have an example of passing a mutable reference and then dereferencing it.

Listing 1-14. Passing the variable as a reference and dereferencing it to get set

```
pub fn run() {
    let mut x = 5i32;
    println!("1 > {:?}", x);
    alter(&mut x);
    println!("2 > {:?}", x);
}

fn alter(x : &mut i32) {
    *x = 3i32;
}
```

Traits

Most of the Rust we have discussed are fairly common features between languages (most languages have concepts of methods or functions and variables). Traits are very different and are how we create abstraction in Rust. Traits are abstraction layers that work on `structs` to add functionality to yours or to existing `structs` within the framework. We will see in the chapters to come they are used extensively to create functionality for existing middleware.

Let's start in Listing 1-15 with an existing `struct` that has an implementation with it.

Listing 1-15. A Person struct and its optional implementation

```
pub struct Person {
    pub name: &'static str,
    pub address: &'static str
    //pub extensions: TypeMap,
}

// pub is implied and not needed here
impl Person {
    //fn address
    pub fn say_hello(&self) -> String {
        format!("Hello {}", self.name)
    }
}
```

Here we have a `struct` of People, containing a name and address, and even have an implementation to add a say_hello() call to the `struct`. Now let's get into traits; the trait is going to define certain abstractions for your `struct`; the nice thing about traits is they can be applied to more than one `struct`; you will just have to implement them for each. So in Listing 1-16, we define a trait of students.

Listing 1-16. A student trait

```
pub trait Student {
    // sets the name
    fn new(name: &'static str) -> Self;

    // gets the name
    fn name(&self) -> &'static str;

    // enrolls in the class
    fn enroll(&self, class: &'static str) -> bool;
}
```

The trait defines functions needed for it, but not the implementations, although we could define an implementation there if we need to, but that is not the usual case. Finally, let's attribute the trait Person to the Student in Listing 1-17.

Listing 1-17. Implement student on the person

```
impl Student for Person { ①
    fn new(name: &'static str) -> Person {
        Person { name: name, address: "" }
    } ②

    // gets the name
    fn name(&self) -> &'static str {
        self.name
    } ③

    // enrolls in the class
    fn enroll(&self, class: &'static str) -> bool {
        println!("Enroll the student in {}", class);
        true
    }
}
```

① The syntax to say the implementation of trait Student for Person.

② A new to construct the trait. This is optional.

③ Finally, one of the methods used.

At this point, you have your trait, and person has been implemented for the trait; all that's left in Listing 1-18 is to instantiate and use it.

Listing 1-18. Instantiate and use the trait

```
use super::people::Student;

// have to include all the fields
let mut p: Person = Student::new("joseph");

println!("Person W/Trait:: {}", p.name);
p.enroll("CS 200");
```

You will actually instantiate the structure using the trait itself. This is optional, but then it allows the compiler to know that we have `Person` with a `Student` trait attached. Thus, any other functions you pass it to would not know those methods were allowed. This leads us to the other case of using traits; what if we have a trait on an existing `struct` but want to use the trait in our function? In Listing 1-19 we look at that use case.

Listing 1-19. Using a trait without instantiating it on a struct

```
mod run2 {
    use super::people::Person;
    use super::people::Student; ①

    pub fn run(person: Person) {
        person.enroll("CS 200");
    }
}
```

① Adding this line in your module allowed the compiler now is required in this case.

The addition of the `Student` along with the `Person` allows the compiler to know the `Person` will have `Student` functions as well; this is what allows us to add traits to `structs` that we didn't create in our application.

Typemap

One quick final topic about traits, if you noticed we could add different traits to one struct, but since they are only allowed to define functions, it's hard to add any extra data functionality to separate the traits out. You can only work with the data, and you really don't want to add data fields for one that you don't use for the other. For example, a `student` trait may have classes, advisor, and so on. And a `faculty` trait could have classes taught and so on. One useful way around this limitation is with `TypeMap` (`https://github.com/reem/rust-typemap`). `TypeMap` allows us to store key/values in a tuple that are tied to a struct and then look them up that way accordingly. In Listing 1-20 we have an example of using the `TypeMap`.

Listing 1-20. Typemap example

```rust
use typemap::{TypeMap, Key};

struct KeyType;

#[derive(Debug, PartialEq)]
struct Value(i32);

impl Key for KeyType { type Value = Value; }

#[test] fn test_pairing() {
    let mut map = TypeMap::new();
    map.insert::<KeyType>(Value(42));
    assert_eq!(*map.get::<KeyType>().unwrap(), Value(42));
}
```

We will use this later with the iron framework to add middleware data to Requests. In addition, there are a few other features using Arc<Mutex<>> and the async/await pattern that we will dive into in later chapters when we actually need to use them.

Cargo

Compiling and running code is obviously a must have for any code written, and while we can always compile and run applications from the command line with the language compiler, eventually (usually early on) a package manager (or 8 if you are Java) comes out. Rust is no exception to that of course, and hence we have Cargo. Cargo is the default package manager used by Rust and for Rust projects and in all the coming chapters is what we are going to be using to run our examples and applications. Luckily, Cargo is distributed with by default so we do not have to take any extra steps to get it working.

Cargo will set up a fairly straightforward directory structure for you; you will have a src folder and inside a main.rs with a fn main method. This will be the default entry point into the application. There a few commands we can use to run it:

- cargo run – Runs the binary or the source application

- cargo test – Runs all the tests in the application

- cargo doc – Creates the documentation from the application using the commenting

- `cargo bench` – Benchmarks the package

- `cargo build` – Builds the application into an executable

The two commands you will use the most are `run` and `test`. The `build` you will normally run when performing a release, so that will occur when you run `cargo build --release`. There are also third-party extensions to add more functionality to your cargo releases. You can find a various amount here: `https://github.com/rust-lang/cargo/wiki/Third-party-cargo-subcommands`.

Feature Flags

Feature flags are a way of activating code at compile time or runtime based on a given feature. We will use this when importing crates in the application. With feature flags, you may want to activate certain set of code vs. other sets. For example, inside the ORM we will be using for the database, you could use different versions of the UUID crate. This is quite common in Rust. Feature flags are first defined in your `Cargo.toml` file and then activated at compile time in your code by encapsulating the method, block, and module with `#[cfg(feature = "feature-name")]` that would then activate that set of code when the `feature-name` is supplied. I wanted to mention them because while I won't actively be using them in the chapters, I will be using them in the source code. Most of our code builds up on itself as we go along either by adding new services or new modules. However, there are many instances that as we progress from chapter to chapter, we have to change a method signature or drastically update. In these instances, I have added feature flags to the code that accompanies this book. The flag `full` will always be for the final book, but often I use `ch05` to compile the code for that specific chapter. The `README.md` for each module will tell you which flags are supported for that application; of course, you can also look at the `Cargo.toml` to find out as well.

Creating a Release

One of those extensions is a cargo-release that adds extra functionality to the cargo build release process. You can install the `cargo-release` plug-in with the command `cargo install cargo-release`; the only requirement is your project needs to be managed by `git`:

1. It first will check that the current working directory is `git clean`; now this usually won't affect you since releases should be performed on a build system, but it's useful to know you do not have any outstanding commits before creating a release.

2. It bumps the release level if set. This one is a bit more complicated, in that there are different rules based on the level you are releasing, and has to do with the version you set in your `Cargo.toml`. If you had marked it as pre-release (i.e., 0.1.0-pre), it will simply remove the `pre`. If the level is a `patch` and there is no pre-release associated with it, then it will bump the minor version. If the level is `minor`, it will bump the minor (i.e., 0.1.0-pre to 0.2.0), and if the level is `major`, it will bump the major version (0.1.0 to 1.0.0). You can also use `alpha`, `beta`, and `rc` for levels as well. We will use this for our application on the hardware being released, but won't be using it for.

3. Run `cargo publish` if you want to publish this project; this is useful for crates you are creating for public consumption.

4. It generates the `rustdoc` and pushes to `gh-pages` (optionally); again this is good for a projection that is for a public crate hosted on `github`.

5. It generates a git tag with the number of the version; this is required so that you can easily see the source code associated with a given release.

6. In the main, it will then bump the version for the next development cycle.

7. Finally, it pushes these changes, the bump and the tag, to git.

Summary

In the introduction, we presented the requirements and goals of the book and described the applications we will be creating for it. We also covered some topics related to web and board applications as well as ran through some basic Rust language tutorials. In the next chapter, we will start coding our first microservice.

CHAPTER 2

Server Side

In the previous chapter, we went through the basics of the Rust language. This was of course not a complete course in the Rust language; there are entire books for that, but I hope for those that are not familiar with Rust, it at least gives you the basics to follow along with the coding samples in this chapter. We also started to go over the goals of this book; this will be our first chapter diving in writing code for our eventual completion of that goal and a creation of a full-service IoT application.

The next few chapters will build up on another to create the web application portion of the IoT application. We will be working on this to deploy to the cloud, but really could be deployed to your local server, a Raspberry Pi server or whatever you want. And we will look at different ways to deploy the application later. Part of what makes this chapter difficult is we will be connecting all the moving parts together. We won't dive into complex business logic so as we can focus on the architecture and frameworks needed to put the application together.

We will be building upon this application for the next couple chapters; much of it will remain the same, others we will add and update to. The one thing to understand before we dive in is the state of Rust and the web applications. Rust was not initially designed to do full web-blown features; as such, some of the libraries are either not maintained or very transient. Right now, much of the focus is on threading that many of these libraries will benefit from when completed. However, do not take that as a reason to not use Rust. Its design is actually very good for the Web and can cover the same spectrum that Golang applications use. But because of this, some of the topics that we cover here, the exact library may be different a year or two.

© Joseph Faisal Nusairat 2020
J. F. Nusairat, *Rust for the IoT*, https://doi.org/10.1007/978-1-4842-5860-6_2

Goals

After this chapter is complete, we will have the following steps complete:

1. Retrieval service microservice.

2. Learned and implemented Iron web framework.

3. Created custom middleware for Iron.

4. Set up the database we are going to use and integrate the microservice with it.

Microservice Architecture

If you've been developing for a while or coded at a more traditional shop, you might be used to the traditional monolithic application model. Monolithic applications create one application that covers all the requirements for the site. This application would contain everything – your website and generated/stored HTML – run your backend services, and manage the database connectivity. The application would be ALL of your site. Then the nature of the web and mobile applications changed everything. Backend services needed to serve both web and mobile content. In addition, we started using a more MVC architecture for websites via tools like React. This meant backend servers were no longer generation HTML but generation JSON content that can then be shared by mobile and Web. This cut back on the size of the application server, but it was still fairly large.

There are upsides and downsides to the monolithic application model. Upsides are that you have one application to manage, one docker image to manage, and when QA tests the application, they have much better guarantees what they are testing is what's fully going to be deployed. However, monolithic applications are difficult to sync deployments among many teams since you have to coordinate deployments. Also a failure in one part of the application that crashes will crash the entire application. Coordination on the deployment of the monolithic app goes beyond just the application but database rollout since generally one application points to one database with multiple schemas or structures. Microservices help address all these needs and more. Microservices divide up your application by service areas. Then each service area has its own database. This decoupling then treats each service as its own application. Microservices can then communicate with each other over TLS so that you aren't losing cross-service communication. The biggest downside that might come to mind is what about the endpoint from the outside. If it's different applications, are they different endpoints? The answer is no; you can use a variety of techniques from ingress controllers (we will cover in Chapter 7), or if you are using GraphQL, you can perform schema stitching to create a seamless endpoint.

Why Microservices?

Oftentimes when I'm off to teach classes or give presentations, you get push back in the software world that we are creating complexity for the sake of being complex; software developers do tend to like the shiny new object. But much of that is because the question of what we are trying to solve keeps changing due to consumer demand and technology availability (by way of iPhones, Alexa, Google Home, etc.).

Microservices can work in any environment, but they are truly suited for a cloud high availability site. Your traditional corporate internal application, let's say an application for insurance companies to sell insurance over the phone. They have a fixed set of users (those they hired to answer the phones) and a set schedule that they know, and often they are using the full application in their daily routines (searching, quoting, binding), albeit binding may happen less often than the other two. And most importantly, you are running and deploying from your own internal servers that you've had for years.

Now take an external application you are launching for the first time. This application has a registration and searching, and you can purchase goods from it. Traffic here is not always known, but a few things can happen. When you launch the application, you often get a spike of registrations at the beginning and then it slowly goes down, or a spike if the site gets lots of press. Also if you are selling goods, around the holidays, you will have sales and specials and get higher checkouts than you would during the rest of the year. And the most important aspect, you have deployed to the cloud, so now you are having a variable cost.

If you created a few large instances in the cloud to handle normal traffic, then what happens during these spikes? Well you are getting more traffic, and your web service can only handle so many simultaneous connections, so you would have to keep scaling up your large instance to more large instances. And you are using the large instances because of the size of your application.

But what if we separated registration, searching, and checkout to their own microservices? You could put each part in their own small instances, and that way during spikes, you would only have to add extra small instances or increase the memory/speed of existing instances. The end result is not only faster throughput but more importantly cheaper cost. In Figure 2-1, we have a graphical example of how to scale up registration independently.

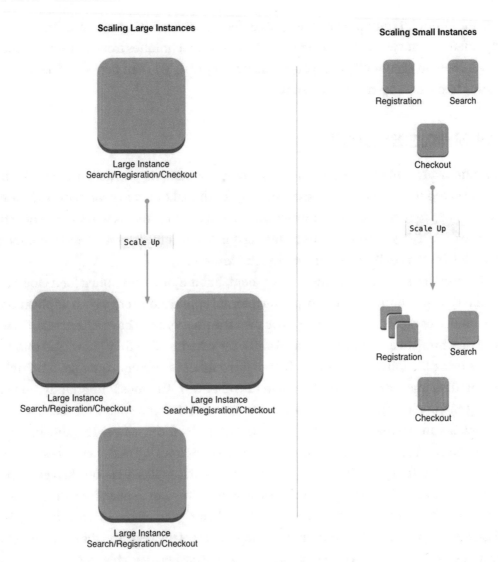

Figure 2-1. *Shows the difference in scaling between large and small instances*

In Table 2-1 we have a few of our endpoints will be using for the application as well. I would also argue it's also much easier to make patch changes and being able to work on code separately without getting in the way of others work with microservices. If you have any further questions about microservices, I highly recommend reading Martin Fowler's blog on them at https://martinfowler.com/articles/microservices.html.

Backend Design

This brings us to the design for our application, at least for this chapter. We will add on and change the endpoints over the next few chapters, but this architecture is the basic one we are going to develop.

First is the problem we are solving for this chapter. From a high level, we want to create an application that allows us to upload and download files (preferably media applications). In addition, we want to store information about the files uploaded and then be able to run queries to find the files by name and uploaded time and then be able to download those applications back to us. Since we are creating these applications in an IoT RESTful world, all the applications should interact with us via REST commands.

To help us get used to creating microservices, we will create two basic services: one for uploads/downloads and another for querying of the data. The upload/download service will also need a persistent storage to be able to have a place to retrieve the data later. The retrieval service will be the sole service to call out to the database. Keeping these separate does help; if one service is hacked, they don't have access to everything. In Figure 2-2, we have the basic pattern of two microservices communicating with each other and independently communicating with storage.

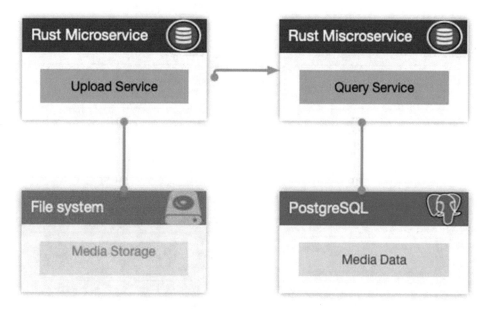

Figure 2-2. *Showing the basic design of our microservice architecture*

Database Design

The database design for this application will be rather simple for now, and I've added a bit extra just to make it more interesting for future work though. All we have to do is store a file to the database and then retrieve it later. The first table will be the `media_datas` table and will contain everything we need to know about the media data; in addition, it will contain the `uuid` for the device the media data originates from.

The next table will be linked to it in a one-to-many relationship; the `comments` table will be able to contain a list of comments on the table. Eventually, when we discuss authorization, we will add users to both so that we know who made the media and who the comments are from. In Figure 2-3 we have the database design.

Backend Application Design

Database Tables

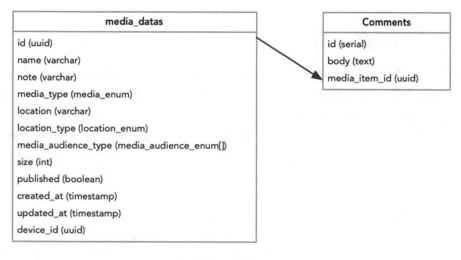

Postgres Enums

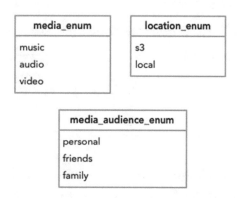

Figure 2-3. *Showing the basic design of our database architecture*

In order to spruce up the table a bit, I also added some enumerations. These will be useful later and useful for data references that do not change often. Hence, why I created these instead of a relational table. Now if you look deeper in there, you will notice we have three columns that use the enumerations: media_type, location_type, and media_audience_type. The first two use a standard enumeration. The last one actually takes an array of enumerations which will allow us to tag a media file as for friends, family, or personal.

While much of this database table is generic, there will be specifics particular with enumerations that use Postgres exclusively. So for this book, realize the code will only work with Postgres without any modifications.

RESTful Endpoints

Now that we have our database design, our microservice design, how do the services communicate? Through RESTful endpoints of course. (Note: In future chapters, some of these will be changed to GraphQL endpoints.)

We will dive into how each endpoint works further in the chapter, but for now, here is a list of the endpoints we are creating.

Table 2-1. *RESTful endpoints*

Service	Type	Endpoint	Parameters
Upload Svc	POST	/api/upload	MultiPart File
Upload Svc	GET	/api/download/:id	none extra
Query Svc	PUT	/api/comment/add/:media_item_id	comment: the text of the comment
Query Svc	PUT	/api/media/add	{ size: <media_size>, location: <file_loc>, uuid: <uuid> }

Deploying

For this chapter, we won't be deploying the application, so we do not have to worry about bundling the application yet. However, in future chapters, we will deploy using the following tools:

Docker – For creating images of our application

Kubernetes – For creating the deployment environment

Helm – For package managing our deployment environments

Docker

We won't be using Docker till later; however, in the "Database" section, we will use docker to create a postgres instance for us to test locally with. So in order to have you ready to do that, you should go ahead and download and install docker now from here: `www.docker.com/get-started`.

Later in the book, we will get into specifics on how to use Docker; if you have Postgres installed on your computer using our docker, Postgres is optional.

Web Framework

The heart of any modern application is the backend server running our web framework that serves up static and dynamic data as well as allows for updates and queries to the database. Regardless of what the mobile application, website, or the device does, the backend not only moves the bits and the bytes but handles the logic to process these bits and bytes. It is almost ironic that we still call these "web frameworks" since the primary service of these frameworks is not going to be for a web page, nor do they often serve up websites. In reality, we should call them "backend web exposed secure services using REST"; of course, that's way too long and isn't even 100% accurate when we get to the CQRS section. This section will be a combination of example code and code we directly apply to our system. If you don't see a file reference in the listing, that means it's not directly in our final application.

Choosing a Web Framework

Many of the "new" languages that have come out over the past 10–15 years like Elixir or Clojure or to a lesser extent Kotlin or older languages like Ruby that have become popular have done so due to someone designing a web framework to use with it. Rust really wasn't born like that. While it's certainly picked up speed recently due to its web frameworks, it was popular because of its pure shell side running. Rust has been consistently voted as the #1 favorite language by Stack Overflow Developer Survey. I say this because the state of its web frameworks is in flux and made the decision which framework to use for the book more difficult.

Hyper is a core framework used for low-level http binding and calling. It's a great framework to use if you are writing a CLI that needs to access a web service, but it would be rather difficult to use to create a full-blown web application. In fact, you'd have to write so much code you'd be writing Iron.

Iron is based on hyper. It's not low level, but it's not as feature-rich as other frameworks by default. In fact, in order to get in most of the features, you have to bring in a variety of other middleware designed to work with Iron. This is nice when wanting to write a light web application but annoying in that you have to constantly find dependencies to use with it. Also there is some issue with how often it's updated; a year ago, there was some issue with not many people working on the code base, but since then its seemed to have more repo commits. So with Iron, you get a good quick framework that is very extensible, but you have to pick and choose what to extend, and for beginners, this can be difficult to know.

Rocket is a full-featured web framework more in line what most people are used to when they have picked up a modern framework like Phoenix, Grails, or Spring. It's quick and works well but has one giant caveat. The framework at the time I wrote the book was based off of nightly builds of Rust.

And here was the crux of my problem. Do I chase a nightly build, hoping by the time the book is done, it's good to go and on a stable build. Or do I take Iron? In the end, I decided for what this chapter wants; we will use Iron. Thus, we will be ironborn for this book (*GOT* reference intentional).

Start Up Basic Iron

To get started, let's go over how to make some basic calls to Iron; we will then progress to more and more advance calls culminating with writing the application we are using.

Hello World

To get things started, let's start off with the most rudimentary example, the Hello World example in Listing 2-1.

Listing 2-1. Creating our basic Hello World example

```
use iron::prelude::*;
use iron::status;

fn main() {
```

```
Iron::new(|_: &mut Request| Ok(Response::with((status::Ok, "Hello World
Rust"))))
    .http("localhost:3000");
}
```

This is the most basic example one can create. This will start a server binding the application to `localhost:3000`. Once bound, you can call the endpoint with `http` `http://localhost:3000` which will return `Hello World Rust`. In fact, the way it is created, it is just bound to the `localhost:3000` so any call to it regardless of path and type will return `Hello World Rust`. This obviously is not ideal for most applications but works for our Hello World example. Let's take a further look at how this works. If you've ever worked with web applications, you know at the root of how it works are three things:

1. Request – That defines the incoming request; this includes the request type (get, post), body parameters, multipart, and the route – everything you want to use to define the application. We take it for granted that server's route and control are based on this information, but it is up to the server to decide what to do with it.

2. Response – The return values, or redirects. A combination of status codes, headers, and data usually defines our return and defines how the client uses the data we return.

3. Port binding – And finally the port we are binding to. When starting up, this is the port that every web server has to bind to and clients then call to. By default, this is port 80 but can be anything.

How does this tie into the previous listing? Because all that information is there and it's how we are going to expand on it. The `Iron::new` takes in just one function that receives one parameter and returns one thing. That one parameter is the request, and the return is a response. This is all you need for a web server. This allows iron to start and run faster than most applications because it doesn't assume you need the kitchen sink to use it. This request/response function we pass in is called the handler, and rust allows a plethora of crates to customize the functionality of how it works; we will use a variety of handlers as we go on.

I like using the application `https://httpie.org/` to test my code. It's a bit easier to make requests and to read the responses. Thus, most of the examples in the book will use it.

Redirects

Another feature is we can redirect the endpoint to another server in Listing 2-2.

Listing 2-2. Redirects all request to rustfortheiot.com

```
use iron::prelude::*;
use iron::{status, Url};
use iron::modifiers::Redirect;
use router::Router;

fn main() {
    let url = Url::parse("http://rustfortheiot.com").unwrap();

    Iron::new(move |_: &mut Request| {
        Ok(Response::with((status::Found, Redirect(url.clone()))))
    }).http("localhost:3000");
}
```

You can redirect all or just partial endpoints; in this case, we created just one handler to use.

Response Codes

Iron has the standard variety of response codes to use when responding from an endpoint. The default you see in most of the example applications is the status::Ok; this correlates to a 200 status code, but everything is available via iron::status which brings in the codes from the hyper underlayer of hyper::status::StatusCode. To use a different status code, you can simply change the response creation like in Listing 2-3.

Listing 2-3. Using different status codes

```
Ok(Response::with(status::Created));
```

Or even in Listing 2-4 is a more fancy request where we return a 500 based on an internal exception and a 200 when everything passes.

Listing 2-4. Responding with different status codes

```
extern crate iron;

use iron::prelude::*;
use iron::status;

fn echo(request: &mut Request) -> IronResult<Response> {
    // let body = request.get_body_contents().map_err(|e| {
    let body = request.body.map_err(|e| {
        IronError::new(
            e,
            (status::InternalServerError, "Error reading request"),
        )
    })?;
    Ok(Response::with((status::Ok, body.clone())))
}

fn main() {
    Iron::new(echo).http("localhost:3000");
}
```

Parsing Parameters

One of the next common concepts is to retrieve parameters. Almost all the requests you are going to work with in a RESTful application will have to have parameters submitted. Iron with the help of some middleware crates supports retrieving request parameters in three different ways. Following are the three ways you can retrieve request parameters:

1. Your standard URL encoded query or post parameter – This is the standard form data translated to multiple parameters.

2. REST parameters – These are parameters on the REST string itself; if you have http://app/add/:id, you want to be able to access the id parameter. (Note: That isn't a real URL but an example.)

3. JSON data being passed in via the body – This is growing to be one of the more standard ways to send data requests with RESTful endpoints.

Let's go over how to retrieve parameters each of those ways.

Params Parsing

Let's begin with the first item, good old-fashioned parameter parsing. But what exactly is parameter parsing? When we talk about parameter parsing, we are really referring to four different types of parameters that you receive in any web application:

- JSON data (Content-Type: `application/json`)

- URL-encoded GET parameters

- URL-encoded Content-Type: `application/x-www-form-urlencoded` parameters

- Multipart form data (Content-Type: `multipart/form-data`)

These are the typical parameters that have been around for decades to retrieve properties. We can use the `params` plug-in to get all of these various parameters; you can install the plug-in with the crate listed in Listing 2-5.

Listing 2-5. Adding the params plug-in, in file Cargo.toml

```
params = "0.8.0"
```

Now that we have the `params` crate installed, we can use it to get the parameters.

Listing 2-6. Retrieving using the params plug-in, in file src/actions/comment.rs

```
use params::{Params, Value, Map}; ①

    let map = req.get_ref::<Params>().unwrap(); ②

const COMMENT_FIELD: &str = "comment";

fn get_comment(map: &Map) -> String {
    let x: &str = match map.find(&[COMMENT_FIELD]).unwrap() { ③
        Value::String(s) => s.as_ref(),
        _ => "none",
    };
    String::from(x)
}
```

① Brings in the Params and Value from the params crate to be used.

② This line is what converts the parameters into a map of keys and values.

③ Finally, the last part will go through the map and find the attribute you are using.

And here you have it; it's not as simple as one would like, but you can reuse the method. One thing to note here, in this sequence of code, I passed in the map, not the request; this is because I need to reuse the request later to get the rest ID, and it caused too many borrow issues trying to pass the mutable request around.

URL REST Parsing

The use of RESTful interfaces has been popular for over a decade now, and we often still have endpoints we want to parse. For our adding a comment function, our endpoint was defined in the router in Listing 2-7.

Listing 2-7. The router definition with an id, in file src/http.rs

```
add_comment: put "/comment/add/:media_item_id" => comment::add,
```

You can see on the URL we are passing in a `media_item_id`; this will be the UUID PK (primary key) for the database. In order to access this inside our comment controller, we will use the request extensions to pull the router object off of it like in Listing 2-8.

Listing 2-8. The router definition with an id, in file src/actions/comment.rs

```
fn find_media_id(req: &Request) -> Uuid {
    let id: &str = req.extensions.get::<Router>().unwrap()
        .find("media_item_id").unwrap();
    Uuid::parse_str(id).unwrap()
}
```

JSON Parsing

Finally, JSON parsing, there is a library for that as well. This library is for parsing the body into json data. The application takes the raw json passed into it and parses it into three different types depending on the need:

1. Raw – Raw parse into a string; this is useful if you are just going to store the result into the database or return to another layer.

2. Json – Can be resolved into a Json object. This can be useful if you want to reuse the data in Json form or create searches in Json, or more importantly, it is unstructured data but may have certain fields you need for processing.

3. Struct – For structured data that you plan to store in a database or use with implementations on the struct, this method works great. And this is the example we will show (since in the future, this struct will have an `impl` to save to the database).

For our application, we are going to use the `upload_svc` to receive a media file; it will then process the media into its raw data and send it to the `retrieval_svc` to store. In Listing 2-9, we have the struct of the media data that will 1:1 emulate the json data we will be receiving from it.

Listing 2-9. The `MediaData` struct that emulates the record it will receive, in file src/actions/media_data.rs

```
use crate::database::PgPooled;
use crate::models::metadata::{Image,Video};
use serde_derive::Deserialize;
use crate::database::{MediaEnum, LocationEnum};

#[derive(Deserialize, Debug, Clone)]
pub struct MediaDataAdd {
    pub id: Uuid,
    pub name: String,
    pub media_type: MediaEnum,
    pub location: String,
    pub location_type: LocationEnum,
    pub size: i32,
    pub device_id: Uuid,
    pub image_data: Option<Image>, ①
    pub video_data: Option<Video> ②
}
```

```
#[cfg(feature = "ch02")]
impl MediaDataAdd {
    fn save(self: Self, pool: &PgPooled) {} ③
}
```

①   Only populated for an image object.

②   Only populated for a video object.

③   Placeholder till we discuss databases.

The option for the image and the video is because we will receive either an image or a video back. Now in Listing 2-10, we will receive the JSON string; let the parser run and then call the MediaData.save.

Listing 2-10. media_datas add function using the body parser, in file src/actions/media_data.rs

```
pub fn add(req: &mut Request) -> IronResult<Response> {
    info!("-- add media data --");
    let json_body = req.get::<bodyparser::Json>();
    info!(">>>> JSON ::: {:?}", json_body);

    let struct_body = req.get::<bodyparser::Struct<MediaDataAdd>>(); ①

    match struct_body {
        Ok(Some(media_data)) => {
            info!("Parsed body:\n{:?}", media_data);
            media_data.save(&req.db_conn()); ②
            Ok(Response::with((status::Ok, "OK")))
        },
        Ok(None) => {
            warn!("No body");
            Ok(Response::with(status::BadRequest)) ③
        },
```

```
        Err(err) => {
            error!("Error parsing meta data :: {:?}", err);
            Ok(Response::with(status::InternalServerError)) ④
        }
    }
}
```

① Allows you to pass in a struct to the body parser to create that struct from the body.

② Allows us to use the rendered structure body as an object and use it. This method we haven't implemented yet, but will do so later.

③ Returning a 400 error code.

④ Returning a 500 error code.

You will notice we have three different return states for this. The first is that the body is parsed, and we can then perform actions on the parsed JSON. The next is we didn't receive any JSON body, so we return a 300. And finally, there is a problem parsing the data; this could be due to some internal issue or more likely the data doesn't match the format we expected.

Routing

As I am sure you noticed in the previous examples, we were binding the entire site to one handler regardless of path supplied. This is great for examples, but in real life, we are going to have multiple paths to the application (at least usually). We will use a plug-in to help us with routing. The routing is processed through the `router` crate that can be installed via Listing 2-11.

Listing 2-11. Add the router crate to the Cargo.toml

```
router = "0.6.0"
```

Setting up routing is fairly easy; it only requires three things to define a route. You need a unique key for it, the actual path, and the service you are routing to. The Router can be created by calling out to the `struct` and its `impl`, or you can use a macro that makes it a bit easier to read; we will use the macro. In Listing 2-12, we are going to add the routes for the download service; they consist of a health check, an upload which will take in JSON and MultiPart file, and a download service that just takes an id.

Listing 2-12. Routes for the upload service, in file src/http.rs

```
use router::{Router}; ①
use router::router; ②

fn create_routes(url: &str) -> Router {
    let owned_name = format!("{}", url).to_owned();
    router!(
        health: get "/healthz" => health,
        upload: post "/upload/:device_id" => move | request: &mut Request |
        upload(request, &owned_name), ③
        download: get "/download/:id" => download)
}
```

① This is the struct being returned.

② This allows us to use the macro.

③ Using the move allows us to pass a parameter to the upload aside from the Request.

What is being created here is a handler, much like we had when we created the individual requests, but then this handler delegates to each of the incoming requests based on the request path. In order to activate the router, set it as the handler on the request like in Listing 2-13.

Listing 2-13. Routes for the upload service

```
Iron::new(router).http("localhost:3000").unwrap();
```

When we start the server in our applications, we will be passing command-line variables to the application and parameters for the URL as opposed to hard-coding it.

Middleware

Finally, we will end the web discussion with something we have talked about throughout this chapter, middleware. The middleware is what allows all the extra features we have in combination with macros. We will add more middleware to the mix in the next section, but let's run through a few examples of middleware to gain a better understanding how to use it and what it does. We have handlers to handle incoming requests and outgoing responses; the middleware acts in conjunction with these to control the processing flow of a request. Middleware handlers will act as normal wrappers around your control flow to your actions. The purpose of which is to manipulate the requests and response and even control whether the handler should be used. There are three types of middleware we can create:

1. BeforeMiddleware – This middleware runs before your action gets processed. This can add to the request via the `req.extensions` TypeMap adding functionality, like user information for a logged in user, database connection, or whatever you want. It can also control the flow to actions like it does with the `router` middleware and can even decide if you progress further, in the case of authorization.

2. AroundMiddleware – This wraps around the handlers and is used to manipulate the `Response` object itself. It can change the `Response` passed to subsequent handlers.

3. AfterMiddleware – This is similar to the `AroundMiddleware`, except that it's not for changing the response but for changing headers, logging, and so on.

Creating middleware is actually quite easy; each of the types I discussed earlier are traits. And you will just have to create a struct that implements that particular trait you want to use; your struct can even implement multiple traits if necessary.

Logging Middleware

Let's start with a basic example in Listing 2-14; that just uses the `BeforeMiddleware` and `AfterMiddleware` to perform logging around a request. We are going to perform a `println` before the action is called and after (we won't use this code in our deployed code, but it's here for our first example).

Listing 2-14. Simple logging middleware

```
/// Logging example
/// Example here : https://github.com/iron/iron
use iron::{typemap, BeforeMiddleware, AfterMiddleware};
use iron::prelude::*;
```

```
pub struct LoggerMiddleware; ①

impl BeforeMiddleware for LoggerMiddleware { ②
    fn before(&self, req: &mut Request) -> IronResult<()> {
        println!("Log - Before Start");
        Ok(())
    }
}

impl AfterMiddleware for LoggerMiddleware { ③
    fn after(&self, req: &mut Request, res: Response) ->
    IronResult<Response> {
        println!("Log - End Start");
        Ok(res)
    }
}
```

①   Create a structure that will store our middleware.

②   Implement the `BeforeMiddleware` trait for the struct.

③   Implement the `AfterMiddleware` trait for the struct.

And there you have it, a middleware that is fully created; however, it is not connected to our system yet. To do this, we are going to assume we have the router defined as well. If you didn't have the router, this would just be any action handler. But we are going to use the chain to create a chain of handlers that gets called. This will allow us to add multiple handlers. Our existing code looks like Listing 2-15 for creating an application.

Listing 2-15. Basic existing application

```
let router = create_routes();
Iron::new(router).http("localhost:3000");
```

We will now use `chain` to build up a chain of before and after around the handler. In Listing 2-16 the chain, we need to specify if the `struct` we created is used for before or after or around middleware.

Listing 2-16. Wrapping a chain around the handlers

```
use mount::Mount;
use iron::prelude::Chain;

    let router = create_router();

    let mut mount = Mount::new();
    mount.mount("/", router); ①

    let mut chain = Chain::new(mount); ②
    chain.link_before(LoggerMiddleware); ③
    chain.link_after(LoggerMiddleware); ④

    Iron::new(chain).http("localhost:3000"); ⑤
```

① Mounts our router to the / path; we could just as easily mount it to
   "/api" which is fairly common for a web application. Thus, to call any
   endpoint will be like "/api/healthz".

② Creates the chain using the mount as the handler; we could use the
   router or the individual handler if there was just one.

③ Will attach the struct that has a BeforeMiddleware to be run before
   the chain starts.

④ Will attach the struct that has a AfterMiddleware to be run after the
   chain starts.

⑤ Now with the chain that also contains our mount, which contains our
   routes, we bind that to port 3000 for execution.

And once all this is run, you now have a web application that has routes and supports
a logging middleware.

Timer Middleware

Let's take a look at a slightly more complex example, the timer example. What this
example is showing is that in the before, we can not only retrieve and use the request,
but we can actually insert values onto the request that can then be used in either other
middleware or our handlers. We are essentially storing these into a key/value store.

If you set attributes in a general map on the request, this could pose many problems if you started adding more and more middleware. It would be difficult at compile time to know if we had multiple overwrites of a key. What we do instead is we use the typemap::Key object that then gets set to a struct in our module. Therefore, whenever we reference the key, we are going to use the struct. This also allows us to create complex objects that can be used by our middleware. The struct itself could contain multiple values and have implementations of other functions. When we get to diesel in the next section, we will see a more complex example that then sets the middleware to retrieve our database connectivity in our handler, but in Listing 2-17 we want to just start a timer and then be able to retrieve our AfterMiddleware.

Listing 2-17. Timer example

```rust
// Copiedfrom https://github.com/iron/iron
use iron::prelude::*;
use iron::{typemap, AfterMiddleware, BeforeMiddleware};
use time::precise_time_ns;

pub struct ResponseTime; ①

impl typemap::Key for ResponseTime { type Value = u64; } ②

impl BeforeMiddleware for ResponseTime {
    fn before(&self, req: &mut Request) -> IronResult<()> {
        req.extensions.insert::<ResponseTime>(precise_time_ns()); ③
        Ok(())
    }
}

impl AfterMiddleware for ResponseTime {
    fn after(&self, req: &mut Request, res: Response) ->
    IronResult<Response> {
        let delta = precise_time_ns() - *req.extensions.
        get::<ResponseTime>().unwrap(); ④
        println!("Request took: {} ms", (delta as f64) / 1000000.0);
        Ok(res)
    }
}
```

① Create the struct that is going to hold our start timer.

② Implementing the `typemap::Key` will allow us to use this structure to set in the `req.extensions`.

③ Use the `req.extensions` to add functionality, passing in the `ResponseTime` struct with the value of the time in ms of right now.

④ Retrieve from the extensions the `ResponseTime` that we had set in the `BeforeMiddleware`.

And there you have it, an easy timer to add to monitor how long your particular route took to run. We will add on to more middleware as the chapters go along, some out-of-the-box crates and others customized.

Database with Diesel

Much like our choices with web frameworks, there are a variety of frameworks out there to pick from for calling a database from Rust. Many of the modules out there are dealing with calling to specific databases. And while with this application we are only calling to a specific database, I wanted to use a more full-featured framework with object-relational mapping (ORM) support. And like most frameworks out there, one stood tall, Diesel. Diesel is a well-documented full-featured extensible framework to use for our application.

The schema we are using for the example applications will be the same one we initially used for our application (we will make some changes as we go along and add features). But this will help us be able to test out and get comfortable with Diesel before we dive into integrating it into the web application. Much of the application will be able to be integrated one for one in there, but we will make some slight changes along the way to align with what we are doing.

For reference, the Diesel home page `https://diesel.rs/` has a great getting started as well as API documentation that can be invaluable for new and even experienced users.

Getting Started

Before we get started writing actual code, let's make sure we have the necessary tools installed to work. From Chapter 1, you should already have `cargo` installed, but there is also a `diesel` command-line tool that is valuable in running migrations and deploying the application.

To install the command-line interface, run

```
cargo install diesel_cli
```

If you had issues running that, it could be because you do not have a database backend library for `diesel`. If that's the case, you will need to first make sure you have `Postgres` library files installed (or MySQL, but we just care about Postgres).

Since we are using this to interface with Postgres, you need to install `Postgres` as well (at least the library files). You can install it any way you want; the way I most commonly install applications is via Homebrew, but this only works with OSX and Linux computers. If you have one, I am sure you have it installed; if you don't, you can go to `https://brew.sh/` for installation instructions. Once `brew` is installed, you can install `postgresql` for your Mac or Linux box:

```
brew install postgresql
```

After that, you can try to re-install your `diesel_cli` application, specifying the postgres feature:

```
cargo install diesel_cli --no-default-features --features postgres
```

And finally, if that all doesn't work, do not fret too much; you can still continue; just realize when we are referencing using the `diesel` cli, you will have to perform the operations manually. We will mostly use the cli to set up the database and run our migration scripts accordingly.

Configuring the App

In a new or existing application, let's add the diesel dependency in Listing 2-18; you can add this to the application we already started building.

Listing 2-18. Adding the dependencies, in Cargo.toml

```
# Enable Number, this allows us to use big decimal that we can use in the
place of f64
# serde_json = needed for using JSONb
# uuidv07 : needed for higher uuid versions (in the master this was changed
to just uuid)
diesel = { version = "^1.4.4", features = ["postgres", "r2d2", "chrono",
"uuidv07", "numeric", "serde_json"] }
dotenv = "0.15.0"
```

Two things you notice, you will see we have the standard add but also the `features`. We will need to activate the feature for the corresponding database you are writing to. In our case, we are using `postgres`. I also included the `dotenv`; this is not necessarily needed for our `diesel` but will be needed by our connection script to read our database URL variable which we will set with an environment variable.

Creating the Database Tables

We have the `cargo` configured; let's start writing some simple database insertion code. `Diesel` has the concept of migrations which will help push us along the process. The migrations are designed to be able to create and drop, so that if you need to revert a change, you easily can. For our situation, the revert will be pretty simple and just drops, but in a full production app, both the update and drops could be at the column level and even move data around. It will be up to you to determine how complex your update gets.

To get things kicked off, we need to create the migrations directory first. The migrations directories are readable timestamp directories with the name of the table we are creating at the end. Now we can create this by hand, but it's a bit easier to have `diesel` do it for us. To create the first table, run the following from the root of your project directory:

```
diesel migration generate comment
```

This in turn will create a directory under `migrations` with a timestamp + `comment` and inside of that will have two files, the `up.sql` and `down.sql`. The up is for the SQL generation, and the down is for the revert. Let's create a comments table in Listing 2-19 and add two fields to it.

Listing 2-19. For our create table for comments

```
CREATE TABLE comments (
  id SERIAL PRIMARY KEY,
  body TEXT NOT NULL,
  media_item_id UUID NOT NULL references media_datas(id),
  created_at TIMESTAMP NOT NULL DEFAULT CURRENT_TIMESTAMP,
  updated_at TIMESTAMP NOT NULL DEFAULT CURRENT_TIMESTAMP
)
```

Listing 2-20 is a fairly simplistic listing but gets the point across of what we are building. The down.sql will simply list our drop statement for the comments table.

Listing 2-20. To drop the comments table

```
DROP TABLE comments;
```

Generating the Database with Docker

Now that we have the start of our databases, the next step will be to generate the tables; but to do it requires a few more steps. The biggest step of course is that we need a database to write to. If you already have Postgres installed and want to use that instance, you can skip the next part, but I actually prefer this method than simply having Postgres run all the time.

If you are like me, you do quite a bit of work from your laptop, but you also do quite a few projects from there. You could be writing a Postgres-Rust app one day; another day, you may want to demo a Redis+Mongo+Spring app for another client. Your needs change, and I don't want to have to get into a habit of always remembering what database I have to configure, where to pull it from, and did I use brew for one and a package installer for the other. The solution to make your life easier is docker. Docker is a brilliant image container, and there are many custom images out there. Besides the default postgres images, you can even find postgres images that have database information embedded into them as well, which is actually what we want to use for performing future geographic information system (GIS) queries. The default image you could use is postgres, but we want one with GIS, so we will be using mdillon/postgis.

Without diving too much into docker (we will get more into it in Chapter 7), docker contains image repositories both remotely and locally. The remote repositories are good at storing known images you want to share, and the local allow a local copy of either those ones or ones you need to use. Basically for us, we can keep an image of all the different database, tools, and applications we may want to run. But for now, let's stick with installing postgres. In Listing 2-21, we run the image in our docker container.

Listing 2-21. Downloading a Postgres GIS and running it

```
docker network create -d bridge iot ①
docker pull postgres ②
docker run --name rust-iot-book --net=iot --volume ~/.docker/volumes/post
gresgisiot:/var/lib/postgresql/data -p 5433:5432 -e POSTGRES_USER=user -e
POSTGRES_PASSWORD=password -e POSTGRES_DB=rust-iot-db -d mdillon/postgis ③
```

① Creates a bridge network, useful for allowing multiple docker images to talk to each other.

② Pulls the Postgres database.

③ Runs the docker image command.

Make sure the database you use in your application is the one created here; the one created by diesel does not have the GIS active and will affect our application in the next chapter.

Line 1 will pull the postgres GIS database into our local docker image repository. Line 3 is where it gets more interesting; this is what actually starts up the repository. Now you could have started it up with a simple docker run mdillon/postgis, but that wouldn't have been as helpful. It is important to understand what is going on here. The image created is not being run as a local application; it is being run in its own image in its own virtual machine (VM). So the files it writes to and the ports it binds to are not by default accessible to the user unless we explicitly say otherwise, and how do we accomplish this, we send arguments to the run. Let's take a look at what each of these arguments does:

--name – This will give us an easy name to start and stop the server once we initially run the container and be able to give a name to the running container (as opposed to a docker id). Now we will be able to start/stop the server using the name rust-iot-book.

--volume – As I stated earlier, the image is not run in our local environment; however, we may want the image to have access to a local volume. This is for a number of reasons. In a traditional application, you may want to share data, but here, it's mostly so we can persist the data between starts and stops and computer reboots. In postgres /var/lib/postgresql/data is where the underlying data for the database is stored. This is why we will map a local folder to that directory, so during stops, we don't have to recreate the data.

-p – I mentioned earlier that the containers run in their own environment not exposed to the external environment (which would be our local). For a database, this wouldn't work for us; our Rust app ran from the command line would never be able to read/write to the database. What this parameter does is gives you a from and to, to expose the port. The port in a postgres application is 5433 so we have to use that as the to, but to make things simple, I use the from as the same. To simplify, think of 5433:5432 as local:docker_port. I set it to forward to port 5433 since its PostGis may interfere with an existing database you have installed and wanted to make this seamless.

-e – You will notice multiple -e's throughout our call, which stands for as you may have guessed environmental variable. These are the environmental variables the application will use at startup. For postgres, these will create a default database named diesel_demo as well as creating a user named user with password password; that account though will allow us to dynamically create more schemas in the application when we run the diesel scripts.

-d – Finally, one of the more important options is -d; this specifies the docker image we are going to use to spin up the virtual machine with. And this is our postgres GIS database.

That set of commands will start up the application; let's go over a few more commands that you will find useful when using docker.

Docker Running Containers

If you want to view all the docker containers running, you can type docker ps and you will get a list of all the containers as well as when they were created and how long they have been up for.

Stopping Docker

If you want to stop the container running, you can use docker stop rust-iot-book to stop the image we created earlier.

Starting Docker

If you have manually stopped the docker container or it's stopped due to restarting, you can restart it. (Note: Reboots do not automatically restart a container). Luckily, you do not need to run the preceding long script since the container has already been created; you can simply run `docker start rust-iot-book` and it will start up the image again with all the parameters we set earlier.

Running the Generation Scripts

Now back to `diesel`. We have created our migration scripts and started up a `postgres` instance; we are now ready to set up our database and run our migrations; we just need to do a few things more to get ready.

Diesel has quite a few mechanisms to help automate our database creation, but to take advantage of them, we have to tell it where our database exists. You can do this via an environmental variable on your system, but the easiest way is via an `.env` file in the root of your project like in Listing 2-22.

Listing 2-22. Our environmental variable with the database URL, in file .env

```
DATABASE_URL=postgres://user:password@localhost:5433/rust-iot-db
```

This sets up an environmental variable named `DATABASE_URL` that the `diesel` will read and use to create the database. The preceding example uses the username and password we created earlier and creates a database schema named `diesel_db_example`. Now we are ready to use the rest of the `diesel` commands to create the database.

First thing you need to do is set up the database, which is run with the `diesel setup` command; this will do a few things. This will create a schema (assuming it has privileges to do so) in your database and will also run your initial set up script. This will be creating a folder named `00000000000000_diesel_initial_setup` with an `up.sql` and `down.sql` in the `migrations` folder, much like our other migrations (the folder name is picked so it's guaranteed to always run first). The file adds one basic item that you can see in Listing 2-23.

Listing 2-23. Showing the initialization script for our database

```
CREATE OR REPLACE FUNCTION diesel_manage_updated_at(_tbl regclass) RETURNS
VOID AS $$
BEGIN
    EXECUTE format('CREATE TRIGGER set_updated_at BEFORE UPDATE ON %s
                    FOR EACH ROW EXECUTE PROCEDURE diesel_set_updated_
                    at()', _tbl);
END;
$$ LANGUAGE plpgsql;

CREATE OR REPLACE FUNCTION diesel_set_updated_at() RETURNS trigger AS $$
BEGIN
    IF (
        NEW IS DISTINCT FROM OLD AND
        NEW.updated_at IS NOT DISTINCT FROM OLD.updated_at
    ) THEN
        NEW.updated_at := current_timestamp;
    END IF;
    RETURN NEW;
END;
$$ LANGUAGE plpgsql;
```

This will also add a trigger to automatically update the updated_at column on your tables if they have one. This makes it easy and useful to have your database updated_at field automatically updated by the database.

After running diesel setup in your application, there are a few more commands you can choose to run:

- diesel migration pending – This will let us know if there are any migrations that need to be applied to the database that are not there. The way the system keeps track of if we have migrations is by checking the database table _diesel_schema_migrations which will track the migrations run.

- diesel migration run – This command will run any of the pending migrations.

- `diesel migration list` – This command lists all the migrations that have been run and any that are in a pending state. This becomes useful as you have more and more database tables and migrations.

- `diesel migration revert` – Finally, it can become necessary to revert a migration; this often happens in design when you realize you want to change what you created or if you want to back out a migration. This command will only revert the last previously committed change, but can be rerun to revert subsequent ones as well.

There are many more commands, but these are the most common that you will use.

Schema File

There are a few side effects of running the preceding scripts. The first one is when you run `diesel setup`, it will also create a `diesel.toml` file. This has quite a few configurations we aren't going to talk about here, but you can learn more at `http://diesel.rs/guides/configuring-diesel-cli/`. The main thing it does is define a file path for the `schema.rs`.

The `schema.rs` is actually a generated file that will contain our table definitions based on our database migrations. These are encapsulated in a rust macro, and we will use it to do our ORM querying, updating, and so on from the database in our Rust code. And when we get to database enumerations, we will actually have to modify the file directly. In Listing 2-24 is the manual modifications of it.

Listing 2-24. Showing the database schema generated from adding our comment table

```
table! {
    comments (id) {
        id -> Int4,
        body -> Text,
        media_item_id -> Uuid,
        created_at -> Timestamp,
        updated_at -> Timestamp,
    }
}
```

```
table! {
    health_checks (id) {
        id -> Int4,
        device_uuid -> Uuid,
        data -> Jsonb,
        user_id -> Uuid,
        created_at -> Timestamp,
        updated_at -> Timestamp,
    }
}
```

As you can see, this tells Rust what the table name is for reference, the attributes, and their types as well as what type is the primary key. Later, we will look at one that has joins and other attributes in it as well. But first, let's learn how to do basic querying, updating, inserting, and deleting against it.

Basics

Before we start diving into how to do queries in diesel, I feel there are some fundamental differences between diesel and other ORMs that we should discuss. Most ORMs follow a pretty typical model of mapping a database relation to a concrete object. So that if you have a comments table, you have a comment object/struct/class whatever your system is using to store objects. These relations tend to be 1:1; for every comment table, you have one comment struct and then you use that for everything – for adding, deleting, updating, modifying, querying, and so on. But this is not necessarily and not often the case with diesel. You will create a struct for what you are trying to do since often the fields will be different; you will then use traits so that struct knows what it can do, whether it can query, insert, and so on. One of the reasons you do this is because when inserting you may not have an id, but on querying, you will. On first look, this seems weird, but in practice, it makes things easy and useful, and since you can easily place multiple structs in one file, your code still stays very organized.

Inserting

Now that we have everything set up, the first thing you want to do is insert into the database. There are quite a number of different ways to do this; we will go over a few of them here.

Our first example is in Listing 2-25; you can create a database record passing in the column types individually and then setting them on the table. This methodology is easy for inserts that are small in number or run ad hoc.

Listing 2-25. Create a comment passing a string, in file src/models/comment.rs

```
pub fn add(conn: &PgPooled, media_id: Uuid, bod: String) -> i32 {
    use diesel::{RunQueryDsl, ExpressionMethods};
    use diesel::insert_into;

    info!("insert into the comment database");

    match insert_into(comments)
        .values((body.eq(bod), media_item_id.eq(media_id))) ①
        .returning(id) ②
        .get_result::<i32>(&*conn) { ③
        Ok(val) => { ④
            val
        },
        Err(e) => {
            warn!("insertion failed, likely invalid reference : {}", e);
            -1
        }
    }
}
```

① The body in this code represents the body field in schemas::table.

② You can pick the column to return; id is the most usual since it's the unknown at insertion time for a serial db type.

③ You have to give the type for the id, in this case, i32.

④ Checks the return of a result, returning negative 1 if it doesn't create any.

The other way to insert is to have a `struct` use a macro; this will be a struct that is a subset of the full record and items like the serial primary key; the auto created dates are not a part of the struct. The struct only contains what we plan to insert. In addition in Listing 2-26, we use a `diesel` macro that allows it for insertion.

Listing 2-26. Creates a new struct that has the macro `derive(Insertable)` on it for insertion, in file src/models/comment.rs

```
use diesel::Expression;

// need to bring in the comments module for this to work
#[derive(Insertable, Queryable, PartialEq, Debug)]
#[table_name="comments"]
pub struct NewComment {
    pub body: String,
    pub media_item_id: Uuid,
}
```

With that object in Listing 2-27, you can then pass that into your function and save it directly on the table; we will be using this methodology in Chapter 3 to insert the media data information.

Listing 2-27. Pass in an object to add to the table

```
fn create_comment_execute<'a>(conn: &PgConnection, c: &'a NewComment) ->
usize {
    use schema::comments::dsl::*;

    let inserted_rows = insert_into(comments)
        .values(c)
        .execute(&*conn).unwrap();

    inserted_rows
}
```

Alternatively in Listing 2-28, we could have saved it but then returned the resulting result object as well.

Listing 2-28. Pass in an object to add to the table

```
insert_into(comments)
    .values(c)
    .get_result(&*conn)
    .expect("please don't error out")
```

Deleting

Deleting is a pretty simple task as well. We can delete based on any attributes on the table. In the Listing 2-29 example though, we will delete based on ID since it is the most often use case.

Listing 2-29. Deleting an object from the database, src/model/comment.rs

```
pub fn delete(conn: &PgPooled, comment_id: i32) -> DbResult<u32> {
    use diesel::{QueryDsl, RunQueryDsl, ExpressionMethods};
    use diesel::delete;
    //use diesel::prelude::;

    let result = delete(comments.filter(id.eq(comment_id)))
        .execute(&*conn);

    match result {
        // Convert since we get it as Usize
        Ok(rows_deleted) => Ok(rows_deleted as u32),
        Err(error) => Err(error),
    }
}
```

You will notice we also grab the result and use a matcher against the result to determine the rows deleted so we know if the rows are deleted.

Querying

Another common operation with database is to query the data. This as well can be handled multiple ways. There is a DSL layer built on top of connections to perform querying operations, as well as calls to find all or find by primary key. In Listing 2-30, we will retrieve all published posts.

Listing 2-30. Querying from the database

```
use diesel_demo::schema::posts::dsl::*;

    let connection = establish_connection();
    let results = posts.filter(published.eq(true))
        .limit(5)
        .load::<Post>(&connection)
        .expect("Error loading posts");

println!("Displaying {} posts", results.len());
for post in results {
    println!("{}", post.title);
    println!("----------\n");
    println!("{}", post.body);
}
```

We will go into more examples as needed throughout the book when the time for each query comes.

Your Queryable struct has to have the fields in the same order as they are in the table! definition.

Field Order

Using #[derive(Queryable)] assumes that the order of fields on the Post struct matches the columns in the posts table, so make sure to define them in the order seen in the schema.rs file.

Using Enumerations

When creating database applications, we often have data that is used for drop-downs, selectors, and anything that is a type. There are two ways to represent the data usually. The first is to have a table with a one-to-many relationship to the main table. This is good for information that can be changed frequently. And even if the data is not changed often, the data could just be used for displayable purposes. However, often the data never changes, and more importantly, that data is needed for use in the application to make decisions. Take our application; we are going to store data in S3 or local file store. We also want to have different options for handling audio, video, or photo data. The way we generally handle these situations in code is via enumerations, and that is how we are going to handle them here. Different databases have different support for enumerations. MySQL will make you use an int with a sequence to represent the data; however, Postgres does have an enumeration type we can map the type to. We can also store an array of enumerations to one field to perform some multi-selection stores. This will allow us to query the database faster than having a multi-table querying with a many-to-many; you would normally need to perform this operation. How we do this will take a few steps and is not super simple but not overly complex either. Enumerations themselves are part of the Rust language; we just need to use a library to hook it into the database. In Listing 2-31 we define our location enum.

Listing 2-31. Our location enumeration to determine whether to write to S3 or Local

```
pub enum LocationEnum {
    S3,
    Local
}
```

A fairly straightforward enumeration, we will have three totals in our code. We won't have all the examples in the book, but they will be in the code for the book. So now that we have an enumeration written, let's look at how to create enumerations in Postgres. In Postgres, we can create custom enumeration types so we will start with creating three of those in Listing 2-32.

Listing 2-32. Creating the enumeration types for the database

```
CREATE TYPE media_enum AS ENUM ('image', 'video', 'unknown');

CREATE TYPE location_enum AS ENUM ('s3', 'local');

CREATE TYPE media_audience_enum AS ENUM ('personal', 'friends'' family');
```

In here, we have created enumerations for the different types of media, the location it's stored in, and the audience type. Now let's apply them to our media_datas table. But first the media_audience, we could really apply more than one to a piece of media, so let's make that an array so we can save more than one. In Listing 2-33, we added our media types to the media_datas table.

Listing 2-33. Adding the media_datas to the table

```
media_type media_enum NULL,
location_type location_enum NOT NULL,
media_audience_type media_audience_enum[] NULL
```

Diesel Derive Enum Crate

OK, now that we have our database updated, the enumerations in place, it's time to integrate this change with Diesel. Out of the box, we do not have tight integration; luckily, there is a diesel enumeration crate that gives us a hand. The diesel derive enum crate (https://github.com/adwhit/diesel-derive-enum) can be added to our dependencies in our Cargo.toml in Listing 2-34.

Listing 2-34. The crate for the diesel-derive-enum

```
diesel-derive-enum = { version = "0.4", features = ["postgres"] }
```

One thing to remember is since every database treats enumerations differently, you will have to activate the feature for the trait you are using. In this case, we will be using postgres; you can select either the aforementioned postgres, mysql, or sqlite. Then in order to use the diesel_derive_enum, we need to apply the trait DbEnum to our enumerations like in Listing 2-35.

Listing 2-35. For having an enumeration

```
#[derive(DbEnum, Debug, Eq, PartialEq, Deserialize, Clone)]
#[DieselType = "Media_Audience_Enum_Map"]
#[derive(GraphQLEnum)]
pub enum MediaAudienceEnum {
    Personal,
    Friends,
    Family
}
```

What this trait does is create a custom type that can be used by diesel for the schema mapping. By default, this trait will use the name of the enum as the custom type we have to define in the schema. But we can also create our diesel type name like in Listing 2-36.

Listing 2-36. For having an enumeration

```
#[derive(DbEnum, Debug, Eq, PartialEq, Deserialize, Clone)] ①
#[DieselType = "Media_Enum_Map"] ②
#[derive(GraphQLEnum)]
pub enum MediaEnum { ③
    Image,
    Video,
    Unknown,
}
```

    ①   Applying the DbEnum and other traits to this enumeration.

    ②   Changing the diesel type name that will be used.

    ③   Defining our enumeration.

The real purpose of using this is if you want to use the diesel cli print-schema command, with the cli it is going to derive the type from the database type, and with databases we usually separate types by underscores, but with Rust structs we use camel case. This would make *media_enum* enum type in the database to the Rust enumeration *Media_enum*, hence the usefulness of this. The next part gets a bit tricky – how to make this all work with our schema. For the most part, our schema is derived when you run migrations and does get overwritten each time you run a new migration. However, since these types are only created when the trait is created, we will have to manually modify the schema.rs, specifically the table! macro that you have the enumerations in. In Listing 2-37 we have our modifications ot the schema.

Listing 2-37. Manual modifications to the schema

```
table! {
    // Manual edition
    use diesel::sql_types::{Integer, Array, Text, Bool, Timestamp,
    Nullable, Uuid}; ①
    use super::Media_Enum_Map; ②
    use super::Location_Enum_Map;
    use super::Media_Audience_Enum_Map;
```

```
media_datas (id) {
    id -> Uuid,
    name -> Text,
    note -> Nullable<Text>,
    media_type -> Media_Enum_Map, ③
    location -> Text,
    location_type -> Location_Enum_Map,
    device_id -> Uuid,
    media_audience_type -> Array<Media_Audience_Enum_Map>, ④
    size -> Integer,
    published -> Bool,
    created_at -> Timestamp,
    updated_at -> Timestamp,
}
}
```

① Manually bringing in the sql types for diesel.

② The three enumeration types that we defined in the mod.rs file.

③ Mapping using our custom diesel_type.

④ Our array using the name of the structs directly without the custom override.

Probably the most startling line is the #1 point bringing in the sql_types. But this is necessary; if not, it won't be able to find the types once we started creating custom types. At this point, we now have a database with schemas and queries we can make use of.

Relationships

Diesel supports all your standard relationships, the one-to-many, many-to-one, and many-to-many. When you create your database entry with a relationship, it will automatically get reflected in the schema.rs and then be able to be used for querying. In Listing 2-38 is the added reference to *schema.rs*.

Listing 2-38. Showing relationships in diesel

```
joinable!(comments -> media_datas (media_item_id));
```

Using a UUID

Most of the time, our database primary keys are sequence numbers, and usually they are created by the database themselves. This works to ensure the PK in the database is a unique number. However, this only works if the data object we are creating only needs to know that PK at the time of insertion. What if you are using a read/write CQRS system (like we are going to in a few chapters), or what if you have one system talking to another system, which is often the case with microservices, and they need to know the PK of the object to be stored before it's stored? Let's examine our choices:

1. If System 1 has data, it creates a local sequence PK for that data; when it calls System 2, then System 2 can store System 1's ID in a column on the database. That way when System 1 needs to query System 2, it has something it knows how to talk.

2. In a reverse situation, System 2 can respond with its PK and System 1 can store it.

3. Use UUIDs.

The first two are utterly complex and sloppy; what we really want to do is use the SAME PK, but how do we do that with a sequence id that may not be the same? The answer is Unique Universal Identifiers (UUIDs). UUIDs give us the ability to transmit data and store it back and forth. In our use case, we are going to store our media files in our upload_svc and then transmit the data including the UUID to the retrieval_svc so that we always have a correlation between the two.

Please note that we will be keeping the comment's PK as a serial ID since the way it stores its data is only via the retrieval_svc.

UUIDs work very well with cargo, and there is a good crate to make UUIDs work, so the process to have our database use UUIDs is quite simple. Step 1 in Listing 2-39 will be to change the primary key from serial to UUID; UUID is a type in Postgres, so no customizations are needed.

Listing 2-39. Setting our primary key for the table

```
CREATE TABLE media_datas (
  id UUID PRIMARY KEY,
```

However, we do have to slightly change our configurations to let `diesel` know we want to use a UUID sql type. In your `diesel` dependency, you will have to activate the UUID feature as well as bring in the UUID crate, although the latter is simply so we can create UUIDs. (Note: In the previous example, the uuidv07 is also listed; I am showing it in Listing 2-40 to illustrate the specific feature that was needed for it.)

Listing 2-40. Activating the UUID in our diesel app and adding the UUID crate

```
diesel = { version = "^1.4.4", features = ["postgres", "uuidv07"] }
uuid = { version =  "^0.8.0", features = ["serde", "v4"] }
```

At this point when your `schema` file is generated, it should now use the UUID diesel trait; I did run it with everything on there since it's a final copy, but you would have needed the `uuid` trait to get it to fully work. In Listing 2-41, we have it.

Listing 2-41. The UUID being reflected in our schema.rs file

```
media_datas (id) {
        id -> Uuid,
```

Finally, the last thing to do is to use it. If you reference Listing 2-18, you will notice one of the features we brought in was v4; this is because the UUID crate will let you use any versions 1–5 for the UUID. The v3 and v5 are used to generate a UUID off a given name; however, with video and file upload, we can't guarantee uniqueness; we just want pseudo-random numbers, for which v4 is our best choice to do. For our application, we will have a bit of a unique use case; since we are using the UUID in upload_svc, we will have to instantiate the UUID and then convert it to a string for the filename; we can then use that identifier when creating our JSON and pass it to the `retrieval_svc`. In Listing 2-42, we see the UUID being instantiated and passed to our save_data function.

Listing 2-42. Manual modifications to the schema

```
let uuid = Uuid::new_v4();
debug!("File to save :: {:?} to {}", filename, uuid);

match save_data(&uuid, &data, &filename,uuid.to_hyphenated().to_string()) {
```

Now that we have our database all designed (or as much as we need for now), let's see how we integrate it into our `iron` application.

Integrating with Our Application

We have gone over how to use `diesel`, creating our own schemas and implementing queries we need for our schemas. We also have gone over examples for the queries in our application and how to use them. Now we actually need to glue that all together with `iron`. Simply put, we could use the code we've been writing and use it directly with the data coming in; it works fine. However, if you notice for every call, we have been calling the `get_connection` which instantiates a new connection each time. If you have ever written web applications, you will know most of the time we use a connection pool. There are a number of reasons for this; the first is a database itself has a limited number of connections, and this way we can control it through some central process in the application. The other is of course performance, so we are not spending the time to create a new connection each time. I am going to step you through creating your own `middleware` to handle pool connections, and after we will use a slightly out-of-the-box solution. Both examples will use the `r2d2` crate (`https://github.com/sfackler/r2d2`); this is a very powerful `crate` that is designed to create a connection pool in `rust` for a variety of different backend and frameworks. There is support for all the major databases as well as pooled connections for many of the NoSQL databases. The most up-to-date list will be at the `github` repo I mentioned previously. But our custom and the solution we use will both make use of `r2d2`.

Diesel Write Your Own Middleware

We went over creating middleware when we were talking about `iron`; the concepts and steps will also apply here but with a bit more complex example. Let's first define our goals:

1. Create a connection pool to the database using `r2d2` as the mechanism.

2. Expose this connection in our controller layer of the application without having to instantiate anything directly.

To do this, I am going to work our way back from the controller, to creating the middleware, to creating the database connection.

I initially started this example because the `iron_diesel_middleware` did not work with the latest versions of diesel. However, the author is very open to patches; and after I got done writing this chapter, he incorporated my patch. Thus, we are still going over how to create it because it's a very good use case and learning experience, but this code will not be in the full example application since the latest version of the plugin incorporates the necessary fixes.

Let's start. First up in Listing 2-43, the most common way to extend your middleware to add features is to add on to the `iron::Request`, through the `extensions` attribute also directly on the request itself. This is somewhat counter-intuitive for those coming from languages that have injection everywhere, but injection is expensive and problematic; adding to the request we can guarantee more compile-time use and memory allocations needed for it. Let's call the database connection we want as `db_conn`.

Listing 2-43. Exposing the middleware on the request

```
use middleware::database::DieselReqExt; ①

pub fn comment(req: &mut Request) -> IronResult<Response> {
    let conn: PgPooled = req.db_conn(); ②
    insert_into_db("test", &conn); ③

    Ok(Response::with((status::Ok, "OK")))
}
```

①   The trait applied to allow db_conn to be on the request.

②   We are retrieving the database connection from db_conn on the req.

③   We pass in the connection received to a function to process the database insert.

As you can see, this makes our controllers clean and concise with little extra work needed, allowing our functions to be readable controllers. Let's go into the next step in Listing 2-44; we need to instantiate the middleware component and add the middleware component to the chain.

Listing 2-44. Instantiating the middleware

```
// Setup our middle ware
let diesel_middleware = DieselMiddlewareConnPool::new("DATABASE_URL"); ①

// Link the chain with our middleware object
let mut chain = Chain::new(mount);
chain.link_before(diesel_middleware); ②
```

①   The first step is to instantiate the middleware from the
DieselMiddlewareConnPool.

②   Since we need to have the connection before the function, we set it
via link_before.

Now we get to the meat and the potatoes creating the actual middleware struct,
DieselMiddlewareConnPool. The struct is pretty simple; it just needs to contain a
connection pool. This connection pool is what gets passed back into the db_conn being
called by the request in our controller. The simple struct is in Listing 2-45.

Listing 2-45. Struct for the DieselMiddlewareConnPool

```
pub struct DieselMiddlewareConnPool {
    pool: PgPool
}
```

After this, there are three extra steps we need to take all performing operations on
this struct to make. There are essentially three remaining steps we need to do to make
everything work:

1.   Have an implementation that will create a connection to the
connection pool.

2.   Have the DieselMiddlewareConnPool inserted for the
BeforeMiddleware trait so that the chain knows when to fire it off.

3.   Using a trait, add a function db_conn to the Request that will pull
in the DieselMiddlewareConnPool and return it to the controller.

Implementing the Connection Pool

Let's start with creating the connection pool; this part in Listing 2-46 is super easy; we
are just going to implement our struct and set a new that passes in as an environmental
string that we should find the connection pool on. From there, we can establish our
connection pool.

Listing 2-46. Implements the new on our struct to create the connection pool

```
impl DieselMiddlewareConnPool {
    /// Creates a new pooled connection to a sql server
    pub fn new(connection_env_var: &str) -> DieselMiddlewareConnPool {
        let pg_pool: PgPool = establish_connection_pool(connection_env_var);
        DieselMiddlewareConnPool {pool: pg_pool}
    }
}
```

The connection pool method in Listing 2-47 will look much like the establish connection we created earlier, except adding the connection pool manager.

Listing 2-47. Code to actually create the connection pool

```
pub type PgPool = Pool<ConnectionManager<PgConnection>>; ①

pub fn establish_connection_pool(db_env_var: &str) -> PgPool {
    dotenv().ok();
    let database_url = env::var(db_env_var)
        .expect("DATABASE_URL must be set");
    let manager = ConnectionManager::<PgConnection>::new(database_url);

    // Get the pooled connection manager
    Pool::new(manager).expect("Failed creating connection pool") ②
}
```

① We set a new type to point to a much longer type, because simply that would be too much to type when setting in each function.

② This is the main addition from what we created before, and it puts the connection manager inside the pool.

Adding the Middleware

Next we need to add to the BeforeMiddleware in Listing 2-48 a before function implementation.

Listing 2-48. Creating our BeforeMiddleware

```
pub struct Value(PgPool);

// to use the Value we need to have a typemap implementation for the Diesel
Middle ware pool
// implement the trait
impl typemap::Key for DieselMiddlewareConnPool { type Value = Value; } ①

// Our middleware we are creating
// inspired by https://github.com/darayus/iron-diesel-middleware/blob/
master/src/lib.rs
// and  git@github.com:DavidBM/rust-webserver-example-with-iron-diesel-
r2d2-serde.git
impl BeforeMiddleware for DieselMiddlewareConnPool {
    fn before(&self, req: &mut Request) -> IronResult<()> {
        req.extensions.insert::<DieselMiddlewareConnPool>(Value(self.pool.
        clone())); ②
        Ok(())
    }
}
```

① Using the typemap::Key to store the value Pool object.

② Inserting the value object on the req.extensions.

You can see here is where we insert on the *req.extentions* a clone of the connection pool. We need to perform the clone because this is going to be called many times, and if we kept trying to use the same object, we would be trying to borrow it constantly and would get a cannot mot out of borrowed content error, since you can't have the same object borrowed and never returned (much like a library book).

Adding a Method to Request

Most of this you have seen before via the timer middleware we wrote, but this the coup de grace to make it a bit fancier and easier to use. If you recall in Listing 2-43 you saw on the controller, we used a trait DieselReqExt before the controller call; here is where we create and define that trait.

Listing 2-49. Adding the trait `DieselReqExt` and implementing it on the `Request`

```
pub trait DieselReqExt {
    fn db_conn(&self) -> PgPooled;
}

impl<'a, 'b> DieselReqExt for Request<'a, 'b> {
    fn db_conn(&self) -> PgPooled {
        let pool_conn = self.extensions.get::<DieselMiddlewareConnPool>().
        expect("Diesel MW Conn Pool Retrieval");
        let &Value(ref pool) = pool_conn;

        return pool.get().expect("Failed to get DB Connection in the
        request");
    }
}
```

We start off by creating the trait with one function db_conn; then in the following section, we implement that trait for the Request so that when applied in context with the trait, we have a connection pool.

Diesel Middleware

There you have it, a clean controller that allows us to create connection pools on the fly. Of course, the most logical thing you'd think to yourself is to wrap this up into a crate and make it easy to use for each project. Luckily, there is one project out there from @darayus that does just that (https://github.com/darayus/iron-diesel-middleware), called iron-diesel-middleware. However, there is a small issue with the project, in that he makes use of the crate r2d2-diesel which was an r2d2 for diesel; that project has since been deprecated and that code is baked into diesel and activated by adding the r2d2 feature. What I ended up doing is forking the project and patching it to use r2d2 from diesel. It's pretty simple to use. For the dependency, you will have to reference the git repo like in Listing 2-50.

Listing 2-50. Add the middleware to the Cargo.toml

```
[dependencies.iron_diesel_middleware]
git = "https://github.com/nusairat/iron-diesel-middleware.git"
```

Now that we have the crate, we can apply it; the structs and functions in the crate are very similar namewise (intentional). In Listing 2-51, you can see adding the request function.

Listing 2-51. Using the `iron-diesel-middleware` in our code

```
use iron_diesel_middleware::{DieselMiddleware, DieselReqExt};
type DieselPg = DieselMiddleware<diesel::pg::PgConnection>;

fn create_links(chain: &mut Chain, url: &str) {

    // Create the middleware for the diesel
    let diesel_middleware: DieselPg = DieselMiddleware::new(url).unwrap();

    // link the chain
    chain.link_before(diesel_middleware);
}
```

More Web Framework

I wanted to jump back into the web framework world a bit more. We will do that from time to time. But I wanted to go over a few extra crates; that is going to hopefully make your life easier in any Rust application. Some of these are specifically for the Web, but others are more generic and could be used for anything.

Command-Line Parameters

As you have noticed already from using the application, we run everything from the command line. The same will be when launching the web application or using the application on a device. As you saw as well, we even pulled the database url from the environmental variable; this is how we will also set things once we go to production in future chapters with Helm, Kubernetes, and so on. This means that when we want to run the applications, we need to use either the command line or environmental variables. Luckily for us, there is a great tool to do command-line parsing supporting both methods. And that's Clap Rs (https://github.com/clap-rs/clap). Clap is a great tool, in that it not only allows us to pass in arguments on the command line but also allows us to pass default values and environmental values for those arguments. This makes it great for ease of use with development. Let's get started by importing the clap crate in Listing 2-52.

Listing 2-52. The Cargo.toml with the clap crate

```
# Used for Argument Matching And Applications
clap = "2.33.0"
```

Let's take a look at a small example in Listing 2-53 to see the power it provides and all the options allowed for it for each command.

Listing 2-53. Argument matching for one argument, the port argument

```
use clap::{App, Arg};
use iron::prelude::*;
use iron::status;

fn main() {
    let matches = App::new("Title")
        .version(env!("CARGO_PKG_VERSION")) ①
        .about("Our description.")
        .arg(Arg::with_name("PORT") ②
                .short("P") ③
                .long("port") ④
                .takes_value(true) ⑤
                .required(true) ⑥
                .env("PORT") ⑦
                .default_value("3000") ⑧
                .help("The value to start the server on"))
        .get_matches();

    let port = matches.value_of("PORT").unwrap(); ⑨

    Iron::new(|_: &mut Request| Ok(Response::with((status::Ok, "Hello World
    Rust"))))
        .http(format!("localhost:{}", port));
}
```

① This sets the version that we use from the Cargo file.

② We will use this name to reference the call later.

③ When calling from the command line, this is the short variable.

④ When calling from the command line, this is the long variable.

⑤ Specifying whether the value will be supplied at runtime.

⑥ Whether or not this value is required.

⑦ The environmental variable that can be supplied with the PORT.

⑧ The default value to use; really useful for development.

⑨ How to actually retrieve the values; the value_of uses with__name set
of PORT.

Right now if you run that application, the application will start up normally. But what happens if you turn off the default flag? You will get an error that is actually useful. Let's view the error in Listing 2-54.

Listing 2-54. Showing the error when there is no default value

```
error: The following required arguments were not provided:
    --port <PORT>
USAGE:
    cli --port <PORT>
```

You can rerun this example by passing in --port 3000 to the executable binary. Doing this in development mode is a bit different than if you had the compiled rust binary. Listing 2-55 shows how to run the command from cargo run.

Listing 2-55. Running the clap locally

```
→ cargo run --bin cli -- --port 3000
```

We will make great use of this as we go along for any external services that may require configurations that can change. For us about every argument we use will be the matcher, with a combination of string and integer values depending on the argument. Some of our applications like retrieval_svc will have nine attributes to match. If you look back on Listing 2-53, adding eight more attributes could make that very ugly very fast. What we are going to do is set up each argument in its own module under the args module. Thus, the port attribute will be stored in a file like in Listing 2-56; here we apply constants to the values and settings. Each of our arguments will have a similar method.

Listing 2-56. Argument matching for the PORT, in file src/args/port.rs

```rust
use clap::Arg;

pub const HELP: &str = "The Port the App is bound to ";
pub const LONG_HELP: &str = "\
Our Port for our application";
pub const LONG: &str = NAME;
pub const NAME: &str = "port";
pub const SHORT: &str = "p";
pub const DEFAULT_VALUE: &str = "3010";
pub const TAKES_VALUE: bool = true;
pub const VALUE_NAME: &str = "PORT";

pub fn declare_arg<'a, 'b>() -> Arg<'a, 'b> {
    Arg::with_name(NAME)
        .short(SHORT)
        .long(LONG)
        .env(VALUE_NAME)
        .value_name(VALUE_NAME)
        .required(TAKES_VALUE)
        .help(HELP)
        .long_help(LONG_HELP)
        .default_value(DEFAULT_VALUE)
}
```

Now when we have to perform an argument matcher against nine arguments, the code is still readable. In Listing 2-57, we have our argument matcher along with two subcommands (this application is run twice, one to serve as an RPC and the other to serve as rpc the other to perform automatic migrations; we will get into these applications later). But for now, take away how much cleaner that looks.

Listing 2-57. Argument matching for the application, file in src/main.rs

```
fn start_app_and_get_matches() -> ArgMatches<'static> {
    App::new(APP_TITLE)
        .version(env!("CARGO_PKG_VERSION"))
        .author(env!("CARGO_PKG_AUTHORS"))
        .about(APP_DESCRIPTION)
        .setting(AppSettings::ColoredHelp)
        .arg(args::database::declare_arg())
        .arg(args::server::declare_arg())
        .arg(args::port::declare_arg())
        .arg(args::rpc::declare_arg())
        .arg(args::auth::declare_arg())
        .arg(args::event_store_host::declare_arg())
        .arg(args::event_store_port::declare_arg())
        .arg(args::event_store_pass::declare_arg())
        .arg(args::event_store_user::declare_arg())
        .arg(args::event_store_web_port::declare_arg())
        .subcommand(SubCommand::with_name("migration")
            .about("runs the migrations for diesel"))
        .subcommand(SubCommand::with_name("rpc")
            .about("runs the RPC server"))
        .get_matches()
}
```

Error Handling

Right now, most of the way we are handling errors is we aren't. We are using the expect() call and letting the function just crash. However, often we want to have customized errors for each type of error. This is out of the box possible to do with Rust but becomes cumbersome with lots of coding. You will have to write an error for each and track where the errors are, which becomes a bit of a pain. Introducing error_chain (https://github.com/rust-lang-nursery/error-chain). This will allow us to more easily create and return errors to the system. In Listing 2-58 we add our out of the box formatting for our error.rs file.

Listing 2-58. Our errors module with the error_chain! macro

```
use error_chain::*;
use std::result;

// We can define our error chains in here
//https://docs.rs/error-chain/0.12.0/error_chain/
error_chain! { ①

}


// Couple custom errors
pub type MyResult<T> = result::Result<T, Error>; ②
```

① Defining our macro necessary for the error_chain.

② A wrapper for the Error that will get returned from the chain to use in the application.

That's all we need now to start using the error chain; we can add in customizations to define the custom responses for each error. This gives the developer a central area to handle the errors that are in the application. We will be adding to this as we go along, but for your production systems, it can be invaluable to learn the errors and trace the root causes. We can implement this by adding .chain_err instead of an .expect to any error calls where you want to use error_chain. In Listing 2-59 we add it to the *save_text_to_file* method.

Listing 2-59. Using our chain error to add a message to the error handling

```
fn save_text_to_file(path: &str, name: &String, data: &String) ->
MyResult<()> {
    std::fs::write(format!("{}/{}", path, name), data)
        .chain_err(|| "unable to write to file")?;

    Ok(())
}
```

This uses the message to create a custom error. I will be using the error chain throughout the application, sometimes more than other places. I'm not going to dive into the application every time. Honestly, there are quite a bit of competitors in the error space right now including snafu and thiserror that look interesting. thiserror seems more for libraries, but snafu seems very promising (https://crates.io/crates/snafu).

Loggers

We have used the println! macro for most of the book, but that is such a newbie thing to do; it's time to look at how to use a logger. Loggers are great because you can format the levels that get displayed, format the display with time zones, thread IDs, and so on. But most importantly, you can control those levels between development and production so you don't blow up your error logs. Let's begin by bringing in the proper crate for this. For logging, we are going to use in Listing 2-60 a log (https://github.com/rust-lang-nursery/log) crate but also use the pretty-env-logger (https://github.com/seanmonstar/pretty-env-logger) which helps make it look prettier.

Listing 2-60. The Cargo.toml with the logging crate

```
log = "0.4.8"
pretty_env_logger = "0.4.0"
env_logger = "0.7.1"
```

The code is pretty straightforward to write; we are setting the RUST_LOG here, but this could also be fed in via an environmental variable, but we are allowing for a default RUST_LOG to use while we are in development. Next in Listing 2-61, we are initiating the pretty logger, and this will start the logging for our entire application.

Listing 2-61. Example of initializing the logger and writing log tests

```
use pretty_env_logger;
use std::env;
use log::*;

fn main() {
    env::set_var("RUST_LOG", env::var_os("RUST_LOG").unwrap_or_else
    (|| "debug".into())); ①
    pretty_env_logger::init(); ②
```

```
    debug!("Testing Debug"); ③
    info!("Testing Info");
    warn!("Testing Warn");
    error!("Testing Error");
}
```

① Setting the RUST_LOG env variable needed for the logger. We can do this externally as well.

② Initializing the pretty logger.

③ Our various logger options.

The preceding code when ran produces the following output in Listing 2-62. The logs actually color-code the different levels on the console, but that is a bit hard to see in a black and white book; you will just have to trust me or run it on your own. All the logs calls are to macros as you can see by the exclamation point and logging will be used throughout the book.

Listing 2-62. Output from the logs

```
DEBUG logs > Testing Debug
INFO  logs > Testing Info
WARN  logs > Testing Warn
ERROR logs > Testing Error
```

Loggers are fairly simple, but we want to use them as much as possible instead of println!; those have a habit of entering the code and never leaving till you go to production, and now your app is spending far too much I/O time writing output due to a println! you forgot about, whereas you can more easily control loggers output flow.

As we go along, we will add extra crates that universally help make our programming more readable and concise.

Summary

In this chapter, we set up our first iron-based microservice that integrated with the database. This gave us RESTful endpoints to be able to query and insert into the comments and media data tables. In addition, we had all the plumbing around logging, error catching for a modern application. In future chapters, we will build up on this file and add even new endpoints. In the next chapter, we will dive into the upload service and how to upload a file and communicating that metadata back to the retrieval service.

CHAPTER 3

File Uploading and Parsing

In the previous chapter, we went over the design for the application, including our microservice architecture. Part of that architecture was starting the pipes to have the upload_svc call the retrieval_svc. Majority of last chapter though, we focused on really two things, setting up iron for the web server and creating our database to store media files. Most of the coding focused on the retrieval service and integrating it with the database to store comments and media data. In this chapter, we are going to expand and dive into the upload service. We will be looking at how to upload, download, and parse the media data. Media data often contains extra information about it that tells us track, authors, camera use, and so on, and that is good metadata to store in the database.

Before we start coding, you should go create the upload_svc. We are not going to build it from scratch, since you just did it. We are not going to start the upload service from scratch. It will be your typical Iron framework application with error chain and loggers. This should be relatively easy since you just wrote the same structure in the previous chapter.

But what we want to dive into more is the file upload process for our IoT app – the ability to upload the files and store them on our system as well as parsing the files metadata for information we can feed for retrieval. We are only going to be focused on video and still image files and processing data from those files. However, much of the same code could be used to expand to audio and other formats. We will look at a variety of crates that will help us parse image and video data as well as store those files. In addition, we will also head back to the retrieval service and show how to store the metadata from the uploaded files. In later chapters, we will show how to perform more queries against the media data.

© Joseph Faisal Nusairat 2020
J. F. Nusairat, *Rust for the IoT*, https://doi.org/10.1007/978-1-4842-5860-6_3

Goals

After this chapter, you should learn to do the following pieces of code:

1. Upload media files to the upload service.

2. Parse EXIF data from an image file.

3. Parse video data from a video file.

4. Call the retrieval service from the upload service.

5. Store the metadata into the database.

There are many different video and image types and quite a bit of data you can gather and analyze when using the image and video parsers. The metadata we will get back ranges from the camera exposure, aperture, date and time, and even GIS location when available. We are not going to focus much on individual sections of data but treat it as a whole; it will be up to you to perform any interesting queries or tasks on the data.

Parsing Image Data

If you have ever taken a picture with your mobile phone or uploaded your pictures to sites like Facebook, you will notice that the pictures often show details about the location of the picture. Further, if you have any modern operating system installed on your computer or viewer, they will show the metadata for any images. For my example, I am using OSX, and when you click a picture, you will find a whole host of information from the location to the device that took the picture, the resolution, aperture, and so on (should be similar for Windows or Linux OS). This information can be useful for knowing the conditions a picture was taken for learning and editing purposes. In Figure 3-1, I click a picture I took of one of my cats.

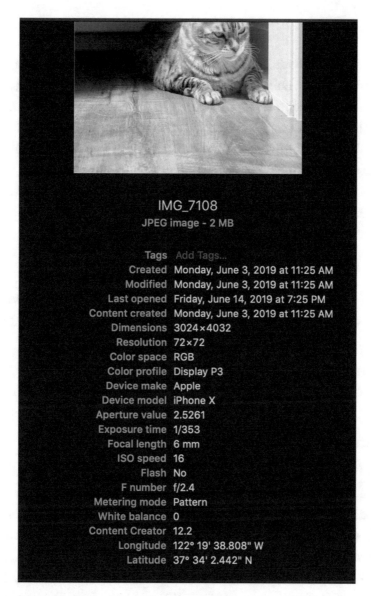

Figure 3-1. *Shows a picture of a cat with details*

That information displayed is all stored on the picture as EXIF data.

EXIF

But what is EXIF? EXIF stands for Exchangeable Image File Format and is the standard that was created in 1995 which specifies the format for digital images and sound. The EXIF structure is borrowed from the structure used by Tagged Image File Format (TIFF), and there is overlap in structure between the standard and various TIFF formats. The EXIF data is embedded within the image itself in a predefined structure; hence, there are various parsers that can then parse the data out since the format is a standard. This means we could parse the data ourselves or more easily use an existing crate that will make it easier for us.

Kamadak EXIF

There are quite a few EXIF cargo crates out there to pick from. This beckons the question: which one to choose? There were two main requirements I wanted when picking the EXIF parser:

1. A parser that is regularly maintained (incidentally this library had two minor increments between writing this chapter and finishing the book)

2. A parser that is natively written in Rust

The second was very important for performance and safety. We could have instead called a Rust crate that wraps a C library or had the application call out to a shell command (via `std::process::Command`) eww. But either of these options would compromise the performance and safety. There was even a crate that wrapped a very well-maintained and performant Go library. However, I wanted to avoid all this, ensure safety, and stick to a natively written library. About the only limitation to consider when using kamadak is that it only supports TIFF, JPEG, and HEIF (most often used by iOS) files; however, that is fine for our use cases. Listing 3-1 references the kamadak crate.

Listing 3-1. kamadak-exif installed parser, in upload_svc/Cargo.toml

```
kamadak-exif = "0.5.1"
chrono = { version = "0.4", features = ["serde"] }
```

You will notice we also included the `chrono` library. The library is used for date/time interchanges between a struct and string or long representations of date/time data. This crate follows the ISO 8601 Date and Time Format standard (`www.iso.org/iso-8601-date-and-time-format.html`) and is commonly used throughout rust crates. In addition, we included the `serde` feature in order to handle serialization and deserialization of `structs` that have date time data. We will be using the struct `DateTime` that is included in the crate to represent date/times throughout the app, but more specifically in this chapter for the date/timestamps from the EXIF data.

Data Structure

This parser will get a large set of data from the file; we are going to use much of that data to store to the database but not all of it. There are more pieces of information you can obtain if you dig deeper into the library. This is just a small subset of the data available. We will add on to this data in later chapters; for now, Listing 3-2 reflects the tags we actually are concerned with.

Listing 3-2. The Image EXIF data structure for image metadata, in upload_svc/src/parsers/image.rs

```
#[derive(Deserialize, Serialize, Debug)]
pub struct ImageMetaData { ①
    exif_version: Option<f64>,
    x_pixel_dimension: Option<u32>,
    y_pixel_dimension: Option<u32>,
    x_resolution: Option<u32>,
    y_resolution: Option<u32>,
    date_of_image: Option<DT<Utc>>,
    flash: Option<bool>,
    make: Option<String>,
    model: Option<String>,
    exposure_time: Option<String>,
    f_number: Option<String>,
    aperture_value: Option<f64>,
    gps_point: Option<Point>,
    altitude: Option<f64>,
    speed: Option<f64>,
    media_item_id: Uuid,
}
```

```rust
impl ImageMetaData {
    pub fn empty(id: Uuid) -> ImageMetaData {
        ImageMetaData {
            exif_version: None,
            x_pixel_dimension: None,
            y_pixel_dimension: None,
            x_resolution: None,
            y_resolution: None,
            date_of_image: None,
            flash: None,
            make: None,
            model: None,
            exposure_time: None,
            f_number: None,
            aperture_value: None,
            gps_point: None,
            altitude: None,
            speed: None,
            media_item_id: id
        }
    }
}

// This is copied from diesel-geography::GeogPoint, which makes it easier
// for JSON conversion
#[derive(Deserialize, Serialize, Debug)]
pub struct Point { ②
    pub x: f64, // lon
    pub y: f64, // lat
    pub srid: Option<i32>, // spatial reference identifier
}
```

   ①   The ImageMetaData structure.

   ②   The Point data structure used to store our GIS data.

The first struct is fairly self-explanatory; this has all the fields we are going to use with a corresponding data types that we retrieve from the EXIF data. We have declared them all optional since depending on the camera, the image, and so on, not all the fields are reported. Resolution is a fairly common one since any image you have will by default have some resolution (whether it's reported in the EXIF data is dependent on the device that recorded it).

The second struct contains our latitude and longitude information. This structure is more strict in that we need to keep it the same fields and types that the diesel GIS is using and when we are mimicking the structure of the GIS crate that we are going to store to in the database. Keeping the structure identical will make it easier when we send the JSON to the retrieval service for storage of data.

Reading the Image

In order to read the image, we will open the image file and use a buffered reader passed to the exif reader. In Listing 3-3, we will then use the reader to parse through various fields.

Listing 3-3. Our parser for the image data, in upload_svc/src/parsers/image.rs

```
pub fn parse(media_id: Uuid, file_path: &str) -> Result<ImageMetaData,
crate::errors::Error> {
    let file = File::open(file_path).unwrap();
    let reader_result = Reader::new().read_from_container(
        &mut BufReader::new(&file));

    match reader_result {
        Ok(reader) => {
            // create the image data
            Ok(ImageMetaData { ①
                exif_version: get_float(&reader, Tag::ExifVersion),
                x_pixel_dimension: get_int(&reader, Tag::PixelXDimension),
                y_pixel_dimension: get_int(&reader, Tag::PixelYDimension),
                x_resolution: get_int(&reader, Tag::XResolution),
                y_resolution: get_int(&reader, Tag::YResolution),
                date_of_image: get_datetime(&reader, Tag::DateTime),
                flash: get_flash(&reader),
```

```
                make: get_string(&reader, Tag::Make),
                model: get_string(&reader, Tag::Model),
                exposure_time: get_string(&reader, Tag::ExposureTime),
                f_number: get_string(&reader, Tag::FNumber),
                aperture_value: get_float(&reader, Tag::ApertureValue),
                gps_point: get_geo(&reader),
                altitude: get_float(&reader, Tag::GPSAltitude),
                speed: get_float(&reader, Tag::GPSSpeed),
                media_item_id: media_id
            })
        },
        Err(e) => {
            // This can happen if there is no EXIF data
            warn!("Error :: {:?}", e);
            Ok(ImageMetaData::empty(media_id))
        }
    }
}
```

① Creating the ImageMetaData by using data read in from the EXIF data.

Each line when initializing our data is made up of a getter for the type and a Tag. The getter will correspond to the type you are setting to. The second field on the method will be the type of EXIF data we are trying to retrieve. This is an enumeration that is set by the kamadak-exif crate.

The get_float, get_int, and so on are all custom methods to retrieve the data returning the correct type. These wrapper functions make it easier to retrieve data when we create the structure initially. The methods will perform the conversion based on the type of data we are accessing. In the next section, we will run through each of the parsers.

Parsing Data Types

We are going to create four fairly standard types of parsing and two custom parsers that are highly specific to the data we are retrieving:

- Integer

- Float

- String

- Date time

- Boolean for the flash

- GIS coordinates

The first four are fairly straightforward; the GIS one is more complicated, but we only have one set of coordinates, and the flash is unique because we are going to parse a string text to make a boolean out of it. We will go over each of the parsers and spend particular time on GIS parser.

Let's start off with the more standard parsers: the float, integer, and string in Listing 3-4.

Listing 3-4. Parsers for float, int, and string, in upload_svc/src/parsers/image.rs

```rust
fn get_float(reader: &Exif, tag: Tag) -> Option<f64> {
    reader.get_field(tag, In::PRIMARY)
        .and_then(|field| match field.value {
            Value::Rational(ref vec) if !vec.is_empty() => Some(vec[0].
            to_f64()), ①
            _ => None
        })
}

fn get_int(reader: &Exif, tag: Tag) -> Option<u32> {
    reader.get_field(tag,In::PRIMARY)
        .and_then(|field| field.value.get_uint(0) ) ②
}

fn get_string(reader: &Exif, tag: Tag) -> Option<String> {
    reader.get_field(tag,In::PRIMARY)
        .and_then(|field| Some(field.value.display_as(tag).to_string()) ) ③
}
```

① Our float parser matching on a rational number and converting to float.

② The integer parser parses the value to unit.

③ Using the standard display_as function and then converting the string slice to a string.

These are all fairly straightforward matchers; you will notice I used the and_then function that will just return None if it doesn't have a Some value for the Option. This is a bit of a shortcut in writing instead of using your regular matcher.

Next let's look at our date parsing function. The date we are receiving from the system is in an ASCII format like 2013-08-30 13:06:55.933; we want to convert this to a Coordinated Universal Time (UTC) timestamp that we can then send to the retrieval service to be stored. In Listing 3-5, we have the date convert function.

Listing 3-5. Parses the field for a date time, in upload_svc/src/parsers/image.rs

```
use chrono::{Utc, DateTime as DT};

fn get_datetime(reader: &Exif, tag: Tag) -> Option<DT<Utc>> {
    use chrono::offset::TimeZone; ①

    match reader.get_field(tag, In::PRIMARY) {
        Some(field) => {
            let val = field.value.display_as(tag).to_string(); ②
            Utc.datetime_from_str(val.as_str(), "%Y-%m-%d %H:%M:%S").ok() ③
        },
        None => None
    }
}
```

① Include the trait in order to use the Utc.datetime_from_str.

② Retrieve the date time field as a string.

③ Convert the date time from a string format to a DateTime<Utc>`.

In here, we are first retrieving the field as a string to serve as an intermediary before we convert it to the DateTime<Utc>; the preceding format matches the same format we are using to parse the string with. The actual parser returns a Result struct, but since we want an Option<>, we use the ok() function at the end converting the Result to an Option. It will convert any Result that returns without error to Some() of the unwrap(), and any Result that is an Err will be returned as None.

The flash parsing is a bit interesting as it returns a string with details of if there was a flash and what types. However, all I cared about was whether the flash was fired or not. In the case of the flash being fired, the `display_as` will return a string like "fired, no return light detection function, forced". We aren't concerned with the details; all we care about is the "fired" part of that text; hence, we will check if the string starts with "fired"; if it does, we will return a boolean like in Listing 3-6.

Listing 3-6. Checking whether the flash was fired, in upload_svc/src/parsers/image.rs

```
fn get_flash(reader: &Exif) -> Option<bool> {
    match get_string(&reader, Tag::Flash) {
        Some(flash) => {
            Some(flash.starts_with("fired"))
        },
        None => None
    }
}
```

Parsing GIS

The geographic information system (GIS) was first thought up in 1968 by Roger Tomlinson as a system to track the land capability in rural Canada. It wasn't untill 1986 though that people started using GIS for personal computers, and by the 20th century, this exploded even more with the Internet and the needed ability to view and analyze GIS data. Today it is ubiquitous in our modern life, and some governments around the world use it to know everything their citizens do. We will use it for more innocuous purposes of being able to determine where our pictures or videos where taken.

Let's start with retrieving the data. The end goal that is needed is to store the data into the database that has GIS support. The Postgres GIS database we installed in the previous chapter will then allow (when stored correctly) us to do queries based on the location. The format the database wants for GIS is a latitude and longitude decimal degrees; however, that is not the format we are retrieving from the exif crate. The crate is going to return the degrees, minutes, seconds, and reference (N,S,E,W) of the image location. We will need to convert it from degrees, minutes, seconds (DMS) to decimal degrees. When converted, 1 degree 0 minutes 0 seconds is equal to 1.0. Each 60 minutes you will have another degree; hence, the degree can also be thought of as an hour when calculating. The decimal value also makes use of positive or negative values; this is translated from the DMS using the N/S/E/W notation where North and East are positive and South and West are negative for their corresponding latitude and longitude.

In Listing 3-7, you will see how to retrieve those objects from the EXIF data for conversion.

Listing 3-7. Prep the DMS data for conversion to a point, in upload_svc/src/parsers/image.rs

```
fn calculate_pointe(reader: &Exif, dms: Tag, dms_ref: Tag) -> f64 {
    // get latitude
    match reader.get_field(dms, In::PRIMARY) {
        Some(field) => {
            match field.value {
                Value::Rational(ref vec) if !vec.is_empty() => { ①
                    let deg = vec[0].to_f64();
                    let min = vec[1].to_f64();
                    let sec = vec[2].to_f64();
                    let ref_factor = calculate_ref(&reader, dms_ref);
                    convert_point(deg, min, sec) * ref_factor
                },
                _ => 0.0
            }
        },
        None => 0.0
    }
}

/// Convert longitude values that are in the western hemisphere or
/// latitude values that are in the southern hemisphere to negative decimal
degree values.
/// f64 cause we are going to multiply it
fn calculate_ref(reader: &Exif, dms_ref: Tag) -> f64 {
    match get_string(&reader, dms_ref) {
        Some(field) => {
            match (field.as_ref()) { ②
                "N" => 1.0,
                "S" => -1.0,
```

```
                "E" => 1.0,
                "W" => -1.0,
                _ => 1.0
            }
        },
        None => 1.0
    }
}
```

① The DMS comes in from the exif crate as a vector in the order of degree, minutes, seconds.

② Calculating the reference factor, North and East are always positive numbers, and South and West are negative numbers.

Listing 3-8 shows how we calculate it for one decimal degree. The way one converts from DMS to decimal degrees is rather simple if we keep in mind 1 degree is equal to one hour which is equal to 60 minutes or 3600 seconds. Thus, the formula is Decimal Degrees = degrees + (minutes/60) + (seconds/3600).

Listing 3-8. Final degree min sec conversion to a point, in upload_svc/src/parsers/image.rs

```
fn convert_point(deg: f64, min: f64, sec: f64) -> f64 {
    (deg + (min / 60.0 ) + (sec / 3600.0 ) ) ①
}
```

① Using the formula we discussed earlier to convert DMS to DD.

Now that we have everything to do the conversion, Listing 3-9 shows how to combine this into one set.

Listing 3-9. Converts our GEO coordinates into a GIS DD point, in upload_svc/src/parsers/image.rs

```
fn get_geo(reader: &Exif) -> Option<Point> {
    let latitude = calculate_pointe(&reader, Tag::GPSLatitude,
    Tag::GPSLatitudeRef);
    let longitude = calculate_pointe(&reader, Tag::GPSLongitude,
    Tag::GPSLongitudeRef);
```

```
if latitude == 0.00 || longitude == 0.0 {
    None
}
else {
    Some(Point {
        x: longitude,
        y: latitude,
        srid: None
    })
}
}
```

We retrieve the latitude and longitude and then set the point with longitude first and latitude second so the DMS value we convert will look like [37.39, -15.25].

Parsing Video Data

Video data is not like image data where there is embedded EXIF data to read on the file; this is partially due to the nature of videos. Videos aren't one static image but a collection of frames and have data move along buried in each track and section that can be parsed. Hence attributes of the data you have could be adjusted along the video's timeline. Much of that data is about the video itself: the size, the duration, the length and height, and the codecs. We mostly use the data to feed to video players to know how to read and render the data to the user, since different codecs require different ways to output the audio and video. In addition, these parsers can often have header data that they can store extra information like your GIS coordinates or other user-specific information. This is useful for your mobile device to be able to tag where this video has taken.

The nature of creating video parsers is not easy; there is not a huge selection to choose from. However, there is one, and it's an amazing one as in Listing 3-10. As you may recall, Rust started as Mozilla project, and because of that, there is a nice mp4parser to get track metadata for Firefox, and it's also open sourced (https://github.com/mozilla/mp4parse-rust). We will be using this parser to parse our track and other data. Unfortunately, this parser does not parse out some of the other misc header data like GIS data. This is unfortunate, but maybe someone with some free time reading this book will dive into that fix (hint hint).

Mp4Parser

Let's start by referencing the mp4 parser in our `Cargo.toml`.

Listing 3-10. MP4Parser, in upload_svc/Cargo.toml

```
mp4parse = "0.11.2"
```

Our Data Structure

Before we start parsing, let's figure out what kind of data we will pull for the videos. Like the image parsing, there is quite a bit of data available from the parser to retrieve. We are only concerned with a small subset since we are using the data more for analysis and not information related to playback. Most of the data we are going to retrieve is around the video and audio quality, size, and so on. On the video side, we will retrieve the following:

- Duration – In milliseconds of the video

- Width – The width of the video display in pixels

- Height – The height of the video display in pixels

- Codec – A string representation of the codec used to encode the video

And for the audio, we will retrieve two fields related to audio quality:

- Duration – The length of time the audio track is for

- Codec – A string representation

We represent all of this data in a `VideoMetaData` struct in Listing 3-11.

Listing 3-11. The VideoMetaData structure, in upload_svc/src/parsers/video.rs

```
#[derive(Deserialize, Serialize, Debug)] ①
pub struct VideoMetaData { ②
    video_duration: Option<u64>,
    video_width: Option<u32>,
    video_height: Option<u32>,
    video_codec: Option<String>,
    audio_track_id: Option<u32>,
    audio_codec: Option<String>,
```

```
        media_item_id: Uuid,
}

impl VideoMetaData { ③
    fn new(id: Uuid) -> VideoMetaData {
        VideoMetaData {
            video_duration: None,
            video_width: None,
            video_height: None,
            video_codec: None,
            audio_track_id: None,
            audio_codec: None,
            media_item_id: id,
        }
    }
}
```

①   Serialize and Deserialize will be necessary later when we want to
      serialize this to a JSON object to send to retrieval service.

②   The VideoMetaData struct and its constituent parts.

③   The implementation to create a new structure.

Here we also default everything to optional since we are not sure what data will be
provided depending on the video type. Additionally, the way we are going to parse the
data is by iterating over each track to find the information relative at each point, so at
initialization of the data, we won't have all the data unless we set them to intermediate
variables. This is unlike the image data where it was easy to create the data in one
method. Thus, we are creating a new to initialize all data to None to start with.

Reading the Video

Like our image parser, we are going to start with passing the path to the file in Listing 3-12;
this will allow this module to be more self-contained if we ever want to use it for other
purposes. Then the mp4parse crate will handle the parsing of the file into the context
object.

Listing 3-12. Initializing the reading of the file, in upload_svc/src/parsers/video.rs

```
pub fn parse(uuid: Uuid, file_path: &str) -> Result<VideoMetaData,
crate::errors::Error> {
    use crate::errors::ErrorKind::Mp4Parse;

    let mut file = File::open(file_path)?;
    let mut context = MediaContext::new(); ①
    match mp4parse::read_mp4(&mut file, &mut context) { ②
        Ok(_) => {
            // return the meta data
            Ok(create_meta_data(uuid, context)) ③
        },
        Err(e) => {
            warn!("Error reading Mp4 : {:?}", e);
            // return a blank object
            Ok(VideoMetaData::new(uuid))
        }
    }
}
```

① Create a new MediaContext object to store the output from reading the data.

② Parser that reads in the data from the file and stores it into the media context.

③ We pass the object to create the metadata.

Allowing the read_mp4 to perform the parsing allows the crate to optimize the parsing of large files and not our code.

Next in Listing 3-13, we will take the filled context object and precisely retrieve the data that we want from the video metadata to fit our VideoMetaData model. A video file often contains tracks on top of each other; video and audio are actually two different tracks that then get played together. The context will thus contain many tracks, each with different types of data, so we need to parse and set our VideoMetaData accordingly.

Listing 3-13. Our video data parsing, in upload_svc/src/parsers/video.rs

```
fn create_meta_data(uuid: Uuid, context: MediaContext) -> VideoMetaData {
    info!("Movie extend box : {:?}", context.mvex);

    let mut vmc = VideoMetaData::new(uuid);
    check_tracks(context.tracks,  vmc)
}

fn check_tracks(tracks: Vec<Track>, mut vmc: VideoMetaData) ->
VideoMetaData {
    for track in tracks { ①
        match track.track_type {
            mp4::TrackType::Video => { ②
                vmc.video_duration = Some(track.duration.unwrap().0);
                // Reference is here if not we will get a borrow err below
                match &track.tkhd {
                    Some(tkhd) => {
                        vmc.video_width = Some(tkhd.width);
                        vmc.video_height = Some(tkhd.height);
                    },
                    None => {}
                };
                vmc.video_codec = retrieve_codec(&track);
            },

            mp4::TrackType::Audio => { ③
                vmc.audio_track_id = Some(track.track_id.unwrap());
                vmc.audio_codec = retrieve_codec(&track);
            },

            mp4::TrackType::Metadata | mp4::TrackType::Unknown => {}
        };
    }

    vmc
}
```

① Iterating through each track to parse.

② Retrieving the video data.

③ Retrieving the audio data.

And finally as part of that, we have a separate function that helps us parse the codec in Listing 3-14.

Listing 3-14. Retrieving the audio codec, in upload_svc/src/parsers/video.rs

```
fn retrieve_codec(track: &Track) -> Option<String> {
    match &track.stsd {
        Some(stsd) => {
            match stsd.descriptions.first() {
                Some(v) => {
                    match v {
                        mp4::SampleEntry::Video(v) => {
                            Some(stringify!(v.codec_type).to_string()) ①
                        },
                        mp4::SampleEntry::Audio(v) => {
                            Some(stringify!(v.codec_type).to_string()) ②
                        },
                        _ => {
                            None
                        }
                    }
                },
                None => {
                    None
                }
            }
        },
        None => {
            None
        },
    }
}
```

① Retrieve the video codec.

② Retrieve the audio codec.

With these video parsing functions, we have generated all the metadata that we need for the `VideoMetaData` object; we will use the video and image parsers in the next section to parse the incoming files.

File Uploads

We now have all our parsers created and ready to be used in their modules. The next step is going to be uploading the file, parsing the data, and sending it to the retrieval service for storage in the database. We are looking at four essential steps:

1. Upload the various types of data.

2. Determine the parser to use for the data by the file type.

3. Parse the file to retrieve the metadata.

4. Send the data to the retrieval service in JSON format.

Upload File

With all the requests we were sending over in the last chapter, these were simple HTTP requests. We had a set of JSON and sent it to the endpoint. Most of the requests you create on servers follow this model, your retrieval of data by search field and your updating of data or deleting of data. This works because they are all the same set of data. You have one set of JSON or set of request parameters. When transmitting files, it becomes different. We are sending different types of data; we are sending plain http request information about the item, but also sending binary data. We can't send data the same way as we normally would; instead, we have to use a concept called `multipart`. Multipart is part of the W3C spec defined to be used when sending "one or more different sets of data are combined in a single body".[1] And when we are sending image or

---

[1] `www.w3.org/Protocols/rfc1341/7_2_Multipart.html`

110

video data, both of which are binary we are doing just that. We are going to send to the server the file and also the UUID of the device the file originated from (in addition, there is other default metadata that is sent, but we won't be covering that; this is standard for all HTTP request).

But the important thing to take away is that with file upload, you won't be able to use your previous way of retrieving requests. To help with this, we will use another crate, the `multipart` crate, which will assist in uploading files. This crate will take a file and allow us to return it as textual data, a file, or byte array depending on how the file upload was used. In Listing 3-15 is the crate we are using to upload the file.

Listing 3-15. The multipart file uploader, in upload_svc/Cargo.toml

```
# For file uploading
multipart = { version = "0.16.1", features = ["iron"] }
```

You will notice that since this multipart uploader can be used with various web frameworks, we have to turn on the feature for `iron`. Now that we have the feature turned, let's look how we parse and access the data.

In addition to being able to upload the file, point #4 was that we wanted to send the file to the `retrieval_svc`, and to do that, we are going to add the `reqwest` crate in Listing 3-16 which will allow us to send HTTP requests from `upload_svc` to `retrieval_svc` to store the metadata in the database.

Listing 3-16. The crate used to send HTTP requests, in upload_svc/Cargo.toml

```
reqwest = {version =  "0.10.4", features = ["blocking", "json"] }
http = "0.2.0"
```

At this point, we have all the crates we are going to need to code this. Because this could be called from the Raspberry Pi, I've decided to make it an easier REST quest via Iron. Let's start with the action method that is going to receive the request. In Listing 3-17 is the `upload` function, and two pieces of data are submitted to us:

1.   Device Id – The unique id of the Raspberry Pi this originated from

2.   Multipart file – The uploaded video or image

Listing 3-17. The upload request that our router has mapped to, in src/actions/upload.rs

```
use params::{Params, Value, Map};

const DEVICE_ID_FIELD: &str = "device_id";

pub fn upload(req: &mut Request, retrieval_svc_url: &str)
              -> IronResult<Response> {
    use router::Router;
    let mut id: &str = req.extensions.get::<Router>().unwrap()
        .find(DEVICE_ID_FIELD).unwrap();

    let device_id = Uuid::parse_str(id).unwrap();
    info!("Upload for Device ID :: {}", device_id);

    save_multipart(req, retrieval_svc_url, device_id)
}
```

Next in Listing 3-18, the previous function will call `save_multipart` that will take the request and get the entries from the multipart request. This could contain multiple entries; for us, it will contain just one.

Listing 3-18. The multipart receiving the entries from the request, in src/actions/upload.rs

```
fn save_multipart(req: &mut Request, retrieval_svc_url: &str, device_id:
Uuid)
    -> IronResult<Response>{
    if let Some(entries) = req.extensions.get::<Entries>() {
        debug!("{:?}", entries);
    } else {
        debug!("Not a multipart request");
    }
```

```rust
// In case you want to eventually make the location S3
let location_type = LocationEnum::Local; ①

// Save the entries for multipart requests
if let Some(entries) = req.extensions.get::<Entries>() { ②
    debug!("-- Multi Part Requests");
    match save_entries(&entries, retrieval_svc_url, location_type,
                        device_id) {
        Ok(status) => { ③
            info!("Succeeded : {:?}", status);
            Ok(Response::with((status::Ok, "OK")))
        },
        Err(e) => { ④
            error!("error saving the file {}", e);
            Ok(Response::with(status::InternalServerError))
        },
    }
} else {
    Ok(Response::with(status::NotFound)) ⑤
}
}
```

① We will be saving the file locally as opposed to an S3 bucket.

② Gets the entries that are added to by the middleware.

③ Returns OK if the entries were processed and saved successfully.

④ A 500 internal server error if the entries were not able to be saved.

⑤ A 401 if there were no entries passed back.

The multipart crate is a middleware crate that stores the entries on the req. extensions. Next in Listing 3-19, save_entries we iterate through the list of entries. This function will go through the entries and allow us to parse out the multi-file uploads.

Listing 3-19. The multipart parser that will iterate and process the entries, in src/actions/upload.rs

```rust
use std::path::PathBuf;

fn save_entries(entries: &Entries, retrieval_svc_url: &str,
                location_type: LocationEnum, device_id: Uuid)
                -> MyResult<()> {
    for (key, value) in &entries.fields { ①
        // the file part will show up as "file" the others will be the
        field name
        if key.as_ref().eq("file") {
            info!("{} / {:?}", key, value);
            for field in value {
                let filename = &field.headers.filename; ②
                let size = field.data.size(); ③
                let data = &field.data; ④

                save_data_matcher(data, filename, size,
                                  retrieval_svc_url, &location_type,
                                  device_id); ⑤
            }
        }
    }
    Ok(())
}
```

①   Iterate through all files that have been uploaded.

②   Get the filename for this entry.

③   Receive the size of the data for the entry.

④   Retrieve the data object itself the SavedData reference.

⑤   Call the save_data_matcher passing in the data.

Bullets 4 and 5 are the important and unique details to pay attention to here. The SavedData is an enumeration that has three different struct tuples:

- Text – This contains a string of the file contents.

- Byte – This contains a Vec<u8> of binary contents.

- File – This contains two objects a PathBuf and the size of it stored in a u64 size.

We now have the SaveData type, the filename, and location; we are ready to parse this file and send it the retrieval svc. In Listing 3-20, we will call out to save_data to save the data locally and then on successful save call send_to_retrieval_svc.

Listing 3-20. Matcher for the files ready to be processed

```
fn save_data_matcher(data: &SavedData, filename: &Option<String>,
                     size: u64, retrieval_svc_url: &str,
                     location_type: &LocationEnum, device_id: Uuid) {
    let uuid = Uuid::new_v4();
    debug!("File to save :: {:?} to {}", filename, uuid);

    match save_data(&uuid, &data, &filename,uuid.to_hyphenated().to_
    string()) {
        Ok((file_saved_name, file_meta_data)) => {
            info!("Saved with MetaData :: {:?}", file_meta_data);
            send_to_retrieval_svc(retrieval_svc_url, filename,  size,
            location_type.clone(), file_saved_name,
            uuid, file_meta_data, device_id);
        }
        Err(error) => {
            error!("Encountered an error saving the data {}", error);
        }
    }
}
```

We are creating the UUID initially here because we are going to use that as a filename. While all our filenames should be unique coming from the Pi, I find it best to not take the risk that they aren't. We will thus in Listing 3-21 call the save_data passing that id as the file_id.

Listing 3-21. Processing the various SaveData enumerations, in
src/actions/upload.rs

```rust
fn save_data(uuid: &Uuid, data: &SavedData, filename: &Option<String>,
file_id: String)
    -> MyResult<(String, FileMetaData)> {
    // Match and handle the type of data we have
    match data {
        SavedData::File(file, bytes) => { ①
            info!("File data");
            debug!("Move file :: {:?}", file);
            save_file_to_file(uuid,
                            retrieve_path(),
                        get_extension_for_name(filename),&file_id, &file)
        },
        SavedData::Text(txt) => { ②
            info!("Text data");
            save_text_to_file(retrieve_path(), &file_id, &txt)
        },
        SavedData::Bytes(byes_data) => { ③
            // Not tested yet
            info!("Byte Data");
            save_byte_to_file(retrieve_path(), &file_id, byes_data)
        }
    }
}

// Strips the extension from the back of a file name
fn get_extension_for_name(filename: &Option<String>) -> String { ④
    match filename {
        Some(name) => {
            let x: Vec<&str> = name.split(".").collect();
            x.last().unwrap().to_string()
        },
        None => "unk".to_string()
    }
}
```

116

① Process normal files.

② Process text files.

③ Process byte data.

④ Get the extension for the filename passed in.

This checks if the data is a file, text, or bytes. For our use, we will only fully support the file type save for full parsing of the metadata; we won't parse metadata from the bytes or text type. The fourth part getting the extension will become more obvious when we parse the file data. But before we do that, let's quickly look at how to parse the text and bytes; we won't be using them much, but it's good to know how it works for other use cases. The various save functions will return a tuple of (String, FileMetaData). The string is a location on the local path the file is saved to, and the second part is an enum with a struct that is defined in Listing 3-22.

Listing 3-22. FileMetaData enum, in src/parsers/mod.rs

```
pub mod image;
pub mod video;

use image::ImageMetaData;
use video::VideoMetaData;

#[derive(Debug)]
pub enum FileMetaData {
    Image(ImageMetaData),
    Video(VideoMetaData),
    None
}
```

This enum contains structs of the parsed metadata of the files. This allows the return to have the complete metadata of the files; the metadata that will be parsed for ImageMetaData and VideoMetaData; we will go over their struct structure in a bit; for now, just realize that is what is being parsed.

For reference the functions save_text_to_file and save_byte_to_file are below. We won't be using them to create our parsing and saving but are for your own use if you ever need to parse bytes or text from the multipart.

```
[source,rust]
----
include::../code/full_example_app/upload_svc/src/actions/upload.
rs[tag=save_file2]
----
```

<1> Function to save a text data to a file.
<2> Function to save bytes to a file.

Saving the File

In Listing 3-23, we are going to save the file that was uploaded to a specific location in our file system. Interestingly enough, we do not have to do anything to process the file upload; as part of the multipart process, it has already uploaded the file to our file system, but it's not in a permanent location, so we are going to move it to a new spot using the format of <UUID>.<file_extension> using the information we retrieved earlier.

Listing 3-23. Function to saving the file data, in file src/actions/upload.rs

```
fn save_file_to_file(uuid: &Uuid, path: String, extension: String, name:
&String, file_path: &PathBuf)
    -> MyResult<(String, FileMetaData)> {
    use crate::errors::ErrorKind::NoMetaData;

    info!("Save to file {}, {}, {:?}", path, name, file_path);

    // need to do this in 2 steps so we can have the memory saved longer
    //let file_name = format!("{}", name, extension);
    let path_to_save_name = format!("{}/{}.{}", path, name, extension);
    let path_to_save = Path::new(&path_to_save_name);

    info!("Save from : {:?} to {:?}", file_path, path_to_save);

    std::fs::copy(file_path, path_to_save)
        .chain_err(|| "unable to write to file")?;

    match parse_metadata(uuid, extension_type(extension),
                        path_to_save.to_str().unwrap()) { ①
        Ok(metadata) => Ok((name.clone(), metadata)), ②
```

```
        Err(err) => Err(NoMetaData.into()) ③
    }
}

fn extension_type(extension: String) -> FileType{ ④
    debug!("Extension :: {}", extension);
    match extension.to_lowercase().as_str() {
        "tiff" => FileType::Image,
        "jpg" => FileType::Image,
        "jpeg" => FileType::Image,
        "mov" => FileType::Video,
        "mp4" => FileType::Video,
        "m4v" => FileType::Video,
        _ => FileType::Unknown
    }
}
```

① Call the metadata parser with the file information.

② When retrieving the metadata, we return it with the filename in a result object.

③ Return an error if we are unable to parse the metadata.

④ Return a FileType enumeration based on the extension type.

There are better ways to determine file types, mainly by reading the file headers to determine if it's REALLY a particular type. But for this level, we are going to just enforce a policy of the extension names being correct.

The FileType can be of three types: Image, Video, or Unknown; the first two we will perform parsing on. We have the FileType defined in Listing 3-24.

Listing 3-24. Definition of the file type, in file src/actions/upload.rs

```
#[derive(Debug)]
enum FileType {
    Image,
    Video,
    Unknown
}
```

The next step is to parse the metadata; the two pieces of information we need to do this are the path to the file to parse and the type of parse we want to run against it. The extension method helps us in calculating which parser to use. The other item to take note is our error. This is a custom error we define in our `errors.rs` file as part of the `error-chain` crate. But now we are ready to parse the data.

Creating the Metadata

In the previous sections of this chapter, we created the code to parse the metadata; in here, we will only have to call the parsers based on the file type. In Listing 3-25, we call our parsers.

Listing 3-25. Call our parsers in the other modules, in file src/actions/upload.rs

```
use crate::parsers::image::parse as image_parse; ①
use crate::parsers::video::parse as video_parse;
use crate::errors::ParseResult;

fn parse_metadata(uuid: &Uuid, file_type: FileType, path: &str) ->
ParseResult<FileMetaData> {
    use crate::errors::ErrorKind::NoMatchingParser;

    info!("Parse Meta Data :: {:?}", file_type);
    match file_type {
        FileType::Image => Ok(FileMetaData::Image(image_parse(uuid.
        clone(),path)?)), ②
        FileType::Video => Ok(FileMetaData::Video(video_parse(uuid.clone(),
        path)?)),
        // in theory we could try and see if either video or image could
        parse this
        // since it could be just a bad extension but correct file headers
        FileType::Unknown => Err(NoMatchingParser.into())
    }
}
```

① Imports our parser modules to be used.

② Parses the metadata for the application.

At this point through all the methods we have covered, we have our file stored on the file system, and we have the metadata created for that. All that is left is to create an object to send to the retrieval service.

Upload File

If you remember back to Listing 3-20, we mentioned we'd circle back to send_to_retrieval_svc; well at this point with the file stored, the metadata parsed the functions will return, and as long as they are successful, we will call send_to_retrieval_svc.

We are going to take the metadata created earlier and convert it to a struct of FileUpload that will then be sent to retrieval_svc. The FileUpload is defined in Listing 3-26.

Listing 3-26. The struct of the data we will send to the retrieval service

```
// Mimics the Enums in Retrieval Svc
#[derive(Deserialize, Serialize, Debug, Clone)]
pub enum MediaEnum {
    Image,
    Video,
    Unknown,
}

#[derive(Deserialize, Serialize, Debug, Clone)]
pub enum LocationEnum {
    S3,
    Local
}

#[derive(Deserialize, Serialize, Debug)]
struct FileUpload {
    id: Uuid,
    name: String,
    media_type: MediaEnum,
    location: String,
    location_type: LocationEnum,
    size: u64,
    image_data: Option<ImageMetaData>,
```

```
    video_data: Option<VideoMetaData>,
    device_id: Uuid
}
```

This struct contains all the parts of the file that the retrieval service needs. Much of that we created in Chapter 2; for us, the location and UUID will be the same, but we could always change that if the need ever arises. But the other important aspects we have are the optional ImageMetaData and VideoMetaData that we created in the parsers.

Send Data to Retrieval Services

Finally, let's now create the struct and send the data over in Listing 3-27.

Listing 3-27. Creating the struct and sending over an HTTP request

```
use reqwest::blocking::Client;
use http::status::StatusCode;

///
/// Send the meta data to the retrieval data service.
///
fn send_to_retrieval_svc(url: &str, filename: &Option<String>, size: u64,
                         location_type: LocationEnum,
                         file_saved_name: String, uuid: Uuid,
                         file_meta_data: FileMetaData,
                         device_id: Uuid) -> MyResult<StatusCode> {
    let name = filename.to_owned().unwrap_or("none".to_string()); ①

    let location = format!("/api/media/add/{}", file_saved_name); ②

    let file_upload = match file_meta_data { ③
        FileMetaData::Image(image) => FileUpload::new_image(uuid,
                    name, location, location_type, size, image, device_id),
        FileMetaData::Video(video) => FileUpload::new_video(uuid,
                    name, location, location_type, size, video, device_id),
        _ => FileUpload::new(uuid, name, location, location_type, size,
        device_id)
    };

    // Create the URL
```

```
    let mut add_media = url.to_owned(); ④
    add_media.push_str(&ADD_MEDIA_DATA);

    info!("Send HTTP Request {}", url);
    info!("Sending Data :: {:?}", file_upload);

    send_json(add_media.as_str(), file_upload)
}

fn send_json(add_media: &str, file_upload: FileUpload) ->
MyResult<StatusCode> {
    let c = Client::new() ⑤
        .put(add_media) ⑥
        .json(&file_upload) ⑦
        .send();
    match c {
        Ok(response) => {
            // TODO : This will also return success for 500 errors
            // TODO: Check the status code and do a retry? or log the error.
             info!("Put successfully sent: {}", response.status());
             Ok(response.status())
        },
        Err(error) => {
            error!("Error sending : {:?} : error:: {:?}", add_media, error);
            Err(Http.into())
        },
    }
}
```

① Get the filename in a safe way; if there is none, then use none.

② Append the UUID to the location string for the download. This way, we are dictating what the URL is to retrieve it, not the retrieval service.

③ Create the FileUpload struct given the size, name, and location, and adjust based on if we supplied image or video data.

④ The URL is allowed to differentiate based on environments, but the relative endpoint will stay the same, so add that and create a URL we can call.

⑤ Use reqwest Client to create a URL request.

⑥ In our case, we are calling put; this could have also been get, post, or delete depending on the request method we wished to use.

⑦ The .json tells the Client we are sending in a struct that we want to convert to JSON. This is also why all our structs have implemented Serialize and Deserialize so they can be converted to JSON.

And that was the final step in processing our files for the upload service. From there, the file is sent to the retrieval service to be processed. But now, we have all of our updates for this chapter that we need for the retrieval service to work.

Storing the Metadata

At this point, we have the service we just created to send the file metadata to the retrieval service, and we also, from the previous chapter, have the action ready to accept the media_data. We also have the basics of the database in place that has the location, name, and file. We are ready to start and can at least skip the basics of creating the actions. We are going to focus on what's missing, and that is

1. Update the database to include the metadata.

2. Update the structs to reflect the new data.

3. Parse the incoming JSON into the new structures.

4. Save the data to the database.

Let's first start with what crates we are going to bring in to help us with these steps. The two crates we have to bring in deal with parsing and storing the GIS data and converting the incoming JSON to a `struct`. In Listing 3-28, we are bringing in the bodyparser; this will allow us to take the complete body coming in and converting it either to a string, json, or a `struct`. We will only be using it here for converting the body to a `struct`.

Listing 3-28. The bodyparser to convert the body

```
persistent = "0.4.0"
bodyparser = "0.8.0"
```

In addition as we mentioned previously, we need to store the GIS data in the database. This is a special column type that we have to use; luckily, there is a crate to wrap this and make it fairly transparent to the end user. In Listing 3-29, we will add in the `diesel-geography` crate.

Listing 3-29. The diesel geographic that will work with serde parsing

```
diesel-geography =  { version = "0.2.0", features = ["serde"] }
```

Let's continue; now that we have the crates installed, we will start addressing each of the features.

Update the Database

We had already created the `media_data` table in the previous chapters; now we need to add our metadata for the images and videos. The structure will reflect the structure we used for the `structs` in the previous section. We will start with defining the `video_data` in Listing 3-30.

Listing 3-30. The migration script for the video metadata

```
CREATE TABLE video_metadatas (
  id SERIAL PRIMARY KEY,

  video_duration numeric null,
  video_width numeric null,
  video_height numeric null,
  video_codec varchar null,
  audio_track_id numeric null,
```

```
  audio_codec varchar null,

  media_item_id UUID NOT NULL references media_datas(id),

  created_at TIMESTAMP NOT NULL DEFAULT CURRENT_TIMESTAMP,
  updated_at TIMESTAMP NOT NULL DEFAULT CURRENT_TIMESTAMP
)
```

This contains all the fields we used for defining the video; let's move on to the image data to notice the one important difference in Listing 3-31.

Listing 3-31. The migration script for the image metadata

```
CREATE TABLE image_metadatas (
  id SERIAL PRIMARY KEY,

  exif_version decimal null,
  x_pixel_dimension int null,
  y_pixel_dimension int null,
  x_resolution int null,
  y_resolution int null,
  date_of_image timestamp null,
  flash boolean null,
  make varchar null,
  model varchar null,
  exposure_time varchar null,
  f_number varchar null,
  aperture_value numeric null,
  location geography(point, 4326) not null, ①
  altitude numeric null,
  speed numeric null,

  media_item_id UUID NOT NULL references media_datas(id),

  created_at TIMESTAMP NOT NULL DEFAULT CURRENT_TIMESTAMP,
  updated_at TIMESTAMP NOT NULL DEFAULT CURRENT_TIMESTAMP
)
```

① Geographic type used to define the endpoint.

Here you see the geography type being used; if you examine the database tables, you will also notice there is a spatial_ref_sys table from when we initialized the database. This table contains over 3000 known spatial reference systems.

Update the Structs

Next let's create the struct that reflects the video and image database tables we created. In Listing 3-32, we create the extra structs.

Listing 3-32. The extra structs for the Image and Video

```
use crate::database::schema::image_metadatas;
use crate::database::schema::video_metadatas;

use crate::models::media_data::NewMediaData;

use diesel_geography::types::GeogPoint; ①
use bigdecimal::BigDecimal;

//use chrono::{Utc, DateTime as DT};
//#[derive(Debug, Deserialize, Clone)]
#[derive(Insertable, Associations, Debug, Deserialize, Clone)]
#[belongs_to(NewMediaData, foreign_key="media_item_id")]
#[table_name="image_metadatas"]
pub struct Image { ②
//    pub id: i32,
    exif_version: Option<BigDecimal>,
    x_pixel_dimension: Option<i32>,
    y_pixel_dimension: Option<i32>,
    x_resolution: Option<i32>,
    y_resolution: Option<i32>,
    // uses RFC3339 out of the box
    //https://serde.rs/custom-date-format.html
    //#[serde(with = "my_date_format")]
    date_of_image: Option<NaiveDateTime>,
```

```
    flash: Option<bool>,
    make: Option<String>,
    model: Option<String>,
    exposure_time: Option<String>,
    f_number: Option<String>,
    aperture_value: Option<BigDecimal>,
    location: Option<GeogPoint>, ③
    altitude: Option<BigDecimal>,
    speed: Option<BigDecimal>,
    media_item_id: Uuid
}

// #[derive(Debug, Deserialize, Clone)]

//#[derive(Insertable, Queryable, Debug, Deserialize, Clone)]
#[derive(Insertable, Associations, Debug, Deserialize, Clone)]
#[belongs_to(NewMediaData, foreign_key="media_item_id")]
#[table_name="video_metadatas"]
pub struct Video { ④
    video_duration: Option<BigDecimal>,
    video_width: Option<BigDecimal>,
    video_height: Option<BigDecimal>,
    video_codec: Option<String>,
    audio_track_id: Option<BigDecimal>,
    audio_codec: Option<String>,
    media_item_id: Uuid
}
```

① Uses the GeogPoint from the diesel-geography crate.

② The Image metadata struct.

③ The GeogPoint is our latitude, longitude location.

④ The Video metadata struct.

Now that we created the extra structs, let's look at the parent struct in Listing 3-33.

Listing 3-33. The NewMediaData struct

```
use crate::models::metadata::{Image,Video};
use crate::database::schema::image_metadatas;

// NewMediaData has to have Deserialize/Clone to work with bodyparser
// #[derive(Debug, Deserialize, Clone)]
#[derive(Insertable, Debug, Deserialize, Clone)]
#[table_name="media_datas"]
pub struct NewMediaData{
    pub id: Uuid,
    pub name: String,
    pub note: Option<String>,
    pub media_type: MediaEnum,
    pub location: String,
    pub location_type: LocationEnum,
    pub size: i32,
    pub device_id: Uuid
}
```

Parse the Incoming Data

Now let's head back to the action and parse the data coming in from the request and create a NewMediaData struct that we can then persist to the database. Luckily, parsing the body is really easy. In Listing 3-34, we have the action.

Listing 3-34. The NewMediaData struct with the extra fields

```
pub fn add(req: &mut Request) -> IronResult<Response> {
    info!("-- add media data --");
    let json_body = req.get::<bodyparser::Json>();
    info!(">>>> JSON ::: {:?}", json_body);

    let struct_body = req.get::<bodyparser::Struct<MediaDataAdd>>(); ①

    match struct_body {
        Ok(Some(media_data)) => {
            info!("Parsed body:\n{:?}", media_data);
```

```
                media_data.save(&req.db_conn()); ②
                Ok(Response::with((status::Ok, "OK")))
        },
        Ok(None) => {
            warn!("No body");
            Ok(Response::with(status::BadRequest))
        },
        Err(err) => {
            error!("Error parsing meta data :: {:?}", err);
            Ok(Response::with(status::InternalServerError))
        }
    }
}
```

① In the bodyparser, we pass in the struct that we want the incoming body to create.

② Now call the add function on the media_data passing in the database connection.

Save the Data

The final step is saving the data; we made the call, but we need to add the implementation to the media data to save the data. In Listing 3-35, we save the implementation.

Listing 3-35. An impl on NewMediaData to save the data

```
impl NewMediaData {
    // adding the self: &Self to make it a method instead of associated
    function
    // https://doc.rust-lang.org/reference/items/associated-items.html
    pub fn add(self: &Self, conn: &PgPooled) {
        use diesel::insert_into;
        use diesel::RunQueryDsl;
```

```
    insert_into(media_datas)
        .values(self)
        //.get_result(&*conn)
        .execute(&*conn)
        .expect("Insertion of new media error");
    }
}
```

Summary

This chapter focused on a core piece of our application, the uploading and parsing of video and image data. We won't actually upload the images till Chapter 11, but this allows us to receive and process the images and have two microservices communicate with each other. All of these techniques are usable in real-world applications as well. We haven't tackled it here, but combining this with what you learned in Chapter 4, you could use the metadata to make more complex GraphQL queries.

CHAPTER 4

Messaging and GraphQL

In this chapter, we are going to modify an existing service and create an entirely new service. First up, we are going to add support for message queues (MQs); as you will learn, MQs are invaluable for communication in an IoT system. This chapter we will set up the plumbing for a basic insecure message queue. But as we move along, we will add security and more in later chapters. In addition, we will also discuss GraphQL, which, if you've only used REST, you are in for a treat. GraphQL helps solve many of the limitations and frustrations that come in a RESTful system.

Goals

After completing this chapter, we shall have the following added to our app:

1. Understand the key role message queues (MQTT) play in IoT design.

2. Create an MQTT service with endpoints to a health service topic watcher that can feed into our database.

3. Understand the need for GraphQL in our system.

4. Implement GraphQL for the retrieval service.

This code will expand on our existing topology with the addition of our third microservice. With this, we will have three services that can all communicate with each other.

GraphQL

If you are not familiar with GraphQL yet, you should, and by the end of this, you will be. There are many technologies and concepts that have changed in software over the last 20 years; some seem trendy, and others seem like we are just chasing the latest shiny

© Joseph Faisal Nusairat 2020
J. F. Nusairat, *Rust for the IoT*, https://doi.org/10.1007/978-1-4842-5860-6_4

object (MongoDB being used for everything as one). GraphQL is not one of those things. Let's first start by talking about what it's replacing, REST. Representational State Transfer (REST) has become ubiquitous with creating backend HTTP applications for over a decade now. And REST has become even more important over the last 10 years with the advent of smart phones. Now we are required to have one backend endpoint that can serve smart watches, smart phones, smart TVs, and websites. And this has been great for development.

Problems with REST

However, all of this has come with quite a bit of cost. And that cost is in traffic and complexity. REST was designed to cut back on the complexity and the expense of processing data, especially on the web tier. Instead of having the servers process the data and translate the pages to HTML, we made the clients heavier. This was a smart move in the current ecosystem where we have to handle millions and hundreds of million users. Cloud servers cost money; a good way to reduce your cost is to reduce how much work the cloud is doing and the size of the traffic. In fact, Netflix spends quite a bit of money and time doing just that in the way it compresses and serves up data.

How are we affected by complexity in REST? Let's think of a simple example using our application. What kind of calls do we need to make?

- GET /retrieve_media/list/ – Retrieve all the media data for a given user.

- GET /retrieve_media/detail/<UUID> – Retrieve the details for a given media data.

- GET /comments/get/<MEDIA_UUID> – Retrieve the comments for a given media UUID.

In addition, we also have lots of puts, deletes, and so on to store the data, delete the data, and anything we want users to do. This complexity becomes ever more difficult in two ways: first, the sheer amount of URLs the backend team has to keep track of for being active and for the consumers of that data to know the URLs are active and second the details to expose and notify changes of that data. The more complex the system, the more of a headache this becomes. The BIGGER issue is what if you are on a details page that wants just the details, or the details and the comments. In the latter, this now becomes two calls to the system. With single-page applications (SPAs), this can become even more annoying because you could have dozen calls to the system to get all the data. This not only taxes the servers and increases the cost to serve the data more but slows down the loading of the page.

GraphQL to the Rescue

However, there is a solution, and that solution came from a company who has to serve an exponential amount of data with one of the biggest user bases to websites and phones, and that is Facebook. Facebook created GraphQL in 2015 and has been gaining traction by the mainstream developers ever since. GraphQL not only reduces the noise but allows for greater interface by the consumers to use the application. First, how does this work? GraphQL exposes ONE endpoint for the clients to access; this endpoint will then allow the user to send in structured JSON to tell the server exactly what it wants. This is done by using GraphQL query language, which we will go over each part of the syntax here, but you can find more at `https://graphql.org/learn/queries/`. Let's dive into some examples on how that query language looks.

Query

In our REST example, if we wanted to find all the media data names (just names), you would have to do a query to `/retrieve_media/list`, and then it would return a JSON like in Listing 4-1.

Listing 4-1. Example output for a RESTful query

```
{
    "data": [
    {
        "name": "Front Door",
        "id": "c0b7f4a8-debe-4f72-b075-d752d82fa69c",
        "note": "Our Notes",
        "media_type": "Video",
        "location": "Local",
        "media_audience_type": ["Family"],
        "size": 3,
        "created_at": 1562622727,
        "updated_at": 1562622727
    },
```

```
    {
        "name": "Kitchen",
        "id": "619f0036-2241-4b95-a544-b000a83262ac",
        "note": "Our Notes",
        "media_type": "Video",
        "location": "Local",
        "media_audience_type": ["Family"],
        "size": 3,
        "created_at": 1562622727,
        "updated_at": 1562622727
    }
]
}
```

Now multiply that by 100, and that gets quite a bit of data back that we simply don't want; how would this look in GraphQL? Listing 4-2 shows the query we'd use to query all names in the media data.

Listing 4-2. Find all the media data by name

```
{
    allMedia {
        name
    }
}
```

In the query, we are stating only the fields we want and not the fields we don't. It is then up to the consumer to decide which fields we want; the output for this is in Listing 4-3.

Listing 4-3. Example output for the previous query

```
{
  "data": {
    "allMedia": [
      {
        "name": "Front Door"
      },
```

```
    {
      "name": "Kitchen"
    }
  ]
}
}
```

We could have of course added more fields to that and even add struct fields that may require a separate query like comments, only doing that query when we have the field specified. With the REST query, it becomes dangerous to add any connected objects because if you don't need them all the time, then you don't want to automatically perform the database join, since it will slow down retrieval. With GraphQL, we have the ability to only use the attributes we want. In Listing 4-4, we show the input with a query including the comments and example output.

Listing 4-4. Example input and output of all media with comments

```
{
    allMedia {
        name
        updatedAt
        comments {
          body
        }
    }
}
{
  "data": {
    "allMedia": [
      {
        "name": "Joseph",
        "updatedAt": 1562625410,
        "comments": [
          {
            "body": "Our first comment"
          }
```

```
      ]
    },
    {
      "name": "George",
      "updatedAt": 1562625410,
      "comments": []
    }
  ]
  }
}
```

Mutations

In addition to querying, we also use REST to alter the database. GraphQL uses mutations to add, update, and delete any data. The mutations can expect one to many objects including GraphQLObjects. With the mutations, you generally define the method with the parameters to call, and then the query variables are separate. That way, you can reuse the method when needed. In Listing 4-5, I have the mutation along with the query variables.

Listing 4-5. Example input and output of all media with comments

```
mutation add($id: Uuid!, $bod:String!) { ①
  addComment(mediaItemId: $id, body: $bod) { ②
    success ③
    value
  }
}

{
  "id": "fc5b6acc-816d-4afb-80ee-2c47c8c9180c", ④
  "bod": "Our first comment"
}
```

① Defining a name for our mutation; this can be totally random. The variables need whatever is needed to fill in the next step.

② The addComment is the name of the mutation we define in our system.

③   The `success` and `value` are the fields we want returned from the mutation.

④   Our query variables, the id references `$id` and bod references `$bod` when used for the mutation.

In that example, we will create a new comment which references the media data id and has a body value that we reference in bod. The output of the result of this when successful is in Listing 4-6.

Listing 4-6.   Mutation output with a successful result

```
{
  "data": {
    "addComment": {
      "success": true,
      "value": 23
    }
  }
}
```

Subscriptions

The last feature I want to touch on with GraphQL is subscriptions. Subscriptions are used to allow consumers to create a socket connection to the application and have changes pushed to it when data changes. This can be very useful for UIs to be able to dynamically update without constant queries. We won't be covering subscriptions in this book. At the time of writing of this chapter, they were not complete. However, they are now and I welcome their use for your future applications.

Playground

The final concept I wanted to go over is the playground, also referenced as the explorer. This is probably one of my favorite features when it comes to GraphQL and will make your life easier. This is also how I tested and produced the output from the previous examples. GraphQL essential provides a playground to test your queries with against the server. Since the queries we are supplying can be more complex, it allows an easy way to run the queries and test against. When the server is launched, the playground endpoint can be exposed, and you will be able to write queries, mutations, or subscriptions (if supported) like in Figure 4-1.

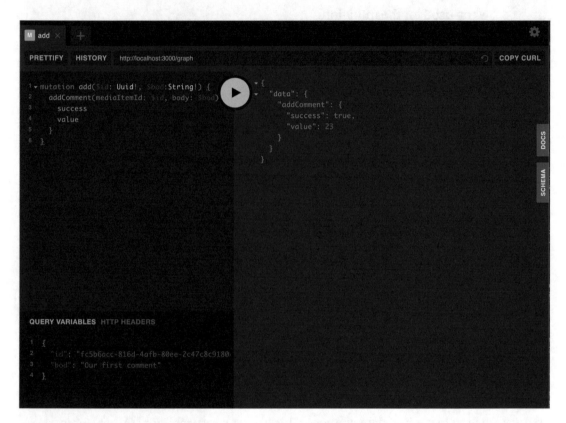

Figure 4-1. *Shows the mutation for addComment*

In addition, the other feature is the self-documenting nature of the application. All the GraphQL mutations, queries, and subscriptions will show up including the possible params and the objects they return. Some iOS and React components can read these to help assist in creating the queries necessary to run your application. Figure 4-2 shows an example of our documentation.

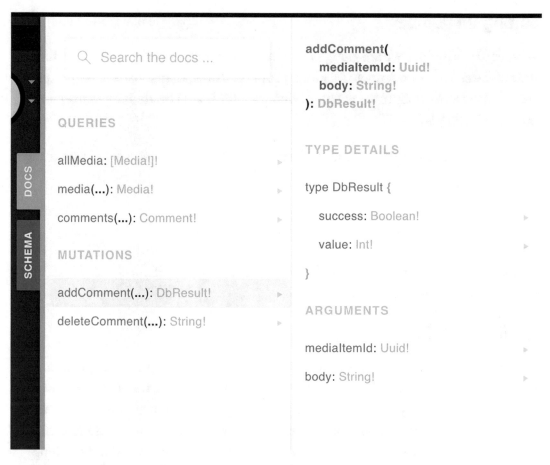

Figure 4-2. *Shows the available GraphQL queries*

The other great feature is that when you do change or add, anyone using the application can easily see the changes without having to write extra documentation; it is an example of the code, being the documentation, and it will never be able to get out of sync like a wiki page can.

Juniper

Now that you've seen what makes GraphQL work, let's show how to make those queries we used earlier actually work in our application. We will be using the Juniper crate to implement GraphQL on our application (`https://graphql-rust.github.io/juniper/current/`). These libraries seemed the most complete from the ones out there, and they have built-in support for Iron as well.

Setting Up Juniper

In order to use Juniper, we are going to have to use the Juniper crate, in addition, the crate of the custom web framework juniper supports; in our case, that will be `juniper_iron` to allow us to easily integrate the endpoints with `iron`. The addition of the juniper crate is in Listing 4-7.

Listing 4-7. Adding Juniper and juniper iron; this will be in the file Cargo.toml

```
[dependencies]
juniper = "0.14.2"
juniper_iron = "0.6.2"
[patch.crates-io]
juniper = { git = "https://github.com/nusairat/juniper",
branch = "v14.2/add-uuid" }
```

Creating the Context

Now let's set up our context object. With our normal web flow process, we are in iron action functions and have full access to the `iron::Request` object; this object can contain extra parameters, or as you've seen, we can add configuration from custom middleware. In order to do the same with Juniper, we are going to have to create a custom implementation of the `juniper::Context`. You can add a variety of fields from the request and anything else that you can set to it. This will then be accessible in our queries and mutations.

In Listing 4-8, we create a custom `Context` that will contain the `remote_addr` and the database `pool`; we aren't going to use the `remote_addr`, but just adding it for fun.

Listing 4-8. Creating the custom context; this will be in the file graphql/context.rs

```
pub struct Context { ①
    pub pool: PgPooled ②
}

impl juniper::Context for Context {} ③

pub fn context_factory(req: &mut Request) -> IronResult<Context> { ④
    Ok(Context {
        pool: req.db_conn() ⑤
    })
}
```

142

① The custom context we will use in our queries and mutations.

② Setting the database pool so we can pass it into our queries and updates.

③ Need to set the Context created to be a juniper::Context to work with juniper.

④ Set up the context factory.

⑤ Using our DB Pool middleware to pull the request connection.

Setting Up the Schema

Next let's set up our GraphQLObjects; these are going to be the struct that can be used as return data from the queries or even be used for passing data for the mutations. For our two examples, we will use them as the return. These are actually quite easy to create; you just need to make sure the struct implements the GraphQLObject trait; you can also add descriptions that are then reflected in the playground and even deprecate fields so the consumer knows to eventually move away from that object or field. In Listing 4-9, we implement the GraphQLObject for Media and Comment. Please note that while we use snake case in Rust, GraphQL uses camel case, so any object names you define here in snake case will be converted to camel case for GraphQL. This is quite common throughout GraphQL utilities; the Elixir Absinthe plug-in does the same thing.

Listing 4-9. Creating the schemas; this will be in the file graphql/schema.rs

```
#[derive(GraphQLObject)]
#[graphql(description = "Media objects for the application")]
pub struct Media { ①
    pub id: Uuid,
    pub name: String,
    pub note: Option<String>,
    pub media_type: MediaEnum,
    pub location: String,
    pub location_type: LocationEnum,
    pub device_id: Uuid,
    pub media_audience_type: Vec<MediaAudienceEnum>,
    pub size: i32,
```

```rust
    pub published: bool,
    pub created_at: NaiveDateTime,
    pub updated_at: NaiveDateTime,
}

#[derive(GraphQLObject)]
#[graphql(description = "Comments given to the item")]
#[derive(Queryable, PartialEq, Debug)]
pub struct CommentG { ②
    pub id: i32,
    pub body: String,
    pub media_item_id: Uuid,
    pub created_at: NaiveDateTime,
    pub updated_at: NaiveDateTime
}
```

① The Media GraphQLObject.

② The Comment GraphQLObject.

Creating a Query

Now let's get to the meat and potatoes of making GraphQL work, creating our queries and after this our mutations. Each will be defined relatively the same way. The queries we want will be a struct that implements various functions. This struct can be named whatever you want; for consistency sake, I would call it Root or Query. We are going to call ours Root and then implement various functions on it. These will be functions that are then exposed in the GraphQL as queries, and the parameters are the same parameters we used in the playground previously. In Listing 4-10, we create our struct, implementing three different queries.

Listing 4-10. Creating the query; this will be in the file graphql/context.rs

```rust
use crate::graphql::schema::{CommentG, Media, MediaComment};
use crate::models::media_data::MediaData;
use crate::models::comment::Comment;

pub struct Root; ①
```

```
#[cfg(feature = "cqrs")]
#[juniper::object( ②
    Context = Context,
)]
impl Root { ③
    fn all_media(context: &Context) -> Vec<MediaComment> { ④
        MediaComment::all(&context.pool) ⑤
    }

    fn find(device_id: Uuid, context: &Context) -> Vec<MediaComment> {
        MediaComment::find(device_id, &context.pool)
    }

    fn comments(media_id: Uuid, context: &Context) -> Vec<Comment> {
        let pool = &context.pool;
        Comment::all(media_id, &pool)
    }

    fn health(user_id: Uuid, context: &Context) -> Vec<Uuid> {
        HealthData::find(user_id, &context.pool)
    }
}
```

① The struct for the GraphQL Query.

② Sets up the context that we created previously to be injected.

③ An impl to create all the different queries for the Root.

④ Our first query, the all_media, will be translated to allMedia for GraphQL.

⑤ Queries all the media data and returns a vector of the media model.

You should notice two things here, the first being that we add the Context trait that we set up previously. This is then added to each query call (note that part is not exposed in the GraphQL). And this is what allows us to get access to our database or message queue pool. Also note the naming just like earlier for the schema; the snake case will be converted to camel case.

Creating a Mutation

Now the flip side of creating the queries is the mutations. The mutations have essentially the same format in setting up in our code as the queries except this will be used for changing the underlying database as opposed to querying. In addition, your results are often not the object itself but some way to mark the transaction as being successful, perhaps passing back the UUID of the object created. In Listing 4-11, we add two mutations related to comments.

Listing 4-11. Creating the mutation; this will be in the file graphql/context.rs

```rust
use crate::models::comment::Comment as CommentDb;

#[cfg(feature = "ch04")]
#[derive(juniper::GraphQLObject)] ①
pub struct MutationResult { ②
    success: bool,
    value: i32
}

#[cfg(feature = "ch04")]
pub struct Mutations; ③

#[juniper::object( ④
    Context = Context,
)]
impl Mutations { ⑤
    fn add_comment(&self, media_item_id: Uuid, body: String, context:
    &Context) -> FieldResult<MutationResult> { ⑥
        // Validate inputs and save user in database...
        info!("Add comment :: {}, {}", media_item_id, body);
        let val = add_comment(self, context, media_item_id, body);
        let result = MutationResult {
            success: true,
            value: val,
        };
        Ok(result) ⑦
    }
```

```rust
    fn delete_comment(comment_id: i32, context: &Context) ->
    FieldResult<bool> {
        // Validate inputs and save user in database...
        info!("Del comment :: {}", comment_id);
        let success = match CommentDb::delete(&context.pool, comment_id) {
            Ok(_) => true,
            Err(_) => false
        };
        Ok(success)
    }
}

#[cfg(feature = "ch04")]
fn add_comment(mutations: &Mutations, context: &Context, media_item_id:
Uuid, body: String) -> i32 {
    CommentDb::add(&context.pool, media_item_id, body)
}
```

① Applying the struct to be a GraphQLObject.

② The MutationResult will be a standard result we will return for our mutations.

③ The struct for GraphQL mutations.

④ Setting up the context that we created previously to be injected.

⑤ An impl for the Mutations.

⑥ The add_comment mutation will be translated to addComment in our application as well as media_item_id to mediaItemId.

⑦ Returning the MutationResult successfully.

Integrating with the Iron Router

We now have everything set up for the GraphQL; the last part is the actual integration with the iron framework that we created and managed in our http module. There is only one endpoint you have to integrate to, and that is the /graph one, the GraphQL handler. However, we also want access to the playground, so we will have two endpoints for our implementation. The `juniper_iron` crate we brought in earlier comes with three different handlers we use to our application:

- GraphQLHandler – The main handler that will take the query and mutation struct we used earlier to perform all the necessary GraphQL functions.

- PlaygroundHandler – The handler that will create the playground UI we used earlier; this will take in the relative URL to the GraphQLHandler.

- GraphiQLHandler – This handler creates another UI similar to the look of the playground UI but simpler; this will also take in the relative URL to the GraphQLHandler. Generally speaking, you would use either the PlaygroundHandler or the GraphiQLHandler.

Let's create the handlers and mount endpoints to the handlers; we will use /graph for the GraphQLHandler and /play for the PlaygroundHandler. In Listing 4-12, we create all the handlers and endpoints.

Listing 4-12. Adding Juniper and juniper iron; this will be in the file http.rs

```
use juniper_iron::{GraphQLHandler, GraphiQLHandler, PlaygroundHandler};
use juniper::{EmptyMutation, FieldResult};
use crate::graphql::context::{Context, context_factory, Root, Mutations};
use event_sourcing::eventstore::OrgEventStore;

let playground = PlaygroundHandler::new("/graph"); ①

let graphql_endpoint = GraphQLHandler::new( ②
    context_factory,
    Root,
    Mutations
);

mount.mount("/play", playground); ③
mount.mount("/graph", graphql_endpoint); ④
```

① Setting up the playground, which will use an endpoint of /graph to interface with.

② Creating the endpoint for the GraphQL to process against; this also references the Root (query) and Mutation we created earlier.

③ The endpoint for our playground tieing the handler to it.

④ The endpoint for the GraphQL that the consumer apps will use; this also needs to be the same endpoint that was used in bullet 1.

Now if you go to your console and run `cargo run`, you will be able to go to the /play endpoint and start testing queries and mutations against our application. You can use the query and mutations we created earlier as examples to start with.

Messaging

Messaging is going to be one of our core components to creating an IoT system. This is what will drive much of the communication between the device and the cloud and allow it to be fault-tolerant services. For those of you that have never used a message queue before, it uses publish-subscribe protocol that is used for a variety of asynchronous communication for many years now. However, recently it has become very favorable with IoT applications since it would be a security hazard usually, to directly expose endpoints like thermostats or vehicles to the open Internet to have command sent directly to. The MQ we will be using here is Message Queuing Telemetry Transport (MQTT) based on ISO/IEC PRF 20922.[1] Message queues involve having a broker that serves as a high availability system for passing messages between systems. The messages are passed via topics, and the client can decide if it wants to subscribe or publish to a particular topic. The messages are most often sent as JSON objects.

Purpose in the IoT System

Communication between the cloud and your device is one of the most paramount importance with any IoT devices. We need to provide seamless communication between cloud and hardware but still allowed for downtime. The downtime in the cloud can often

---

[1] `www.iso.org/obp/ui/#iso:std:iso-iec:20922:ed-1:v1:en`

be mitigated to close to zero, but it's the device downtime that you will always have the greater issue with. If the device is in the home, you can lose Internet at random times; if the device is part of a vehicle, they can quite often be out of range or underground, same with a personal IoT device (like a phone). Or the device simply can be off. You don't want to lose messages to the device just for being out of range or off.

Additionally, there is the security concern. Suppose we want to remotely be able to start and stop a camera. Without the message queue to be used for communicating, we would have to expose an endpoint on the device itself to communicate against, which then starts a litany of problems. For one, if the home IP changes, that would then have to update the endpoint each time, which can be mitigated by using DNS entry but this is sloppy. Then there is the issue that if you are using any modern router, it probably have a firewall (or should), and you would have to expose the port we are using to the firewall, which would require supplying documentation for each router for the end user to configure, and finally basically the issue of hacking. Imagine if a hacker could hack the endpoint and disable all security cameras. In addition, every time you expose a port on your firewall, you allow another way for a hacker to enter. Simply put, message queues are easier and more secure.

Our Design

Our design will be expanding as the book goes on; for this chapter, we are mostly involved with putting the plumbing in place; we will add on more when we get to other chapters. For now, we are going to add two things, so we can balance out practicing the publish and subscribe. We will start with our health check monitor. This will monitor the `health` endpoint; eventually, the device we are creating will periodically send a message to the cloud to know the status of the system. This will help us in the future able to do inform the user if there is an IoT component down. For now, our service will be fairly simple. The endpoint for our health topic will be in the structure of `health/[uuid]`, with the uuid being the id of the device.

On the publish side, we are going to publish commands to start and stop recording of cameras on an IoT device; for us, each device could contain more than one camera, so we will specify the camera UUID as well. This endpoint will be only two levels as well, with the structure `recording/[uuid]`, the uuid being the id of the device as well. (Note: The Raspberry Pi will then have a corresponding publish of health data and subscribe of recording.)

A bit further thought on the design. I could have easily tied the MQTT interface to retrieval or upload service. But I like to keep one microservice that interacts with the MQTT and then sends the data to the necessary microservices for work. This keeps the service without too many moving parts and also never exposes any endpoints accessible outside of our cluster. This is mostly for security reasons, so that in order to pop the microservice, they'd have to get to another box first. We will dive more into this architecture in our security chapter; for now, just realize this is a separate microservice on purpose.

Starting Up Local Messaging Service

Message queues require a broker to be run on, and much like our database, we are going to use docker to run that broker locally. This will provide us the maximum flexibility and ease to create, run, and manage the message queue for testing – and biggest ease in turning it off or getting rid of it later.

We will be creating this image twice, once in this chapter and another time in the security where we will add authentication mechanisms. For now, we will not worry about authentication.

The docker image we are going to use is devrealm/emqtt; this is the Erlang version of MQTT, and one of the main reasons I chose is its speed and low memory footprint. I've used this at other jobs and has worked very well in even high use cases. Let's start off by pulling the docker image to our local repository in Listing 4-13.

Listing 4-13. Downloading the local docker image

```
docker pull devrealm/emqtt
```

Now that the image is there, in Listing 4-14 we will start it up, exposing some default ports we are going to use as well as a few other settings.

Listing 4-14. Running the docker image for our EMQTT service

```
docker run --restart=always -ti --name emqtt-no-auth -p 18083:18083 -p
1883:1883 -p 8083:8083 -p 8443:8443 -p 8084:8084 -p 8080:8080 -e
"EMQ_LOG_LEVEL=debug" -e "EMQ_ADMIN_PASSWORD=your_password" -e
"EMQ_NAME=emqtt_broker" -d devrealm/emqtt
```

First off, we gave this the name of `emqtt-no-auth`; this will be the name we can reference when starting and stopping the docker container. In addition, we set the admin authentication password to `your_password`; you will use this along with the user `admin` to access the web console for EMQTT portal. We won't be covering the console in depth here, but it can be used to see what sessions are currently logged in and what clients are active. This can be useful in debugging to make sure your device and cloud services are connected and talking to your message queue. There are also quite a few ports; let's take a look at what all of them are for in Table 4-1.

Table 4-1. *MQTT mapping of ports to descriptions*

Port	Description
18083	Our http port to access the EMQTT admin portal. You will be able to log in via `http://localhost:18083`.
1883	The TCP port to access the EMQTT broker; we will be using this port in our application.
8083	The web socket port to access the broker.
8883	Not exposed, but it is the port that SSL connects to the broker.
8084	The secure web socket port to access the broker.
8080	The api socket to access the broker; this can be used to access the EMQTT to find items like sessions active and so on.

Now that you have your broker up and running, let's show you how to use it without writing any Rust code.

Calling Messaging Service Locally

Before we start coding, let's use some tools to test out the message queue with; this will allow us to run a few tests and to understand what we expect to see when running our code. We will also be using the same set of tools later when testing out the application since we do not have a device running yet. You can really use any message queue client; the one I prefer to use is Eclipse Mosquitto. It's a great easy-to-use broker/client, and we can use it to test authenticated and non-authenticated services. If you have `brew` on your computer, you can use `brew install mosquitto` to install it. If not, you can go to `https://mosquitto.org/download/` and follow the instructions to install based on your system.

Once installed, there are a few different commands that it provides us; the two we are going to use is `mosquitto_sub` and `mosquitto_pub`. The first `mosquitto_sub` subscribes us to a topic and will print out to the console any messages that are picked up by that topic. The topic in this can be a fixed topic, or we can use wildcards to subscribe to what potentially could be a multitude of topics. Since each of our devices will publish to their own topic, this will be useful to us in our application to be able to have one service monitor all health topics. The second `mosquitto_pub` will publish a specific file content to a topic.

Let's take a look at an example we will use in conjunction with our health application. For our health application, we are going to have the devices send messages to `health/[UUID]` for each of its health check. We will have them send over information in the form of a JSON like we have in Listing 4-15.

Listing 4-15. JSON example of the health data; put this in a file named `health.json`

```
{
  "uuid":"9cf81814-1df0-49ca-9bac-0b32283eb29b",
  "status": "Green",
  "msg":"Here we define what could be going on with our application and its
  items.",
  "timestamp":1562453750553,
  "peripherals":[{"name":"Camera"},{"name":"Temp"}],
}
```

Let's start with the subscribing to that topic; we want our topic to watch all the messages being sent to `health` topic; with MQ, there are two ways to do wildcards. Let's take a look at an example topic of `home/[uuid]/[peripheral]/[action]`, where the peripheral could be of the type `camera`, `temperature`, and `humidity` representing three different sensors. And `action` could be `set` or `read`.

Single-Level Wildcard (+)

With a single level, we are only replacing one level. Suppose we wanted to do machine learning on all the temperatures coming back to our system. We could wild card the uuid with the + wildcard and do a subscription to `home/+/temperature/read`; this would then give us all temperature readings across all devices, which can be useful for analysis.

Multi-Level Wildcard (#)

The other way is to subscribe to topics across multiple levels. On the device side itself, you really do not want to set up multiple message monitoring but want to monitor every command coming for the given uuid. Given our device having a UUID of `24f89ac6-e53d-418b-be6d-2a7571aa483f`, we could subscribe with the # wildcard to `home/24f89ac6-e53d-418b-be6d-2a7571aa483f/#`.

Please note you want to be careful especially with the multi-level wildcard that you aren't going to receive too many messages from the broker or you may not have time to process the service. This is generally only an issue on the server side since it will pick up messages from every client, whereas on the client side, you are only receiving messages for it.

Subscribing

Now let's actually subscribe to our health topic to monitor all the outputs. In Listing 4-16, we subscribe to all the `health` UUIDs being published.

Listing 4-16. Subscribing to the localhost health topic

```
mosquitto_sub -d -h localhost -p 1883 -t "health/+" --tls-version tlsv1.2 ①
Client mosq/jvQbjjug7FK8KXaU9q sending CONNECT
Client mosq/jvQbjjug7FK8KXaU9q received CONNACK (0)
Client mosq/jvQbjjug7FK8KXaU9q sending SUBSCRIBE (Mid: 1, Topic: health/+,
QoS: 0, Options: 0x00) ②
Client mosq/jvQbjjug7FK8KXaU9q received SUBACK
Subscribed (mid: 1): 0
```

    ①   Our command to subscribe to the health topic.

    ②   Signaling that subscription was verified.

The subscription confirmation is very important; if you do not see it in your console, the MQTT application is down, or if this is in the real world it could be blocked due to VPN or other firewall rules. Now keep this running and open a separate window so we can publish to it.

Publishing

Let's take that health data file we created in Listing 4-17 and publish it to the topic. In a new window, we will publish to the health topic using the health.json data. We should see a verification in our new window that it's published, and the contents should show up in your previous subscription window.

Listing 4-17. Publishing to the localhost health topic

```
mosquitto_pub -d -h localhost -p 1883 -t "health/24f89ac6-e53d-418b-be6d-
2a7571aa483f" --tls-version tlsv1.2 -f health.json ①
Client mosq/dyjKcKhXJXNetOhbt8 sending CONNECT
Client mosq/dyjKcKhXJXNetOhbt8 received CONNACK (0)
Client mosq/dyjKcKhXJXNetOhbt8 sending PUBLISH (d0, q0, r0, m1,
'health/24f89ac6-e53d-418b-be6d-2a7571aa483f', ... (82 bytes)) ②
Client mosq/dyjKcKhXJXNetOhbt8 sending DISCONNECT
```

① Our command to publish to the health topic. Note the -f used to tell us the file being published.

② Signaling that publication was successfully sent.

Verify everything worked correctly; by verifying, you see the JSON in the subscription window like in Listing 4-18.

Listing 4-18. Subscription window with the JSON output

```
Client mosq/jvQbjjug7FK8KXaU9q received PUBLISH (d0, q0, r0, m0,
'health/24f89ac6-e53d-418b-be6d-2a7571aa483f', ... (82 bytes))
{
 "status": "Green",
 "msg": "Everything is fine",
 "timestamp": 1562453750553
}
```

We can use these commands throughout this and other chapters to verify and test publishing messages to the MQ. We are now ready to create our Rust application service.

Create the Messaging Service

As I stated earlier, this is going to be another microservice to add to our collection; we will use the standard `iron` framework with logging and routing to set up the application. We won't cover those parts since much of the initial set up is reuse from our previous applications. What we will dive into is parts of creating the client and making our subscription and publishing actions work.

There are a few different crates out there that we can use to create your MQ application; they range from very low-level to high-level wrappers. One of the issues with many of them is their support certificates (which we will use in later chapters). The crate we are going to use is the `rumqtt` crate (`https://crates.io/crates/rumqtt`). This crate allows for easy use of creating clients with securing connections, publishing, subscribing, as well as handling the callbacks from the system. We will need the `rumqtt` and the `crossbeam-channel` crate to use for our MQ application; we have those imported in Listing 4-19.

Listing 4-19. Rumqtt Crate with chrono feature enabled

```
# Used to generate the name of the connection
sys-info = "0.6.0"
rumqtt = { version =  "^0.31", features = ["chrono"] }
```

With those installed, let's go over what we are planning to create:

1. Client create – We will need a function that given parameters (like url, port) will make a connection to a message queue and start up the client. This method will return two things, a client and a notification handler.

2. Notification monitor – Our create client will return a handle to the notifications; this means we will need to create a method to handle the notifications (usually on subscriptions) to process the notifications coming back.

3. Subscribe function – Given a client and topic, we want to subscribe to a given topic.

4.   Publish function – Given a client, topic, and payload, we want to publish to a given topic.

5.   Iron middleware – Since we plan to use in part in our Rust `iron` actions, we will need to create and expose the client in the middleware.

We will work through those steps for the rest of the chapter; let's start with creating the client. In order to create the client, let's define a `struct` that contains all the necessary configurations for the client. Right now, the `struct` only needs to contain two items, the server and port, like we have in Listing 4-20.

Listing 4-20. Struct for our configurations; this will be in the file mqtt/mod.rs

```
#[cfg(feature = "ch04")]
#[derive(Debug, Clone)]
pub struct MqttClientConfig {
    pub mqtt_server: String, ①
    pub mqtt_port: u16, ②
}
#[cfg(feature = "ch04")]
impl MqttClientConfig {
    pub fn server_name(&self) -> String { ③
        match sys_info::hostname() {
            Ok(name) => {
                name
            },
            Err(error) => {
                "server".to_string()
            }
        }
    }
}
```

①   Variable to hold the server URL (in our case localhost).

②   Variable to hold the server port (1883 since we will connect via TCP).

③   This will be used to help us generate the client id, giving us the name of the server we are on.

The fields for these should be created via environmental variables and set in the main like we did in previous chapters. When creating the client, it's important to note that this name should be unique for connections to the server and also should be somewhat meaningful so that if you are viewing it on the web UI, you have an idea what client it is. With that in mind, we are going to create the client, passing in the config, and a unique name for the client. In Listing 4-21, we have our create_client function.

Listing 4-21. The create_client function; this will be in the file mqtt/client.rs

```rust
use rumqtt::{MqttClient, MqttOptions, QoS, ReconnectOptions, Notification,
Receiver}; ①

use super::MqttClientConfig;

const CLIENT_NAME: &str = "mqtt";

#[cfg(feature = "ch04")]
fn create_client(config: &MqttClientConfig, name: &str)
                        -> (MqttClient, Receiver<Notification>) {
    let client_id = format!("{}-{}-{}", CLIENT_NAME, name, config.server_name()); ②

    debug!("Create the connection ... ");

    let reconnection_options = ReconnectOptions::Always(10);

    let mqtt_options = MqttOptions::new(client_id, config.mqtt_server.
    as_str(), config.mqtt_port) ③
        .set_keep_alive(10)
        .set_reconnect_opts(reconnection_options)
        .set_clean_session(false);

    MqttClient::start(mqtt_options).expect("Issue trying to make a client
    connection") ④
}
```

① Imports needed from rumqtt for use by the client.

② We create a custom client using a generic name for the MQ, the name passed in, and the server name. The last is needed when you have multiple developers trying to code against a remote service and do not want collisions.

③   Creates the `MqttOptions` given the config we passed in and other
variables.

④   Starts up the client returning `MqttClient` and the `crossbeam_channe`
`l::Receiver<Notification`.

When this is called, we will have an active client we can make requests against.

One topic I want to address that we will use next is the quality of service (QoS). This
is common in message queues, and if you have never used one, it is good to learn about
how they work or more importantly how they guarantee delivery. The following are the
three levels of QoS used in MQTT:

- QoS 0 – At Most Once

- QoS 1 – At Least Once

- QoS 2 – Exactly Once

These QoS are used when publishing and subscribing and can be used based on
networking reliability and application rules. We need to define these based on how
important it is for a message to be delivered and how detrimental it is for it to be a
duplicated message. Remember, with topics, you can have multiple clients publishing and
multiple clients subscribing. Now the tricky thing here is that the subscriber and publisher
do not have to use the same QoS level; what happens in that case? In the case of a subscriber
defining a lower QoS than it was published with, the broker downgrades the messages and
sends to the subscriber with a lower QoS. Let's take a look at what each QoS level means.

At Most Once – QoS 0

This is the least guaranteed method in our delivery system, but also has the least amount
of overhead. When publishing this message, the client fires the message to the broker
and forgets about it. There is no guarantee of delivery; it simply sends to the broker and
goes on its business. This is good for messages that are immaterial to the application
working correctly. In our application, the `health` check can be a QoS of 0. If the message
gets lost or not delivered, it's not the end of the world, and another health check will
come shortly anyways.

At Least Once – QoS 1

The second method, with a QoS of 1, is a two-way communication. The publisher sends
a packet and waits for the broker to acknowledge that it received the packet by sending
a PUBBACK packet. However, if the PUPBACK is not received, it will send another message.

Now the message may not have been delivered due to network congestion, slow broker, and so on. In this case, it is possible that the broker will see the same message twice, and thus any clients will receive it twice. This will be fine for topics like `recording`; we want to guarantee that when we say to start or stop a recording, the broker receives it; however, if the broker sends two `starts` to a client, it won't make a difference since it already started.

Exactly Once – QoS 2

The final one is the most expensive in terms of network traffic, but it guarantees that not only does the broker receive the message, but it receives it only once. This is achieved by a four-part handshake. QoS of 2 should only be used if a client receiving the same message twice could cause unintended consequences. We will not be using it for our system, but imagine if you were sending commands to a robot car, and you sent "turn left" obviously receiving one "turn left" vs. two "turn lefts" would cause very different behavior.

Now that we have our client created and understand QoS a bit, let's turn to subscribing to a topic.

Subscribe to the Health Topic

For our use case, we will be subscribing to the health topic. To subscribe to a topic, we are going to need to define a non-blocking call to subscribe to the topic, since the topic could receive data at any point, but we want to continue with our processing. Part of the tuple returned in the `create_client` is a notification receiver that will contain any notifications from the subscription. To help with the processing, I have created a generic set of code that we can feed the receiver to in order to process the notifications for subscribers; that code is in Listing 4-22.

Listing 4-22. The `monitor_notifications` function; this will be in the file mqtt/mod.rs

```rust
use rumqtt::{Receiver, Notification}; ①
use rumqtt::Notification::{Publish};
use std::{thread, str};
use log::{debug, error};

// Monitor the notifications from the notification receiver.
#[cfg(feature = "ch04")]
pub fn monitor_notifications(notifications: Receiver<Notification>, url:
String, f: fn(&str, String, String)) { ②
```

```
thread::spawn(move || {  ③
    for notification in notifications {
        debug!("Notification {:?}", notification);
        match notification {
            Publish(p) => {  ④
                // Retrieve the payload and convert it to a string.
                let pl = String::from_utf8(p.payload.to_vec());
                debug!("The Payload :: PKID: {:?}, QOS: {:?},
                Duplicate: {:?}", p.pkid, p.qos, p.dup);
                match pl {
                    Ok(payload) => f(url.as_str(), p.topic_name,
                    payload),  ⑤
                    Err(error) => {
                        error!("Error sending the payload: {:?}", error)
                    },
                };
            },
            _ => debug!("n/a")
        }
    }
});
}
```

① Imports needed for the `monitor_notifications` function.

② Our function signature containing the notifications we received, a
    client, and a function that will be used to forward the message.

③ We spawn a thread to do a forever for loop. The thread is necessary
    so we do not block other method calls.

④ The notification can have multiple types, mostly acknowledging the
    packet. All we care about though is the actual `Publish` notification.

⑤ Forward the payload to the function we passed in.

You will notice that I have created this to be very generic, as I stated earlier, most
of what I do with messages is I pass them on to other microservices. We could have
just as easily made this a struct holder containing all the environmental variables or

even a generic struct to pass in. Also notice we are sending a function in each time, this function will have to have the same signature across all uses of it; it has three function parameters:

1. url – The url we just mentioned; if this is not needed, you could always pass in a blank string.

2. topic – The topic subscribed to; this is necessary in case the topic contains important details like the UUID in the case of the health topic.

3. payload – This is the actual message received and needing to be processed.

The monitor is actually the second half of the equation to create the subscription; the first is the subscribe function itself. In Listing 4-23, we call the subscribe on the application passing in the three necessary items, the client, topic, and our QoS.

Listing 4-23. The subscribe function; this will be in the file mqtt/client.rs

```
pub fn subscribe(client: &mut MqttClient, topic: &'static str, qos: QoS) {
    info!("Subscribe and process: : {:?}", topic);
    client.subscribe(topic, qos).unwrap();
}
```

Now that we have and understand the monitor_notifications and subscribe, let's take a look at how we will use this with the health subscription. In Listing 4-24, we set up a call to monitor the health subscription.

Listing 4-24. The monitor function; this will be in the file actions/health.rs

```
use crate::mqtt::client::{subscribe, create_client};
use crate::mqtt::{MqttClientConfig, monitor_notifications};

const MOD_NAME: &str = "health"; ①

pub fn monitor(config: &MqttClientConfig, retrieval_svc_url: String) {
    let (mut mqtt_client, notifications) = create_client(&config, MOD_NAME); ②
    ////emqtt::subscribe(&config,"vehicle/+/pulse", &mandalore_url,
    heartbeat::process);
    info!("Subscribe to the device health ...");
```

```
    subscribe(&mut mqtt_client,"health/+", QoS::AtMostOnce); ③
    debug!("Monitor the notifications ... ");
    monitor_notifications(notifications, retrieval_svc_url,process); ④
}
```

① Part of the unique name that will make up the client id.

② Calling the create client and returning a tuple that contains the client and notifications.

③ Call to the subscribe function we defined earlier.

④ Call to the monitor_notifications we defined earlier passing in the function we are going to be using process.

One important takeaway is that we need to create a process function that will actually process the payload. For our method, we are going to take the payload, convert it to a struct, and call to a send_to_service method. For now, this method will just output the contents, but in later chapters, we will actually hook it up to the retrieval_svc. In Listing 4-25, we have the process function along with its helper functions.

Listing 4-25. The process function; this will be in the file actions/health.rs

```
pub fn process(url: &str, topic: String, pl: Vec<u8>) {
    info!("Payload Size :: {} ", pl.len());
    let pl = String::from_utf8(pl);
    match pl {
        Ok(payload) => process_and_send(url, topic, payload),
        Err(error) => {
            error!("Error sending the payload: {:?}", error)
        },
    };
}

fn process_and_send(url: &str, topic: String, payload: String) {
    info!("Process Health :: {} :: {}", topic, payload);

    // UUID and data
    let uuid = convert_uuid_input(topic.as_ref()); ①
```

```
    let mut health_data: HealthData = serde_json::from_str(payload.as_
    str()).unwrap(); ②
    health_data.uuid = uuid;

    send_to_service(url, &health_data);
}

fn convert_uuid_input(input: &str) -> Option<Uuid> { ③
    match extract_uuid(input) {
        Some(uuid_str) => {
            let uuid = uuid_str;
            Some(Uuid::parse_str(uuid).unwrap())
        },
        None => {
            None
        }
    }
}

fn extract_uuid(input: &str) -> Option<&str> {
    debug!(" Input :: {}", input);
    lazy_static! {
        //static ref RE: Regex = Regex::new(r"health/(?P<uuid>[0-9a-
        zA-Z_-]*)/check").unwrap();
        static ref RE: Regex = Regex::new(r"health/(?P<id>(.*))").unwrap(); ④
    }

    RE.captures(input).and_then(|cap| {
        debug!("CAPTURE: {:?}", cap);
        cap.name("id").map(|uuid| uuid.as_str()) ⑤
    })
}

pub fn send_to_service(url: &str, data: &HealthData){
    info!("We are sending {:?} to {}", data, url); ⑥
}
```

①   The UUID is in the topic; we need to extract it.

②   Use serde_json to convert the JSON into a struct.

③   Function to convert the topic to a UUID.

④   Regex to identify the id from the topic.

⑤   Uses the regex name mapped to ID to get the ID and return it as a string slice.

⑥   Prints out the final object; this is placeholder code for our later chapter.

As you can see, we are making use of the regex to parse the string; the regex itself is static and won't change. However, we can't define consts that require a function call to compute the value, hence our use of lazy_static; the lazy_static macro allows us to create statics that require heap allocations, vectors, hash maps, or as in our case function calls in order to be initialized. Let's also take a look at the struct we are creating; we have it defined in Listing 4-26.

Listing 4-26. The HealthData struct; this will be in the file actions/health.rs

```
use chrono::prelude::*;
use chrono::naive::serde::ts_milliseconds::deserialize as from_milli_ts; ①

// combination of :  use num_traits::{FromPrimitive,ToPrimitive};
use enum_primitive_derive::Primitive;

#[derive(Serialize, Deserialize, Debug, Primitive, PartialEq)]
pub enum Status { ②
    Green = 0,
    Red = 1,
    Yellow = 2
}

#[derive(Serialize, Deserialize, Debug)]
pub struct Peripheral {
    pub name: String
}
```

```
#[derive(Serialize, Deserialize, Debug)]
pub struct HealthData {
    pub uuid: Option<Uuid>,
    #[serde(deserialize_with = "from_milli_ts")] ③
    pub timestamp: NaiveDateTime,
    pub status: Status,
    pub msg: String,
    pub peripherals: Vec<Peripheral>
}
```

① Using one of the built-in serde converters for NaiveDateTime, you can also create your own custom one.

② Possible values for the status.

③ Converting from the supplied long value to the NaiveDateTime.

Had we just wanted to forward this along as JSON to another endpoint, the conversion would not have been necessary but could have been beneficial. The conversion could have still served as a validation step that the JSON retrieved was in the form of values that our downstream processes could understand since any JSON format could be sent to the message queue. Ideally, we should still do that here to handle the error casing of bad JSON. I will leave it up to the reader to add that code.

Publish to the Recording Topic

Let's take a look at the flip side of a subscription, the publishing. With publishing, we essentially fire and forget, at least from a code point of view. Depending on the QoS under the covers, it may do more. The client will perform the same create client call we made before, but now we will be calling a publish function like in Listing 4-27.

Listing 4-27. The publish function; this will be in the file mqtt/client.rs

```
pub fn publish(client: &mut MqttClient, topic: &str, payload: String, qos:
QoS) {
    info!("Publish to the topic : {:?}", topic);
    client.publish(topic, qos, false, payload).unwrap();
}
```

All we have to do is create the client and pass our client, topic, and payload to send over and we are done. However, the issue is how we plan to make this work. We want this message queue to be triggered by an outside call to our service. To do this, we will expose an iron action that our services can call, which will then trigger the message queue. The router for that action is defined in Listing 4-28.

Listing 4-28. The `action` for running the recording function; this will be in the file http.rs

```
recording: post "/recording/:id/:type" => recording::run,
```

Here we are passing in the UUID of the device, type (start, pause, stop), and the uuid for the camera. Now how do we get the client to be exposed in the action? The answer as you may have guessed is the same way we exposed the database to our iron application in the previous chapter via middleware.

Message Queue Middleware

We are going to create a middleware piece that allows us to expose the client in the iron action. What follows are the steps to go through in creating the middleware; I won't overly dive into what each part does since we've created middleware twice now. But to start with, the main entry in initializing the MQ middleware is to pass the config into the application. In Listing 4-29, we set up the middleware to accept our `MqttClientConfig` that we previously created.

Listing 4-29. The middleware definition; this will be in the file mqtt/middleware.rs

```
use super::MqttClientConfig;
use super::client::create_client;

pub struct MqttClientMiddleware {
    config: MqttClientConfig,
    client: Option<MqttClient>
}

impl MqttClientMiddleware {
    pub fn new(config: MqttClientConfig) -> MqttClientMiddleware {
        MqttClientMiddleware {
            config: config,
```

```
            client: None
        }
    }
}
```

Next we run through the steps of implementing the BeforeMiddleware trait for the struct we just created as well as creating a trait that will expose the method call to our extensions on the Request. All of this is written in Listing 4-30.

Listing 4-30. The middleware implementation; this will be in the file mqtt/middleware.rs

```
// Our tuple struct
pub struct Value(MqttClientConfig, Option<MqttClient>); ①

// This part still confuses me a bit
impl typemap::Key for MqttClientMiddleware{ type Value = Value; }

impl BeforeMiddleware for MqttClientMiddleware {
    fn before(&self, req: &mut Request) -> IronResult<()> {
        req.extensions.insert::<MqttClientMiddleware>(Value(self.config.
        clone(), None)); ②
        Ok(())
    }
}

// TODO See if i can get working if not remove
//impl AfterMiddleware for MqttClientMiddleware {
//    fn after(&self, req: &mut Request,  res: Response) ->
      IronResult<Response> {
//        let config_val = req.extensions.get::<MqttClientMiddleware>().
          expect("Mqtt Client");
//        let Value(ref config, client) = config_val;
//        match client {
//            Some(mut client_val) => {
//                client_val.shutdown();
//            }
//            _ => {}
```

```
//        }
//        Ok(res)
//    }
//}

pub trait MqttRequestExt {
    fn mqtt_client(&mut self) -> (MqttClient, Receiver<Notification>); ③
}

impl<'a, 'b> MqttRequestExt for Request<'a, 'b> {
    fn mqtt_client(&mut self) -> (MqttClient, Receiver<Notification>) {
        debug!("Get Client Request");
        let config_val = self.extensions.get::<MqttClientMiddleware>().
        expect("Mqtt Client");
        let Value(ref config, _) = config_val;

        // Create the client here for each request
        let (client, note) = create_client(&config, random().as_str()); ④
        // save the client
        self.extensions.insert::<MqttClientMiddleware>(Value(config.to_
        owned(), Some(client.clone())));

        return (client, note);
    }
}

fn random() -> String { ⑤
    use rand::{thread_rng, Rng};
    use rand::distributions::Alphanumeric;

    thread_rng()
        .sample_iter(&Alphanumeric)
        .take(5)
        .collect()
}
```

① Setting the Value to the config.

② Inserting the config before the method call.

③ Exposing a trait that we can use in our action that exposes `mqtt_client()` method.

④ A call to the `create_client` that we created previously.

⑤ A randomizer to use as the name for the client creation.

The one interesting piece to note is the randomizer. In our subscriber pattern, we would only ever have one subscriber per server. There was never a chance of name collisions. But here we are not really sure which publisher is using it, but also we could have many simultaneous requests for the same publish, and we would not want to cause client conflicts. Small note here, we are not pooling our connections yet. We ideally want to do this since there could be an insane amount of clients being created.

Recording Module

Let's make use of this new trait for our requests in the recording module. This module will receive an endpoint /recording/:id/:type/:camera and will be responsible for sending that to the MQ which will then get picked up by the IoT device. Let's start in Listing 4-31 with setting up the struct we are going to convert that URL information into.

Listing 4-31. The middleware implementation; this will be in the file actions/recording.rs

```
#[derive(Serialize, Deserialize, Debug)]
enum RecordingType { ①
    Start,
    Stop
}

#[derive(Serialize, Deserialize, Debug)]
struct Recording { ②
    uuid: Uuid,
    rtype: RecordingType
}
```

① The enum for the recording type.

② The Recording struct we are creating.

Now let's implement the run function will which process the iron request and send the data over to the message queue. In Listing 4-32, we take the request data convert it to a struct and then send that as JSON data to the recording/ topic.

Listing 4-32. The run endpoint for our recording; this will be in the file actions/recording.rs

```rust
use crate::mqtt::middleware::MqttRequestExt;
use crate::mqtt::client::publish;
use rumqtt::QoS;

pub fn run(req: &mut Request) -> IronResult<Response> {
    info!("Recording Start/Stop");

    let recording = Recording { ①
        uuid: super::get_uuid_value(req, "id"),
        rtype: get_recording_type(req)
    };
    info!("Set Recording Type to : {:?}", recording);

    // Send the data over
    let (mut client, _ ) = req.mqtt_client(); ②
    let topic = format!("recording/{}", recording.uuid);
    let json = serde_json::to_string(&recording).unwrap(); ③

    publish(&mut client, topic.as_str(), json, QoS::AtLeastOnce); ④

    Ok(Response::with((status::Ok, "OK")))
}

fn get_recording_type(req: &Request) -> RecordingType {
    match super::get_value(req, "type").as_ref() {
        "start" => RecordingType::Start,
        "stop" => RecordingType::Stop,
        _ => panic!("You have bad code")
    }
}
```

① Create the `Recording` struct based on the parameters supplied on the URL.

② Call the `mqtt_client` from the middleware we just created; you will notice the that we used "_" on the notification tuple return since we will not use it.

③ Convert the `Recording` struct to a JSON String.

④ Call the `publish` on the MQ client and send over our payload to the correct topic.

I have not included all the code to do all the value conversions; they are based off the `Router` extension we used in the previous chapter, as well as some parsing. The code is in the source material though, but we didn't need to go over it. Also like I mentioned earlier, we used a QoS of `AtLeastOnce`, since sending over multiple messages will not alter the state of the device adversely.

While creating the middleware piece was a bit cumbersome, in the end, we now have a very clean and easy-to-read code that can be replicated repeatedly for other MQ publish scenarios.

Summary

In this chapter, we focused on the GraphQL and messaging. The GraphQL is able to replace using RESTful APIs and replace with a structured format. We can still perform all our actions but in a more descriptive nature. GraphQL is very useful when sharing between mobile and web applications as well. In addition, we went into MQTT messaging; the MQTT is one of the keys to any IoT application because it allows us to support communication with our devices even while offline. Message queues serve that useful barrier of accepting outside commands even when the IoT device is down (and vice versa but less likely to happen). In the next chapter, we will work more on the `retrieval_svc` optimizing calls to it.

CHAPTER 5

Performance

One of the most common problems with any application and IoT ones in particular is cost and performance. Remember IoT devices may have to transmit huge amounts of data and depending on the device may have bad or random Internet connectivity (think of an IoT-connected vehicle or a device outside your house far from your Wi-Fi monitoring). We expect our devices to communicate quickly and without lag. No one wants to send a command to the IoT device and wait too long for the command to be processed by the device. This cost is not just in processing time, but it's a practical cost; cloud providers charge for the amount of data being transferred. Hence, you want to reduce that cost, and there are essentially two ways:

1. Reduce the amount of times you transfer data.

2. Reduce the size of the data you transfer while still transmitting all the information you need.

Another area of cost by cloud providers is the actual cost of the servers (the use of CPU/RAM). We went over in the first chapter the difference in large and small instances. And these all take an actual monetary cost in usage. And all of this is a balance between performance and cost. You can have a super-fast app that handles many simultaneous connections, but it may cost you money. And you may not make money off that app minus the initial hardware sale (i.e., Nest cameras can stream for free but charge for recording). There are a couple ways we can keep high performance and control cost. And while there are different areas to achieve optimized performance, we will discuss and optimize for two of them. The first is optimizing the actual computational cost of data via the serialization and deserialization of data. This occurs while converting JSON to Strings and vice versa. This often has a high CPU and I/O cost associated with it. Another is your latency when making a request. Many of the requests perform numerous writings to a database; what if on simple items like inserts we return a response immediately and let the application perform the actual processing in the background?

© Joseph Faisal Nusairat 2020
J. F. Nusairat, *Rust for the IoT*, https://doi.org/10.1007/978-1-4842-5860-6_5

There are many strategies in how to solve for these, but the two we will be using in this chapter are Cap'n Proto and CQRS. These each handle different aspects of processing.

CQRS is going to help solve the issue of response time to the user; it works by allowing part of the process to happen and the rest of it being processed asynchronously. The Cap'n Proto is going to be used to lower the cost of sending messages between services both in size of the messages and also CPU and memory use of the services.

Before we start, I want to make it clear that neither of these solutions is 100% use case solutions nor the "end all be all" to solve all problems. There are many who disagree with using these models mostly for the amount of extra framework code necessary to run them and also for potential increase where errors can occur. But these two topics I found imperative to discuss if we are going to discuss modern IoT applications backend, since they come up again and again. And at least now, you will be able to see for yourself if you like them and can pick them for use in your IoT application. And I have used both at times in IoT, so they are valuable tool sets to learn.

Goals

After completing this chapter, we shall have covered the following topics:

1. Understanding how and why we use CQRS and eventual consistency for our applications.

2. Implementing CQRS for Comment Adds/Deletes.

3. Using Eventstore to integrate with our CQRS system to be used as a storage for the events.

4. Understanding the role of binary serialized data has in our application.

5. Implementing Cap'n Proto to serialize and deserialize a message.

6. Implementing Cap'n Proto to use RPC to process a message.

In this code, we will be using three services: the message queue service, the retrieval service, and a new health client service.

CQRS

Command Query Responsibility and Segregation (CQRS) was a technology that has been out for a while but was brought to your average developer by Martin Fowler (@martinfowler) in 2011, in what is now a famous blog post about it (https://martinfowler.com/bliki/CQRS.html). Fowler first learned about CQRS from Greg Young (@gregyoung) who has quite a few great articles and videos on CQRS if you want to learn even more. The heart of CQRS is about the separation of layers – and separation of responsibility.

If you look back before 2011 (and even current day), many of our applications are Create/Read/Update/Delete (CRUD) applications. These are your standard applications that we often show in books, demos, and so on. Think of your bookstore model or, for something even more advance, your taxes. In the end, we often feed your tax data into a CRUD database. We then pull from this database with a set of queries. Figure 5-1 shows a model of how this typically looks.

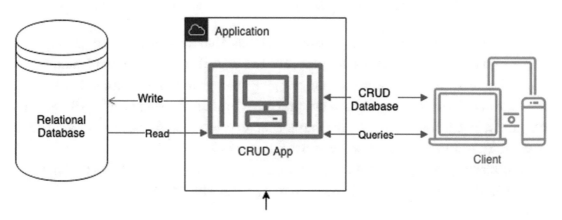

Figure 5-1. *Your typical model for a CRUD interaction with a database*

I've written these types of models many times, and they do work for the simplest of cases and are perfect for a standard admin portal or to alter simple settings. The problem can be when you go beyond your standard design. Most of the more interesting pages involve complex queries that do not necessarily model the exact data we stored. For example, we rarely just input a movie and want that movie. We may want a search for a list of movies with Schwarzenegger or movies that are all the action flicks between 1980 and 1990 (the best decade ever for action movies). As these models for command (used for the changing of data) and the querying become more complex, so do our need to separate them. In Figure 5-2, we see how you'd separate out command and querying.

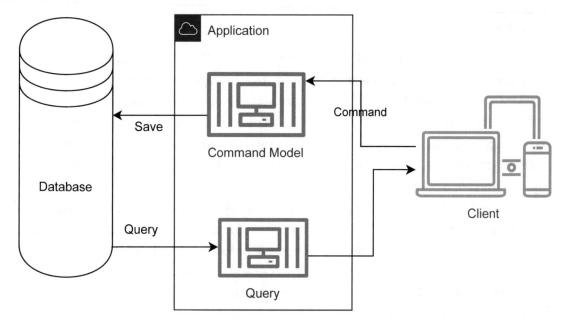

Figure 5-2. *Your most typical CQRS model*

This CQRS model allows us to separate the reads from the writes, not only from a process point of view but a modelling one. The writes go through a command model that writes to the database, and the querying goes through another set of services to read from the database. In here, you have two processes running the client which will send a command that gets written to the database. Then the client could also in another thread or the same send a query that would retrieve from the data.

The other upside is that CQRS easily fits into other patterns that work well with it. Martin Fowler identities five other patterns that fit well with CQRS:

- Task-based UI

- Event-based programming models
  (https://martinfowler.com/eaaDev/EventNarrative.html)

- Eventual consistency (www.allthingsdistributed.com/
  2008/12/eventually_consistent.html)

- Eager read derivation
  (https://martinfowler.com/bliki/EagerReadDerivation.html)

- Event poster (https://martinfowler.com/bliki/EventPoster.html)

- Domain-driven design

I have provided links you can look at for a few of those; the one I am most interested that fits our needs is eventual consistency. Eventual consistency is the idea that events are eventually consistent. This means that when commit an event to our application, it may not get persisted or processed right away, but eventually it will. This allows for quick calls and responses from the server, while it goes ahead and processes the data. This obviously only works well for nontransactional type data. With eventual consistency, the events first stored to a write event store; this can be a traditional database or a streaming database like eventstore. From there, the events get picked up and sent to the normal CQRS pattern, and the data is now written to the CQRS database.

In this scenario, you have a read and write database. The read database is what the client will call to perform its queries, and the write is the EC-tied database that the client will call when performing a write operation. This can be a bit confusing, but realize the read database gets written to by the CQRS; it's just not directly written to by the client.

Part of the reasoning behind all this is also to create more readable and maintainable code. When adding EC, we are going to add a secondary data store. (Note: This is not necessary, but we are going to do it.) The architecture of this is listed in Figure 5-3.

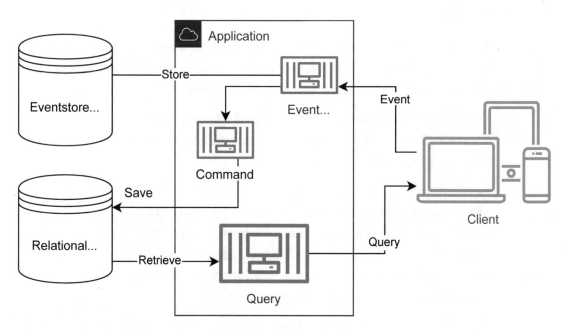

Figure 5-3. *Your typical model for a CQRS transaction*

This puts an asynchronous layer between our event and the CQRS. The event handler will receive the event and send it to the data store before sending a command to the event handler. You end up with a read database and a write database. Although this can be a bit confusing at first, the database you actually write to is the read database. This can help in performance optimization for your system, if you perform writes more than reads or reads more than writes. With developing microservices for a deployed application, you always want to consider the cost to your deployed infrastructure; this can easily get eaten up by a poor bloated design. Another interesting aspect is how reads/writes work with eventual consistency; since all your work is stored in the writes, initially it becomes a catalog of what has happened in the past. This will also allow you to rerun from certain times in the past to repopulate your read database, even applying new logic if need be along the way. However, be warned if you changed your Command or Event structure along the way, this could lead to some duplicitous behavior.

Let's break down step by step what happens in the command model. CQRS uses particular labels and wording for each step.

CQRS Steps

Each step has a particular purpose; in addition, in each step when we define the struct or enum for it, we will use a certain set of grammar, noun, or verb. This isn't a must of course, but it's the nomenclature most CQRS systems go for:

1. Data will enter your controller from a RESTful or GraphQL endpoint. This has already been written for us, and we will just integrate with our existing code.

2. In the controller, you will translate this to a command. Commands dictate that there are actions to happen; hence, the command enums are named as action verbs in the present tense. The commands are a CQRS command that could be directly plugged into the CQRS system or in our case will be sent to the event store. This all depends on what the dispatcher is doing.

3. From the command, you get fed into an Aggregate. The Aggregate is the glue that combines everything together. The aggregate takes the current state and applies the command to it, outputting an event. In here the aggregator can ignore or use the previous state; it's up to you. We will get into more in our example.

4. The aggregator will then return from it 0 to many events.

5. The name of the event object should be in the past tense. This is the action that has happened. We can use this to do a number of tasks and triggers, and the event is where the CQRS framework really interacts with the application.

In addition, depending on the CQRS system you are using, there are handlers and managers. The biggest key to understand is the Command-Event-Aggregate model; I have broken that out for you in Figure 5-4. This model is the flow most CQRS + EC applications take in processing.

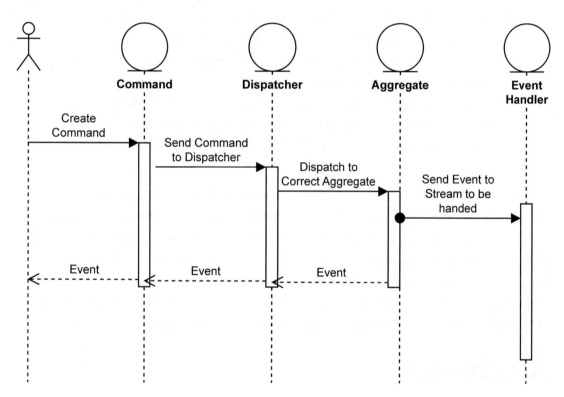

Figure 5-4. *The Command-Event-Aggregate model*

Which CQRS to Use?

I hope this gives you a basic understanding of CQRS. I would also suggest reading Martin's blog on it. I've tried to cover enough for you to understand the problem and the solution we are going for. The idea is simple in its nature but then gets more complex when implementing. And this is where it gets a bit tricky for us in Rust. There isn't one "end all be all" fully functional CQRS applications. There are in other languages, but like I've said before, Rust is only recently coming into its own on the Web. Part of that is because the threading won't be resolved till late 2019, and that is key for a good CQRS solution. With my research, I found three solutions I liked:

1. Riker CQRS – Seemed like a very basic but good base model, but still seemed raw (`https://github.com/riker-rs/riker-cqrs`).

2. Chronicle – This seemed very much on its way to be a full-fledged CQRS, but work has stopped on it and hasn't been worked on for two years (`https://github.com/brendanzab/chronicle`).

3. Event sourcing – Started off as a medium.com article, and then a follow-up created a framework based on the second article. Still very fresh and the author recently altered it and made it easier and smoother to use (note to author of the crate, thanks I had to rewrite this chapter because of it.) But in addition, I really liked the Event Store database tie in which makes it easier for us to perform eventual consistency along with it (`https://github.com/pholactery/eventsourcing`).

None were what I'd consider full CQRS implementations, but for the book, we are going to go with the third. It's also easier and a better start than us trying to write our own from scratch. I liked the passion behind event sourcing, and the added portion of the `eventstore` gave it a good way to hook into the events once created. Again most importantly, we are going over the concepts of CQRS in this section. We will use this one going further. I believe what is really needed is a company to have a need for CQRS and create an open source application that allows for a public and private input on it.

Event Sourcing

The `event sourcing` crate creates a standard set of commands, aggregations, and events. However, it's how you use the events that is different than in other models. The `event sourcing` can use (and we will use) Event Store database under the covers to store all our writes. The Event Store database is an open source database that can allow for 15,000 writes per second and 50,000 reads. This will allow our application to have considerable throughput and only have to worry about bottleneck when we have to read the event and then process the event. This database was designed for stream data, so it's a perfect fit for event sourcing (`https://eventstore.org/`).

Implementing in Our Application

The code in this demo application will be designed to work in the `retrieval_svc`, in our `/comment/add` endpoint. This endpoint right now is called via a standard http command that will call to our database and save a comment. This does not have any added business functionality, but for now imagine other side effects could be calling out to a notification server to let someone know of a new comment on their video.

Another reason to choose the comment adds is that this service is one of our endpoints that could potentially receive heavy traffic. Because of that, we wanted to tie eventual consistency with it. EC tells us that the application will EVENTUALLY be correct and contain the right data. We are able to do this because of the Event Store we are using. The actual work on the event will occur by monitoring the eventstore stream, allowing us to return a response to the user before the event has been stored in the database. Figure 5-5 illustrates our flow for the application.

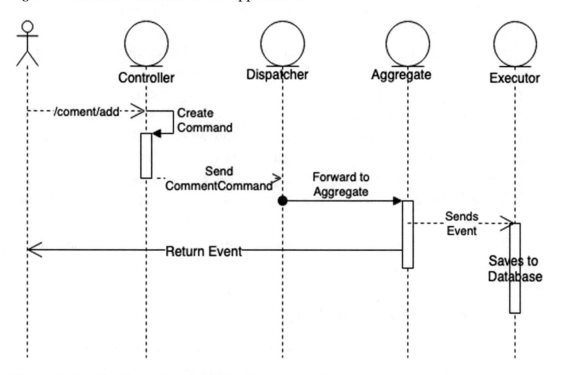

Figure 5-5. *The flow of our application*

The key to making this fast and responsive is we are able to continue processing even after the controller returns to the user. This allows us to have a fast response to acknowledge to the user that they received their comment but before the comment has actually been persisted, so make sure any validation occurs before we return. If after you receive an acknowledgment you sent a delete, the beauty of the event stream is that it will be queued up and will simply get processed after so you do not have to worry about one event happening before another. It's all a sequential ordering of processing.

Gotchas

Because of the nature of EC, it is imperative you only do it for things where a transactional state does not matter. In shopping carts, for example, you do not want to confirm a purchase has been completed until the purchase has actually been completed and the credit card is confirmed. However, I would argue in many of the transactions we do not need this absolute level of control. Functions like changing the temperature or turning a light on and off can be events that EC works great for. In the real world of course, this isn't taking minutes but maybe seconds at most, usually micro seconds, but if you've ever worked with a database before, you know one of the longest aspects of your CRUD interactions is the database persistence part.

Another thought about our use of eventual consistency is that it fits in very nicely when you use GraphQL subscriptions. Since you may want acknowledgment when a command has been fully processed and stored into the database, one can add a subscription event to the user. With subscriptions, we can have socket notifications of a change. In our example of a light turning on, you could request the light turn on and get an immediate call back, and then in your actual section of code that shows the light is on, it would send a socket request to your app notifying you it was successful. And then your app can reflect the change accordingly. This allows good symmetry with low latency in your application.

Of course, one of the best ways of learning for me is doing, so let's implement the application.

Setting Up Our Environment

Let's get started; to start, we mentioned we are using Event Store as the streaming database to store the events. Much like our other services, we are going to use docker to install it. We have done this a few times now, so you should be getting the hang of it. In Listing 5-1, we retrieve the eventstore for local install.

Listing 5-1. Pull and install our event stream giving the name eventstore-node

```
docker pull eventstore/eventstore

docker run --name eventstore-node -it -p 2113:2113 -p 1113:1113 eventstore/
eventstore
```

Our Event Store will be named eventstore-node and will expose two ports for our use. The 1113 will be used to launch and connect to our consumers of the eventstore. The 2113 endpoint will be used to store our event into the eventstream and also will be used as the port for the web application. Speaking of which, when running the docker image, open the web browser that can browse the data. You can launch the application at http://localhost:2113; the default admin account user is admin and the password is changeit. Note on restart of docker or your computer, you will have to run docker start eventstore-node to have the eventstore start up again.

Cargo Update

Let's open up your retrieval_svc application; this is the microservice we will be updating to use CQRS. We are going to add the event sourcing crate to the application. In Listing 5-2, we will add the event sourcing and event sourcing-derive crate.

Listing 5-2. Adding the event sourcing crates; this will be in the file Cargo.toml

```
event sourcing = { version = "0.1.5", features = ["orgeventstore"],
git = "https://github.com/nusairat/eventsourcing.git" }
event sourcing-derive = "0.1.3"

## For the event store database
eventstore = "0.7.4"
```

I am using my own branch here, because I needed to add the functionality to add user authentication when talking to the orgeventstore. By the time you read this, this may not be necessary as the owner may have updated it by then. You will also notice we activated the feature orgeventstore. The CQRS pattern requires that we store the events into an intermediary store before it gets processed; this is the write store, and this is what will be used to write to the Eventstore streaming database. Let's start coding.

Creating Our CQRS Objects

First off, we are going to start by creating the necessary command and event objects. The command and event are what drives the CQRS system to save to the database. Comments are made of three items:

- id – This is the UUID that identifies a unique comment.

- body – This is the actual comment text.

- media_item_id – This is the video or picture the comment is referencing.

Ideally, we'd also have a user, but in our imagery world, all comments are anonymous. We are going to achieve two functions for this:

- Adding – Adding a comment to the database

- Deleting – Deleting a comment from the database

Both of these will require a command and a corresponding event. In addition, we want to group all CQRS commands and events for a particular type together via an enum. We will thus create two enums CommentCommand and CommentEvent that will contain an entry for adding and deleting.

Command and Event

In Listing 5-3, we have the CommentCommand and CommentEvent defined for our add and delete comment.

Listing 5-3. Adding the event sourcing command and events; this will be in the file src/domain.rs

```
use uuid::Uuid;
use event sourcing::prelude::*; ①
use event sourcing::Result;
use event sourcing::eventstore::EventStore;
use serde_derive::{Serialize, Deserialize};
use crate::database::PgPooled;

const DOMAIN_VERSION: &str = "1.0";
```

```
pub enum CommentCommand { ②
AddComment { body: String, media_item_id: Option<Uuid> },
    DeleteComment { id: Uuid }
}

#[derive(Serialize, Deserialize, Debug, Clone, Event)]
#[event_type_version(DOMAIN_VERSION)] ③
#[event_source("events://iot-rust/comment")]
pub enum CommentEvent {
    CommentAdded { id: Uuid, body: String, media_item_id: Option<Uuid> }, ④
    CommentDeleted { id: Uuid }
}
```

①   Crate imports we need for the macros and traits for CQRS.

②   Our enumeration keeping all of our different events.

③   Adding the macro to define these event types and defining a source for the events. Also defining an event_source, you can set this to something unique often reflecting your git entry.

④   Our CommentAdded event.

There are a few things to highlight in this code. The first thing you will notice is while each event is a struct, they are a struct in an enum. This is mostly to allow more concise processing and boilerplate code. Also recall earlier I said to label commands as verbs in the present tense and events as verbs in past tense. You will see that we have "Add" and "Delete" both verbs in the present and "Added" and "Deleted" both verbs in the past tense.

We also did group all the comments together; if we had another, we could have a MediaData one to group all the media data changes. This can be a bit confusing to look at initially, but does make it easier to process when we get to the aggregate phase.

After writing quite a bit of CQRS, there are two fairly common patterns I've encountered when tieing commands with events:

1. Command → event directly – The one-to-one ratio pattern. Like in our system, each command will create exactly one event to process the command.

2. Command → multiple events – Not all systems create one command to one event; in this pattern, your command can spurn multiple events. We aren't doing this for this particular task, but a comment could trigger the database addition, but also could trigger notification being sent to the original poster that a comment was posted. You would want to treat these as two different events.

But the route we go all depends on what we decide in the aggregator.

Aggregator

The Aggregator in CQRS moves the command to the event phase. In our event sourcing crate, it is a trait that we will implement for our comments. The trait is defined in the crate as having these functions listed in Listing 5-4.

Listing 5-4. The Aggregate trait. This is defined in the event sourcing source

```
pub trait Aggregate {
    type Event: Event;
    type Command;
    type State: AggregateState + Clone;

    fn apply_event(state: &Self::State, evt: Self::Event) ->
    Result<Self::State>;
    fn handle_command(state: &Self::State, cmd: Self::Command) ->
    Result<Vec<Self::Event>>;
    fn apply_all(state: &Self::State, evts: &[Self::Event]) ->
    Result<Self::State>;
}
```

Here you define the Event, the Command, and the State. The command and the event we already discussed, and the state we only briefly touched. The state is the current state of the event. It's used and altered as we go along and can be used to know what happened the previous time a comment was added. The apply_event will apply the events to the current state producing a new state; this is called when re-recording what happened. The handle_command is what will produce 0 to many events from a command. And the apply_all will reapply all events on the package. In our application, we are going to create just one event per command; however, we have this defined in Listing 5-5.

Listing 5-5. The aggregate and the states for our application; this will be in the file src/domain.rs

```rust
#[derive(Debug, Clone)]
pub struct CommentState { ①
pub body: String,
    pub media_item_id: Option<Uuid>,
    pub generation: u64
}

impl AggregateState for CommentState { ②
fn generation(&self) -> u64 {
    self.generation
}
}

pub struct CommentAggregate;
impl Aggregate for CommentAggregate { ③
type Event = CommentEvent; ④
type Command = CommentCommand;
    type State = CommentState;

    // Apply events to state, producing new state.
    fn apply_event(state: &Self::State, event: &Self::Event) ->
    Result<Self::State> { ⑤
        info!("Apply event");
        // needs to implement the event on the state itself
        unimplemented!()
    }
```

```
/// 2. Handle commands, producing a vector of outbound events, likely
candidates for publication.
fn handle_command(_state: &Self::State, cmd: &Self::Command) ->
Result<Vec<Self::Event>> { ⑥
    info!("Handle Command");
    // validate

    // Only if validation passes return the events for it
    Ok(vec![cmd.into()]) ⑦
}
}
```

① The CommentState is our struct that defines the state; this should include properties from the command and event.

② The AggregateState is a trait from event sourcing that at each state produces a new state with a one higher sequence number.

③ The CommentAggregate is an aggregate without properties that implements the Aggregate trait we mentioned before.

④ We define the Event, Command, and State to match the CommentEvent, CommentCommand, and CommentState we created early. These will be the events.

⑤ The apply_event method; we are not implementing this for now.

⑥ The handle_comand that will funnel our commands we created.

⑦ An into on the command to convert the command to the events we created.

Few things to dive deeper here, inside the handle_command, we can add validators and converters if needed to change the command to an event. We aren't going to define any here since we are relying on the validation on the client side, which we own. The second part is the into; this actually gets derived when you define the From trait on a struct. The trait method will take in its Self and return another predefined struct that is converted. We are going to use this in Listing 5-6 to create the enum event from the enum commands.

Listing 5-6. Implementation of the From trait on the CommentCommand; this will be in the file src/domain.rs

```
// Used to convert from one type to another
impl From<&CommentCommand> for CommentEvent { ①
    fn from(source: &CommentCommand) -> Self { ②
        match source {
            CommentCommand::AddComment{body, media_item_id} => { ③
                CommentEvent::CommentAdded{
                    id: Uuid::new_v4(), ④
                    body: body.to_string(),
                    media_item_id: *media_item_id
                }
            },
            CommentCommand::DeleteComment { id } =>
            CommentEvent::CommentDeleted { id: *id } ⑤
        }
    }
}
```

① Implementation of the From trait on the `CommentCommand` for the `CommentEvent`.

② The only function that needs to be implemented is the `from`.

③ Matches the `AddComment`.

④ This is where we create the Uuid for the event.

⑤ Matches for the `DeleteComment` creating a `CommentDeleted` event.

Dispatcher

Now we have our command, event, state, and aggregate working; the last piece that is needed to tie it all together is the dispatcher. The dispatcher or router in other CQRS frameworks is what's going to feed in event and move it through the system with the output of the dispatch being a `CloudEvent`. We have the event defined in Listing 5-7.

Listing 5-7. The Dispatcher trait; this is defined in the event sourcing source

```rust
pub trait Dispatcher {
    type Command;
    type Event: Event;
    type State: AggregateState;
    type Aggregate: Aggregate<Event = Self::Event, Command = Self::Command,
    State = Self::State>;

    fn dispatch(
        state: &Self::State,
        cmd: Self::Command,
        store: &impl EventStore,
        stream: &str,
    ) -> Vec<Result<CloudEvent>>;
}
```

This is a trait the user can define for whatever their implementation. Luckily for us the framework hooks into the Event Store; we will use the `derive` macro to create the dispatcher, which will tell the dispatcher which aggregate to use. In Listing 5-8, we have defined our dispatcher with the `CommentAggregate`.

Listing 5-8. Implementation of the CommentDispatcher; this will be in the file src/domain.rs

```rust
#[derive(Dispatcher)]
#[aggregate(CommentAggregate)]
pub struct CommentDispatcher;
```

Calling Our Commanded Endpoint

At this point, we have everything created for the CQRS to make it functional, but alas, there are two steps left to make this work in our application. The first and most obvious is calling the dispatcher with our command. This will require us to do a few things; the first and most obvious is create the command itself and to have it dispatched. The second and not as obvious is create the state; this will define the initial state, although for comments right now they are additive. If we added a modified, we would use the

UUID to track and know what the previous state is. This can be useful in tracking adds vs. updates or if you want to perform a different function based on the previous properties. I've used this mostly for tracking statuses and determining difference if a status moves from one state to another.

We are going to be having the events called by a GraphQL mutation as opposed to a RESTful endpoint, so the code will replace the `graphql/context/add_comment` we created in the previous chapter and will now call our own CQRS version.

But first, we need to make some alterations to the `Mutations` struct itself; it will need a reference to the OrgEventStore so that we can pass the command to the event stream. There are a few modifications we will need to make one in `http.rs` and the other in `schema.rs`; we will place those both in Listing 5-9.

Listing 5-9. Instantiating the OrgEventStore and passing it to mutations, in the file src/http.rs

```
#[cfg(feature = "cqrs")]
pub fn start(   server: &str, port: u16, auth_server: &str, database_url:
                &str, event_store_host: &str, event_store_port: u16, ①
                event_store_user: String, event_store_pass: String) {

    use juniper_iron::{GraphQLHandler, GraphiQLHandler, PlaygroundHandler};
    use juniper::{EmptyMutation, FieldResult};
    use crate::graphql::context::{Context, context_factory, Root, Mutations};
    use event sourcing::eventstore::OrgEventStore;

    // mounts the router to the
    let mut mount = Mount::new();

    // Api Routes we will setup and support
    let router = create_routes();
    mount.mount("/api", router);

    // need to pass in the endpoint we want in the mount below
    // no subscription URL
    let playground = PlaygroundHandler::new("/graph");
```

```
// Setup for Org EventStore
let event_store = OrgEventStore::new_with_auth(event_store_host,
                                              event_store_port, ②
                                              event_store_user, event_
                                              store_pass);

let graphql_endpoint = GraphQLHandler::new(
                                          context_factory, Root,
                                          Mutations{org_event_store:
                                          event_store} ③
);
```

① Pass the eventstore user, password, host, and port to the function; this will be derived from command args module we have been using previously.

② Create the OrgEventStore struct from the given variable.

③ Pass that variable to our mutations.

Now in Listing 5-10, let's update the Mutation struct to include the OrgEventStruct.

Listing 5-10. Instantiating the OrgEventStore and passing it to mutations, in the file src/graphql/context.rs

```
#[cfg(feature = "cqrs")]
pub struct Mutations {
    pub org_event_store: event sourcing::eventstore::OrgEventStore
}
```

Finally, let's update add_comment in Listing 5-11 which will take the mutation data passed in, creating a command and executing the dispatcher, which will add it to the event stream.

Listing 5-11. The `media_add` iron request; this will be in the file
src/graphql/context.rs

```
#[cfg(feature = "cqrs")]
fn add_comment(mutations: &Mutations, context: &Context, media_item_id:
Uuid, body: String) -> Uuid {
    comment_add(&mutations.org_event_store, media_item_id, body.as_str())
}

use crate::domain::{CommentCommand, CommentState, CommentDispatcher,
CommentEvent};
use crate::models::health_check::HealthData;

// Send via the CQRS
pub fn comment_add(eventstore: &OrgEventStore, media_id: Uuid, comment:
&str) -> Uuid {
    use uuid::Uuid;
    // dispatcher trait
    use event_sourcing::Dispatcher; ①
    // For the event sourcing
    use event_sourcing::eventstore::OrgEventStore; ②

    // You create the command you want to execute
    let command = CommentCommand::AddComment { ③
        body: comment.to_string(),
        media_item_id: Some(media_id),
    };

    // our state, the initial one, aggregate should emit this.
    // this is the returned state that should then be used for subsequent
    calls
    let state = CommentState { ④
        body: "".to_string(),
        media_item_id: None,
        generation: 0
    };
```

```
// Successful call will return the Event
debug!("Dispatch ...");
let res = CommentDispatcher::dispatch(&state, &command, eventstore.
clone(), crate::cqrs::STREAM_ID.clone()); ⑤
let data = &res[0].as_ref().unwrap().data; ⑥
let id = data.get("CommentAdded").unwrap().get("id").unwrap();
let uuid_created = match id {
    serde_json::Value::String(st) => {
        Some(Uuid::parse_str(st).unwrap())
    },
    _ => { None }
};

uuid_created.unwrap() ⑦
}
```

① Adds the trait for the dispatcher.

② Also loads the OrgEventStore that we will use to define the destination for the event.

③ Defines our AddComment command.

④ Our initialized state for the comment.

⑤ Runs the Dispatcher passing in our state, command, the store, and the stream name to store the comment against.

⑥ Gets the return from the dispatcher which will be the event, and retrieving the id we created for it so we can return to the user the ID that was created.

⑦ Returns the UUID created for the object back to the mutation. The caller can then use this UUID to perform a subscription, query, and others on the comment after it gets saved.

Bullet 6 is critical; you will notice the last parameter we are using is a constant; this is set in a different module that we will get to in a bit. Just realize the value stored is my_comment; this is the stream name, and knowing the name will become important in a bit. We are going to be using persistent streams so the stream data will be saved during restarts. We will use this name again later to retrieve the stream and also when viewing the stream on the Event Store website.

Bullet 7 if you aren't familiar with Rust is a bit of a mess, and the reason is the application returns the CloudEvent, but the data we are really interested is on the event which is buried in there in a vector (remember commands can return 0 to many events).

At this point, go ahead and run the application and make a sample request to the comment. You will use the mutation code you wrote in Listing 4-11 to write a comment out. You will get a UUID returned.

In addition, we can view the comment in the stream itself. When you started eventstore, you exposed a web port at 2113. If you go to http://localhost:2113/, you will be asked to log in using the generic username and password for eventstore which are admin and changeit, respectively. Once logged in, click Stream Browser at top; you will get an image that looks like Figure 5-6.

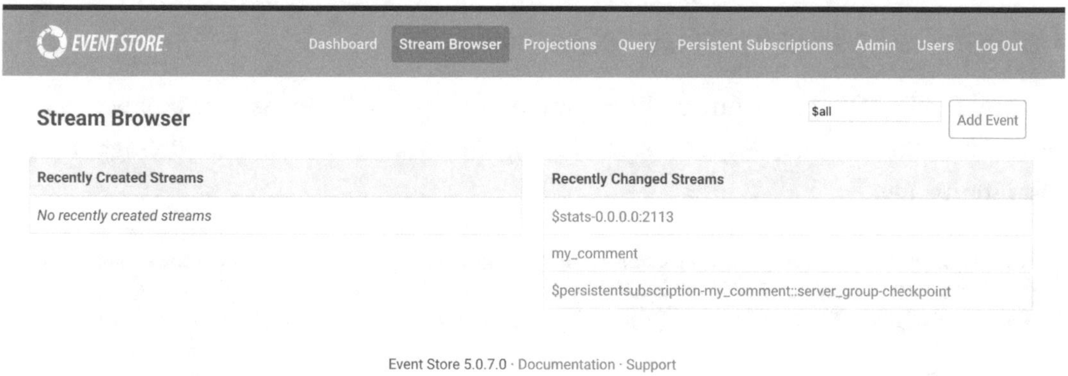

Figure 5-6. The Event Store browser stream

We are using persistent streams, and if we have added to it, you should see our stream name under Recently Changed Streams. Click the name my_comment to get a detailed list of all the streams; if you've run this a few times, it should look like Figure 5-7.

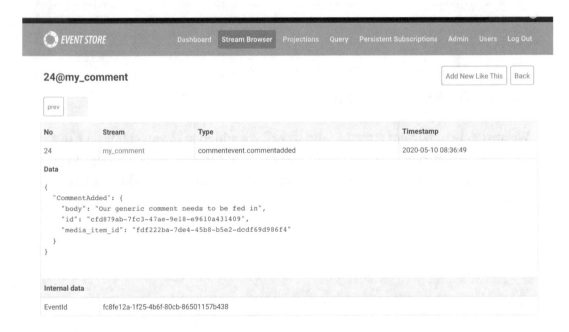

Figure 5-7. *The list of streams for my_comment*

And finally, if you click one of the stream names, you will see the data that was passed into the stream in Figure 5-8. Reviewing the data can be useful for debugging or just monitoring.

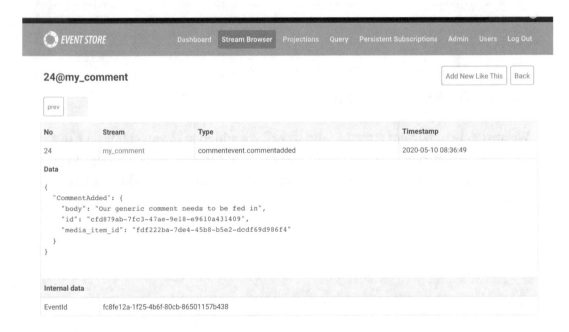

Figure 5-8. *The details of one stream event*

Processing the Event Stream

At this point, we have submitted the data to the event stream; we can verify that it is in the event stream; now let's process it. Out of the box the event sourcing package does not have event handlers. It's common for projects at this level, but more full-fledged CQRS systems do have that. But that is why we are writing to the eventstore which does have quite a bit of hooks we can create to handle the events stored. We are going to go over how to create a struct to actually handle the events as well as the framework to subscribe to the stream we created earlier for comments. I'll also show you how these are handled asynchronously to allow continued processing while our application runs. Since we are performing asynchronous operations, we will need to make sure to import tokio into our Cargo.toml in Listing 5-12.

Listing 5-12. Use the tokio dependencies; this will be in the file Cargo.toml

```
tokio = { version = "0.2.17", features = [ "full" ] }
futures = "0.3"
async-std = "1.5"
```

Creating the Executor

First up is what I am calling the Executor; this is where the actual business logic will take place for processing the CommentAdded event. This set of logic will have no knowledge of the eventstore and even the CQRS system. We will create a trait with a run method for the CommentEvent, and when anyone calls it, it will execute an add on the comment. In Listing 5-13, we have that code.

Listing 5-13. The executor trait and implementation of it; this will be in the file src/domain.rs

```
pub trait Executor { ①
    fn run(&self, pool: &PgPooled) -> bool;
}

impl Executor for CommentEvent {
    fn run(&self, pool: &PgPooled) -> bool {
        debug!("Execute our comment {:?}", &self);
        match &self {
```

```
            CommentEvent::CommentAdded{ id, body, media_item_id }=> { ②
                comment_add(id, body, media_item_id, pool)
            },
            _ => false
        }
    }
}

fn comment_add(id: &Uuid, body: &String, media_item_id: &Option<Uuid>,
pool: &PgPooled) -> bool { ③
    use std::{thread, time};
    use crate::models::comment::Comment;;

    info!("Execute our add Comment '{}' / {:?}", body, media_item_id);
    info!("----> {}", id);
    // TODO Store the comment data
    Comment::add(pool, media_item_id.unwrap(), body.to_string()) > 0 ④
}
```

①   Our executor trait; this is designed to be generic so our handlers later
     can run on any enum that implements this trait.

②   Implementation for the CommentAdded event.

③   The function that does the actual work; this would convert the enum
     to our data store and store it.

④   Save the data to the database.

This function right now is not interacting with our database; you can add that or you will find it in the master code. I have added a temporary 5-second delay, so we can view this in the order of which the responses get processed in our code. Now that we have the executor written to handle processing our events, let's see where this gets called at.

Subscription Stream Monitor

Now that we have the executor, we still need to retrieve the data from the event stream. This part of the code is immaterial to using event sourcing, and you could use it for any set of applications that wanted to interact with EventStore database. We will write a consumer that can retrieve events for a particular message queue and process them. When we retrieve an item off the queue, the data brought back is not only the event itself, but metadata about the event, when it was added, what stream, the order it was received, and so on.

This is going to take three steps for us to create, and we will perform this in reverse order of how the code flows:

1. Create our subscription handler; this will monitor the my_comment stream for new data; when the data is received, it will then retrieve the data and execute our Executor we just created against it.

2. Create a connection to the event store; this set of code will create a connection and pass it to the subscription for monitoring.

3. In our main module, we will configure the http runners to run both the http service and the cqrs service, since we need both running to have our application work.

Reading the Connection Stream

Starting with reading the connection stream, we are going to first create the persistent connection and then connect to it. The first step is optional if the connection already exists, but seems no harm in having it. Afterward, we will retrieve the stream data, get the event and convert it to a CommentEvent, and then call our executor. In Listing 5-14, we have the subscription function.

Listing 5-14. Creates the asynchronous connection to the stream and processes any messages against it; this will be in the file src/cqrs.rs

```
// Constants
pub const STREAM_ID: &str = "my_comment";
const GROUP_NAME: &str = "server_group";

async fn subscription(connection: &Connection, database_url: &str)
                    -> Result<(), Box<dyn Error>> {
    use crate::domain::Executor; ①
    info!("Start Subscription ...");
```

```
// Can do programmatically or create here
let _ = connection ②
    .create_persistent_subscription(STREAM_ID.clone(), GROUP_NAME)
    .execute()
    .await?;

let (mut sub_read, mut sub_write) = connection ③
    .connect_persistent_subscription(STREAM_ID.clone(), GROUP_NAME)
    .execute();

// Database Connection
let pool = establish_conn(database_url);

// Iterate over to send the event
while let Some(event) = sub_read.read_next().await { ④
    let originalEvent = event.inner.get_original_event(); ⑤
    let mut data: crate::domain::CommentEvent = originalEvent.as_
    json().unwrap(); ⑥
    info!("Data From Stream >> {:?}", data);
    data.run(&pool); ⑦

    sub_write.ack_event(event).await;
}

Ok(())
}
```

① Uses the executor trait to allow us to run the struct we are receiving.

② Creates the persistent connection stream my_comment.

③ Subscribes to the stream returning a reader and writer to it. The reader will read the events, and the write will be used to acknowledge the events were read.

④ Starts our look of reading in the stream.

⑤ Retrieves the next available event from the stream.

⑥ Converts the event to JSON and we deserialize that json to a struct.

⑦ Runs the executor we created in Listing 5-13.

This subscription handles only the events on my_comment; if we had more events to monitor, we'd have to create more subscription calls for each, although in that case, we could have created a more generic method that would take in stream parameters.

Creating Connection to Stream

Next in Listing 5-15, we will create a single-node connection to the EventStore server and pass in our subscription stream.

Listing 5-15. The creation of the subscription connection to the server; this will be in the file src/cqrs.rs

```
#[tokio::main]
pub async fn start(database_url: &str, host: &str, port: u16) {
    use std::net::ToSocketAddrs;

    let url = format!("{}:{}", host, port);
    debug!("Connect to : {:?} and database : {:?}", url, database_url);
    info!("ES Connect :: {:?}", url);

    // Create socket address.
    let endpoint = url.to_socket_addrs().unwrap().next().unwrap(); ①

    // start up our connector
    let connection = Connection::builder() ②
        .single_node_connection(endpoint)
        .await;

    // Subscription
    subscription(&connection, database_url).await; ③
}
```

  ① Converts the URL to a SocketAddr.

  ② Creates a single-node connection.

  ③ Calls the subscription asynchronous function awaiting its processing.

Launching the CQRS Monitor Service

Finally, we need to launch this monitoring of the eventstore. This isn't a server, but it is an asynchronous process that will monitor the CQRS; in addition, you will have to also launch the http server that we had created earlier. Few areas to watch out for, we are using variable names like the event store host in both the http and the cqrs monitor (one to send one to receive). We had to clone those. We are also creating threads for each of the runs. This will allow us to run and launch both sets of the puzzle in Listing 5-16.

Listing 5-16. The launcher for HTTP and the EventStore monitor; this will be in the file src/main.rs

```
#[cfg(feature = "cqrs")]
fn run_http(app: Application) {
    use std::thread;

    let server = app.server;
    let port = app.port;
    let auth_server = app.auth_server;
    let database = app.database.clone();
    let es_host = app.event_store_host.clone();
    let es_port = app.event_store_port;
    let es_user = app.event_store_user;
    let es_pass = app.event_store_pass;
    let es_web_port = app.event_store_web_port;

    // For CQRS call
    let es_host_cq = app.event_store_host;
    let es_port_cq = app.event_store_port;
    let db = app.database.clone();

    let mut children = vec![];

    children.push(thread::spawn(move || {
        info!("Starting up application");
        http::start(server.as_str(), port, auth_server.as_str(),
        database.as_str(),
```

```
                    es_host.as_str(), es_web_port.clone(),
                    es_user, es_pass);
    }));

    children.push(thread::spawn(move || {
        info!("Starting up CQRS");
        cqrs::start(db.as_str(),es_host_cq.as_str(), es_port_cq);
    }));

    // Now join execute
    for child in children {
        // Wait for the thread to finish. Returns a result.
        let _ = child.join();
    }
}
```

Run It All

At this point, you can start up the demo and run the application and then send a GraphQL call to the application; you will notice output similar to Listing 5-17. One of the big takeaways from the output is you will notice we are still processing even after we have returned to the client, and that is the beauty of eventual consistency.

Listing 5-17. This is the shell of our run of the code

```
INFO  cqrs > Start it up!
START!
 INFO  cqrs::http > Start Server on localhost:8888
 INFO  eventstore::internal::driver > Connection established:
 7ede7b5c-7e87-45e6-8c9a-cb235f11e2c8 on V6([::1]:1113).
 INFO  eventstore::internal::driver > Connection identified:
 7ede7b5c-7e87-45e6-8c9a-cb235f11e2c8 on V6([::1]:1113).
 INFO  eventstore::internal::operations > Persistent subscription
 connection [37d9416e-8cf1-4b9d-960a-5cd3984bb002] is confirmed
COMMENTADD!
 INFO  cqrs::domain                         > Handle Command
```

```
HERE2 >> CommentAdded { id: cfd879ab-7fc3-47ae-9e18-e9610a431409, body:
"Our generic comment needs to be fed in", media_item_id:
Some(fdf222ba-7de4-45b8-b5e2-dcdf69d986f4) }
ITS A STRING!
```

INFO cqrs::http	> ID value :: Some(cfd879ab-7fc3-47ae-9e18-e9610a431409)
INFO cqrs::http	> Return to Client :: {"uuid": "cfd879ab-7fc3-47ae-9e18-e9610a431409"}
INFO cqrs::domain	> Execute our add Comment 'Our generic comment needs to be fed in' / Some(fdf222ba-7de4-45b8-b5e2-dcdf69d986f4)
INFO cqrs::domain	> ----> cfd879ab-7fc3-47ae-9e18-e9610a431409

We have implemented a basic CQRS pattern that hopefully creates a smoother and faster comment add and delete for the end user.

Cap'n Proto

The second part of this chapter is going to deal with our "insanely fast data interchangeable format and and capability-based RPC system" (the Cap in Cap'n is from the capability-based ACL).[1] This is another technology that has been out for a while but only really made popular in the last 3–5 years. And it makes sense based on what they are for. Cap'n Proto was inspired by and similar in structure and function to protocol buffers (Protobuf) which are used for serializing and deserializing of structured data and performing this task efficiently, meaning speed and memory use. The original purpose of protocol buffers was for data exchange between systems. Protobufs were first created by Google in 2001 and first made publicly available in 2008. This allowed Google to store and transmit structured data between systems at Google. They specifically use Remote Procedure Call (RPC) as the communications mechanism between the systems. All of this is to lead to quick speed and low latency between systems.

---

[1]https://capnproto.org/

They came about as a way to replace XML as the messaging data between systems (remember this was 2001), but today it is used as a replacement for JSON as well. Using XML was always an expensive operation for highly scalable systems, but it allowed easily reproducible and verifiable structure. And while JSON grew to replace XML, it still suffers from some performance despite its more compact size to XML. There is still a large serialization/deserialization cost. In addition, JSON's advantage is it does not need to be structured data, but that can also be a disadvantage. Cap'n Proto and Protobufs both allow for structured data that also is much faster to serialize and deserialize. Both pass around and create messages; the messages can not only define the data but also the structure of the endpoints to be executed against. Once you create the message, they are serialized into binary structure that is not self-describing, meaning that without the format translating, you will not know what is in the structure just by looking at it. This does make it a bit more secure, but also can make debugging a bit harder since you can't just watch what messages get transmitted.

While Protobuf was originally written in C++, there are various translations for other languages; this particularly is needed given the nature of Protobufs being used to transmit data between services either via RPC or other means. The Protobuf message though is written in a language-agnostic way; in Listing 5-18 is an example of a message for a health check.

Listing 5-18. Example of a simple Health message Google Protobuf

```
syntax = "proto2";

message Health {
   required string uuid = 1;
   required int64 timestamp = 2;
   required string status = 3
   optional string msg = 4;
}
```

A few important takeaways here, when we create the messages, we define the type for each property. This is necessary so we know how to translate the byte data back; in addition, you will notice the sequential number after. The number is there to define the order of fields; good rule of thumb is to always be additive in order to preserve backward compatibility with older messages. Since you will still be able to translate old version if you are only adding new fields. As I mentioned, there are a variety of Protobuf implementations; you can find the different implementations on the github page for Protobuf (`https://github.com/protocolbuffers/protobuf`).

Cap'n Proto

For our implementation, we aren't going to use the standard Protobuf by Google; we are going to use Cap'n Proto, which is a competitor to Protofbuf's but as I said is very similar in nature and structure. This is a framework originally designed by Kenton Varda, the primary author of protocol buffers version 2, and is property of Sandstorm.io, of which he's a co-founder of. And what makes it cooler is the encoding/decoding step is basically nonexistent, making it faster and more cpu efficient. Cap'n Proto is designed to make use of the way a CPU runs in order to make the data creation as optimized as possible. It uses little-endian byte order in order to create objects of fixed widths, fixed offsets, and proper alignment. Any elements that do not have a fixed size like lists are embedded as pointers; however, even those are optimized to be offset based and independent.

As you'd expect, all of this leads to messages that are much smaller than your JSON, but in addition to make it even smaller, there is a Cap'n Proto compression schema to remove all the zero bytes and make the messages even smaller. In most tests, this leads to same or smaller messages than Protobufs as well (one reason why we are using Cap'n Proto).

One small note, the preceding data is based on documentation from the Cap'n Proto page. I have not had a chance to run the numbers myself yet.

Advantages of Cap'n Proto

However, these are not the only advantages for Cap'n Proto; there are many more advertised advantages to Cap'n Proto. You can read the documentation for a complete listing, but here is a highlight of a few:

- Incremental reads – You can read in the message before all the inner objects of the message have been received. This is due to using pointers for those objects as opposed to be read sequentially.

- Single property reads – You can read just one property without parsing all the properties; this is due to the properties being of fixed order and size.

- Memory map – You can read all the properties in memory without having the OS access it.

- Inter-language support – Cap'n Proto supports multiple languages, meaning it serves as a perfect resource to communicate between applications.

- Inter-process messaging – You can share messages via memory between multiple processes running on the same machine, meaning there is no CPU cost.

- Memory allocation – Cap'n Proto uses an "arena" or "region" style of allocating to avoid issues that Protobuf had with memory allocation bogging down the system.

- Smaller – Both the code generation and the libraries are smaller in Cap'n than in Protobuf.

- RPC – The RPC allows for the call result to be returned before the request comes back to the server. They call this the time travelling RPC.

If you have any more questions about Cap'n Proto, check out their documentation at their site `https://capnproto.org/` for a more in-depth look.

Cap'n Proto RPC

While we can transfer Cap'n Proto and Protobuf messages via any mechanism, the main mechanism it uses for dispatching patches to other subroutines is via RPC. RPC allows inter-processing communication and will communicate with different virtual addresses even though the physical address is the same. RPC used to be much more popular before REST and was the standard way of communicating between services, often as SOAP (or XML-RPC). RPC works by exposing public methods that two systems can then communicate between as long as at least one implements the server (of course, if the other doesn't, it can only serve as a client sending messages to that system and receiving responses). However, the use of SOAP to transmit message data often with XML became heavy. There were extra calls and processing, and the code was more complicated. REST gave you easier and smaller payloads with less of the headache, but you also lost much of the ability to create guaranteed contracts both on endpoints and payloads.

Cap'n Proto implements four different feature levels:

1. The use of promise and futures pipelining to make requests.

2. Restore and save, allowing persistent capabilities of the message. This allows you to save your message returning a token that then allows you to restore that message later.

3. Multi-machine interactions. This allows you to have three-way interactions between Cap'n Proto vats. With three-way vats, you can have machine #1 call to machine #2 a reference to machine #3, and machine #2 will be able to retrieve that reference.

4. This builds up on Level 2, but allows you to have multiple machines guaranteeing the integrity of the data you stored. This is the basis of how many distributed data systems work; it forces all the data to point to the same underlying objects. It also makes it harder to hack, since if you only get access to one server, you won't be able to change the underlying data without also accessing another vat.

Cap'n Proto for Rust

I mentioned earlier that there are multiple languages and framework support for both Protobuf and Cap'n Proto; most major languages have implementations for at least the messaging portion; luckily for us, Rust has a crate that implements the messaging and the RPC (to note there is no Java packages for the RPC). The crate we are going to use is by David Renshaw (@dwrensha) and is a pretty full functional implementation with some great examples in the code. Some of the examples assume you have a good knowledge of Cap'n Proto, so hopefully here we can go through how to implement this in our code with some more detailed explanations.

Implementing in Our Application

Our implementation will be a replacement for an earlier service we wrote, the health check. If you recall earlier, the health check sent out a status to the MQTT that we would then take and forward to our database service. In that service, our MQ accepted a JSON, converted to a `struct` and forwarded on to the next service.

We are going to adjust our normal process we did for health check retrieval and storage to the database. Before we did your normal flow from client to message queue to our retrieval service passing JSON between each layer. However, performing this the traditional way took more processing in not only size but also CPU cost for our serialization and deserialization. Let's look at the difference in steps in Table 5-1 between how we accomplished this with JSON and how we will accomplish this with the Cap'n.

Table 5-1. *Cap'n Proto vs. JSON*

Area	JSON	Cap'n Proto
Client	Create the `struct` for the health check and then serialize to JSON.	Create the Cap'n Proto message for the health check.
Sending to MQTT	Message is sent as JSON.	Message is sent as Cap'n Proto.
Receive from MQTT	Receives byte array serialized to JSON.	Received byte array creating a Proto message (Note: Since we aren't examining the data here, we don't serialize any of the parts).
Send to Retrieval Svc	Sends via HTTP request to retrieval_svc.	Sends via RPC to retrieval_svc.
In Retrieval Svc	HTTP endpoint is picked up serialized to JSON.	RPC endpoint is picked up.
Saving to the database	JSON is converted to a `struct` and saved to the database with diesel.	Proto message is converted to a `struct` and saved to the database.

The preceding data will serve as a guide to what we are building this chapter. To do this, we are going to have to add Cap'n Proto in three microservices:

- client – This will be our generic client that will send health data to the MQ; this code will eventually be used on our Raspberry Pi.

- mqtt_service – This will be the gateway on the MQ that will pick up the health data sent from the client and then forward the data to the retrieval_svc via RPC.

- retrieval_svc – This will receive the health data via RPC and store it to the database; this is where our last and only serialization step will occur.

Installing Cap'n Proto

Regardless of the implementation of Rust you are using, they all require the Cap'n Proto C++ binaries. The binaries are required by the capnp builders to generate the source code for the messages. This is what helps to make the messages universal across applications. There are a variety of ways to install the binaries; if you are on Mac, you can use `brew install capnp`; if you aren't, head to `https://capnproto.org/install.html` and follow the various instructions for your system, including downloading the git binaries for install.

In addition, let's get all the `capnp` rust libraries we are going to use for this application. We are going to need to install not only the `capnp` crates but a few other helper crates that we will use later. In Listing 5-19, we have the crates listed and their uses.

Listing 5-19. Example of the crates needed for Cap'n Proto; this will be in the file Cargo.toml

```
# CANPNP
capnp = "0.9.4" ①

# For the Derive for the Enumerations
enum-primitive-derive = "0.1.2" ②
num-traits = "0.2"

# Canpn RC
capnp-rpc = "0.9.0" ③
tokio = "0.1.18"
futures = "0.1.25"
```

① This is the main capnp crate that will be used for all the message building and manipulation.

② These two traits are used for our manipulation of enumeration numbers to our standard rust `structs`.

③ These are for the capnp RPC `structs`; we will make use of these later in the chapter and are for communicating capnp messages via RPC.

Define the Message

Now that you have the Cap installed, let's start creating our health data message. We can use the Health data JSON we created earlier as a starter to reflect the message we are creating. In Listing 5-20, we have the JSON we created in the previous chapter.

Listing 5-20. Example of a simple health JSON

```
{
 "uuid": "9cf81814-1df0-49ca-9bac-0b32283eb29b",
 "timestamp": 1562453750553,
 "status": "Green",
 "msg": "Here we define what could be going on with our application and its
 items.",
 "peripherals":[{ "name": "Camera" }, { "name": "Temp" }]
}
```

Here is one of the downsides of using JSON; by looking at it, we aren't sure what all those field types are or the size. For example, is the status an enumeration, a free forming string, or something else? If the timestamp came in as nil, would it be a long, a string that needs parsed, and so on? This is where proto binary messages and their structured data really become powerful in a distributed microservice process. The parameters we have are as follows:

- uuid – A UUID field which is a Text field

- timestamp – An unsigned int64

- status – An enum with allowed values Red, Green, Yellow

- peripherals – A list of Peripheral that has the field name on it

Let's use the capnp messaging profile to create a message that contains all these fields in Listing 5-21; this will look similar to the Google Protobuf you saw earlier but with some differences.

Listing 5-21. The Message; this will be in the file schema/message.capnp

```
@0xca254782cfb5effd;
struct Health @0xdfdf80ca99cd265c { ①
  # Used as the struct to send out Package Updates
  uuid @0 :Text;
  timestamp @1 :UInt64;
  status @2 :Status; ②
  msg @3 :Text;
  userId @4 :Text;
  peripherals @5 :List(Peripheral); ③

  enum Status { ④
    green @0;
    red @1;
    yellow @2;
  }

  struct Peripheral { ⑤
    name @0: Text;
  }
}
```

    ①   This starts the structure of our definition including an id.

    ②   For our status, we are using a custom enumeration.

    ③   Properties can also be lists of other `structs`.

    ④   An enumeration definition of Status.

    ⑤   The struct `Peripheral` which we referenced earlier as a list.

You will notice we have the enum and structs inside the struct itself. This is because we aren't using those structs outside of the struct at all. If we had planned to use the structs outside of use in this one or in multiple structs, then you would have put the inner struct outside the external struct. But for readability and brevity, I prefer this way.

Let's circle back on that first line where you have those random digits after `Health`; that is the Capnp id and is required to be somewhere in the schema. This ID is a 64-bit id with the first 8 bytes being derived from the MD5 hash of the parent's scope id. This

ID is used to help provide an easy way to remove ambiguity between schemas across context. Normally, this is achieved in most languages with package or module structures. Consider it similar to that but fancier. There is still a chance for collisions but rare. You place the capnp id on the first line of the file and on the line for each structure/interface. If you omit the ID, one will be assigned dynamically during the schema generation. How do you create this id? You use the `capnp` tool we installed earlier; you can see this tool being used in Listing 5-22.

Listing 5-22. Creating the capnp id on the command line

```
➜ capnp id
@0xfeb3c1c63721c118
```

Just copy and place it into your message at the appropriate areas.

Generating the Source Code

The message we created earlier was placed in `schema/message.capnp`; however, now we need to take that schema and convert it to meaningful rust code that we can use. This occurs via the Cap'n compiler; it will take a Protobuf message and generate source code that reflects the message as well as adding necessary builders and readers. In Listing 5-x, we added all the crates we needed to run the application, but we need add one more in a section of the `Cargo.toml` that we haven't used before, and that's the `build-dependencies`. The `build-dependencies` are used in conjunction with the `build` section of the `package`. The build reference in the `package` is used to help in compilation of our application, and the `build-dependencies` are any dependencies needed for to run whatever rust file is defined in the `build` of the package. For our application, we are going to have cargo generate the message code before it starts to compile the application using the `message.capnp` as a reference. The builder can be created with boilerplate code that we have in Listing 5-23.

Listing 5-23. This will be the message builder; this will be in the file build.rs

```rust
fn main() {
    ::capnpc::CompilerCommand::new()
        .src_prefix("schema") ①
        .edition(capnpc::RustEdition::Rust2018) ②
        .file("schema/message.capnp") ③
        .run().expect("compiling schema");
}
```

① The prefix of the source location.

② The RustEdition, if not set, defaults to Rust2015 which would not work for our application.

③ The location of the message.capnp we created.

In order to compile the build.rs, we are going to require the capnpc (capnp compiler) crate. This is defined in the Cargo.toml file in Listing 5-24.

Listing 5-24. This is the message builder; this will be in the file build.rs

```
[package]
name = "mqtt_service"
version = "0.1.0"
authors = ["Joseph Nusairat <joseph@nusairat.com>"]
edition = "2018"
build = "build.rs" ①

[features]
full = []
ch04 = []

[build-dependencies]
capnpc = "0.9.3" ②
```

① The location of the build.rs file we created earlier.

② The build dependency with the builder compiler crate.

Now run your cargo build and the message_capnp.rs will be created. The location of the generated file will vary, but in general, you will find it in target/debug/build/<project_name>/out/message_capnp.rs. Try to find the file and take a look at it; a takeaway from it is it doesn't actually generate a struct with properties but with readers and writers instead which helps the speed of using Cap'n. The only set of code that may look more familiar to you is the Status enum. I want to show that in Listing 5-25 since it has some interesting traits.

Listing 5-25. The status enum that is generated; this will be in the generated message_capnp.rs

```
#[repr(u16)]
#[derive(Clone, Copy, PartialEq)]
pub enum Status {
    Green = 0,
    Red = 1,
    Yellow = 2,
}
impl ::capnp::traits::FromU16 for Status {
    #[inline]
    fn from_u16(value: u16) -> ::std::result::Result<Status,
    ::capnp::NotInSchema> {
        match value {
            0 => ::std::result::Result::Ok(Status::Green),
            1 => ::std::result::Result::Ok(Status::Red),
            2 => ::std::result::Result::Ok(Status::Yellow),
            n => ::std::result::Result::Err(::capnp::NotInSchema(n)),
        }
    }
}
```

What you will notice is that the source automatically generates a sequence id for each status and provides a trait for creating the Status from the int. This makes it easier to have a reference to the status outside of the application without importing and working directly on it. We can interact with just a number. Also realize much like our properties the Statuses are additive; it will be easy to add, but to subtract is not backward compatible.

Referencing the Source Code

One final item, we need to reference this generated source code in our application in order to actually use it in our application. We are going to create a module that wraps all the source code that we created. I've put this in the main.rs file of each of our services. In Listing 5-26, we have the reference for the message_capnp.rs file that is created by the build.rs in the out directory of our project.

Listing 5-26. This will be the module that wraps the generated source; this will be in the file src/main.rs

```
pub mod message_capnp {
    include!(concat!(env!("OUT_DIR"), "/message_capnp.rs"));
}
```

The code and the messaging creation we created earlier will be used in each of the three services we need, so assume adding that block of code to the `main.rs` for each service.

Creating the Client

Let's start with creating the client; when the client code is run, it will set up an MQTT client, then create a generic health data object, and finally publish it to our queue. When building the message, the generated code is not creating structs, but using a builder pattern instead. The builder pattern allows us the Cap'n Proto libraries to be more tightly coupled with the objects we create and able to store them the way it wants to for optimal serialization and deserialization. We are building this client code here to go over and for testing purposes. However, the code itself will live in the `rasp-pi-mq` application since it will be run directly from the Raspberry Pi.

Let's go over the steps we need to build our message:

1. Create a mutable builder message object; this will be the same across all Cap'n Proto messages we create.

2. Using the message, initialize a mutable `Health` object based on the `health::Builder` so that we can start adding fields to the health data. Remember, using the builder pattern helps us avoid some of the serialization cost.

3. Set all the fields that you want to set on the `Health` message. The Peripherals will be built via their own type of builder.

4. Finally, convert this message to a byte array to send to the MQ.

In Listing 5-27, we use the preceding steps to create the Vec<u8> message; you will notice all the variables are passed in to be set; the full code is in the examples attached with the book.

Listing 5-27. The client builder for the message queue; this will be in the file rasp-pi-mq/src/mqtt/client.rs

```
fn build(status: u16, msg: &str, peripherals: Vec<&str>, uuid: &Uuid,
time_in_sec: Duration) -> Vec<u8> {
    use crate::message_capnp::health; ①
    use crate::message_capnp::health::Status;
    use capnp::serialize_packed;
    use capnp::traits::FromU16; ②

    let mut message = ::capnp::message::Builder::new_default(); ③
    {
        // Use a Scope to limit lifetime of the borrow.
        let mut health = message.init_root::<health::Builder>(); ④
        // Get the user id (TODO hard-code for now)
        health.set_user_id("JOSEPH1234");
        // Give it a unique ID
        health.set_uuid(uuid.to_string().as_ref());
        health.set_timestamp(time_in_sec.as_secs());
        // This could error if the result isn't 1-3, should validate or wrap
        health.set_status(Status::from_u16(status).unwrap()); ⑤
        health.set_msg(msg);

        // needs to occur after or you will get "value borrowed here after
        move" for the other setters
        let mut health_peripherals = health.init_peripherals(peripherals.
        len() as u32); ⑥
        {
            for i in 0..peripherals.len() {
                health_peripherals.reborrow().get(i as u32).set_
                name(peripherals[i]); ⑦
            }
        }
    }
```

```
// write the message to stdout
let mut buffer = Vec::new();
serialize_packed::write_message(&mut buffer, &message).unwrap(); ⑧

debug!("Payload {:?} ", String::from_utf8(buffer.clone()));
buffer
}
```

① The crate imports for the capnp health data derived from the module we set up in the previous section.

② This import is to add the FromU16 trait that creates a status from an id.

③ Creates our default builder.

④ Initializes the builder for our health data object.

⑤ Uses the from_u16 trait to convert our integer to a status.

⑥ Initializes the peripherals list with the size of the array we passed through.

⑦ Iterates through the list of items we pass in, setting each on the way.

⑧ Serializes the message we created to a byte array, packing it.

The reborrow() you see earlier is necessary because after creating the health_peripherals we want to use this again. There can be a bit of a trick in the ordering of items to avoid borrow errors. For example, if you tried to do the init_peripherals and setting of them before you set the properties on the object, you would get a borrow of moved value; there are ways to resolve that in Rust by controlling the lifetime of the variable. Also, note on point #8 we used the serialize_packed; there is also serialize; I choose packed because I want to minimize the size of the byte array going over the Internet since AWS, GCP, and so on are going to charge us by the amount of data transferred, and in any mobile apps, you greatly want to minimize potential cost.

Publishing the Message

We have gone over publishing messages before, but before we were passing JSON around, now we are going to publish a byte array instead. And while the code is basically the same, it's good to review it once more in Listing 5-28.

Listing 5-28. The client builder for the message queue; this will be in the file rasp-pi-mq/src/mqtt/processor.rs

```
pub fn publish_bytes(client: &mut MqttClient, topic: &str, payload:
Vec<u8>, qos: QoS) {
    info!("Publish to the topic : {:?} / {:?}", topic, qos);
    client.publish(topic, qos, false, payload).unwrap();
}
```

I wanted to preserve the other endpoint so this endpoint sends to /health/byte.

I keep mentioning the size of the packages we are sending over, and to save not only time to send but also cost to you the IoT creator in terms of cloud usage cost. While I can't get into a total cost by cloud provider since it varies from company to company, we can look at a comparison of the size for the messages. The examples of message we had earlier I sent through MQTT are JSON, Cap'n Proto, and Cap'n Proto compressed. Here are the results:

- JSON – 223 bytes (when we minimize the JSON)

- Cap'n Proto – 216 bytes

- Cap'n Proto compressed – 159 bytes

The JSON vs. the compressed Protobuf is a 29% savings in size; that is quite a bit of savings when spread over thousands and millions of messages. And in fact, there is more compression you could add if you wanted to achieve even smaller messages; Cap'n Proto recommends using further compression. We won't do it for this book, but it's easy to look up gzip, zstd, and so on compression.

Message Queue Layer

In our MQTT layer, it is going to change drastically. Instead of getting a JSON message and sending via HTTP to the retrieval_svc, we will be receiving a Cap'n Proto message and sending it via RPC to the retrieval_svc. Logically, this is fairly straightforward but programmatically very different. The monitor_notifications will remain mostly unchanged. Before it received a Vec<u8> and converted it to a string; now we will just pass the Vec<u8> directly to our processing method. Once in there, we will create our health message from the byte array and then the health::Reader to the RPC server for processing. This first part is fairly straightforward; in Listing 5-29, we take the Vec<u8> and convert to a health::Reader that we can then send to the RPC.

Listing 5-29. The deserializing of the packaged message; this will be in the file
src/rpc.rs

```
pub fn run_health(host: &str, port: u16, buffer: Vec<u8>) -> Result<(),
::capnp::Error> {
    use capnp::serialize::OwnedSegments;

    let deserialized: capnp::message::Reader<OwnedSegments> =
    capnp::serialize_packed::read_message( ①
        &mut buffer.as_slice(),
        capnp::message::ReaderOptions::new()
    ).unwrap();

    let health = deserialized.get_root::<health::Reader>(); ②

    run(host, port, health.unwrap()) ③
}
```

① Remember, we used the `serialize_packed` before to create the array
   so we have to use the same to read that array.

② Now that we have the unpacked message, we can get the
   `health::Reader` off of it.

③ The RPC calls that we will be creating in a bit.

Now that it is in the Reader, you could in theory create a struct and save it to the
database or do processing on the object directly depending on what the message request
is for. For us, we are forwarding it to another microservice.

Creating the RPC Interface

Creating the reader from the MQ was half the battle; the second is sending it over
the RPC. Remember, when we discussed before about the RPC, it a "time travelling"
RPC. This works by using the future and promise model. The promise and future model
is actually an older concept originally created in 1976 by Daniel Friedman and David
Wise who wanted to devise a system to get immediate response of a request. The future
is defined as a read-only placeholder where you will know what value is being returned.
The promise is the "promise" that it will set the future variable to be read. The value
in this is the future doesn't necessarily have to care who sets its promise but that the

promise will be fulfilled. In our case, this results in the request being sent, but allows for immediate continued processing while waiting for that future to complete. We will be making use of promises and futures to deliver the RPC interface.

But to start, let's talk about this RPC interface; we need to define a function we are sending and the attributes of that function. In order to do that, both the client and the server have to agree on this interface definition, so because of that, we are circling back to the message.capnp. In here, we will add an interface which allows us to make the RPC calls. We will be then defining a function to send our health update. And finally, another interface to read the returned value, since this is all being done with promises and futures.[2] You can also add security in the RPC to make sure that the recipient has access to the addressed object; we won't be doing that for our examples though. We are going to go over the code for the interface in Listing 5-30.

Listing 5-30. The deserializing of the packaged message; this will be in the file schema/message.capnp

```
interface ProcessUpdate @0xeb03883f58bd9352 { ①

  # Interface to update the items
  call @0 (update :Health) -> (passed :Value); ②

  interface Value { ③
    read @0 () -> (value :Bool); ④
  }
}
```

① Defining our outer ProcessUpdate interface that will contain our function to send the Health message.

② The method call we will be using to send the Health object, returning a Value interface to be read in the future.

③ The Value interface; we kept this as an inner interface since it is only used by the call. This wraps the value in an RPC object.

④ The solo read method returning the boolean value that it was added successfully.

---

[2]https://capnproto.org/language.html#interfaces

Using the interface as a return for the value is for performance and keeping with the promise/future model; it allows the value to be used in subsequent evaluate requests without waiting for the client to finish its evaluation. This code also will generate corresponding source code and put into the message_capnp.rs like the message was.

Creating the RPC Client

Now it's time to create the RPC client. This will also make use of the tokio crate for our asynchronous runtime processing. It should be noted here that the Cap'n Proto for Rust only implements Level 1; thus, our examples are only going to be for Level 1.

The basics of what we are doing are pretty simple. Create a socket connection to our RPC server to stream the data. Once that is set up, we can create a network between the client and the server reader to communicate between each other. From there, the RPC will make a request to the call method on our server, sending the health data, all while we wait for the promise back returning the boolean whether it was successful or not. The steps are a bit complicated, but I've tried to parse the explanations down the best I can. So read the code in Listing 5-31 and then read all the bullets for explanation of what the code is doing.

Listing 5-31. The sending of the message to our server; this will be in the file src/rpc.rs

```
fn run(host: &str, port: u16, health: health::Reader) -> Result<(),
::capnp::Error> {
    // Set up the socket
    use std::net::ToSocketAddrs;

    // Create a socket address
    let socket_address = format!("{}:{}", host, port); ①
    info!(" Start Run Client: {}", socket_address);

    let socket_addr = socket_address.to_socket_addrs().unwrap().next().
    expect("could not parse address");

    // this is the executor
    // runtime calls the poll on the future until its value is returned
    let mut runtime = ::tokio::runtime::current_thread::Runtime::new().
    unwrap(); ②
    // is a nonblocking connect call
```

```
let stream = runtime.block_on(::tokio::net::TcpStream::connect(&soc
ket_addr)).unwrap(); ③

stream.set_nodelay(true)?;
let (reader, writer) = stream.split();

let network =
    Box::new(twoparty::VatNetwork::new(reader, std::io::BufWriter::
    new(writer), rpc_twoparty_capnp::Side::Client,
    Default::default())); ④

let mut rpc_system = RpcSystem::new(network, None); ⑤
let process_update: process_update::Client = rpc_system.
bootstrap(rpc_twoparty_capnp::Side::Server); ⑥

// This is just to capture any errors we may have gotten and
acknowledge them.
// spwans the variious tasks?
runtime.spawn(rpc_system.map_err(|_e| ()));
{

    // Call was dderived from us using the word call in our
    interface adding _request
    let mut request = process_update.call_request(); ⑦

    let mut builder = request.get().set_update(health); ⑧

    let value = request.send().pipeline.get_passed(); ⑨
    let request = value.read_request(); ⑩
    runtime.block_on(request.send().promise.and_then(|response| { ⑪
        info!("Response :: {}", pry!(response.get()).get_value()); ⑫
        Promise::ok(())
    }))?;

    info!("Request sent ...");
}

Ok(())
}
```

① Creates the socket address; this will be the same address we use on the server.

② Creates the mutable reactor that is backed by the operating system's event queue. The `runtime` is critical in giving us an ability to poll futures and streams and knowing when they will be completed and responding to the system. Using a poll allows us to continue running the thread without blocking.

③ Sets up our socket stream to the RPC server. We block here because if we can't connect to the server there isn't much else to do.

④ Vats are what Cap'n Proto refers to as nodes. This sets up a connection between our client and the server. Since this code is serving as the client, the input is the reader stream and output is the writer stream. Also notice we are using `Box::new` which will allocate memory for this on the heap.

⑤ This is the Cap'n Proto RPC implementation of the `VatNetwork` we just created earlier. This is rather simplistic right now because we are using Level 1 RPC. When Level 3 gets implemented, this will get increasingly more complex.

⑥ The `process_update::Client` refers to the name of the interface we created, `ProcessUpdate`; this bootstraps and sets the client to talk to the server. We have to define the type here because the compiler won't be able to infer the type without it.

⑦ This sets up a reference to the `call` method we created earlier; the format this gets generated in is `<method>_request`.

⑧ This sets the parameter on request; since we named the parameter update in the message, this becomes `set_update` and takes as a variable the `health::Reader` that was passed in to the function.

⑨ Finally, we send the request and in the pipeline get the return value which is named `passed`, hence the `get_passed` as the method. This returns us the interface we created of `Value`.

⑩   In order to get the value off the interface method read, we use the
same format for calling that we performed in bullet 7, and that was to
use <method>_request which will be read_request.

⑪   In this line, we send the request for the value of the return;
however, in order to get the value, we have to wait for the server to
send us a value back. Hence, in this we will block_on to wait for
the promise back.

⑫   Since this is a promise, we can't evaluate the response
immediately. Here we make use of pry!, which is like a try but for
promises. This wraps returning our value in get_value().

This completes setting up the client; we can actually perform a small test now if you
are on a Unix machine and have netcat installed (it comes with most Unix boxes). If you
do, go ahead and run netcat on the same server and port we are using for the RPC. Then
run the mqtt_service, and use the health service to send a message to the MQ. If
everything is set up correctly, you should see the byte array appear like in Listing 5-32;
this will be mostly unformed logic of course.

Listing 5-32. Monitoring traffic on localhost port 5555

➜ nc -l 127.0.0.1 5555

```
R=689d4721-251e-4199-ade3-517b227b902aHere we define what could be going
on with our application and its items: *CameraTemp
```

Retrieval Service Layer

Now that the client is set up, let's finish this piece by setting up the server to receive the
data and then to process and store it in our database. While we are going to keep this
code on our retrieval_svc, we are going to want to actually run the RPC and the HTTP
server as separate services with a command-line flag to differentiate which one we are
running. You can check out the main in the example app to see how we did this. For our
server, there are going to be about three steps we need to make this all work:

1. Create a server for each of the interfaces we created in the message.capnp. That means you will need a server for the ProcessUpdate and another for the Value.

2. Create a function to take the data we received on the health::Reader and store it to the database.

3. Set up the RPC listener on the same port that the client is on.

Creating the RPC Server

Before we set up our listeners and threading, we need to create the implementations of the Cap'n Proto interfaces we defined in the message.capnp. Since we do not have the concept of interfaces in Rust, these are created by the code generators as traits. Thus, for each method on your interface, you will have a struct that you can name whatever you want, but then you will have to create an implementation of the generated trait that contains a method signature similar to what was defined in our message.capnp. These methods take in three parameters:

1. Self – This is self-explanatory; it contains the properties of that interface.

2. Parameters – The parameters that are passed into the method.

3. Result – The result is the result value we are setting for the return. This of course is mutable since we need to alter it in order to set the results.

You may think logically why is that we are setting the results as opposed to just returning the results like most methods. This is because we are using promise/futures, and what we are actually returning is a Promise instead. In addition, the parameters are not generic but specific and name based on the parameters we created.

Evaluate the Method

To be clear, the end result of everything we are doing is to take the health::Reader we created way back in the health client application and store that data into the database. In Listing 5-33, we make that call to the database converting the health::Reader into a HealthData model that reflects the database model we created earlier.

Listing 5-33. Will evaluate the health data and send to our diesel app to save the
data; this will be in the file src/rpc.rs

```
use capnp::primitive_list;
fn persist( health_reader: health::Reader,
            conn: PgPooled,
            params: Option<primitive_list::Reader<f64>>)
            -> Promise<i32, Error>
{
    use crate::models::health_check::{HealthData,Peripheral};
    use capnp::traits::ToU16;

    let peripherals: Vec<Peripheral> = health_reader.get_peripherals().
    unwrap().iter().map(|p| Peripheral {name: p.get_name().unwrap().to_
    string()}).collect();

    let data = HealthData::new(health_reader.get_uuid().unwrap(),
                                health_reader.get_user_id().unwrap(),
                                health_reader.get_timestamp(),
                                health_reader.get_status().unwrap().to_u16(),
                                health_reader.get_msg().unwrap(),
                                peripherals);

    let id = data.save(&conn);

    Promise::ok(id)
}
```

Implementing the Value Interface

The first interface we are creating is the simplest one; that is the ValueImpl; this interface
is simpler because it does not take any parameters and responds with a boolean as
opposed to struct. Responding with a primitive type is easier than responding with an
object that requires a reader. We are also going to set a boolean on the struct we are
creating; this way, we can have the call method set that boolean for us to make it easier
to know the result to return. In Listing 5-34, we create our ValueImpl for our read @0 ()
→ (value :Bool); method.

Listing 5-34. Server implementation for value interface to be returned; this will be in the file src/rpc.rs

```
struct ValueImpl { ①
value: bool
}

impl ValueImpl {
    fn new(value: bool) -> ValueImpl {
        ValueImpl { value: value }
    } ②
}

impl process_update::value::Server for ValueImpl {
    fn read(&mut self,
            _params: process_update::value::ReadParams, ③
            mut results: process_update::value::ReadResults) ④
            -> Promise<(), Error>
    {
        debug!("Read the Result");
        results.get().set_value(self.value); ⑤
        Promise::ok(())
    }
}
```

① Create the struct with a boolean as a property.

② Create a helper function to make the code cleaner when we create the ValueImpl later.

③ Bring in the parameters, which we have none of.

④ A mutable result list of ReadResults, which name is derived from the method capitalization + Results.

⑤ Set the value on the results; the set_value is derived from the parameter being named value.

This gives us the implementation for the Value returned to the RPC client; now let's set up the ProcessUpdate::call method which will as part of its functionality call out to the ValueImpl.

Implementing the ProcessUpdate Interface

The ProcessUpdate interface, if you recall, had one method call @0 (update :Health)
→ (passed :Value);. Let's look at how this gets translated into an implementation in
Listing 5-35.

Listing 5-35. Server implementation for process_update interface; this will be in
the file src/rpc.rs

```
struct ProcessUpdateImpl { ①
database_pool: PgPool
}

impl ProcessUpdateImpl {
    fn new(db: &str) -> ProcessUpdateImpl {
        ProcessUpdateImpl {
            database_pool: ProcessUpdateImpl::establish_connection_pool(db)
        }
    }

    fn get_db(&self) -> PgPooled {
        self.database_pool.clone().get().unwrap()
    }

    fn establish_connection_pool(database_url: &str) -> PgPool {
        use crate::errors::ResultExt;
        use crate::errors::DbResult;

        let manager = ConnectionManager::<PgConnection>::new(database_url);

        // Get the pooled connection manager
        // unrecoverable fail
        Pool::new(manager).expect("Failed creating connection pool")
    }
}
```

```
impl process_update::Server for ProcessUpdateImpl { ②
fn call(&mut self, ③
        params: process_update::CallParams, ④
        mut results: process_update::CallResults) ⑤
        -> Promise<(), Error> {
    info!("** received a request for process update");

    let eval = persist( pry!(pry!(params.get()).get_update()),
                        self.get_db(), None); ⑥

    Promise::from_future(async move {
        let passed = { if eval.await? >= 0 {true} else {false}};
        info!("Evaluate future ... {}", passed);

        results.get().set_passed(
            value::ToClient::new(ValueImpl::new(passed)).into_
            client::<::capnp_rpc::Server>()); ⑦
        Ok(())
    })

}
}
```

① Creates our struct; we will use this later in the RPCSystem to set as the Server for outside connections.

② Implements the source code generated trait process_update::Server.

③ The call method that matches the signature of the parameter we defined in the message.

④ The CallParams is the name of the method capitalized with Params added.

⑤ Similarly, the CallResults is the name of the method with Results as a suffix.

⑥ We return a promise so this starts the promise we are returning to the caller. In here, we call out to an evaluate method. This evaluate method performs all the work.

⑦ Uses the ValueImpl we created before to set the boolean passed. We evaluate the boolean if there is a non-0 number (meaning the database row was crated), we return true.

On bullet 6, we called a persist method; this method will be where we perform the functionality of using the reader and are saving it to the database. We are going to go about this the easy way and convert the reader to a struct and then serialize that to JSON and store the complete JSON in the database, returning the id that is generated. In Listing 5-36, we save our HealthData to the database.

Listing 5-36. Saves the health reader to the database; this will be in the file src/rpc.rs

```rust
use capnp::primitive_list;
fn persist( health_reader: health::Reader,
            conn: PgPooled,
            params: Option<primitive_list::Reader<f64>>)
            -> Promise<i32, Error>
{

    use crate::models::health_check::{HealthData,Peripheral};
    use capnp::traits::ToU16;

    let peripherals: Vec<Peripheral> = health_reader.get_peripherals().
    unwrap().iter().map(|p| Peripheral {name: p.get_name().unwrap().to_
    string()}).collect(); ①

    let data = HealthData::new(health_reader.get_uuid().unwrap(),
                              health_reader.get_user_id().unwrap(),
                              health_reader.get_timestamp(),
                              health_reader.get_status().unwrap().to_
                              u16(), health_reader.get_msg().
                              unwrap(), peripherals);
```

```
let id = data.save(&conn); ②

Promise::ok(id) ③
}
```

① Convert the peripherals into a Vec<Peripheral>.

② Create a HealthData struct.

③ Persist the JSON conversion of the struct to the database.

Implementing the RPC Server

The final step is to create the RPC server itself; this will look a bit like the client since we are using the same libraries to establish the connections; one of the big differences is we are using a tcp listener as opposed to a tcp stream for our socket connection. In addition, we will be referring to this system as the server for our VatNetwork as well. Let's look at Listing 5-37 for the RPC server.

Listing 5-37. The receiving of the server; this will be in the file src/rpc.rs

```
pub fn start(host: &str, port: u16, database: &str) -> Result<(),
::capnp::Error> {
    use std::net::ToSocketAddrs;

    info!("Start RPC Server : {}:{}", host, port);
    let socket_address = format!("{}:{}", host, port);
    let socket_addr = socket_address.to_socket_addrs().unwrap().next().
    expect("could not parse address");

    // spawns a local pool
    let mut exec = futures::executor::LocalPool::new();
    let spawner = exec.spawner();

    let result: Result<(), Box<dyn std::error::Error>> = exec.run_
    until(async move {
        // Set up the socket
```

```
let listener = async_std::net::TcpListener::bind(&socket_
addr).await?; ①

// Set the server that we implemented
let pu =
    process_update::ToClient::new(ProcessUpdateImpl::new(databa
    se)).into_client::<::capnp_rpc::Server>(); ②

// listen on the incoming socket
let mut incoming = listener.incoming();
while let Some(socket) = incoming.next().await { ③
    // unwrap it
    let socket = socket?;
    socket.set_nodelay(true)?;
    let (reader, writer) = socket.split();

    let network =
        twoparty::VatNetwork::new(reader, writer,
                                    rpc_twoparty_capnp::Side::Server,
                                    Default::default()); ④

    let rpc_system = RpcSystem::new(Box::new(network),
    Some(pu.clone().client)); ⑤

    // Spawns the local object
    spawner.spawn_local_obj(Box::pin(rpc_system.map_err(|e| warn!
        ("error: {:?}", e)).map(|_|()))).into()).expect("spawn")

}
Ok(())
});

info!(" Done with Run Server");
result.expect("rpc");
Ok(())
}
```

① Binds our socket and listens for a connection.

② Creates the `ProcessUpdate` server; this uses a `ProcessUpdateImpl` that we created previously.

③ Listens on the socket for an incoming connection and processes the inner code when received.

④ Creates our `VatNetwork` similar to the one we created previously, but noticeably different is the `side` we are on is the `Side::Server` side.

⑤ This is where we create the heap memory for a new RPC on the network with the `ProcessUpdate` bootstrap.

You now have all the pieces complete to run this microservice application with the client. In order to run this, just do these:

- Start up the MQTT service.

- Start up the retrieval RPC service.

- Run the client health app.

And watch all the screens; you can then check your database in the end for the persisted JSON.

The goal of this chapter was to introduce you to two performance techniques common with IoT applications. You can see the amount of extra plumbing that goes with them, but in the end, they can help with throughput and fix bottlenecks. It's sometimes good not to over-optimize before you need to, but often you can see where bottlenecks are going to happen. When we worked on OTA for our cars, we could tell right away the status messages for it were numbering in the thousands for one car, and these messages would come back in a relatively short period of time. And this was for one car, so it was easy to see where a bottleneck was going to occur. I hope this helps in developing your own IoT stack.

Summary

In this chapter, we discussed optimizing our existing application in the sake of performance. We didn't add any functionality but just altered how to do existing functionality. This chapter was important to me because both topics while they have been around for a bit have gained more recent popularity. CQRS and especially eventual consistency in conjunction are good ways of handling applications of scale. They assist in allowing users to not hang on long connection timeouts while allowing the application to still process all the needed data. Serialized messaging over RPC (Cap'n Proto) has become increasingly popular not just as a communication between backend components but also between JavaScript web layers and the backend. I currently use Protobufs on other applications to talk between a Vue.js application and a backend server. And at the very least, it will educate you to know what these tools are, whether you use them in the future or not.

CHAPTER 6

Security

If we deployed our site the way it's currently designed, it would not be a very secure site; in fact, right now anyone could access our message queues and add data to them or hit all of our endpoints in the microservice. This could somewhat work if you were running on a home network (although still vulnerable to any one who gets on your network). In fact, we don't even have users; this obviously would not make a great application to use in a multi-customer environment. Even as a home project, we'd be locked into one person.

Regardless, we'd be remiss if we didn't discuss how to secure our application. There are many tools and methodologies to secure a modern website. For this book, I am going to focus on just two of them for our application:

- REST/GraphQL layer

- MQTT layer

The first layer is our endpoints exposed on the microservice to be used by either internal applications talking to each other or external entities wanting to gain information from that layer. We will be making use of the REST and GraphQL endpoints created so far. For those endpoints, we are going to add authentication checking since all of our endpoints (except health) require an authenticated user via OAuth 2, which is fairly standard for any site. For the message queues, we will use SSL certs to secure the communication between the endpoints. These will be a set of X509 certs that makes sure the traffic is not only encrypted but secured by the endpoints. Don't worry if some of those terms are confusing; we will get into what everything means and how to glue it together in a bit.

© Joseph Faisal Nusairat 2020
J. F. Nusairat, *Rust for the IoT*, https://doi.org/10.1007/978-1-4842-5860-6_6

237

What We Aren't Covering

To make a truly secure site, there are many other items you want to add to your site. Security is its own department at most large companies, and they even conduct formal architecture reviews of applications to make sure they are secure. If you actually consider the data we will be storing (personal video data), security is VERY important because you wouldn't want to have yours or customer videos exposed to the Web. We won't be able to get into all the techniques used for an application. However, one of the biggest pieces of software large and small companies make use of is monitoring software. Monitoring software can help you determine denial-of-service attacks and other attempts to penetrate your network. In addition, they are good for triage later after an attack to determine what vulnerabilities they were attempting to exploit and what they couldn't. There are many paid and open source solutions for this that you can explore on your own.

One of our biggest hits is our communication between the microservices will not be over TLS; it will be over plain HTTP. This is far from ideal, but I didn't want to set up TLS communication between the endpoints in the book. In a bigger environment, this is where I'd often recommend a service mesh like Istio that can help control the flow of traffic to the services and between services in a secure manner. With tools like Istio, mutual TLS becomes automatic and is just another way to make sure your endpoint traffic is secure.

Goals

Alas, we won't be covering either of those, but what we will cover will be these:

1. Setting up and configuring an account with Auth0 to be used for security

2. Setting up logged in communication between a user and our services

3. Creating authenticated connections between microservices

4. Learning how to use certificates for MQTT

5. Creating self-signed certificates

6. Starting up the eMQTT with self-signed certificates

7. Using self-signed certificates between client and MQTT

Authenticate Endpoints

In this section, we are going to go through how to secure the endpoints in our microservices with authentication. This will allow us to prevent users or hackers from using application to read/write without authentication. In addition, this will allow us when creating media data and querying the data to know the user. For our application, we are going to use tried and true technologies to create this; we will use an Open Authorization 2.0 (OAuth 2) authorization with Auth0 providing the login portal tools. First, let's talk a little about how we got here to use OAuth 2 and Auth0.

In the first 10–15 years of the World Wide Web's mainstream existence, most applications were web based, and even more often those web applications were intrinsically tied to its backend servers, which had content generating the HTML itself for the application. Everything was highly coupled. We used our own databases; on our own servers, we'd create everything from scratch. This isn't much different from days of the first computers when each manufacturer had their own languages for their own computers. Everything that was on the site was generally coded uniquely for the site. And even when we used frameworks, the storing of data was still centralized to the application. However, this model of all under one roof started to change, especially when it came to authentication.

As the use of the Internet evolved, we started to have more complex website and even mobile sites. As the Web evolved instead of creating one application that has the web code and backend code, we started to segregate out those units into their own more stand-alone parts. With the addition of mobile, this became another stand-alone application. Each of these applications still spoke to the same backend but no longer were you generating HTML from that backend. And even within the backends, they had to communicate to other servers with knowledge of the user. All of those lead us to creating a standard OAuth to allow authentication and authorization across different systems.

On the actual code for authentication, it's hard to perform securely so that no one hacks it, and by its nature, it's fairly generic. The login across lines of business is relatively the same. You have a login and password, as well as the ability to recover a forgotten password. I've implemented this myself many times, and it's relatively repetitive. But doing it yourself, you have to constantly worry about security; what if someone were to hack your site? You would expose tons of customer emails, at which point you have to disclose embarrassingly that their info was disclosed. However, if you do not manage it on your own, you lower the risk to storing any personal identifiable data; all they have

239

is UUIDs they can't correlate; there is less of an embarrassment or risk. This leads to companies specializing in OAuth services with low subscription costs, and it just made more sense to spending money for it than spending time.

Authorization vs. Authentication

These two concepts go hand in hand, and we will use them throughout this section to discuss how we are going to work with securing the endpoint for a given user. However, I think it's important not to conflate the terms and use them to understand what each is. Lets define what Authentication (AuthN) and Authorization (AuthZ) means.

Authorization

Authorization is your system that decides whether you should have access to a particular set of resources to perform tasks. This can decide whether a subject (in our case, usually the user) can access a particular endpoint and what they do. It is even used to determine whether two microservices can talk to each other; this helps securing your microservices. Authorization determines what permissions a particular subject is allowed. Most often, the system that one uses for authorization is OAuth 2.

Authentication

Authentication is the process of identifying the subject, most often a user, defining who that subject is and associating a unique identifier to them. This id will then be used to store in your databases and used as a reference when calling the application. This can be your Lightweight Directory Access Protocol (LDAP) system, your Azure AD, or even some homegrown system. Most often, the system that wraps around that interops with OAuth 2; the best implementation of such is OpenID Connect.

OAuth 2

The OAuth framework has been around since about 2006, and the OAuth 2 spec came shortly thereafter and has been in use ever since without any major changes. OAuth has become the industry standard for authorization and is developed as part of the OAuth 2 Authorization Framework.[1]

---

[1]https://tools.ietf.org/html/rfc6749

OAuth 2 allows applications to grant access to services and resources by using an intermediary service to authorize requests and grant user access. This allows you to enable resource access without giving unencrypted client credentials. Users can use a JSON Web Token (JWT) or an opaque token for an authorization server that can then be used to access various resources. These tokens can then be passed to various other services with an expiration date as long as the token is not expired. The client that is doing the requesting doesn't even have to be aware at each call what resource the token belongs to.

OpenID Connect

Open Id is the authentication layer that easily sits on top of OAuth 2.[2] Open ID allows you to do authentication returning JWTs that are easily usable in the OAuth 2 world. These JWTs contain claims that tell you additional information about the user. Standard properties to include are name, gender, birth date, and so on. JWTs can also be signed. If they are and you have the keys to confirm the signature, you can generally trust that data; if not, you can use the JWT to query an endpoint for this information instead.

Applying AuthZ and AuthN

Authentication is pretty standard for most applications, and you've probably never built an application without it even if you didn't set it up yourself. The difference for this application might be how you are authorizing. In most applications you work with, we have a standard web portal or even a forwarded portal via your mobile application. These allow for authentication of the user through a standard username and password. And this works well on your iPhone or desktop because you have a full-size keyboard at all times. However, on most IoT devices, even with a touch screen, we won't always want to make them type the username and password authentication out all the time. It can be time-consuming and error-prone causing a poor user experience.

There is another way of course, and you've probably used it before even if you weren't aware of it at the time, the device authentication flow. With the device flow instead of using the device to log in directly, you will use a website. What happens is the device will prompt us to log in; it will then supply a URL and device code. We will then go to the website and log in using the device code when prompted. In the meantime, our

---

[2]https://openid.net/specs/openid-connect-core-1_0.html

application will ping the authorization server to see if the user has been authenticated. Once the user is authenticated, the system will get a response that the user is authorized that will include an access token and optionally user token. At that point, the device will consider itself authenticated and will continue performing whatever actions it needs to to get the rest of the data.

In Figure 6-1, we have an authorization flow that shows how we can use authentication services to request data.

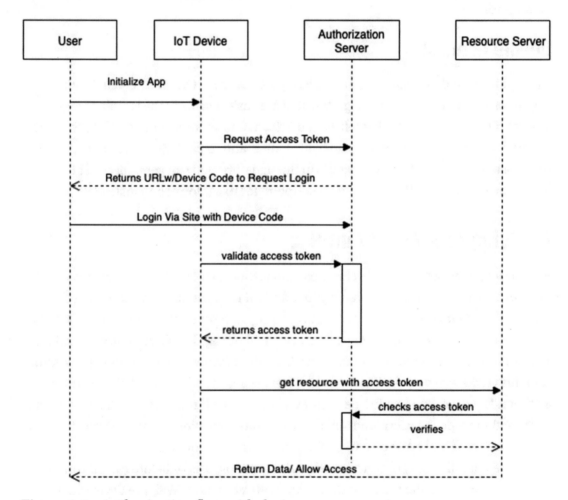

Figure 6-1. *Authorization flow with device*

Auth0

When using OAuth 2 with OpenID Connect, there are multitude ways to put this all together. A common approach is to create your own Authorization system but rely on an OpenID Connect to run the authentication flow. This is common when you go to a website and you are asked to log in and you see the redirects for Google, Facebook, and so on. One of the main reasons people use this approach is security and safety. People may not trust adding their username and password to your site, but they trust another. In addition, it makes it, so you don't have to remember the username and password for each site you use. Also it takes away the onus on you having their user data. If your site gets compromised, it's best to have less personally identifiable data than more. However, many people still like to maintain control of their authorization needs, the OAuth 2 portion; part of the reason is because of how many frameworks are out there to easily interoperability with them.

For our application, we are going to use a provider that can handle both aspects for us, Auth0. And for our testing needs, Auth0 will be free for us to use; even in smaller limited quantities, it is still free. Auth0 allows us to choose using either the Google authentication model or its own personal database. If you want more information on the OpenID Connect system, you can go here: `https://auth0.com/docs/protocols/oidc`.

For our system, we are going to use Auth0's ability to use a built-in database (this cuts back on a few extra steps we'd have to take with setting up a flow with Google). Great thing about this is we could even use an existing database in our system for importing into Auth0 if we needed to. Our examples going forward will use the Auth0 authentication/authorization endpoints to run our user management and security checkpoints. However, most of the code we are writing could work in any system; you may just have to adjust the parameters since those can differ between providers, but the general flow is the same.

Setting Up Auth0

Let's start with walking through setting up Auth0; it's a fairly straightforward process but always good to be on the same page. Head to `https://auth0.com/` and click Sign Up. In Figure 6-2, you will need to pick your method for signing up; I just used my Github sign-in, but it's up to you.

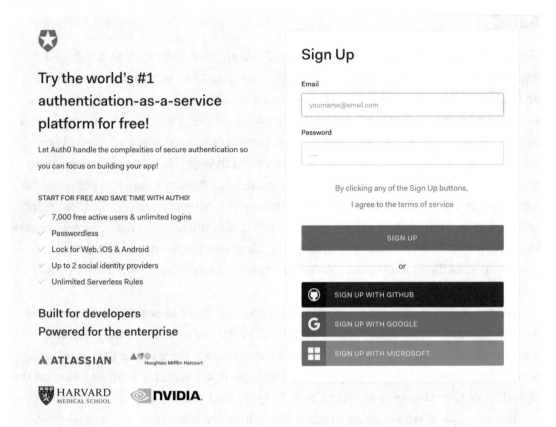

Figure 6-2. *Start*

Once signed in, you may need to pick the plan, although for most the free plan should have been selected automatically; in Figure 6-3, I'm picking the free plan. It is limited to 7K active users, but for a demonstration app or even a beginning application, it should be more than enough.

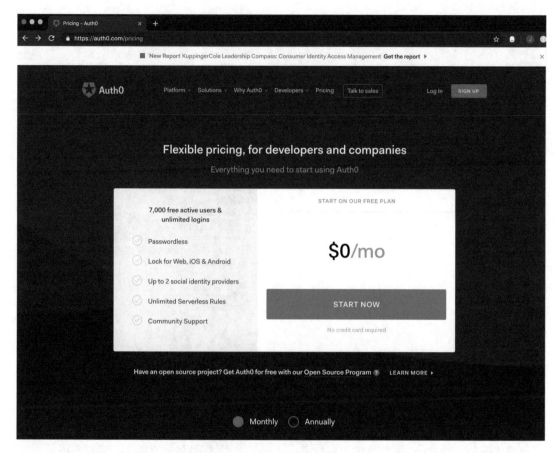

Figure 6-3. *Click the START NOW for $0/month plan*

Now we will start with configuring the application. In Figure 6-4, you will start one of two steps; in the first step, decide on a subdomain name for your Auth0 app and a region majority of your clients will be located (you obviously can't use mine).

Welcome to Auth0

Help us setup your first tenant and start
authenticating.

STEP 1 OF 2

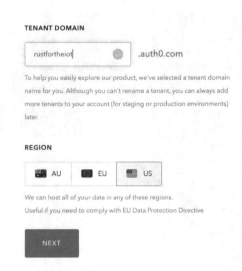

Figure 6-4. *Pick our domain name and region*

Next in Figure 6-5, choose the ACCOUNT TYPE; this part does not matter and I
barely filled it in.

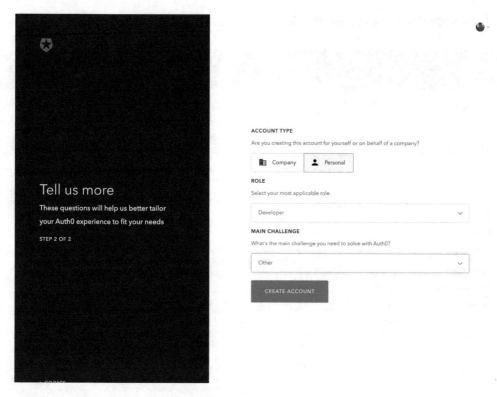

Figure 6-5. *Fill in more relative information*

Once completed, we will get the dashboard that appears in Figure 6-6.

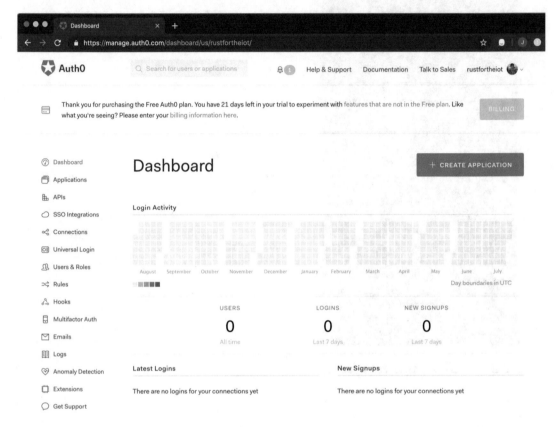

Figure 6-6. *The interactive dashboard for our Auth0 managed application*

At this point, we have our dashboard and a login set up but nothing that actually can interact with the application. We need to add two things: one is a user, and the other we need to add is to create an application to use. This will provide us a client id that our framework can interact with. The applications are independent of our user database, and we can have them interact with many or just a few of them. Each application allows for different types of authentication flows, from a web flow, to device flow, to service, to service communication. Let's go through the process of creating an application that will work with device flows.

Create Authorization

On your left-hand navigation, you will see Applications; click the link and select CREATE; you will get a set of options like in Figure 6-7.

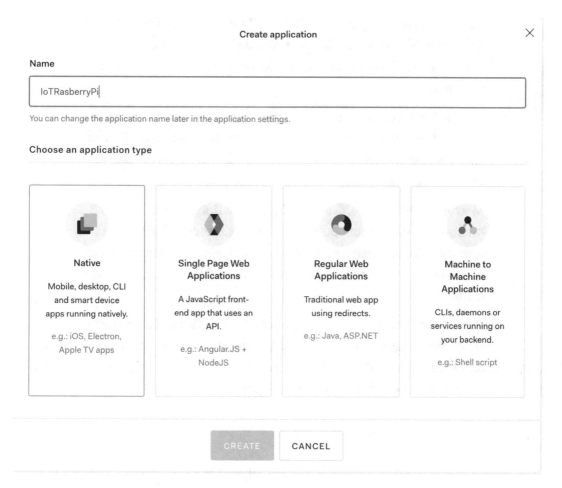

Figure 6-7. *List of application types we can create*

There are four different options, and we can use two of them for our applications:

- Native applications – The best way to describe these is any application that requires a login that is NOT from a website. This will be your mobile apps, Apple TV apps, and any device applications, which in our case are your IoT device apps.

- Single-page web applications (SPAs) – These are your React, Angular, and any modern web application. You'd likely use this as well if you wanted a support application, but the coding of this is out of scope for our book.

- Regular web applications – These are more traditional, older style applications – your Java and ASP.NET apps. Many more traditional shops would use this approach, but to be fair, the SPAs are the more common way of creating web applications these days.

- Machine to machine – These are for applications in your microservice world that do not have a user associated with them. This includes any batch application that needs to access endpoints or any service-to-service calls that are allowed for unauthenticated users.

To begin with, let's create the native application first; this will allow us to authenticate and test against a user. Write any name you want and then go ahead and click Submit. Once you submit, you will be brought to the "Quick Start" page; select the second tab "Settings" and it should look like Figure 6-8.

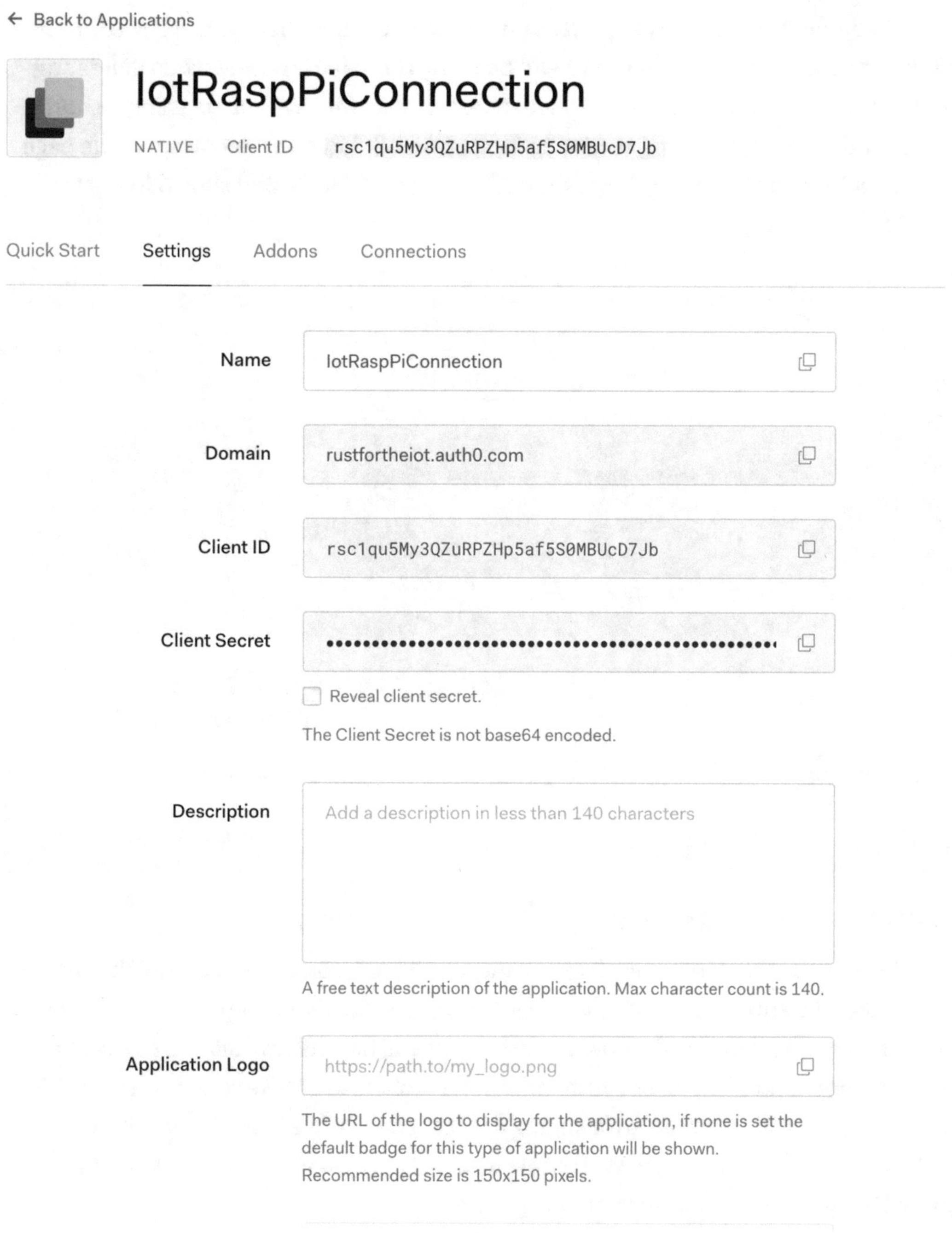

← Back to Applications

IotRaspPiConnection

NATIVE   Client ID   rsc1qu5My3QZuRPZHp5af5S0MBUcD7Jb

Quick Start   **Settings**   Addons   Connections

Name	IotRaspPiConnection
Domain	rustfortheiot.auth0.com
Client ID	rsc1qu5My3QZuRPZHp5af5S0MBUcD7Jb
Client Secret	••

☐ Reveal client secret.

The Client Secret is not base64 encoded.

Description   Add a description in less than 140 characters

A free text description of the application. Max character count is 140.

Application Logo   https://path.to/my_logo.png

The URL of the logo to display for the application, if none is set the default badge for this type of application will be shown. Recommended size is 150x150 pixels.

Figure 6-8. *Native application created*

This shows that our native application has been created; here you will see the client ID and are able to use the secret. We will be using this client ID later when validating our login. So take note of it and copy it to a text editor, since we will be using it shortly. There is one more interesting section to look at; scroll down to the bottom of the page and select "Advanced Settings" and then "Grant Types". I have that shown in Figure 6-9 showing the grant types.

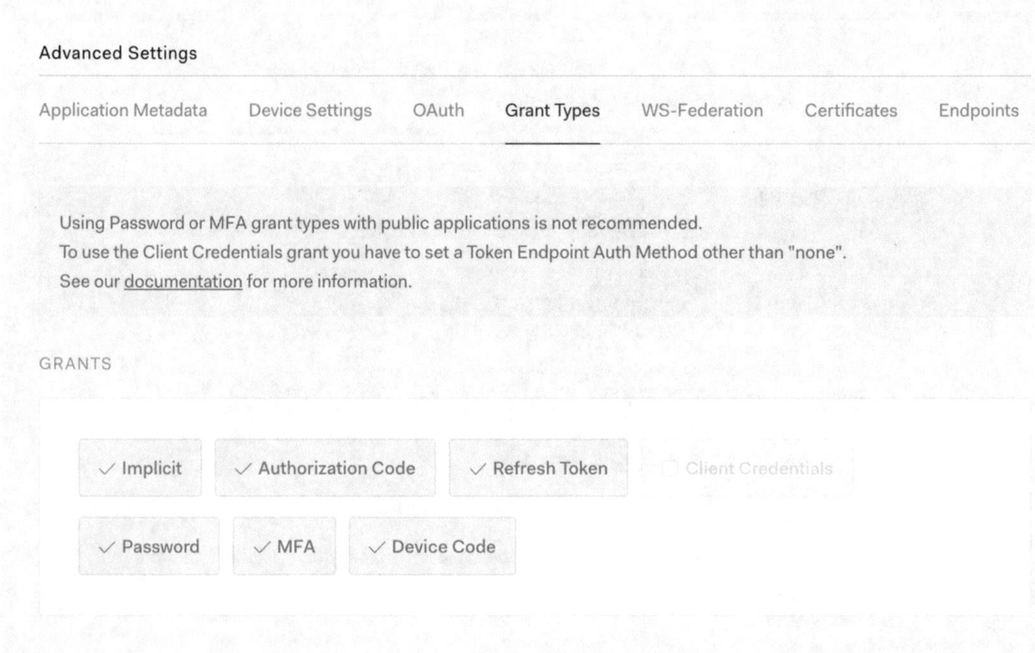

Figure 6-9. *Grant Types for our native authentication*

These will be different for each application type (with some overlap), but they are also what makes the applications unique to each other and the different purposes they serve. As you can see for this one, the Device Code grant will be what will allow us to use the device authorization flow as our authentication mechanism. Make sure it is selected; if not, your first query will return an error stating device code not allowed for the client.

Take note of this screen; we will circle back to it in a bit when we make our first query. For now, let's move on to creating a user.

Create User

We could use Google or Facebook authentication, but for the book, we are going to use the Auth0 existing authentication model. Let's set up an example user to use. Head back to the main dashboard page and click "Users & Roles"; you will get a page like in Figure 6-10.

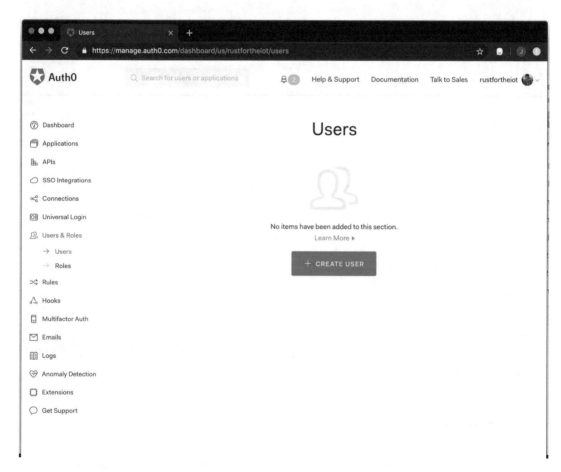

Figure 6-10. *Users to add to*

In Figure 6-11, go ahead and create a user using your email address and whatever password you want.

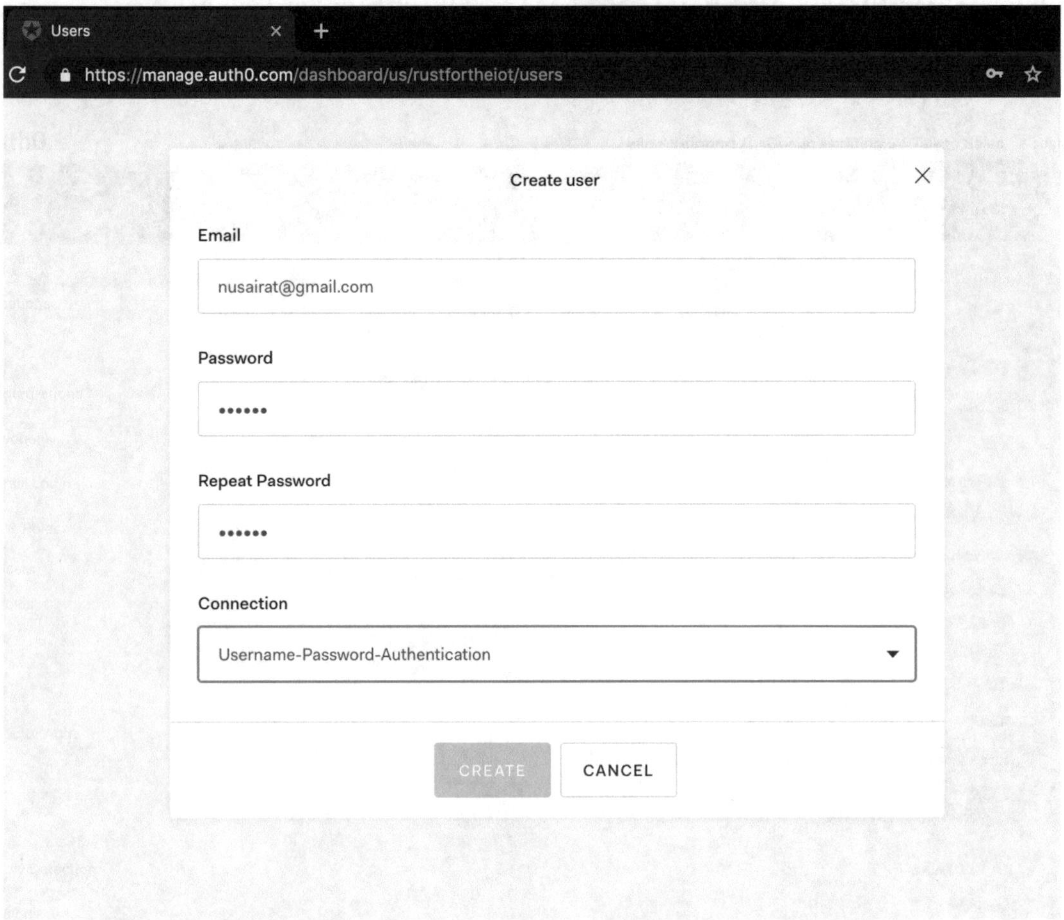

Figure 6-11. *Creating a user*

Once created, you will have a user registered and will be able to start authenticating against that user. Figure 6-12 shows the final screen when the user is created.

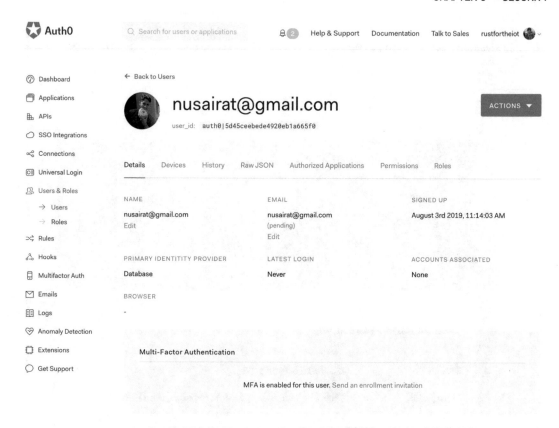

Figure 6-12.   User created screen

However, if you notice under the EMAIL header, it is marked as "pending"; go to your email account and you will have a verification email waiting for you. Figure 6-13 has a sample of that email you should receive, and click "VERIFY YOUR ACCOUNT".

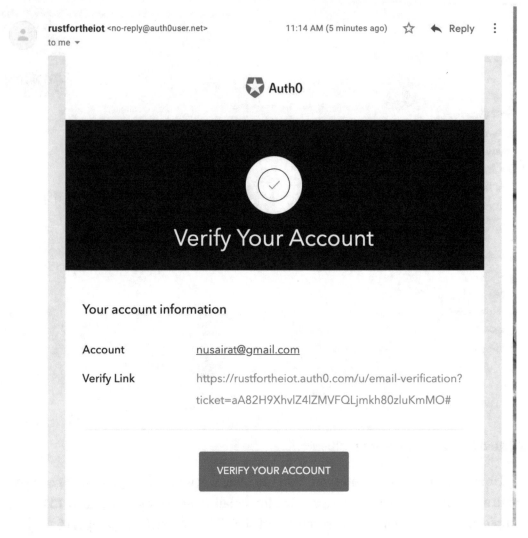

Figure 6-13. *Email verification*

Now that will finish your user setup. As of right now, we have our user set up in
Auth0 as well as an application set up to create Open Id authentication queries against to
receive a JWT that we will be able to use for OAuth 2 interactions.

Authenticating

We haven't focused it yet on our application, but part of what we are going to have to do
is have a user associated with the records. After all, we are building this system to handle
more than just our own personal device. We want this to handle a multitude of devices

and users connecting to our system. What we are going to go over is how to use the command line to trigger the device flow authentication, authenticate, and then use the JWT that is returned to make subsequent user authenticated calls to our retrieval service.

Device Flow

We went over the device flow earlier; now let's implement it. Later we will have the device make these calls, but let's call from the command line for now. We will make a call to the device/code endpoint on Auth0 `https://rustfortheiot.auth0.com/oauth/device/code`. This endpoint takes a few parameters:

- `client_id` – If you recall before when I mentioned we needed to circle back to the client Id, well here is where you need it. Since we can have multiple applications at the `rustfortheiot` endpoint, this determines WHICH application we will choose.

- `scope` – A space separated delineation of what type of token with what access should be created.

The scopes help us define the authorization and what information will be returned by them for use. You can include one or many of the scopes. In Table 6-1, we list what each defines for the authorization.

Table 6-1. *Variety of scopes for Auth0*

Scope	Description
openid	By default, this system will give us back an access token to use that can be traded in for user authentication information. But if we want a JWT that we can use that has user info in it already, supply the openid, and we will get an id_token back as well.
offline_access	If this is going to be a longer-lived request (like with a device), we will need the ability to refresh our access token periodically; if not, the user will have to re-authenticate. This scope will have the response including a refresh_token that can be used for re-authorizing.
profile	By default, the access_token can only be traded in for the subject; if you want the ability to gain more than that, supply the profile scope.
email	If all you need though is the email, you can supply just the email scope to be able to retrieve the user info for it.

We will use all those scopes for our example request, so that we can see the full results. Let's put it all together for a command-line request. In Listing 6-1, we curl the `device/code` endpoint with our parameters. This will give us back a URL and device code that we can go to the site and fill in the request to start the login process.

Listing 6-1. Curl request to get a device code and URL

```
→ curl --request POST \
  --url 'https://rustfortheiot.auth0.com/oauth/device/code' \
  --header 'content-type: application/x-www-form-urlencoded' \
  --data 'client_id=rsc1qu5My3QZuRPZHp5af5SOMBUcD7Jb' \
  --data scope='offline_access openid profile email'

{
    "device_code":"EINQsGUod_tIuDOo5wW2kZ8q",
    "user_code":"KSPT-LWCW",
    "verification_uri":"https://rustfortheiot.auth0.com/activate",
    "expires_in":900,
    "interval":5,
    "verification_uri_complete":"https://rustfortheiot.auth0.com/
     activate?user_code=KSPT-LWCW"
}
```

The JSON returned a few properties; let's take a look at what these properties are:

- `device_code` – This is a unique code we will use for subsequent calls to the system in order to receive back the `access_token` and to check whether the user is logged in.

- `user_code` – This is the code the user will type in, in the `uri` to recognize the device that is trying to be authenticated. This is a short code to make it easy for a person to remember to type into a web page.

- `verification_uri` – This is the URI to go to log in with the user code.

- expires_in – This is the amount of time in seconds that the user has to be able to log in before the device code expires; this is 15 minutes – plenty of time.

- interval – This is the interval in seconds that you should recheck if the user has been authenticated.

- verification_uri_complete – This is the complete URI for verification; this isn't as necessary to use for a visual device authorization, but if your authorization is triggered by a text message or other means, it will be good to use to forward to the system.

The preceding device_code is used to get a status of your login; this will be what our device uses to check if the user is authenticated. We will make a call to the oauth/token to determine whether or not a user is authenticated passing in the preceding device_code and passing in a grant-type of device_code. If you recall from earlier, device_code grant type was unique to our native application, which is why we choose it.

We have to periodically check the server to see if the user has been authenticated; in Listing 6-2, we perform a request against the oauth/token endpoint to do this check. Note: We haven't actually authenticated yet so we would expect it not to work.

Listing 6-2. Curl request to check if the user has been authenticated

```
→ curl --request POST \
  --url 'https://rustfortheiot.auth0.com/oauth/token' \
  --header 'content-type: application/x-www-form-urlencoded' \
  --data grant_type=urn%3Aietf%3Aparams%3Aoauth%3Agrant-type%3Adevice_code \
  --data device_code=EINQsGUod_tIuDOo5wW2kZ8q \
  --data 'client_id=rsc1qu5My3QZuRPZHp5af5SOMBUcD7Jb'

{
    "error":"authorization_pending",
    "error_description":"User has yet to authorize device code."
}
```

The grant_type is a URL-encoded representation of the string urn:ietf:params:oauth:grant-type:device_code and is part of the OAuth 2 spec for device access token request.[3] And it has done that, given us an authorization_pending response since we haven't been authenticated. Besides being successful, let's take a look at what other error conditions we may have, in Table 6-2.

Table 6-2. *Various response errors for OAuth token*

Code	Description
authorization_pending	The user has not attempted to authorize against the given user code.
slow_down	Your application is requesting status of being authorized too much; slow down your requests.
expired_token	The token has expired before the user has been authorized. In our case, this means there was no authorization within 15 minutes.
access_denied	The user has been denied access to the given resource.

How do we get a successful response? Let's go back to that initial URL we are given to and visit the site; in Figure 6-14, we go to the site https://rustfortheiot.auth0.com/activate and enter the user code.

---

[3]https://tools.ietf.org/html/draft-ietf-oauth-device-flow-11

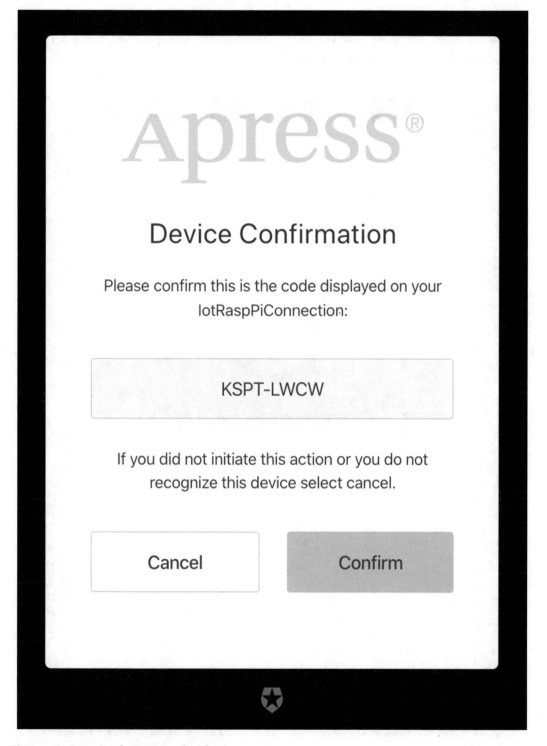

Figure 6-14. *Authorizing the device*

Here you enter the code and select "Confirm"; you will then be requested to log in with the username and password we set up earlier. If everything is valid, you will receive a confirmation message like in Figure 6-15.

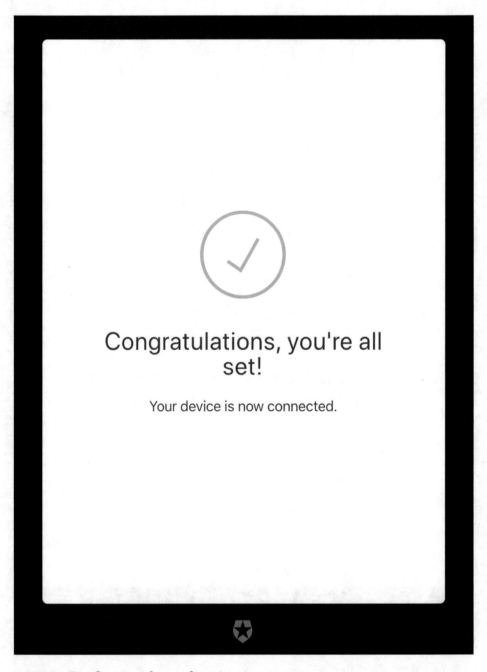

Figure 6-15. *Confirming the authentication*

You will notice I have added the Apress logo; for the login page, you are able to customize those screens in the dashboard of Auth0 as well.

Let's go back to our oauth/token and make another request now that we are authorized; in Listing 6-3, we get a standard OAuth 2 response; that will be familiar to you if you've used OAuth 2 in the past.

Listing 6-3. Using the previous curl here is the new response to the authenticated system

```
{
    "access_token": "sHiy83rLMLEqrxydFMOxjLVyaxi-cv_z",
    "refresh_token": "hnsureBL2jfb62UINDmgjt4F6vZBpOetExeoDja5qGy1Y",
    "id_token": "eyJOeXAiOiJKV1QiLCJhbGciOiJSUzI1N...xTA8WsM3vxCOHwy__2g",
    "scope": "openid profile offline_access",
    "expires_in": 86400,
    "token_type": "Bearer"
}
```

But for those that haven't, let's take a look at what each of these properties means. In Table 6-3, we break down each of the properties from the token. Also note that id_token is usually much longer; I shortened it so it would take up less space.

Table 6-3. *Our tokens for authentication*

Token	Description
access_token	The access token is used as the token that is passed in the authorization phase to check the credentials of the calling application. Token can be used to inform the API that the bearer of the token has been authorized to access the API.
refresh_token	When the access token has expired, the refresh token can be used to go out and obtain a new access token without being required to re-authenticate the user again.
scope	The scopes the tokens have access to.
id_token	The ID token is used to cache and parse the user profile information after a successful authentication. They can then use this data to personalize the user experience.

In our token retrieval, the `acccess_token` has a 24-hour life (computed by the `expires_in`); once that hits, the application should use the `refresh_token` to go out and get another `access_token` before making any more calls to the backend system. The refreshing of the token will be handled by the framework we use, and you won't have to code for it on your own. But we will use all these tokens in our application.

The ID token is not necessary to obtain user information; you could obtain the same information from the `/userinfo` endpoint by sending the access token to it; however, this saves us a call, and since this comes back from the authentication service we know, we know it's a trusted data.

Processing the Tokens

Now that we have our tokens, what do we do with them? We can parse them and use them for access and deciding what to do with the user. For our system, all the calls will be requiring a user for each call, meaning we will need to translate the tokens to our user and use it for access. Let's take a look at each of the tokens we have and how we are going to use them and the code for it.

ID Tokens

The first one to go over is the ID tokens; the ID tokens as we mentioned before are only to be used by the authentication section of the application and only to be used to retrieve more data about the user. You shouldn't use these as an access token and send it to other services. The token is listed in Listing 6-3 with the field `id_token`. The token is a Java Web Token (JWT), and they are easily decomposable to retrieve data from without calling out to any other service. In fact, if you haven't used one before, there is a site `jwt.io` which can help you examine the contents of the token. Go ahead and take the contents of the token output above (from your own screen, maybe a bit hard to copy that entire token from a book) and paste it into `jwt.io` under the Encoded tab. You should get an output similar to Figure 6-16.

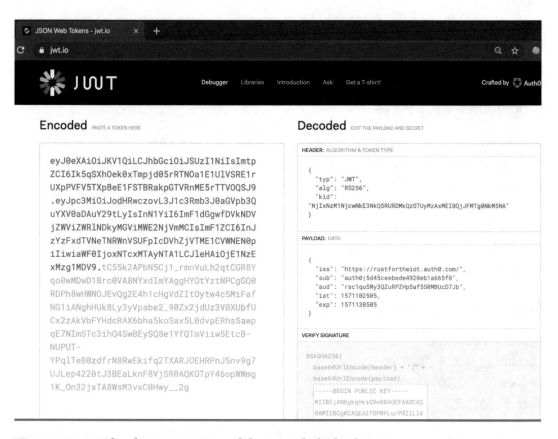

Figure 6-16. *The decomposition of the encoded id token*

This reveals quite a bit of data including the algorithm that is used to encode the signature, subject, expiration, and so on. Of course, the big question is how do you trust this data? Since it's a decomposable JWT, anyone can create one:

1. You called this from a localized microservice authentication, and this was the direct response. Hence, it wasn't given by any middleman service.

2. We can use a public key from the authentication provider in our service to guarantee this originated from the resource we suspected it to be from.

If you look back at Figure 6-4, look at "VERIFY SIGNATURE"; we have an RS256 public key for Auth0 that will be unique for your account. You can download the URL at `http://rustfortheiot.auth0.com/.well-known/jwks.json` (replace the `rustfortheiot` with your domain). We can use this key to help decode the JSON in our application with JWKS. In our code, not only will we be able to decipher the JWT to get the subject or any other fields we want, but the main thing is it guarantees the JWT came from the source we expected it to be from.

Programmatically Parse

Now being able to run curl scripts and decode from the site is all well and good for testing and to verify you have all the right permissions to make everything work. But let's dive into some code. We'll start with parsing an ID token with alcoholic_jwt.

We will need to use JWKS to validate the token; there were not many crates JWT parsing that allowed it. Luckily, I stumbled upon one that isn't often used for JWT but was designed specifically for JWKS validation, that is, alcoholic_jwt. In Listing 6-4, I have the added crates we will use.

Listing 6-4. Crates used to allow parsing of the User ID JWT

```
hyper = "0.10.16"
alcoholic_jwt = "1.0.0"
reqwest = "0.10.4"
http = "0.2.1"
```

Let's create a function that will take our JWT slice, the JWKS, and the authentication URL and validate the slice and return the user (which is stored in the subject). In Listing 6-5, we decode the JWT to receive the User ID from it.

Listing 6-5. Parsing the user ID from the JWT

```
use alcoholic_jwt::{JWKS, Validation, validate, token_kid, ValidJWT};

fn parse_id_token(jwt_slice: &str, jwks: &JWKS, auth_url: &str) ->
UserResult {
    debug!("JWT Slice :: {:?}", jwt_slice);

    // Several types of built-in validations are provided:
    let validations = vec![
        Validation::Issuer(format!("https://{}/", auth_url).into()), ①
        Validation::SubjectPresent, ②
        Validation::NotExpired, ③
    ];
```

```
    let kid = token_kid(&jwt_slice) ④
        .expect("Failed to decode token headers")
        .expect("No 'kid' claim present in token");

    let jwk = jwks.find(&kid).expect("Specified key not found in set");

    //let result: ValidJWT = validate(jwt_slice, jwk, validations).
    expect("Token validation has failed!");
    let user_id = validate(jwt_slice, jwk, validations)? ⑤
        .claims.get("sub").unwrap().to_string(); ⑥
    Ok(user_id) ⑦
}

async fn jwks_fetching_function(url: &str) -> JWKS { ⑧
    use std::io::Read;
    use std::collections::HashMap;

    let jwks_json: String = {
        let url_jwks = format!("https://{}/.well-known/jwks.json", url);
        let mut res = reqwest::get(url_jwks.as_str()).await.unwrap();
        res.text().await.unwrap()
    };

    let jwks: JWKS = serde_json::from_str(jwks_json.as_str()).
    expect("Failed to decode");
    jwks
}
```

① Sets to validate the issuer against the rustfortheiot JWKS.

② Sets to validate the subject is present since we need that to get the user id.

③ Sets to validate that the token is not expired.

④ Extracts the kid portion from the token.

⑤ Uses the validations we created earlier to validate the token.

⑥ Retrieves the subject from the claim.

⑦   Returns the user id as part of the token.

⑧   Functions to retrieve the JWKS and parse it.

This code does not have to be unique for any particular tier and can be used on the backend to deliver content to a website or on our device to display the user to the screen. But let's move on to discussing the role the access token will play.

Access Tokens

The access token is what is used to send between microservices, so that when service A is working with a user, to tell service B about the user, service B can then perform verification of the token to make sure the user is still active and can then trade that token to the authorization service to get more information about the user like email address or other data. Using a token allows service B to be stand-alone and more secure, since if any outside service tried to send a random access token, it wouldn't validate. Having it call back out to the authorization server also makes sure that the token is still active and usable. Access tokens are sent to a server in the header as either opaque or JWT with the formula of

```
Authorization: Bearer <access_token>
```

For Auth0, we will be sending the tokens as opaque. Once your microservice or your api gateway receives the token, it can check the authorization server that this is a valid token, and you can continue on the request. For us, we are going to also get the subject off the token and store it as a user id on the request so that our controllers can perform actions on it. On Auth0, our endpoint is /userinfo to get the user id from the opaque token. In Listing 6-6, we will retrieve from the /userinfo endpoint the data with our access_token we previously retrieved.

Listing 6-6. Retrieving the user data from the user info

```
➜ curl --request GET \
  --url 'https://rustfortheiot.auth0.com/userinfo' \
  --header 'Authorization: Bearer 5BPHIDN84ciNsY4PeOWRyo8OmB_4R69U' \
  --header 'Content-Type: application/json'

{
    "sub":"auth0|5d45ceebede4920eb1a665f0",
    "nickname":"nusairat",
```

```
"name":"nusairat@gmail.com",
"picture":"https://s.gravatar.com/avatar/05927361dbd43833337aa1e71fdd96
ef?s=480&r=pg&d=https%3A%2F%2Fcdn.auth0.com%2Favatars%2Fnu.png",
"updated_at":"2019-10-15T03:17:11.630Z",
"email":"nusairat@gmail.com",
"email_verified":true
}
```

You will notice we get more than the subject back; we also get the nickname, name, picture, and email; this is because earlier we not only asked for the openid scope but also the profile scope which brings back more details for the access token. Let's now use this in our code to check the user id and their authorization level.

The user info retrieval does not check the authentication status, but gets the user.

In Listing 6-7, we take the request, parse out the token from the header, and use the token to retrieve the user info which will contain the subject.

Listing 6-7. Parsing the user ID from the access token

```
fn parse_access_token(request: &Request,  auth_url: &str) -> UserResult {
    // Get the full Authorization header from the incoming request headers
    let auth_header = match request.headers.get::<Authorization<Bearer>>()
    { ①
        Some(header) => header,
        None => panic!("No authorization header found")
    };
    debug!("Auth Header :: {:?}", auth_header);

    let jwt = header::HeaderFormatter(auth_header).to_string(); ②
    debug!("JWT :: {:?}", jwt);

    let jwt_slice = &jwt[7..];
    debug!("JWT Slice :: {:?}", jwt_slice);

    let item = block_on(retrieve_user(jwt_slice, auth_url));

    Ok(item.unwrap())
}
```

```rust
#[derive(Deserialize, Debug)]
struct Auth0Result {
    iss: String,
    sub: String,
    aud: String
}

async fn retrieve_user(jwt: &str, auth_url: &str) -> Result<String,
reqwest::Error> {
    use std::collections::HashMap;
    use http::{HeaderMap,HeaderValue};

    let url = format!("https://{}/userinfo", auth_url);

    // headers
    let mut headers = HeaderMap::new();
    headers.insert("Authorization", HeaderValue::from_str(jwt).unwrap());
    headers.insert("Content-Type", HeaderValue::from_str("application/
json").unwrap());

    let mut json = reqwest::Client::new() ③
                    .get(&url)
                    .headers(headers)
                    .send()
                    .await?
                    .json::<Auth0Result>()
                    .await?;

    Ok(json.sub)
}
```

① From the header retrieves the Authorization Bearer token, making sure it exists.

② Converts the token to a string; this now would contain Bearer `<access_token>`.

③ Calls out to the /userinfo endpoint to trade the token for user data.

Implement Authorization Check

Let's implement this into our API code. With that set of code, we have discussed we can now retrieve the user info. But I don't want to make these calls for each individual Iron action each time. In addition, I want to make sure that for certain calls an access token is ALWAYS supplied, and if not, the call should be rejected. Let's take a look at our requirements to have our framework run automatic verification and injection for each service call:

1.   Use middleware to retrieve the user id from the access token.

2.   Have the middleware return an error if there is no access token.

3.   Only have this middleware called for certain endpoints.

We've created the middleware a few times now, so most of this code should look very familiar. We will start in Listing 6-8 with a struct `AuthorizationCheck` that we will instantiate in our routes to create the authorization middleware. This will take the authorization url as a parameter that we are going to set in the args.

Listing 6-8. Creating the authorization check struct for our authorization

```
use futures::executor::block_on;

pub struct AuthorizationCheck {
    jwks: JWKS,
    // static and this will never change once set
    auth_url: String
}

impl AuthorizationCheck {
    pub fn new(auth_url: &str) -> AuthorizationCheck {
        // Get the jwks
        let jwks = block_on(jwks_fetching_function(auth_url));
        AuthorizationCheck {
            jwks: jwks,
            auth_url: auth_url.to_string()
        }
    }
}
```

Now is the bigger set of functions. This set we've seen before. We are going to create the struct AuthorizedUser to hold the results of the parse_access_token that we created previously. That data will then be inserted into the request extensions (if you recall, this uses the type of the struct as the key in the map to find the data). And finally, we will use the UserIdRequest as a trait that when on our controller can retrieve the user id with the call request.get_user_id. This code is laid out in Listing 6-9.

Listing 6-9. Creating the authorization check struct for our authorization

```
pub struct AuthorizedUser { ①
    user_id: String
}

impl AuthorizedUser {
    pub fn new(user_id: String) -> AuthorizedUser {
        AuthorizedUser {
            user_id: user_id
        }
    }
}

pub struct Value(AuthorizedUser);

impl typemap::Key for AuthorizedUser { type Value = Value; }

impl BeforeMiddleware for AuthorizationCheck {
    fn before(&self, req: &mut Request) -> IronResult<()> {
        let access_token = parse_access_token(&req, self.auth_url.as_str()); ②
        match  access_token {
            Ok(user_id) => {
                req.extensions.insert::<AuthorizedUser>(Value(AuthorizedUse
                r::new(user_id)));
                Ok(())
            },
            Err(e) => {
                let error = Error::from(JwtValidation(e)); ③
```

```
                Err(IronError::new(error, Status::BadRequest))
            }
        }
    }
}

pub trait UserIdRequest { ④
    fn get_user_id(&self) -> String;
}

impl<'a, 'b> UserIdRequest for Request<'a, 'b> {
    fn get_user_id(&self) -> String {
        let user_value = self.extensions.get::<AuthorizedUser>().chain_
        err(|| "No user id, this should never happen").unwrap();
        let &Value(ref user) = user_value;
        // Clones it since we want to pass handling of it back
        user.user_id.clone()
    }
}
```

① The AuthorizedUser struct that will store the results of the parse tokens return.

② The middleware call that will parse the token; if an Ok is returned, we will extract the token from the success.

③ If not Ok, we will return a Json validation error back to the caller.

④ The trait that will be applied to controllers to retrieve the user id.

This sets up all the middleware; now we just need to tie it into our router model. If you recall earlier, we divided up our health and non-health calls to two different chains. We have the /api chain and /healthz. With this, we are going to have the authorization middleware run on the /api chain. In Listing 6-10, you can see the modified create_ links method with the authorization check.

Listing 6-10. Modified `create_links` with authorization check, in file src/http.rs

```
fn create_links(chain: &mut Chain, url: &str, auth_server: &str) {
    use crate::authorization::AuthorizationCheck;

    // Create the middleware for the diesel
    let diesel_middleware: DieselPg = DieselMiddleware::new(url).unwrap();

    // Authorization tier
    let auth_middleware = AuthorizationCheck::new(auth_server);

    // link the chain
    chain.link_before(auth_middleware);
    chain.link_before(diesel_middleware);
}
```

As you can see, the `healthz` will have no extra middleware added, but our media and comments will.

Refresh Tokens

Finally, let's discuss the refresh tokens. As we stated earlier, the access tokens have a time limit and will be up to our device application to know when they expire. When they do, we will have to obtain a new access token that we can use, along with a new id token as well. This is a relatively simple process where we once again call the `ouath/token` endpoint, except this time, we will pass in as the grant type `refresh_token`, so the server realizes we are passing in a refresh_token to it. In Listing 6-11, we make a curl call back to the server to get a new token.

Listing 6-11. Retrieve a new set of tokens using the refresh token as a basis

```
→ curl --request POST \
  --url 'https://rustfortheiot.auth0.com/oauth/token' \
  --header 'content-type: application/x-www-form-urlencoded' \
  --data grant_type=refresh_token \
  --data 'client_id=rsc1qu5My3QZuRPZHp5af5SOMBUcD7Jb' \
  --data client_secret=C4YMZHE9dAFaEAysRH4rrao9YAjIKBM8-FZ4iCiN8G-
    MJjrq7OOalAn9qDoq3YF6 \
```

```
--data refresh_token=hnsureBL2jfb62UINDmgjt4F6vZBpOetExeoDja5qGy1Y \
--data 'redirect_uri=undefined'
```

```
{
    "access_token":"2JbKDWr5BBqT-j5iOlYp-nRbA1nrnfjP",
    "id_token":
      "eyJOeXAiOiJKV1QiLCJhbGciOiJSUzI1NiIsImtpZCI6Ik5qSXhOekOxTmpjdO5r
      RTNOa1E1UlVSRE1rUXpPVFV5TXpBeE1FSTBRakpGTVRnME5rTTVOQSJ9.eyJpc3
      MiOiJodHRwczovL3J1c3Rmb3JoaGVpb3QuYXVOaDAuY29tLyIsInN1YiI6ImF1dGg
      wfDVkNDVjZWViZWRlNDkyMGViMWE2NjVmMCIsImF1ZCI6InJzYzFxdTVNeTNRWnV
      SUFpIcDVhZjVTME1CVWNENOpiIiwiaWFOIjoxNTcxMTkwNTU1LCJleHAiOjE1Nz
      EyMjY1NTV9.km3QnC28qqWnwvhPVO2T2oW8OoEDUFilLUOgerRAas7YHihmFrYg
      SnovVHBmsWjTMKbHkPmX3RCevyOH-AwqZ1DdOe7ckcFopd-lChubpkegxFBEmhdGah
      NQS7xZWY8_JV3y4ytiLlwfgi6LvJaWJYkObcFKg_Sn37X7UoJkZ4hzqOs82bxLKK
      VO1_yLJHspYry9pt_9yokjOMo77jlGU62oZbdHvUHdYqrxZDQOasLGlrkRMNrmG83
      A2U-QlAotIYBbOOKoeGBRG3lTg7Vd4RazlMim9WYHzqslEHV85ksUFGu_oXiIztgN4
      fZEjWzWNzweCxoDJsg4JHJ7AlW_cg",
    "scope":"openid offline_access",
    "expires_in":86400,
    "token_type":"Bearer"
}
```

Now that we have the new set of tokens, use them and set your expiration again.

You can revoke access token either via code or via the UI; you may have this as part of your application to handle situations where a device is stolen or compromised, and you want to prevent that device from talking to the services.

Much of the code you see here and curls will be incorporated when we get to Chapter 8 and start the device coding itself. But I didn't want to overly divide up the concepts of Authorization and Authentication in two chapters. We will revisit some of these calls later, but for now, we have our authorization and authentication.

Securing MQTT

Our first pass of using MQTT for our application, we used TCP for the communication. The TCP connection to the message queue was not only not secure from an authentication perspective, but most importantly it was unencrypted. This means if anyone sniffed our packets being sent from our devices, they would see not only the packages we sent but where we send them to. And before we were using Protobuf, it meant it was even easier to view. This means anyone could not only send data as anyone, but could also receive all the topics that we are deploying revealing customer data. This would be a major breach of data.

There are many ways of solving for security and encryption with a device communicating or your backend services communicating. There are two main ways of solving these problems:

1. SSL (Secure Sockets Layer) – Like most backend application, we use SSL to create secure communication between the client and the server. To do this, we will have to create certificates for the server that the message queue server uses for running the SLL certs. In addition, we will have to create certs for each client that connects to our message queue server.

2. Authentication – Another way to secure the site is to have authentication. This makes it so a particular user can only access the message queue. In fact, you can lock it down even further by only allowing the user to have access to specific topics.

There are a few ways to achieve, but essentially the two are to let the message queue application handle it or have a sidecar handle both. Letting the message queue handle it means using the tools built into the MQ for SSL and Authentication to run the SSL and Authentication. Most MQs out there, and the one we are using, have SSL handlers out of the box as well as authentication. The other way is something that will make more sense in the next chapter when we talk about deployment, and that is using a sidecar injector. A sidecar injector will run along our application and intercept all requests to the service. You can use this to force your calls to all be SSL and authenticated. This can be especially useful in the authentication realm but also if you are not entirely happy with the SSL implementation. In addition, you could replace just one or the other piece with the customization.

If you have good expertise in SSL and Authentication, then the sidecar maybe for you; however, for our implementation, we are going to stick with using MQ SSL model.

Certificates

Certificates are used to communicate and encrypt data between two endpoints so that not only can someone in the middle read the data being transmitted but also so that you can trust that who made the call was the person you thought made the call. The use of certificates has been out since the early days of the Web, but in those days, people only used them to transmit credit cards and other highly secure pieces of data. Today almost every website uses them, and since 2014, Google will give your site a higher ranking when using them. There are essentially two types of certificates, certificate authority (CA) and self-signed.

Certificate Authority (CA) vs. Self-Signed Certificates

We will be talking about using CA vs. self-signed Certificates throughout the next two chapters. By rule, we will be using CA certs for our deployed environments and self-signed for our local environments. Certificate authority certs are certificates that are generated and signed by a recognized certificate authority. The main reason to use them is a guarantee that the domain you are connecting to is truly that domain owned by the person you expect it to be that site. There are various certificate authorities you can use; we will be using letsencrypt. Letsencrypt is free for the amount of requests we would need, and most applications have easy integration into letsencrypt.

When deploying locally, we cannot use signed certificates (well easily). Signed certificates are tied to a domain that can be resolved and are designed for QA and Production testing or any deployed environment. However, we need to test locally against a local MQ and local microservices. To do that, we will use self-signed certificates that will allow us to create the certs and destroy them as needed.

You can deploy self-signed certificates to deployed environments, but then you will have to make sure your system is not enforcing that they are certificate authority signed. You will notice the use of self-signed certificates in websites when they ask you to continue on a cert that is not CA certified.

Creating Server Certificates

For us, we are going to use most of our certs that we create for our MQTT communication.

Before we start, there will be many different file extensions that we will use in this section; it's good to get an overview of the differences:

1. .PEM – This is an RFC 1421 and 1424 file format. PEM stands for Privacy Enhanced Mail and came about as a way to securely send emails, but now it's used for a great many other security chains. This is a base65 x509 certificate that either can contain the public certificate or could contain the entire certificate chain including public key, private key, and the root certificates.

2. .KEY – The .key is mostly commonly used as the private key and will be formatted as PEM file containing just the private key that we should never share.

3. .CSR – This is an RFC 2986 specification in a PKCS10 format. CSR stands for Certificate Signing Request and contains all the information needed to request a certificate to be signed by a certificate authority. The digitally signed certificate will be signed and returned with its public key to be used for digital certs.

Generate CA Root Certificate

First off, we need to generate the private key we are going to use for our self-signed CA Root Certificate. In Listing 6-12, we generate an RSA private key with length of 2048. We are going to name the cert `RustIOTRootCA`.

Listing 6-12. Generate an RSA private key

```
openssl genrsa -out RustIOTRootCA.key 2048
```

This is the private key, the one that if this was a production system, you'd want to keep in a safe place. If someone else got a hold of that key, they could compromise your identity. Usually you use a CA provider to take care of your key that is generated.

Next, we are going to generate the Root Certificate from the key and give it an expiration of 1826 days or roughly 5 years. Could in theory be longer but 5 years is plenty of time for testing purposes. In Listing 6-13, we generate this key.

Listing 6-13. Generate an x509 certificate

```
➜ openssl req -x509 -new -nodes -key RustIOTRootCA.key -sha256 -days
1826 -out RustIOTRootCA.pem ①
You are about to be asked to enter information that will be incorporated
into your certificate request.
What you are about to enter is what is called a Distinguished Name or a DN.
There are quite a few fields but you can leave some blank
For some fields there will be a default value,
If you enter '.', the field will be left blank.
-----
Country Name (2 letter code) []:US ②
State or Province Name (full name) []:CA
Locality Name (eg, city) []:SF
Organization Name (eg, company) []:
Organizational Unit Name (eg, section) []:
Common Name (eg, fully qualified host name) []:localhost ③
Email Address []:
```

① Command to create the RustIOTRootCA cert using sha256 and creating an X509 certificate.

② Add in a few fields like the country name and state.

③ This is normally the fully qualified domain name; since we are running it from localhost, use that instead of a regular name.

The root cert is used as the start of your trust train. Certificates we generate after this will all use the Root to verify the authenticity up the chain. The Root CA can be used to generate any certificate on our site.

Message Queue Server Cert

But first, let's start with creating the cert for the message queue itself. We will generate the private key and the cert for the MQTT, much like we did before with similar commands even. The big difference will be now we have a root CA we can use as well. Like in the previous example, let's start by generating the private key in Listing 6-14.

Listing 6-14. Generate an RSA private key for the MQ

```
openssl genrsa -out EmqttIot.key 2048
```

Now let's use that private key to create a certificate request; the certificate request is used to create a message to the CA requesting a digitally signed certificate. Since we are performing this all as self-signed, we will create that certificate request, then turn around, and create the PEM. In Listing 6-15, we are creating our CSR for the MQTT.

Listing 6-15. Generate a CSR for the MQ

```
➔ openssl req -new -key ./EmqttIot.key -out EmqttIot.csr ①
You are about to be asked to enter information that will be incorporated
into your certificate request.
What you are about to enter is what is called a Distinguished Name or a DN.
There are quite a few fields but you can leave some blank
For some fields there will be a default value,
If you enter '.', the field will be left blank.
-----
Country Name (2 letter code) []:US
State or Province Name (full name) []:CA
Locality Name (eg, city) []:San Mateo
Organization Name (eg, company) []:Apress
Organizational Unit Name (eg, section) []:IoT
Common Name (eg, fully qualified host name) []:localhost ②
Email Address []:

Please enter the following 'extra' attributes
to be sent with your certificate request
A challenge password []:
```

①   Command to create our CSR from the key we created previously.

②   Marking the localhost since we are running this locally.

Now that we have a CSR and a private key, we can use that to create a request for an actual certificate that we will use for the MQ. This will appear similar to the previous PEM creation, except this time we are going to reference the Root CA in Listing 6-16.

Listing 6-16. Generate the certificate for the message queue

```
➜ openssl x509 -req -in ./EmqttIot.csr \ ①
    -CA RustIOTRootCA.pem \ ②
    -CAkey RustIOTRootCA.key \ ③
    -CAcreateserial \ ④
    -out EmqttIot.pem  \ ⑤
    -days 1826 -sha256  \ ⑥
Signature ok
subject=/C=US/ST=CA/L=SF/CN=localhost
Getting CA Private Key
```

①   Command to create a x509 certificate using the previously created CSR as the basis for the request.

②   The Root CA certificate authority file we created previously.

③   The private key for that CA that only the owner should have.

④   This flag creates a file containing the serial number. This number is incremented each time you sign a certificate.

⑤   Defining the file to output the certificate for the MQ to.

⑥   Defining the days this certificate is active for and the cipher to use.

There will be two files generated from this request: the EmqtIot.pem that we defined to be requested and also the RustIOTRootCA.srl serial number that we used.

At this point, we have created our Root CA and the certificate for our MQTT Cert; in addition, we no longer need the EmqttIot.csr that we created, and you can delete it now if you want. We are able to now revisit our MQTT server itself.

Updating the MQTT Server

In order to do this, we are going to have to deactivate our old MQTT server that we created since they will be sharing some port numbers. Go ahead and run `docker stop mqtt-no-auth`; this will turn off the previous MQTT server that did not have certificates.

For the MQTT server, we are going to make use of the certificates we just created to set up the SSL port on the MQTT server so that we can accept only SSL calls with a trusted chain. The EMQTT we are using supports the use of certificates out of the box; it will be up to us to configure them. By default, there is an EMQTT configuration file that is used when running the application, and the docker command we are using can update them with environmental variables.

We need to set two things. One is to set the certificates so that we have SSL connectivity. This will allow us to access the MQ so long as our client is using a trusted Root CA as well for communication. While this will make sure all our traffic is over SSL and thus encrypted, it would still allow anyone the ability to communicate with our endpoint as long as they had a CA certificate.

If you recall, we are also using this as a secure mechanism to control who the clients are; thus, we also need to tell the MQTT server to only accept connections with valid client-side certificates as well. Those certificates can only be generated if one has the Root CA private key, which should be just us.

Let's look at what updates we will need to the configuration files; Listing 6-17 has our eventual settings.

Listing 6-17. Example of the properties we need to set for our certificates to work

```
listener.ssl.external.keyfile = /etc/certs/EmqttIot.key ①
listener.ssl.external.certfile = /etc/certs/EmqttIot.pem ②
listener.ssl.external.cacertfile = /etc/certs/RustIOTRootCA.pem ③
listener.ssl.external.verify = verify_peer ④
listener.ssl.external.fail_if_no_peer_cert = true ⑤
```

① The private key file for the EMQTT client.

② The public certificate for the EMQTT client cert.

③ The public root CA certificate.

④ Verifies the client-side identities by their certificates.

⑤   Ensures that we only allow SSL if there is a verified client-side certificate.

Now this leads to two questions:

1.   Where do we place the files for the docker container to pick up?

2.   How do we tell docker to update the emqtt.conf file with those properties listed in Listing 6-17?

The first is relatively easy; we can use the -v tag in docker to allow a local directory be used as mounted directory in the docker image we are running. The second requires us to use a naming convention used by the image to convert environmental variables to updates to the properties file.

When updating a reference like listener.ssl.external.keyfile, it is converted as an environmental variable starting with EMQ_, then uppercasing the entire string and replacing all the "." with double underscores. Thus, we would have EMQ_LISTENER</emphasis>SSLEXTERNALKEYFILE from the example. This can be used for any of the properties in the EMQTT that you want to adjust. In Listing 6-18, we have our docker create for the emqtt-auth with the necessary environmental variable settings to run our secure EMQTT server.

Listing 6-18. Docker run to create an EMQTT server with SSL enabled and verify SSL turned on

```
docker run --restart=always -ti --name emqtt-auth --net=iot \
-p 8883:8883 -p 18083:18083 -p 8083:8083 -p 8443:8443 -p 8084:8084 -p
8080:8080 \ ①
-v ~/book_certs:/etc/ssl/certs/ \ ②
-e EMQ_LISTENER__SSL__EXTERNAL__KEYFILE="\/etc\/ssl\/certs\/EmqttIot.key" \ ③
-e EMQ_LISTENER__SSL__EXTERNAL__CERTFILE="\/etc\/ssl\/certs\/EmqttIot.pem" \
-e EMQ_LISTENER__SSL__EXTERNAL__CACERTFILE="\/etc\/ssl\/certs\/
    RustIOTRootCA.pem" \
-e EMQ_LISTENER__SSL__EXTERNAL__VERIFY=verify_peer \
-e EMQ_LISTENER__SSL__EXTERNAL__FAIL_IF_NO_PEER_CERT=true \
-e "EMQ_LOG_LEVEL=debug" \
-e "EMQ_ADMIN_PASSWORD=your_password" \
-d devrealm/emqtt
```

① Added the 8883 SSL port and removed the 1883 TCP port from being exposed since we no longer want users to connect via TCP.

② Our local ~/book_certs directory can be mounted to the docker images /etc/ssl/cert.

③ Referencing the directories with escaping the files.

We have our server up and running; it's good to test to make sure it's working as designed. And the way we are going to test to see if it works is if it gives us a correct error back. In Listing 6-19, we attempt to subscribe with just the RootCA.

Listing 6-19. Attempt to subscribe with the RootCA file

```
→ mosquitto_sub -t health/+ -h localhost -p 8883 -d --cafile ./
RustIOTRootCA.pem  --insecure
Client mosq/rL5I4rEQ73Brv2ITSx sending CONNECT
OpenSSL Error: error:14094410:SSL routines:ssl3_read_bytes:sslv3 alert
handshake failure
Error: A TLS error occurred.
```

The error we get is `sslv3 alert handshake failure`; if you receive any other error particularly `certificate verify failed`, that means you set up the installation of the certificate incorrectly. But let's now get the client certificates created. This is because while our server is set up to handle certificates, our client does not have them set up yet.

Creating Client Certificates

Our final step is creating the client certificate; in the future, we will need to be able to create a client certificate for each client. And in our case, each client is the Raspberry Pi devices. Since these are connected devices and we want an ability to control subscriptions, we will make it, so the clients only last for one month at a time. This way, we can control a bit better how long the server device is able to access the server. And in theory if we were doing a monthly billing, if they stopped paying well, they wouldn't have access after that month.

But that will be done programmatically; for now, we are going to do this via the command line like the other certificates. Since this is a bit of a repeat of before, we are going to combine all three steps into one listing. Like before, we will create a private key, create a CSR from that private key, and then using the Root CA create the certificate for the client. In Listing 6-20, we have those steps.

Listing 6-20. Create the client certificate from the Root CA

```
→ openssl genrsa -out PiDevice.key 2048 ①
Generating RSA private key, 2048 bit long modulus
.......................................+++
.........+++
e is 65537 (0x10001)

→ openssl req -new -key ./PiDevice.key -out PiDevice.csr ②
...
-----
-----
Country Name (2 letter code) []:US
State or Province Name (full name) []:CA
Locality Name (eg, city) []:SF
Organization Name (eg, company) []:Apress
Organizational Unit Name (eg, section) []:IoT
Common Name (eg, fully qualified host name) []:localhost
Email Address []:

Please enter the following 'extra' attributes
to be sent with your certificate request
A challenge password []:

→ openssl x509 -req -in ./PiDevice.csr -CA RustIOTRootCA.pem -CAkey
RustIOTRootCA.key -CAcreateserial -out PiDevice.pem -days 3650 -sha256 ③
Signature ok
subject=/C=US/ST=CA/L=San Mateo/O=Apress/OU=IoT/CN=localhost
Getting CA Private Key
```

① Creates the private key for the client.

② Creates the CSR for the private key.

③ Creates the client PEM using the private key created and the Root CA file that was created in the server section.

Pick a slightly different subject than for your clients vs. the Root Certificate. Having the same between the client and the Root will cause issues. Of course, that said, the issuer does need to match. You can double-check the settings for the certs you created with the command `openssl x509 -in <filename> -subject -issuer -noout`. This will give you the subject and the issuer. The `issuer` should all match across certs with the clients having different subjects.

Now that we have created the certificates, let's try to create a connection. In Listing 6-21, we create a connection using the new client certificate we created.

Listing 6-21. Running a mosquitto subscription with the new client certificate

```
→ mosquitto_sub -t health/+ -h localhost -p 8883 -d --key PiDevice.key --cert
  PiDevice.pem --cafile RustIOTRootCA.pem   --insecure
```

```
Client mosq/nHh8mJ922PEe6VeUSN sending CONNECT
Client mosq/nHh8mJ922PEe6VeUSN received CONNACK (0)
Client mosq/nHh8mJ922PEe6VeUSN sending SUBSCRIBE (Mid: 1, Topic: health/+,
QoS: 0, Options: 0x00)
Client mosq/nHh8mJ922PEe6VeUSN received SUBACK
Subscribed (mid: 1): 0
```

Now we have a secure connection to test against and with; however, now we are going to have to update our actual code to switch from using a TCP connection to the SSL connection.

Creating Our New Message Queue Service

We have our MQ running SSL, and slightly more secured by requiring a client key to be used, and shut down the TCP access; the MQTT service we created in previous chapters will no longer work. At this point, the message queue will refuse any connections. We are going to have to convert our `connection_method` for the message queue to use SSL instead of TCP.

Luckily, this is relatively simple. Let's start by defining what extra items we need:

1. Root CA – The root CA to the site that we created; this is the public certificate.

2. Client cert – The client certificate that is generated from the public/private Root CA.

3. Client key – The private key for that certificate.

You can either use the PiDevice certificate we created previously or create a new certificate to use for the MQ service. I am not going to step through all the code, but wanted to highlight two areas. The first is we need to add to our config a few more references; in Listing 6-22, we added the preceding certs to the MqttClientConfig.

Listing 6-22. Updating the MqttClientConfig; this will be in the file src/mqtt/mod.rs

```
#[derive(Debug, Clone)]
pub struct MqttClientConfig {
    pub ca_crt:  String,
    pub server_crt: String,
    pub server_key: String,
    pub mqtt_server: String,
    pub mqtt_port: u16,
    // for the RPC
    pub rpc_server: Option<String>,
    pub rpc_port: Option<u16>,
}
```

Now we need to apply those certificates to the client; before we were using a TCP connection method that didn't require any extra configurations. In Listing 6-23, we alter that to be a TlS connection using the certs provided.

Listing 6-23. Updating; this will be in the file src/mqtt/client.rs

```
pub fn create_client(config: &MqttClientConfig, name: &str)
    -> (MqttClient, Receiver<Notification>) {

    let ca = read(config.ca_crt.as_str());
```

```
    let server_crt = read(config.server_crt.as_str());
    let server_key = read(config.server_key.as_str());

    create_client_conn(config, ca, server_crt, server_key, name)
}
```

And that is it; start up the application, and you can use the test calls we created earlier to send the files to the MQTT and read them over TLS. We now have our message queue system communicating over secure channels instead of insecure ones.

Summary

In this chapter, we covered the very basics of security. I felt authentication was critical since it drives about any Internet-based application. The integration in our layers is less than we probably should do, but good enough for demonstration purposes. You will want to add more as you continue. Same goes for MQTT, certificate-based authentication is very common even for the most basic of items. Remember, with your IoT device, when you first plug it in, you will want it to communicate with a server even without the person being authenticated. This could be to know if it's active, if an update is required, and so on. We will do more callbacks to the authentication layer in Chapter 9 when we allow the user to authenticate with device flow on the Raspberry Pi.

CHAPTER 7

Deployment

The first half of this book is designed to focus on the cloud side of IoT development, while in the second half, we will focus on coding against the device itself that interacts with the backend. However, for this to properly work, we need to get the application off our personal computer and into the cloud and, even more importantly, into the cloud securely. The cloud is obviously the end goal for any application, but for an IoT application, it becomes critical to be scalable; last thing you want is a customer to buy an expensive device and have it not work well. In addition, it needs to be cost-effective. While oftentimes we have subscriptions, many times you make the money on the device and then lose money in the cloud. Netflix in particular spends excessive cycles making sure the amount that is downloaded is not only compressed, only what you need, but it can be done without causing their cloud deployment to be too costly. Why lose money where you don't have to?

For this chapter, we are going to go over how to deploy our application to the cloud and perform this in the best and most reproducible manner. What do I mean by reproducible? Simply put, I am not sure what cloud service you plan to deploy to or if plan to deploy to your own infrastructure. We are going to use Docker and Kubernetes to make easily reproducible deployments with helm charts and then finish it off with using `gitlab-ci` to deploy the application.

What to Deploy

We have developed all the microservices we are going to use for this book and finished configuring them to handle our needs for our device. In addition, we made use of numerous data services. These will all need to be deployed and used in the cloud in order to have our application working. For our solution and for yours, we should do a combined approach. We will deploy all the applications of course, but the data services we will do a combination of using cloud services and deploying our own versions (we will get to this in a bit).

© Joseph Faisal Nusairat 2020
J. F. Nusairat, *Rust for the IoT*, https://doi.org/10.1007/978-1-4842-5860-6_7

Microservices

Let's start with the microservices; we created four of them for our backend application, and each will need to be deployed into our cloud. The microservices we have are as follows:

- http retrieval service

- rpc retrieval service

- mqtt service

- upload service

All of these microservices need to be deployed and scaled correctly in order to provide an optimal end-user experience.

Data Services

The data services consist of all the data store interactions and the pub sub that our application uses. These services are not services we created but based on images we used and customized the settings for. Because of this, we have a few options how we use these services in the cloud. Many of the services, like the database, are often provided by cloud providers. The plus to using the cloud provider once is often guaranteed reliability, automatic scalability, and automated data backups. For many data stores, the added cost is worth the less headache.

Of course, the other way is to simply deploy and manage yourself. The benefit with this is the extra level of control you have in configuring and using your services. Oftentimes, it's not a 100% either/or to use. Let's recall the three data services that we used in our application thus far:

- Event Store

- PostgreSQL database

- eMQTT

The EventStore is a bit unique and not available in all cloud providers, so we will have to deploy that ourselves. With the PubSub, there are many different implementations that can be used and are often provided by cloud providers others out of the box since a PubSub is critical for any IoT solution. For our solution, we are going to use our own PubSub though because I prefer the optimization that comes with eMQTT. The Erlang MQTT is highly scalable and superior broker that will be able to handle higher levels of traffic. That leaves the Postgres database, and this we will use the cloud provider. The extra cost will be worth the extra reliability. And besides, we need to see how it works both ways.

How to Deploy

There are many ways to deploy services to the cloud and many services you can pick from. The traditional methodology is to buy a service instance and create the Linux environment (or make use of one that is existing) and deploy the application directly to there. Or you can simply set up your own server in a data center and set up and maintain the application and deploy directly. This is the way almost everyone did 2 decades ago, and cost quite a bit in maintenance and use. Today, this is still used at very large companies, but even that is shrinking. Many large companies also have a cloud solution using one of the big providers.

The big providers are Amazon Web Services (AWS), Google Cloud Platform (GCP), and Microsoft Azure. If you've done any cloud development, you've probably heard of all three. There are also providers like Aliyum in China. These providers are great; they have data centers all over the world and have high uptime reliability, and most have great options for service and support. These are great if you are a large-scale, or even small-scale, startup. But they are EXPENSIVE. If you are designing an app for hobby or prototype or for a book and don't want to spend hundreds or thousands a month, then there are other options.

There are smaller companies that provide cloud services to users and companies that are more apropos to be used for hobbyists or very small companies. eApps and DigitalOcean are two good examples that will let you deploy to the cloud, run your application, and not break the bank. For that reason, we will use DigitalOcean, and I will step through setting up the account and creating it later.

Deployment Options

We discussed earlier the options to deploy a service directly to the cloud with managed systems; however, this is becoming more of an archaic way of deploying. The alternative that is becoming popular is to use Kubernetes or any type of orchestrated container system.

This allows a configuration-based description for our cloud architecture. In addition, we will be able to use these tools to easily reproduce deployments to any cloud or even local.

Goals

The overarching goal for us at the end of this chapter is to have everything deployed to the cloud. This is quite a large goal and hence a long chapter, and many of the topics we are going to talk about in this book like Docker and Kubernetes have entire books written on. We will be scratching the surface to satisfy our needs, but I will try to cover enough for novices to understand what is going on.

After completing this chapter, the following details should be finished:

1. Creating Docker images for each of our microservices

2. Creating Kubernetes YAML files for deploying our application

3. Creating Helm scripts for our Kubernetes deployments to be able to configure per environment

4. Configuring a CI/CD pipeline to deploy the entire backend

Docker

If you've worked with backend applications over the last few years, you've probably used or at least heard of docker. Docker is a platform-as-a-service (PaaS) product that uses operating system virtualization to create containers that contain the OS virtualization and any other artifacts that we need. Docker first debuted at PyCon in 2013 and was released shortly thereafter. What does this all mean? Why do we need all this? Let's go back in time to what life is like before and if you don't use docker.

One of the common denominators between docker and dockerless deployments is the use of artifacts. No matter how you deploy your code with Rust, we will always be creating releases; with languages like Java, it's a jar or war file. You create the artifact on a build server and can push it through the process of testing on a dev and qa and eventually push the artifact to production. By the time we get to production, we assume it should work because we tested the exact code on each system. However, this was not always the case; far too often, it failed and you had to figure out why. What was the reason if the artifacts were identical? The culprit was often the virtual machines (since rarely do we deploy to one specific full server). There could have been a different server settings, extra software installed, or even a totally different version of the virtual machine. You simply didn't always know. This is what containerization tries to solve. Containers allow you to keep the same virtualized environment whether you are testing locally, in test, or in production. In Figure 7-1, we illustrate how this looks.

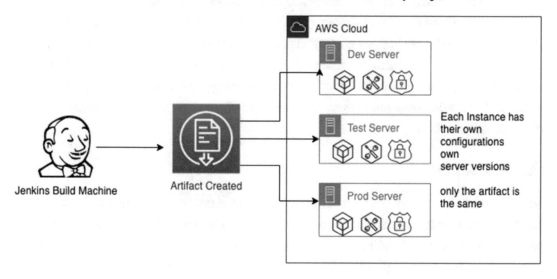

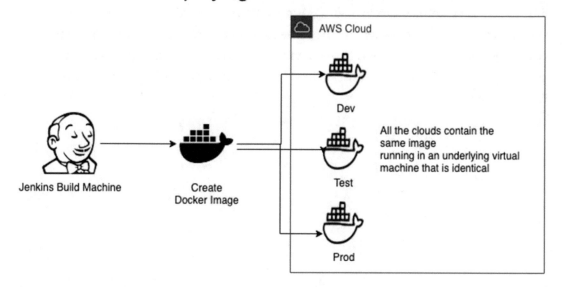

Figure 7-1. *Diagram comparing virtual machine vs. Docker artifacts*

Not only does having container allow you to self-manage your dev to test rollouts, but they also have a way to reproduce and allow the virtual machine to be exactly what you want to contain and nothing more.

What Is Containerization

Containers started as a way of using the Linux container to successfully package images and deploying them to Linux for execution. This was in the start of the Docker world in 2013; since then the docker has spread with partnerships to other systems like Windows. Containers at their core allow an abstraction layer that can run an operating system and multiple applications all on one "server". We often compare them to virtual machines because that is what they most often replaced, and virtual machines in their turn replaced full machines.

Full Machines

By full machines, I mean one rack or server in a data center and that the hardware is 100% dedicated to the application we are writing, most often in a data center and sometimes in someone's house or by a desk. Twenty or so years ago, you would have one server, running one operating system, and then multiple applications could be run off that one system. However, that prevents any sandboxing between applications. They have access to the same system files and same system configurations and allowed little ability to customize system settings for your own application. In addition, your code was co-located with others on the same filesystem which could result in security issues if you weren't careful. While this was not a big issue if you all worked at the same company, if you were a server farm selling services, this was very big. Figure 7-2 reflects this structure.

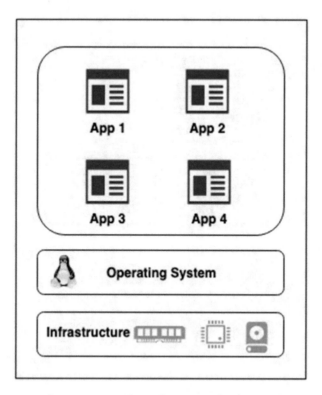

Figure 7-2. *Diagram of our original application deployments*

Virtual Machines

The way this first problem was solved was with virtual machines. You have a virtual machine installed right now on your system if you are using Docker in fact. I know this sounds a bit confusing since we said docker replaces the need for virtual machines, but we'll get into that in a second. If you are a Mac user for the past 10+ years, at some point you may have had a VM running Windows OS on your computer via something like VMware. Virtual machines work by using a common set of infrastructure (your CPU, hard drive, RAM, etc.) and putting a virtual machine monitor on top of it. The virtual machine monitor, often called a hypervisor, creates and runs virtual machines. The virtual machines have their own OS and their own hard drive partition and get access to specific amount of shared ram and shared cpu. You can then put whatever applications you want inside the VMs. These are truly sandboxed environment like we have in Figure 7-3. And they worked well for years.

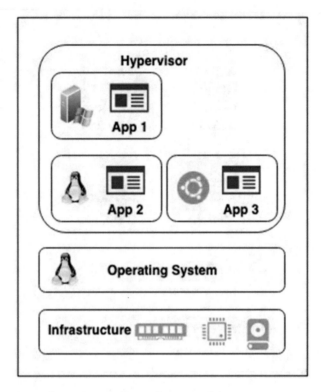

Figure 7-3. *Diagram of our virtual machine architecture*

The problem with these is similar to the full machines; while you can at least segregate multiple applications and teams across a physical server, within the virtual machine all your resources are shared. On your same VM, your applications would still have access to the same file systems, and an application could start processes that would hog all the resources (ram, disk space, cpu). In addition, you still have to do manual updates of the OS and keep up to date with the software patches. In addition, since it is a VM, you will have to install libraries that support all the applications. That means one application could install libraries that the other applications don't need. And now, if that library has a security vulnerability, all the applications are now vulnerable instead of just the one. Virtual machines helped us solve the problem, especially on an enterprise scale, of segregating our teams or even projects on one server but still left us all the vulnerability at an application level.

Containers

That brings us to containers. Containers all use the same OS kernel and infrastructure on a machine. However, instead of a hypervisor, there is a containerization manager that actually runs the containers; for us, this will be docker. Docker allows us to configure our containers and the amount of operating system infrastructure each container is able to make use of. This allows us to have small, fast, compact applications and more of them than we would in a traditional virtual machine environment.

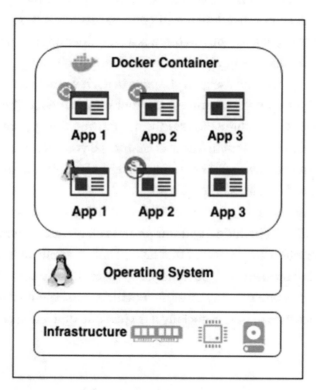

Figure 7-4. *Diagram of our docker architecture*

You will notice in Figure 7-4 I have an Ubuntu and Linux symbol by next to a few of the applications. Each of the containers can contain a base OS image that builds up on the system kernel. This allows your application to run with its own operating system dependencies, depending on what your applications need. This is for your standard features like your bash, what kind of scp, and so on. Lower-level kernel specifics like memory management, the file system, and networking are still run by the kernel and would be hard to divorce from. Because of this, remember, if you require a specific chipset architecture or using features of a specific kernel, you have to target it to the underlying machine that docker is running and the orchestrator is running from. If you notice, two of the applications I didn't attach any OS to, and these are called scratch containers, meaning they contain no extra parts except from what is inherited from the kernel. We will get into how we use both later.

The use of VMs and containers are not mutually exclusive. When you purchase an account from GCP, AWS, DigitalOcean, or any number of companies out there, you are not purchasing an entire machine; that would be very cost prohibitive for most individuals and small companies. You are still purchasing a machine, with virtual machines, except the app we will put on there is a container orchestrator that will allow us to run docker with multiple applications. In addition, each container can define the amount of ram and cpu and assign disk space to each so that you can prevent one application from hogging all the resources. Another huge benefit is the containers are self-contained images that include the OS information and the application code; this makes it very easy and fast to spin up more containers if you ever need to for load, region, or even testing purposes. This structure gives us flexibility in our deployment and our applications all without breaking the bank.

A typical deployed diagram of multiple VMs on a full machine is in Figure 7-5.

I feel remiss if I did not include a counter point to all of this. Remember, every time you add a layer, you add resource use of that layer. That an application sitting on docker, on a VM, and on a full machine will obviously have access to the same amount of CPU, RAM, and disk space as one running on a full machine. Some people prefer deploying to just a VM directly because of this, especially if it's just one or a few applications they have 100% control over.

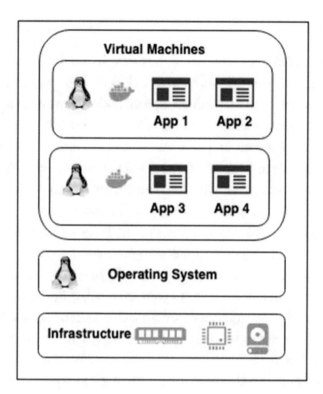

Figure 7-5. *Diagram of a deployment to a machine with multiple VMs and containers*

I am sure in 10 years we will still have docker, but we will also have other options that will gain traction. Server-side application development has been since it started a rapidly changing system to adjust in terms of optimization, security, and cost. And that's what these container and sandbox environments help do; they lower the cost with tighter security and great performance.

Docker Layers

While part of the power of docker comes in the fact you don't need independent virtual machine per service, the other is in its concept of layers. Take the previous figures; we showed that each docker container can contain an underlying OS. In fact, each docker container can contain a number of items, and often when writing microservices, your containers will all contain common parts. They could be getting the same certificates or anything custom. These layers take the form of images that you can create on your own or can be pulled from a repository at docker.com or your own repository. Gitlab, Google, and so on all have private image repositories you can make use of.

While the images on public repositories, especially the certified ones, are fairly safe if you have the resources, I suggest maintaining your own repository of base images built from the source code of the images (and vetted), so as to be sure an image is never changed out from underneath you without your knowledge. Since they are public images, someone could potentially push unknowingly or knowingly a malicious exploit. In general, you will only be customizing your base images by the language and type of application (Web, batch, backend, etc.). And you can have the images vetted by a security or SRE team first. I've also seen images changed and pushed with the same version number; thus, the image essentially changes without you aware at all.

Your layers could be as simple as an Ubuntu OS or a stripped down Ubuntu OS. Most often though, we have layers for the applications we are creating that include the OS as well as all the tools needed to compile and run the application. For example, `rust-lang` maintains multiple docker images with various base images from slim to using the buildpack-deps (contains various build dependencies).

Let's take a look at what one of these looks like. In Listing 7-1, I have the dockerfile to create the debian image with rust for the `rust:1.37` image.

Listing 7-1. The Dockerfile for rust::1.37.0 (I have abbreviated the SHA's for the book)

```
FROM buildpack-deps:buster ①

ENV RUSTUP_HOME=/usr/local/rustup \ ②
    CARGO_HOME=/usr/local/cargo \
    PATH=/usr/local/cargo/bin:$PATH \
    RUST_VERSION=1.37.0
```

```
RUN set -eux; \
    dpkgArch="$(dpkg --print-architecture)"; \
    case "${dpkgArch##*-}" in \
        amd64) rustArch='x86_64-unknown-linux-gnu'; rustupSha256='a46fe...
        c9076' ;; \
        armhf) rustArch='armv7-unknown-linux-gnueabihf';
        rustupSha256='6af5a...caea1' ;; \
        arm64) rustArch='aarch64-unknown-linux-gnu';
        rustupSha256='51862...77a1b' ;; \
        i386) rustArch='i686-unknown-linux-gnu';
        rustupSha256='91456c...182be' ;; \
        *) echo >&2 "unsupported architecture: ${dpkgArch}"; exit 1 ;; \
    esac; \
    url="https://static.rust-lang.org/rustup/archive/1.18.3/${rustArch}/
    rustup-init"; \ ③
    wget "$url"; \
    echo "${rustupSha256} *rustup-init" | sha256sum -c -; \
    chmod +x rustup-init; \
    ./rustup-init -y --no-modify-path --default-toolchain $RUST_VERSION; \ ④
    rm rustup-init; \
    chmod -R a+w $RUSTUP_HOME $CARGO_HOME; \
    rustup --version; \
    cargo --version; \
    rustc --version;
```

① The base image for this dockerfile.

② Sets environmental variables we need for rust including rustup and cargo which we use for building rust applications.

③ Sets the URL for the rust lang and retrieves the archive of the rust language and tool chain.

④ Initializes rustup which will allow us to run or create releases with cargo.

This is not a small image; the size is 1.66 GB which is why we want to use layering, so that every time we have a rust build, its total file size isn't our rust code + 1.66 GB. The beauty about the layering of docker images is that we only need to download the image once on our filesystem to reuse it across multiple applications. There are a variety of images you can choose from when building any application, let alone a rust application. In fact, you could start with a standard debian image and build your own image to compile. Often images follow similar naming formats; the one you will often see uses the `slim` suffix, for example, `rust:1.37-slim`. The slims contain the most basic needed for the operating system so everything you will normally need but nothing else. For rust in order to use it, you need a C++ compiler as well as a few other binaries. The slim version of the preceding rust architecture would get a slim debian instance and add in the binaries we need. In Listing 7-2, we have the beginning `rust:1.37-slim` image.

Listing 7-2. The Dockerfile for rust::1.37.0-slim

```
FROM debian:stretch-slim ①

ENV RUSTUP_HOME=/usr/local/rustup \
    CARGO_HOME=/usr/local/cargo \
    PATH=/usr/local/cargo/bin:$PATH \
    RUST_VERSION=1.37.0

RUN set -eux; \
    apt-get update; \
    apt-get install -y --no-install-recommends \ ②
        ca-certificates \
        gcc \
        libc6-dev \
        wget \
        ; \
# ... the rest of the rust architecture retrieval
```

① Using the debian slim package.

② Installing the binary packages needed for Rust.

The resulting image now becomes 1.06 GB, saving us about half a gigabyte in space and leaving less routes for potential exploits when deployed. Oftentimes, you will start with the big image when creating your own dockerfile and work your way down.

You've noticed a few commands in the dockerfile are already the RUN and ENV; we won't dive into all the commands, but there are a few more you should know and also what's going on whenever you run a keyword (if you noticed on a few of those RUNs they did the && to combine it into one, this wasn't just to write clean scripts).

At each command, we have a different image being created that can be stacked upon; this helps us when using caching to detect if anything is changed. In the preceding listing, you notice they actually ran what's normally a few Linux commands in one RUN statement; the reason for this is to keep it from creating a separate image for each line. This way at the end of the RUN, you have all the extra libraries needed to build your rust application. Now this doesn't mean you want only one RUN command in your dockerfile, but just group them logically. Here are a few more commands we will use:

- COPY – This command copies from the local directory its run form into the docker container. This is how you get your code into docker to begin with.

- RUN – As we've seen before, this runs a command inside container.

- WORKDIR – This is used to set what directory the commands should be run from.

- ENTRYPOINT – This sets the directory you want to execute the command from.

- CMD – This is the command to execute when running `docker run` on your container.

We have already used the `docker run` throughout the book to run applications earlier in the book like emqtt, postgres, and so on. This will be how we execute our rust microservices for local docker testing.

Creating Our Own Containers

The previous was to give you a bit of an understanding of how Docker works and what we are trying to accomplish using layering of images. We will have three microservices that we will have to add docker images for. Before we do that, let's see the basics of implementing the base images we mentioned earlier. To test this, we are going to use a basic hello world application, literally what is created when we type `cargo new basic`, to create and test a basic hello world.

We know how to build an application using `cargo build`; however, that just compiles the application and then requires `cargo run` after. This is not what you'd want to do in a production environment. In fact, in a production environment, we'd want to also remove all the source code after, so that in case your containers were to get compromised, hackers would haven't access to the source. Cargo provides an added flag that allows us to compile all the applications down to one file, a release file. The flag is `--release`; in Listing 7-3, we use the `--release` flag to build our basic application.

Listing 7-3. The output from building with `cargo build --release`

```
➜ cargo build --release
   Compiling basic v0.1.0 (/Users/joseph/Library/Mobile Documents/
   com~apple~CloudDocs/work/rust-iot/code/ch07/basic)
    Finished release [optimized] target(s) in 9.57s

➜ ls -al target/release/basic
-rwxr-xr-x  2 joseph  staff  273360 Sep  2 15:10 target/release/basic
```

Here we have a release we can run and create. So let's use what we've learned to create our first dockerfile. In Listing 7-4, we have our first release that we build this small example application. We execute this code with `docker build -t basic_run -f Dockerfile.run .` where `Dockerfile.run` is the name of that dockerfile.

Listing 7-4. Dockerfile that builds a basic rust application that is executable

```
#  docker build -t basic_run -f Dockerfile.run . ①

FROM rust:1.37.0-slim ②

COPY ./ ./ ③

RUN cargo build --release ④

RUN rm -rf src ⑤

CMD ["./target/release/basic"]
```

    ① Use the slim down rust image as a base image that will allow us to compile rust.

    ② Copy our local code into the container.

③   Build a release for the container.

④   Remove the source code from the image.

⑤   Execute the release when running docker run.

This is a pretty straightforward set of commands; to get a better understanding, let's look at the output from running this in Listing 7-5 and walk through it a bit.

Listing 7-5. Executing the build for the dockerfile

```
➜ docker build -t basic_run -f Dockerfile.run .
Sending build context to Docker daemon  8.704kB ①
Step 1/5 : FROM rust:1.37.0-slim
1.37.0-slim: Pulling from library/rust ②
1ab2bdfe9778: Pull complete
c4720cf120d0: Pull complete
Digest: sha256:6033d46860ec7793dabf22dde84ef84692f233e25c2e11e67aca39e7d88b3e03
Status: Downloaded newer image for rust:1.37.0-slim
 ---> 17110364e319
Step 2/5 : COPY ./ ./
 ---> 6e0fdec3bf73
Step 3/5 : RUN cargo build --release
 ---> Running in c3c3d608b02e
   Compiling basic v0.1.0 (/) ③
    Finished release [optimized] target(s) in 1.38s
Removing intermediate container c3c3d608b02e
 ---> 66cc36d9ebbd
Step 4/5 : RUN rm -rf src
 ---> Running in 564723612b30
Removing intermediate container 564723612b30
 ---> d909b7de775d
Step 5/5 : CMD ["./target/release/basic"]
 ---> Running in 693c925a57ba
Removing intermediate container 693c925a57ba
 ---> 4a1e0f6396b0
Successfully built 4a1e0f6396b0
Successfully tagged basic_run:latest
```

① Sends the dockerfile to the docker daemon for parsing and processing.

② Since this is our first time using the `rust:1.37.0-slim`, it pulls the library from docker hub.

③ You will see the output of each step for this is the output you see when we build a release file.

You will also notice at each level there is an image tag; like we discussed, each step creates another layer that can be built up on. This creates a final container of size 1.05 GB. We can also view each of the history of the image with `docker history <image>`.

Scratch Containers

For me this 1.05 GB file is still a bit too big, even for a slim, plus it contains many items we simply don't need to run it. Since this built a rust executable, we not only don't need the source code, we also don't need the rustup or anything else associated with it. Also we were running commands like `rm -rf`, in order to use those it requires a shell. For production, all we really want is an executable against the underlying kernel. For that, we introduce two notions:

- Multi-stage builds

- Scratch containers

The first, multi-stage builds, allows us to have multiple stages of builds inside one dockerfile, and each stage can access the previous if need be, but the artifacts and any files copied aren't by default in the following stages. This allows you to create a separate container to have whatever you need in it to run the application executable.

The second part, scratch containers, are blank containers. We mentioned them a bit earlier; they have no underlying OS; they simply are whatever you decide to copy in there. Let's take those two concepts and redesign our Dockerfile; we have that in Listing 7-6.

Listing 7-6. Dockerfile that builds the application and then copies it to the scratch container

```
#  docker build -t basic_scratch -f Dockerfile.scratch . ①

FROM rust:1.37.0-slim as build

COPY ./ ./

RUN cargo build --release

FROM scratch as release ②

COPY --from=build /target/release/basic .

CMD ["/basic"]
```

① The from looks similar but with the addition of as build, which names the stage of the build.

② Uses the --from to specify the container we are referencing to copy files from it.

This has about everything we had in our first as far as command goes. The difference is though it builds us a final container that we can run and deploy that only contains the basic release file. Because of this, the final image is only 2.47 MB big. Going from 1 GB to roughly 2.5 MB is an exponential size decrease and is amazing. However, there is one minor gotcha; let's now try to run the application created; in Listing 7-7, we have the output.

Listing 7-7. Running the from scratch container dockerfile

```
→ docker run basic

standard_init_linux.go:211: exec user process caused "no such file or directory"
```

This obviously is not the output we desired. The problem is while you don't need rustup or cargo or anything like that to run a release build of a rust application, that doesn't mean you don't need anything. There are C libraries that are required to run and execute rust applications that are installed on most Linux systems, but on a scratch container, they aren't there.

MUSL

This is solved with using musl. Musl was designed as a standard library to be a static linking library specifically to work on Linux kernels. We can turn the static linking on for our build; we then compile our application but targeting a specific system, in this case, x86_64-unknown-linux-musl. When targeted with this system, it will add the musl libraries and compile to target a barebones container. Luckily for us, someone has already created a container that adds in all the musl dependencies and the default target, so all we have to do is change our first FROM and the copy since the release will be compiled to a different location for the musl target. In Listing 7-8, we have our modified from scratch dockerfile.

Listing 7-8. Dockerfile that builds the application and then copies it to the scratch container, that works

```
#  docker build -t basic_scratch2 -f Dockerfile.scratch2 . ①

FROM ekidd/rust-musl-builder:1.34.2 as build

COPY ./ ./

RUN cargo build --release

FROM scratch as release ②

COPY --from=build /home/rust/src/target/x86_64-unknown-linux-musl/release/
basic .

CMD ["/basic"]
```

    ①   We changed to using a different rust image, one that has the musl libraries.

    ②   Modify the target copy from the musl target directory.

The resulting image is only 1.93 MB big, and this one actually executes.

Ignoring Files

Last item on the docket for docker, I want to introduce you to one final file, the .dockerignore. This is actually a somewhat critical file to use. If you recall when we copy the source code over, we were copying over everything in the directory. This includes the .git subdirectories, and our other IntelliJ or other files, but also contains our target directory which locally can be quite big and even deployed if you are running tests first before creating a container will be big. That's where .dockerignore comes into play, allowing us to ignore files for the COPY process, creating a smaller intermediary image and performing faster. In Listing 7-9, I have the .dockerignore we are using for the basic application and our other examples. You can copy and modify it as you need.

Listing 7-9. The .dockerignore file for our application

```
./.gitignore
.git
Dockerfile
README.md
.idea
target
*.iml
```

This was a broad overview of Docker; if you want to learn more, there are many docker books available by Apress, but this should give you the basics to understand the next steps we are taking to build images for our actual application.

Using Docker in Our Applications

Let's circle back to our applications; we have three applications that we need to create docker files for. Each application will have to create a docker image that we can run, deploy to, and test against. We will automate this later in the chapter. But to start, we will create three Dockerfiles:

1. Upload service

2. MQTT service

3. Retrieval service

Each of these is slightly unique in its own right; we've covered the basics so far, so let's start coding them.

Upload Service

We'll start with the upload service; this will be straight out of the playbook we went over just now. In Listing 7-10, we have our dockerfile to create the upload_svc.

Listing 7-10. The Dockerfile for the upload_svc

```
#FROM rust:1.34.0 as build
FROM ekidd/rust-musl-builder:1.34.2 as build

COPY ./ ./

# Fix permissions on source code.
RUN sudo chown -R rust:rust /home/rust

#RUN cargo build --target x86_64-unknown-linux-musl --release
RUN cargo build --release

FROM scratch

COPY --from=build /home/rust/src/target/x86_64-unknown-linux-musl/release/
upload_svc .

EXPOSE 3001

CMD ["/upload_svc"]
```

As you can see, this creates the dockerfile and creates a runnable upload_svc.

The EXPOSE here doesn't actually do anything; it serves more as documentation to tell a user which port they can connect to.

If you recall from previous chapters, we had used clap args crate to set arguments on our application. We used quite a few defaults when creating it before, but now we start to use one to run the application. In particular, we will be updating the RETRIEVAL_URL to point to our retrieval service we will be deploying in the network. In Listing 7-11, we have the run command to test that our application works.

Listing 7-11. Docker run for upload_svc

```
docker run -p 3000:3000 \
    -e RETRIEVAL_URL="http://localhost:3001" \
    --name up_svc --net=iot -d local/upload_svc
```

MQTT Service

Next is the MQTT service; for this, we are going to initially set it up much like we did the previous, but there are two big differences:

1. Cap'n Proto

2. SSL certificates

If you recall from Chapter 5, when using Cap'n Proto, we were required to install the capnproto C++ libraries as well. This was needed to create and compile our Cap'n Proto schema files, so we will need to add this binary and compile it for our application. Also because we are using SSL certificates for our MQTT communication, we are going to bring in a slightly different musl; this one will have OpenSSL with it. In Listing 7-12, we have the docker build with Cap'n Proto.

Listing 7-12. The Dockerfile for the `mqtt_service`

```
## MUSL with OpenSSL ①

FROM ekidd/rust-musl-builder:1.34.2-openssl11 as build

# Fix permissions on source code.
# Also on where we are installing CAPNP
RUN sudo chown -R rust:rust /home/rust

# need to instapp capnp
# Install capnproto 0.6.1 ②

RUN echo "Intalling Cap'n Proto" && \
  cd /tmp && \
  CAPN_PROTO_VERSION=0.7.0 && \
  curl -O "https://capnproto.org/capnproto-c++-$CAPN_PROTO_VERSION.tar.gz" && \
  tar zxf "capnproto-c++-$CAPN_PROTO_VERSION.tar.gz" && \
  cd "capnproto-c++-$CAPN_PROTO_VERSION" && \
  ./configure && \
  make -j6 check && \
  sudo make install && \
  rm -r /tmp/*
```

```
# add the source code for the build
COPY ./ ./

RUN cargo build --release

FROM scratch

COPY --from=build /home/rust/src/target/x86_64-unknown-linux-musl/release/
mqtt_service .

EXPOSE 8883

CMD ["/mqtt_service"]
```

① Using the `rust-musl-builder` with OpenSSL.

② Dynamically pulling the Cap'n Proto and building it in our system to build.

Now we can run this passing in the MQ certs in Listing 7-13 to execute the MQTT service.

Listing 7-13. Docker run for mqtt_svc

```
docker run -p 8883:8883 --name mq_svc --net=iot \
-v ~/book_certs:/etc/ssl/certs/ \
-e ROOT_CA="\/etc\/ssl\/certs\/RootIOTRootCA.pem" \
-e CLIENT_KEY="\/etc\/ssl\/certs\/PiDevice.key" \
-e CLIENT_CRT="\/etc\/ssl\/certs\/PiDevice.pem" \
-d mqtt_svc
```

Retrieval Service

And finally in Listing 7-14, we have the retrieval service; this one is like the MQTT service in that it uses Cap'n Proto, but the SSL need is on the database side, not the MQTT side.

Listing 7-14. The Dockerfile for the `retrieval_svc`

```
#FROM ekidd/rust-musl-builder:1.34.2 as build
#FROM clux/muslrust:1.34.2-stable as build
FROM clux/muslrust:stable as build
```

①

```
RUN apt-get update && apt-get install -y capnproto

COPY ./ ./

RUN cargo build --release

FROM scratch

COPY --from=build /volume/target/x86_64-unknown-linux-musl/release/retrieval_svc.

EXPOSE 3000

CMD ["/retrieval_svc"]
```

① Install the Cap'n Proto files needed for compiling with Cap'n Proto.

This time I used a slightly different dockerfile; the main reason was this seemed to work better with the database, and since it was debian core, I could just do an apt-get of the CapnProto. There is one code change though we had to do to make this work. The diesel required us when using a musl system to bring in an OpenSSL crate. In order to use it, you will have to add the crate openssl = "0.10.24" to your Cargo.toml as well as add extern crate openssl; to the top of your main.rs. However, as you can see in Listing 7-15, this will run the application well.

Listing 7-15. Docker run for retrieval service

```
-e DATABASE_URL="postgres://user:password@localhost:5432/rust-iot-db" \
    -e RETRIEVAL_URL="http://localhost:3000" \
    -d retrieval_svc
```

Now we have all our docker containers built, tagged, and ready for local use in a Kubernetes system.

Deploying with Kubernetes

Handling a few microservices at a time can be troublesome, but handling an entire ecosystem at scale can be downright impossible, especially when you want to deploy to multiple virtual machines in potentially multiple different cloud environments. When you think globally different regions have better support even among the big tiers, the virtual machine support and configuration offered can be different.. This can force you having to create different deployment scripts depending on the regions and platforms you are deploying to. You also may not want to create deployment scripts that lock you into one particular cloud provider, making it much more expensive to switch providers. And this was a problem Google had early on. The solution to this problem of having to manage at scale led to the creation and use of Kubernetes, which is Greek for pilot or helmsman, which also explains its symbol of a steering wheel.

A little history, Google had created a system called Borg to handle the scheduling and launching of applications. After Docker, they decided to take the bits and pieces to work with it and create a system that has become the de facto standard for deploying and managing large-scale applications across companies. And in 2014 taking what Google had learned from Borg and other systems, they released Kubernetes.

Microservices were not as ubiquitous when Kubernetes first started as they are today, but in many ways, Kubernetes was ahead of its time in providing infrastructure that supports it. Or maybe having such an easy method to deploy microservices leads to more use of them.

How Kubernetes Works

If you've never used Kubernetes before, I think it's important that we at least take a peek under the covers of how it works. Kubernetes provides container orchestration along with a way to allow us to have a full-scale system with load balancers and scaling without the need for knowing the custom types and code in different environments; it is a formidable abstraction layer.

Pods

How does it accomplish this? I like to start in reverse with these things. Our goal in the end is to deploy applications to run. From the previous section, we are running our applications in containers, so what we need is a system that can deploy and manage our containers. We will store our docker containers in pods. A pod often contains one container but can have any number of containers associated with it. For example, you could have your container that runs your application, another that runs migration scripts for the database, and yet another that upgrades traffic to https for any incoming and outgoing requests. But in the end, all these containers are on one pod. They share the same IP address and potentially filesystem. A pod looks like Figure 7-6.

Figure 7-6. *Diagram showing the pod architecture*

In a pod, containers can be run sequentially or they can be run at the same time; we will get into those options later. But it's important to remember that while you can run multiple containers in one pod, there is only one unique internally derived IP address for each pod. This means that all containers local to a pod can talk to each other via localhost. Also remember that while we are using docker containers as the container mechanism, Kubernetes supports alternative containers although Docker is still the #1 used container for it. Pods are also given a unique ID. The purpose of the pod is to do our work; many of the other features you will see support how we create them and the routing of them.

It's important to remember here that while a pod can run multiple containers, it's not designed to run multiple instances of the same container simultaneously for the purpose of scale. In other words, we don't use more containers in a pod to scale the system, rather we use more containers to add more functionality. To scale horizontally, we add more pods in the same configuration. These are defined by the amount of replicas.

Pods can be long lasting or short lasting; while they are often available for months or even a year, the nature of them is for them to not be durable. They need to handle downtime, restarts, and destroys. In fact, you will rarely directly create a pod either.

Nodes

Your pods themselves will live in a node with multiple pods all residing on one node. The node is the actual physical or in most cases a virtual machine hardware that runs part of your cluster. To scale horizontally, you add more nodes; to scale vertically, you can add more memory and CPU to an existing node. In fact, later when we go to set up a cloud service, we will choose the amount of nodes we want and the size. Most often in large-scale applications, you will have multiple nodes which will contain any number of pods on them. With pod sets that have multiple instances of the same pod, these may all be on one node or spread out across nodes. Figure 7-7 shows the node along with the pods inside of it.

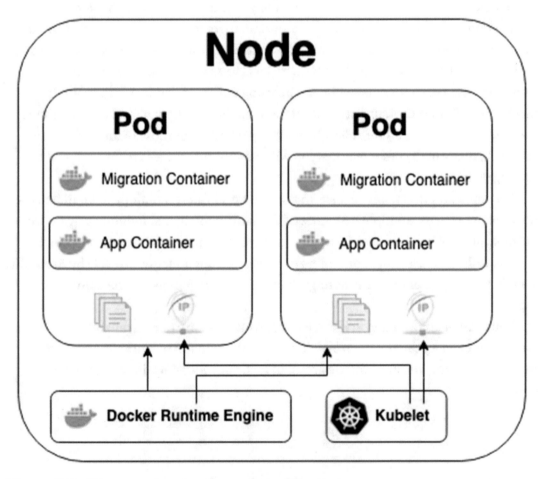

Figure 7-7. *Diagram showing the node architecture*

A node is not just a dumping ground where pods are put; the node itself has to manage the pods. There are a couple processes and applications that help in managing a pod:

1. Kubelet – A background process that runs on the node that manages the pod. The Kubelet is responsible for creating, destroying, and monitoring all the pods and their containers.

2. Container runtime – The runtime that helps the node retrieve the container images to be used to create the pods. This can be configured to be docker or rkt or a few other container types.

3. Proxy – The proxy manager assigns and manages the IP addresses in the node itself. Each node is created with a specific CIDR block that can then determine the range of IP addresses the node can assign to the pod. In most Kubernetes-managed systems, you will never have to set the CIDR block yourself; instead, you manage how many pods you will allow per node. By a default rule, you will have twice as many allowed IPs than you will pods. If you have a 110 maximum pods, you will receive a CIDR block of /24 allowing 256 addresses. The reason for this is when you want to deploy a new set of code to replace an existing, you don't actually just change the pod. You create a new pod; the system verifies the pod comes up and then deletes the old pod. In a worst-case scenario where you update everything at once, it would need twice as many IP addresses as there are pods.

4. cAdvisor – This is not on by default, but it is available as a monitor to collect data about your containers to help determine if they are running, if they are responding. This monitors health and readiness probes on your pods as well as a number of configurable factors to help give you a picture of your network and if there are any issues. Regardless if you use cAdvisor or Prometheus (another monitor), you will want to use something to monitor your infrastructure so you can be reactive in failures and fix any issues before your customers tweet about you.

Nodes are the heart of your Kubernetes-deployed applications, but as I mentioned, you can have more than one node, so there has to be something that sits on top of them.

Control Plane

The control plane is a collection of software that dispatches and controls all the nodes. Whenever you need to make a change to your Kubernetes cluster, you interact with the Kubernetes kube-api-server. The main bridges the control gap between the outside and the nodes. It's made up of four services that help facilitate this:

- kube-apiserver

- etcd

- kube-scheduler

- kube-controller-manager

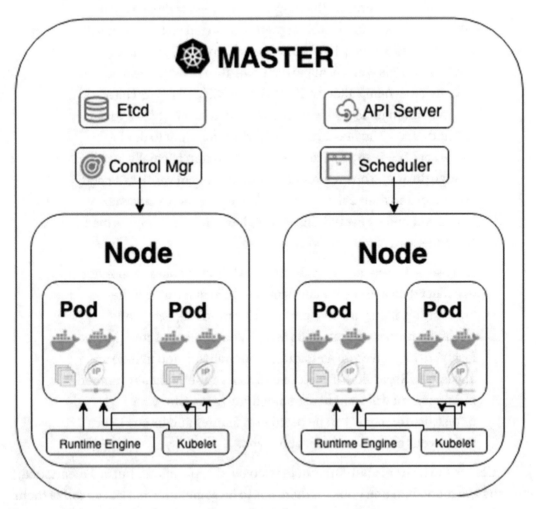

Figure 7-8. *Diagram showing the node architecture*

In Figure 7-8, we diagram the layout of this architecture. When we interact with Kubernetes, we will use an application called kubectl; this application takes in commands and sends them to the kube-apiserver to perform actions. This could range from reading the pods, to configuring the pods, to deleting the pods. This is our main gateway into the system.

The etcd is a distributed key value store that is highly resilient and extremely lightweight and fast. This will store all our configuration data and the current state of the cluster. It's good to back up this data in case of a disaster scenario where your deployed cluster has a catastrophic failure. Having this backed up will reduce your downtime.

The scheduler assigns a worker node for each request to create a new pod. The scheduler takes in multiple factors to balance the distribution across all the nodes in our cluster. The scheduler works in conjunction with the controller manager. Finally, the controller manager runs the controllers. These are processes that manage the pods and the nodes. They make sure that when a request to create a pod is received, its schedule to be created, creates our namespaces, and makes sure all our pods are up and running. In reality, this does quite a bit of heavy lifting.

That is the basic architecture of a Kubernetes system. This also leads to some of the downsides people have with Kubernetes. Suppose you wanted to deploy just one application. This would be quite a bit of work and many services to manage one application, especially if you only had one instance of the application. In addition, when you are buying a cluster from a provider, realize some of that CPU/Ram you have purchased is going to run the Kubernetes cluster, so your applications themselves don't have the full shared power of what you purchased. Hence, you are paying more for this orchestration layer on top.

Generally speaking, in a microservice architecture, I find these problems to not be big though, and in most situations, the pros outweigh the cons in using a containerized orchestrated environment. Now let's take these concepts and deploy our applications to Kubernetes.

Deploying to Kubernetes

We will get into how to deploy to an external managed Kubernetes instance, but for now, we are going to test with Kubernetes locally. There are a variety of options we choose from including Minikube, but the easiest one is to simply use the Kubernetes that is bundled with Docker. Let's make sure you have it on first. On your docker running icon, click preferences and then click Kubernetes. You should see that Kubernetes is enabled and that it is running successfully like in Figure 7-9.

Figure 7-9. *Docker control plane on the Kubernetes tab*

If it's not enabled, enable it; if it is enabled but is not running, try restarting docker or your computer – a very generic solution for sure, but easiest way to debug from a book.

While we will be setting up Kubernetes to run here, please be aware that when you are testing locally, it's still much easier to test against the running docker images locally. This is a bit less overhead and easier to swap out. You do want to keep Kubernetes around to test your deployed infrastructure and any other communication between pods that may need to be tested.

Now that we have Kubernetes set up, let's start using it.

Kubectl

The easiest way to start interacting with Kubernetes is via the command-line tool, kubectl, which is short for Kube Control (and is pronounced that way or sometimes kube cuttle). The kubectl uses certificates stored in the `~/.kube` directory to access various clusters. Let's start by actually downloading and installing Kubernetes. In Listing 7-16, we have the installation for OSX.

Listing 7-16. Installing kubectl on OSX

➜ `brew install kubernetes-cli`

And in Listing 7-17 are the installation steps for Linux.

Listing 7-17. Installing kubectl on Linux

➜ `curl -LO https://storage.googleapis.com/kubernetes-release/release/`
  `` `curl -s https://storage.googleapis.com/kubernetes-release/release/ ``
  `stable.txt`/bin/linux/amd64/kubectl`
➜ `chmod +x ./kubectl`
➜ `sudo mv ./kubectl /usr/local/bin/kubectl`

Now that we have kubectl installed, you can run kubectl version; make sure it is installed correctly and you have an up-to-date version. Also let's make sure the kubectl is pointing to our desktop. In Listing 7-18, we will retrieve all the contexts that have been configured in the `~/.kube/config`; if this is your first time using this application, you probably only have the one.

Listing 7-18. Executing the build for the dockerfile

➜ `kubectl config get-contexts`

CURRENT	NAME	CLUSTER	AUTHINFO	NAMESPACE
*	docker-for-desktop	docker-desktop	docker-desktop	

The name may say docker-desktop or docker-for-desktop; both are the same and are the Kubernetes instance for your docker. If you've used Kubernetes before, you may have other listings; the * indicates which current system you are pointed to. Right now, it should be on docker-for-desktop; if it's not, use the command kubectl config use-context docker-for-desktop to point it to the docker Kubernetes context. We will be using the kubectl for our starting and creating of the files.

Kubernetes Configurations

We now have the tools at our disposal, and we have the background knowledge to understand Kubernetes and have initiated our local cluster. Let's start deploying to the cluster. In this section, we are going to take upload_svc as an example and deploy it to the cluster multiple different ways. This will serve as background knowledge and learning how to design a system. For now, we are going to use smaller examples; in the next section when we use helm, we will dive into full-fledged sets of code with examples. Kubernetes configuration files are yaml files that we spec out what the service needs; the Kubernetes control plane can then parse the yaml to set up our controllers, services, and so on.

While we are going to go over a few of the different kinds for Kubernetes, this is not all of them available, nor are they all the options available for each. We are going to go over what we need to configure the application and only a bit more.

Namespace

The first thing to understand is the idea of namespaces. When deploying microservices, you are more than likely deploying more than one service (like we are doing in our application). But all these microservices are related to deploy for one particular application or piece. At the same time, you may need to deploy multiple applications which contain multiple microservices.

One way of doing this is deploying a different application with multiple microservices to their own cluster. There actually are quite a few advantages in this scenario in terms of segregation of concerns, security, and management. If major work needs to be performed on a cluster, you are only effecting one application. Also assigning memory, CPU limits, and so on is easier.

This all said, this can quickly and easily become a pain. Instead of one cluster to upgrade, you could now have five. Also depending on the size of your applications, this could cost you quite a bit more. What may fit on one medium cluster, you are putting on five smaller ones. In addition, if the clusters need to communicate with each other, this can become more difficult without good site meshing.

Another way of providing this segregation is namespaces. A cluster can have multiple namespaces on it, which allows you to put multiple microservices in one namespace, and you can have multiple namespaces on a cluster. It is also possible to control memory and CPU per namespace as well. We will be using just one namespace for our application.

Let's create an iot namespace; in Listing 7-19, we create the iot namespace.

Listing 7-19. Creating the iot namespace

```
➜ kubectl create ns iot
namespace/iot created
```

Now that the namespace is created, we can start using it with our kubectl commands; for any command we want to use from now on that applies to the namespace, we will use the command kubectl -n iot <command>; go ahead and try kubectl -n iot get pods; it should return nothing since we haven't created any pods yet (these are the same pods we discussed earlier). For brevity sake, whenever I am working on an application, I create an alias for the kubectl command, usually k, and also for the kubectl -n iot command, I will use ki. So, from here on out, all the examples that use ki are referencing a kubectl command for the iot namespace.

Controllers

We have our namespace set up but nothing in the pods yet, and if you recall from what I said earlier, we don't actually create pods on our own; we use controllers to create the pods and manage the pods themselves. There are two types of ways we will create pods, either as Deployments or StatefulSet. Generally speaking, Deployments are used for stateless applications, whereas StatefulSet is used for applications that require state or require specific name and ordering of the pods.

Deployment

Let's start with the easiest type of pods to deploy, the Deployment type. For these examples, we are going to use the upload_svc and test various ways to deploy it, hitting the health endpoint to check and prove that it's up and running. Let's create a deployment that creates stateless pods. We will use the local/upload_svc image we create and will need to define the web port we exposed. In Listing 7-20, we have our deployment spec'd out; we will go over each important line in there.

Listing 7-20. Creating the iot namespace

```
apiVersion: apps/v1 ①
kind: Deployment ②
metadata:
```

```
    name: upload-dep-basic ③
    namespace: iot
spec:
  selector:
    matchLabels: ④
      app: upload-service # has to match .spec.template.metadata.labels
  replicas: 1 ⑤
  template:
    metadata:
      labels: ⑥
        app: upload-service # has to match .spec.selector.matchLabels
    spec:
      terminationGracePeriodSeconds: 10
      containers: ⑦
      - name: upload-service
        image: local/upload_svc:latest ⑧
        # Needed for the docker for desktop use
        # https://github.com/kubernetes/kubernetes/issues/1293#issuecomme
          nt-357326426
        imagePullPolicy: Never ⑨
        ports:
        - containerPort: 3001 ⑩
          name: web
```

①   This is the version of the API we are using; this will differ per the kind of Kubernetes configuration we are using.

②   The kind will tell us what type of Kubernetes configuration we are creating. Since are in a Deployment one, this is Deployment.

③   The metadata allows us to attach labels or annotations to uniquely identify this configuration file.

④   The matchLabels are used to match the configured deployment. We can match them within the configuration, or we can match it to other services that need to reference this deployment.

⑤   The `replicas` tell us how many of the pods we want to create; remember this isn't the pod, just the instructions on how to make the pod.

⑥   The labels here need to match what you wrote in bullet 4, the `.spec.selector.matchLabels`.

⑦   This is the container, the heart of what the application is defining and deploying. You can have only one image per container, although we can have init containers to prep the environments.

⑧   This is the name of the image and its version in the format of `image:version`. Since we didn't specify the version before, we use the latest. This is generally fine for development, but for production, you will want a specific version.

⑨   This is to define when to pull the image; the default is `IfNotPresent`; for us, we want `None` since there is nowhere to pull from since we are using the local docker. If you always want it to pull which you often do in production, you can set it to `Always`.

⑩   The port to expose to the Kubernetes network. This should be the same port we used in our code in the docker image.

This is our basic deployment; in Listing 7-21, we will deploy the deployment which will deploy the pod. We use `ki apply -f <YAML_FILE>` to deploy the deployment. You can then use the command we ran earlier, `ki get pods`, to find all the pods in our namespace.

Listing 7-21. Deploying basic_deploy.yaml, our basic Deployment, and checking the pods are created

```
➜ ki apply -f basic_deploy.yaml ①
deployment.apps/upload-dep-basic created

➜ ki get pods                            ②
NAME                              READY   STATUS            RESTARTS   AGE
upload-dep-basic-8bb5f7cdf-ttcts  0/1     ContainerCreating 0          3s
```

```
➜ ki get pods                                    ③
NAME                                READY   STATUS    RESTARTS   AGE
upload-dep-basic-8bb5f7cdf-ttcts    1/1     Running   0          5s
```

A few takeaways, the creation is pretty straightforward, but then we check the pods. You will notice it does take a few seconds to create the pods and have them ready to access. Also notice the name of the pod is what we defined in `metadata.name` with a random GUID after. The first part of the random GUID is created for the deployment created, and the second set is random for the pods. If one pod is not enough for you, we can create multiple pods; go back to your YAML file and set the replicas line to 2 (`replicas: 2`), and now redeploy the pod configuration: `ki apply -f basic_deploy.yaml`; you will notice it will spin up another pod, and you should see two listed like in Listing 7-22.

Listing 7-22. Deploying two pods for the application

```
 ki get pods
NAME                             READY   STATUS    RESTARTS   AGE
upload-dep-6d989454d9-2p77f      1/1     Running   0          37m
upload-dep-6d989454d9-mt6bk      1/1     Running   0          37m
```

The replicas are part of how we can grow our system horizontally if needed and help to allow higher throughput to our application.

Now remember what I said before; we didn't directly create the pods; we created a deployment which controls the creation of the pods. What happens then if we delete the pod? In Listing 7-23, we delete the pod with the command `kubectl delete pod <pod_name>`, and then right after, we will re-query all the pods.

Listing 7-23. Delete the pods and then re-query for all the pods

```
➜ ki delete pod upload-dep-basic-8bb5f7cdf-ttcts
pod "upload-dep-basic-8bb5f7cdf-ttcts" deleted

➜ ki get pods
NAME                                READY   STATUS    RESTARTS   AGE
upload-dep-basic-8bb5f7cdf-wmbfv    1/1     Running   0          15s
```

As you can see by the ID, the pod we had before was deleted, but then the pod got instantly recreated. This is because the controller is still alive. You can see the controller when you query kubectl get deployment, like we have in Listing 7-24.

Listing 7-24. Query all deployments

➜ ki get deployment

```
NAME                READY     UP-TO-DATE    AVAILABLE    AGE
upload-dep-basic    1/1       1             1            117m
```

This gives us our basic deployment. You will notice the commands for get are repetitive; they are always followed by the kind we are getting. You can use this same pattern for all the different kind we go over. Let's now try to truly delete the deployment; we will use a similar command that we did for the pods. Once we delete the deployment, it should delete all the pods for the deployment as well; in Listing 7-25, we will delete the upload-dep-basic.

Listing 7-25. Delete the upload-dep-basic deployment

➜ ki delete deployment upload-dep-basic
deployment.extensions "upload-dep-basic" deleted

➜ ki get pods
```
NAME                                    READY     STATUS         RESTARTS    AGE
upload-dep-basic-8bb5f7cdf-wmbfv        1/1       Terminating    0           7m6s
```

➜ ki get pods
No resources found.

As you can see, the delete is successful, and the pod will start to terminate and run its shutdown sequence to delete the container and the corresponding pod.

Persistent Volumes

If you recall from our discussions of pods, they have their own file system attached to the pod. And this is large enough for whatever the docker image is defined for. But if you recall for the upload-svc, it is downloading files and needs storage. What's more important is to realize that between pod deletion the files do not persist by default. Anything that exists on the pod will be deleted. What we need is a guaranteed storage mechanism that can also persist between pod creation and deletion.

In order to do this, we are going to use a persistent volume and a persistent volume claim; these two will work hand in hand to set up storage which is permanent that can last beyond the pods. The persistent volume is a declaration of storage being set up that will interact with the kube system it is hosted on. The order in which this gets created looks like Figure 7-10.

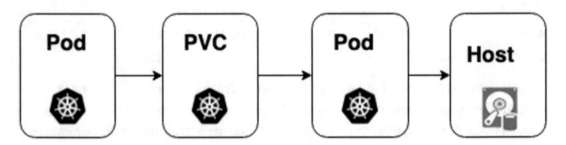

Figure 7-10. *Diagram flow from pod to filesystem*

In some systems, you will have to create it first and then assign the storage to a persistent volume; in others, it will work under the covers. This can also be bound to different types of file systems depending on what type of file system your underlying host virtual machine is, since in the end that is the file system you are writing to. In Listing 7-26, we will define and create our PersistentVolume.

Listing 7-26. Creating the PersistentVolume, in file pvc.yaml

```
apiVersion: v1
kind: PersistentVolume ①
metadata:
  name: upload-iot-volume
  namespace: iot
spec:
  capacity:
    storage: 1Gi ②
  volumeMode: Filesystem
  accessModes:
    - ReadWriteOnce
  storageClassName: manual
  hostPath:
    path: /tmp/iot/download ③
```

① Defining this as a PersistentVolume.

② Defining the storage amount it is allowed to store up to; we will keep this low for development.

③ Defining the location on the file system; I am using the /tmp storage because I want it ephemeral for now.

You can deploy this by typing `ki apply -f pvc.yaml`. If this is successful, you should see an output marking it bound like in Listing 7-27.

Listing 7-27. PersistentVolume successfully bound

```
→ ki get pvc
NAME                       STATUS    VOLUME              CAPACITY  ACCESS MODES
STORAGECLASS     AGE
upload-iot-volume-claim    Bound     upload-iot-volume   1Gi       RWO
manual           3s
```

While the persistent volume creates the volume, the persistent volume claim in Listing 7-28 declares the need for storage. This doesn't necessarily mean there is one but declares the need to get bound and will have to have a status of bound. The way this can be thought of is the same way an asynchronous process like a promise happens. You have a claim for the underlying file system, and it will eventually make sure that item gets bound to a persistent volume filesystem.

Listing 7-28. Creating the PersistentVolumeClaim

```
apiVersion: v1
kind: PersistentVolumeClaim ①
metadata:
  name: upload-iot-volume-claim ②
  namespace: iot
spec:
  accessModes:
      - ReadWriteOnce
  volumeMode: Filesystem
  resources:
    requests:
```

```
    storage: 1Gi
  storageClassName: manual
```

①   Defining this as a PersistentVolumeClaim.

②   The name we will use as a reference when we define this for the deployment.

Once the claim is bound, you will get output similar to Listing 7-29.

Listing 7-29. PersistentVolumeClaim successfully bound

```
➜ ki get pv
NAME                 CAPACITY   ACCESS MODES   RECLAIM POLICY   STATUS
CLAIM                           STORAGECLASS   REASON    AGE
upload-iot-volume  1Gi          RWO                 Retain             Bound         iot/
upload-iot-volume-claim    manual                         8s
```

Let's make use of the persistent volume for our deployment. We add to the spec at the containers level a reference to the pvc we just created. In Listing 7-30, we add the upload-iot-volume-claim to the pvc-data. You will have to delete the deployment and recreate it for the volume to take effect and be attached.

There are many settings like replicas or others you can adjust and redeploy; other settings that are more significant will require you to delete the deployment and recreate the deployment. The documentation on the Kubernetes sites can get into quite a bit more detail on those that we aren't covering.

Listing 7-30. Referencing the PersistentVolumeClaim on the Deployment

```
volumes:
  - name: pvc-data
    persistentVolumeClaim:
      claimName: upload-iot-volume-claim
```

This code should be inserted at the end of the deployment that we created earlier at the same level as - name: upload-service. Once deployed, if you want to see if the volume is attached, we can use another kubectl command to look at the pod in more details. The describe command will show you information about the container including the image deployed, its ID, the IP, the port allocated, and the volumes attached. In Listing 7-31, I've run the command, but for brevity, I am only showing the Volumes section since that's what we are interested in right now.

Listing 7-31. Running describe on the pod created by the deployment

```
➜ ki describe pod upload-dep-6d989454d9-2p77f
Name:               upload-dep-6d989454d9-2p77f
Namespace:          iot
...
Volumes:
  pvc-data:
    Type:           PersistentVolumeClaim (a reference to a
                    PersistentVolumeClaim in the same namespace)
    ClaimName:      upload-iot-volume-claim
    ReadOnly:       false
  default-token-qp2m5:
    Type:           Secret (a volume populated by a Secret)
    SecretName:     default-token-qp2m5
    Optional:       false
...
```

And now we have our persistent volume, the claim, and pvc attached to the pod. There are a few different permutations of the fields you can use, but I wanted to go over one final thing with them. And that is where we set the accessMode; we set this up as ReadWriteOnce. There are three default supported options for this, and we will need to set them to correctly identify what we are trying to do. Let's take a look at what those options are and their meaning in Table 7-1.

Table 7-1. *RESTful endpoints*

Type	Description
ReadWriteOnce	The volume created can be used for read and write purposes by a SINGLE node.
ReadOnlyMany	The volume created can be used for read-only purposes, but can be accessed by MULTIPLE nodes.
ReadWriteMany	The volume created can be used for read and write purposes by MANY nodes.

Now for our situation, we need to have ReadWriteMany if we are going to have more than one pod, and given what the upload_svc does, it will need more than one pod. This can become difficult since many types of disks from cloud providers do not support the ReadWriteMany, for example, Google's GCEPersistentDisk does not. You can find a complete list here: https://kubernetes.io/docs/concepts/storage/persistent-volumes/. What we really need to do is have a PersistentVolumeClaim for each pod created for a deployment; this is not something we easily could code with Deployments though. However, we will be able to do that exact thing when we do StatefulSet.

StatefulSet

StatefulSets are the next type we are going to look at; unlike deployments that should generally remain stateless, the StatefulSet is used for our deployments that need to maintain state or order. State is the ability to store data needed for the application or persistable by the application. This can be for our upload service, or if you wanted to deploy a database which needed to store the data in an area that is persistable and survives, pod restarts.

Order of the pod creation and identify that order matters more with StatefulSet(s). Before when we were creating the deployments, the pods all contained random digits after the pod name; with Stateful, that will not be the case; they will create sequential numbers after the deployment. This means if you were deploying mongo, you would know the primary is the one that ends in -0 and the secondaries are anything that do not end in -0. You can then program the containers to set up variables based on the names of the pods. This all works well for a fully sequential system.

In Listing 7-32, we are creating out StatefulSet for the upload_svc. You will notice that it looks mostly like the Deployment kind we created previously, and for the most part, they do share quite a few attributes.

Listing 7-32. Creating the StatefulSet for upload_svc

```
apiVersion: apps/v1
kind: StatefulSet
metadata:
  ##  Cannot use _ has to be just a dash
  name: upload-ss
  namespace: iot
spec:
  selector:
    matchLabels:
      app: upload-service-ss # has to match .spec.template.metadata.labels
  serviceName: "upload-svc"
```

```
replicas: 2 # by default is 1
template:
  metadata:
    labels:
      app: upload-service-ss # has to match .spec.selector.matchLabels
  spec:
    terminationGracePeriodSeconds: 10
    containers:
    - name: upload-service
      image: local/upload_svc:latest
      # Needed for the docker for desktop use
      # https://github.com/kubernetes/kubernetes/issues/1293#issue
      comment-357326426
      imagePullPolicy: Never
      ports:
      - containerPort: 3001
        name: web
```

This creates our StatefulSet with two pods; much like our deployments, let's take a look at what this looks like. In Listing 7-33, we will run the get pods again.

Listing 7-33. Running get pods for our StatefulSet

```
➜ ki get pods
NAME                         READY     STATUS     RESTARTS    AGE
upload-ss-0                  1/1       Running    0           60s
upload-ss-1                  1/1       Running    0           56s
```

The name is sequential like I promised. Now with the statefulset.yaml as designed, we still have the same issue we had before with no volumes for it. We are going to add a section unique to StatefulSet which is the volumeClaimTemplate, so instead of having to create our own PVC and then attach it in the pod, this will dynamically create a pvc for each deployed pod. In Listing 7-34, we have the spec.volumeClaimTemplate defined after our template for the container. Let's add that to our code and redeploy the StatefulSet; you can simply redeploy like you deployed before ki apply -f statefulset.yaml; it uses the names in the labels to identify the statefulset.

Listing 7-34. The `volumeClaimTemplate` for our `upload_svc` StatefulSet, in statefulset.yaml

```
    volumeMounts:
    - name: upload
      mountPath: /tmp/iot/download
# Creates a new PVC for each one
# Scaling them or deleting a SS wont delete the volumes by default thy
are created
volumeClaimTemplates:
- metadata:
    name: upload
  spec:
    accessModes: [ "ReadWriteOnce" ]
    resources:
      requests:
        storage: 1Gi
```

If we now check our persistent volume claims, we will see two more entries. In Listing 7-35, we re-get the pvc.

Listing 7-35. Running get `pvc` for our PersistentVolumeClaims

```
➜ ki get pvc
NAME                STATUS  VOLUME                                         CAPACITY  ACCESS MODES
STORAGECLASS    AGE
upload-upload-ss-0  Bound   pvc-7f403104-d27a-11e9-aec3-025000000001  1Gi       RWO
hostpath        6m4s
upload-upload-ss-1  Bound   pvc-81a041c4-d27a-11e9-aec3-025000000001  1Gi       RWO
hostpath        6m
```

Now we have the extra pvc to be used by each of the extra pods. One thing to remember, if you decide to delete the `statefulset` later, you will need to manually delete the pvc that was created.

Accessing Deployment and StatefulSets

The question you should be asking about now is how do we access the pod? Right now, the way we have it set up there is no direct way; the pod is running by itself with no route to the pod that you can control as currently configured. But that won't stop us from testing it and testing that individual pod. We can use the Kubernetes api to port forward one of our local ports to a port on a specific pod (either in a local Kubernetes or in the cloud). We use the `port-forward` command to forward from local to remote port on the pod. In Listing 7-36, we forward to the Kubernetes port and then curl to that port. (Note: This was done in two separate terminal windows since the `port-forward` is blocking.)

Listing 7-36. Using port-forward to access the pod

```
➜ ki port-forward upload-dep-basic-8bb5f7cdf-c9482 4000:3001 ①
Forwarding from 127.0.0.1:4000 -> 3001
Forwarding from [::1]:4000 -> 3001
Handling connection for 4000

➜ http http://localhost:4000/api/healthz ②
HTTP/1.1 200 OK
Content-Length: 2
Content-Type: text/plain
Date: Sun, 08 Sep 2019 17:41:52 GMT

OK
```

 ①   Here we make the port-forward and you can see each time a connection comes in.

 ②   Making a call as if on localhost to the port.

This allows us to test our deployed pods, to make sure they are working, performing as expected. But obviously, we still can't access them from the outside world. And in fact when we have multiple pods, how do we know which one to target? This only targets one pod at a time, which can be useful for debugging or testing purposes. Often when testing a local application, I will use port-forwarding if the instance needs to interact with a service in dev or qa.

Logging

We can also view the logs that are generated on individual pods as well. In our preceding statefulset, one of the pods was named `upload-upload-ss-1`; you can run `ki logs upload-upload-ss-1` or `ki logs -f upload-upload-ss-1` if you want the logs to be continuous. We use this often to monitor and troubleshoot. You can do this with production systems as well, but there you usually have an aggregator like splunk instead.

Services

Using `port-forward` is great for testing but is not how we want to expose the application to the outside world. In fact right now, there isn't even a way for pods themselves can communicate with each other since the IP addresses they are assigned to can be changed on pod creation and are only internal IPs. We need to be able to access the pods both from the outside world and internally between pods. To do this, we use the Service kind.

When we define a service, we then define selectors which match the selectors of pods that we have created with deployments and statefulsets. Services use the kube-proxy to route traffic into the correct pods. Every time a service is created, the Kubernetes control plane creates a random port on the local node; this is the proxy port. Any connections that can then be routed to that port can be sent to the service backend. In the end, this allows us to expose a pathway through via the service definitions to the pods.

By default, the mechanism they use to do this is round robin, but there are in fact various modes and various ways we can set the routing. For this book, we are going to go with the most basic (round robin); if you want to read more about the networking possibilities, you can read up on the Kubernetes documentation at `https://kubernetes.io/docs/concepts/services-networking/`.

For now, let's just go over two different types we can create: the cluster IP and the NodePort; both of these examples will use the `Service` kind; they will just differ on the types and options they implement.

Cluster IP

The first type we will look at is the cluster ip. The main goal of the cluster ip is to expose service routes internally for the microservices. If you need your pod to talk to another microservice, you can use the cluster ip to route that traffic internally while still maintaining a load balance and not exposing it externally. In Listing 7-37, we are creating a cluster ip to attach to our statefulset.

Listing 7-37. Using port-forward to access the pod

```
apiVersion: v1
kind: Service
metadata:
  name: upload-svc-service
  namespace: iot
  labels:
```

```
      app: upload_service
spec:
  ports:
    # needs to be the port running on the deployment/SS
  - port: 3001 ①
    name: web
  # Create a cluster IP without an actual IP address for it
  # headless service
  #clusterIP: None
  selector:
    app: upload-service-ss ②
```

① The port we are forwarding the traffic to.

② The selector that matches against the spec.selector.matchLabels
we defined in the StatefulSet.

About the selectors, we only use one for our examples; if you have multiple selector labels, you need to match against all of them. This of course in a big system allows us to be more specific.

Once created, the service upload-svc-service with a dynamic ip address is created; you can see this result in Listing 7-38.

Listing 7-38. Deployed service with a ClusterIP

```
➜ ki get svc
NAME                    TYPE        CLUSTER-IP      EXTERNAL-IP   PORT(S)     AGE
upload-svc-service      ClusterIP   10.108.90.207   <none>        3001/TCP    3s
```

Now the IP address is not going to help you much with a service accessing another service; since if you ever delete the service, a new ip address would be allocated, and you probably don't want to have to redeploy your other apps with the IP address. We can also access this domain internally via a local DNS name. For each service, a DNS A record name will be created in the format <service>.<namespace>.svc.cluster.local using the kube-dns. If you want to use a more standard domain internally, you can run a custom DNS server, but this is usually unnecessary. For our example in order to access, you would use the address upload-svc-service.iot.svc.cluster.local:3001.

This is for internal accessing; however, we can still use port-forwarding on this to test our service access. The port-forwarding will be in the form of svc/<service-name>; in our example, you would call ki port-forward svc/upload-svc-service 3001:3001. Try it locally and use the same call we used earlier.

Headless

Another topic I want to mention is the concept of a headless service. A headless service is one that does not expose an IP and does not use round-robin mechanism. The main purpose of this is for stateful services to access the pods directly. This way, you can use the ordinal number to access the service. This is mostly useful for services that have to specify a primary/secondary relationship in their setups like when configuring a MongoDB stateful service. We won't be using them here, but to configure them, you just need to set the clusterIP: None, and that will be a headless service.

NodePort

Doing the port-forwarding is obviously not ideal; let's go over one way of setting up a service so that we can access it without using a port-forward. The NodePort will expose a static ip on the node bound to the port we define; we can then access that service. In Listing 7-39, we define our NodePort service.

Listing 7-39. Defining a nodeport

```
apiVersion: v1
kind: Service
metadata:
  name: upload-svc-np
  namespace: iot
  labels:
    app: upload_service
spec:
  # Create a cluster IP without an actual IP address for it
  #clusterIP: None
  selector:
    app: upload-service-ss
  type: NodePort ①
  ports:
  # needs to be the port running on the deployment/SS
```

```
- port: 3001
  nodePort: 30001 ②
  targetPort: 3001 ③
```

① Defines the type as NodePort.

② Sets the port on the node we are attaching to.

③ Sets the port we are forwarding to that matches the selector.

Now we are able to access our endpoint without going through the port-forward; in Listing 7-40, we hit the upload-svc endpoint on the statefulset directly.

Listing 7-40. Executing against the node endpoint directly

```
→ http http://localhost:30001/api/healthz
HTTP/1.1 200 OK
Content-Length: 2
Content-Type: text/plain
Date: Mon, 09 Sep 2019 02:07:50 GMT

OK
```

Ingress

NodePorts are great for debugging and development purposes; however, we usually do not use them in production for exposing endpoints. We want to expose into the endpoints one route that can allow a gateway into the system that can then be parsed by host name or url. The easiest way for us to do this is to use an ingress controller; the ingress controller provides a pathway in and then get be pushed from there.

We will create a sample one here; we won't deploy this one right now as this is more for our deployed environment, but we will make more use of it in our helm section. In Listing 7-41, we have the ingress controller for our application.

Listing 7-41. Defining our ingress controller

```
apiVersion: extensions/v1beta1
kind: Ingress
metadata:
  name: ingress-for-rust-iot
```

```
    namespace: iot
spec:
  rules:
  # can have multiple hosts
  - host: www.rust.iot ①
    http:
      paths:
      - path: /api ②
        backend:
          serviceName: upload-svc-service ③
          servicePort: 3001 ④
      - path: /graph ⑤
          backend:
            serviceName: retrieval-svc-service
            servicePort: 3000
    # Can contain multiples
    # kb get pods -o wide --sort-by="{.spec.nodeName}"
```

①   Defines the host name that an external DNS will point to our
    NodePort for this to route requests to.

②   All paths that are /api/* will route to this backend.

③   Defines our service name for the backend.

④   Defines our port on our service for the backend.

⑤   All paths that are /graph will route to this backend.

From here, we will move on to helm; this was a very quick overview of the features of Kubernetes, specifically the features we are going to make use of. The Kubernetes site is VERY well documented, but hopefully this gives you a starting point to examine more when needing to customize.

Helm Charts

In the previous section, we showed how to deploy the application via Kubernetes. This gave us a standard, reproducible way to deploy our application to our clusters (at present we are using just the docker-for-desktop cluster). This, however, was a very manual process where we had to deploy each k8s file. This along the way can create issues:

- How do you manage deployment to different environments?

- How do you dynamically change values in the configuration?

- What happens when you go to a microservice environment?

- How do you initiate rollbacks?

These are all important questions to ask yourself. The first one can easily become cumbersome fast. For development, staging, production, or QA, you will generally have to have different configurations for each. This is often done by creating multiple directories, each with the same files in it.

Oftentimes, things like memory and image location are areas you want to update dynamically, and while you want the event recorded, you may want to do it more across the board to your microservices as opposed to each individual one.

And finally microservices, this is more of a time issue. Imagine you have a system with a dozen or two, let alone hundreds of microservices and want to deploy/redeploy them all. This not only becomes cumbersome to do manually, but what if you forget to do one? That could break your own system. Plus do you really want to create deployment scripts by hand that do each or your Operations owners to run each? Push-button deployments are popular for a good reason, because they increase the safety of your environment.

And finally, one of the most important areas rolls back; if you deploy to production and it causes a failure, you can easily roll back the image, but if more than the image changed, the environment configuration changed and you want that rolled back as well.

What is needed is a deployment package manager, and luckily, we have a solution Helm. Helm is a package manager specifically designed for Kubernetes to make grouping multiple service deployments into one deployable sequence. This will allow us to package our deployments for deploying applications.

What It Does

Helm has two parts to it: a client application and a service running in your Kubernetes deployed environment. The service is used for the client to interact with to know what is deployed and the status of the deployment, whereas the client does much of the heavy lifting of converting our helm marked up Kubernetes files to deployable artifacts and deploying those artifacts. Helm uses Golang style syntax as a markup language with convention style configuration to create scripts and value replacement for the Kubernetes Yaml files.

Aside from allowing services grouped into one deployment, one of the biggest features Helm buys us is allowing us to dynamically allow value replacement for our Kubernetes configurations. Having dynamic values allows us to set field that we can change per deployed environment. A few examples of values you would replace are as follows:

- Image tags – To allow different docker image versions per environment.

- Memory/CPU allocations – To adjust the memory and CPU per environment. Your local and dev environments will likely take less CPU/memory to process. And if you are running in a local VM, you may not have as much memory to use, and if you are deployed, you do not want to overspend for development environments.

- Replicas – Similar to CPU/memory, the amount of pods deployed in production vs. development is usually greatly different. I will say in dev environments, I often still have at least 2–3 replicas running to make sure their services aren't idempotent. This way, we make sure that there isn't a difference calling our application on one running service vs. many.

- Entire Yamls – Since Helm uses actual Golang style syntax, we can write actual coding into our Helm scripts; this includes if statements. This makes it so we can put a giant if statement in a Kubernetes file to declare when it's deployed. This is useful for data services that may be only used in local development.

Installing Helm

To start with, we will need to install helm before we can start running any helm commands. Helm, like many of our other tools, can be installed with homebrew or a various options; in Table 7-2, we have a few different options.

Table 7-2. *Helm installation*

OS	Instructions
OSX	brew install helm
Linux w/ snap	sudo snap install helm --classic
Windows w/ choco	choco install kubernetes-helm
Windows w/ scoop	scoop install helm
Unix misc	$ curl -LO https://git.io/get_helm.sh $ chmod 700 get_helm.sh $ ./get_helm.sh

This will install the client for us and will allow us to make helm calls against our Kubernetes instances. If you are familiar with Helm before 3.0, you also probably remembering having to install tiller on your deployed server. That has been (thankfully) changed in 3.0. We can now move on to using helm.

Creating a Helm Chart

Helm uses a convention over configuration mechanism for defining how to create our helm files and directories. The charts are organized inside of a directory in your project; this can be at the root or in a subdirectory, but you want to give it a meaningful name. For our application, we are going to create a directory of deploy/iot, and this will be where we define our chart, its values, and the templates for the Kubernetes files.

Inside of the helm directory deploy/iot, there will be a few required and optional files/directories; we have that structure in Table 7-3; anything that is a directory will end with /.

Table 7-3. *Chart file structure*

Name	Required	Description
Chart.yaml	Yes	The yaml file containing the details, name, and description of the chart.
values.yaml	Yes	The configuration yaml that will drive the overwritable values we use in our templates.
templates/	Yes	This will contain the Kubernetes templates we will deploy to Kubernetes.
LICENSE	No	The file containing the license for the chart.
README.md	No	A markdown readme file, good for details when deploying to visual repository readers.
charts/	No	Optional directory of extra charts.
requirements.yaml	No	The yaml file that lists our other chart dependencies for our chart (could be items like postgres, etc.).
templates/_helpers.tpl	No	A holder for template helpers that we can reuse across templates.

Let's start with the first file, the Chart.yaml; this is our starting file that defines the name, description, and version for the helm chart. You can define a minimal version of it like we do in Listing 7-42.

Listing 7-42. The Chart.yaml for our iot application

```
apiVersion: v1
appVersion: "1.0"
description: Helm charts for our collection of rust IOT microservices.
name: rust-iot
version: 0.1.0
```

What's in there is a typical set that I try to put in there with a mix of required and optional fields; in Table 7-4, we have a list of the possible fields for the chart.

Table 7-4. *Chart file structure*

Name	Required	Description
apiVersion	Yes	The chart version; always use "v1" until helm has a next version.
name	Yes	Unique name of the chart that will show up in your Kubernetes helm list.
version	Yes	The version for this deployed helm chart; must be in a SemVer format.
appVersion	No	The version of the application contained by the chart.
description	No	A description of the project this helm chart encapsulates.
kubeVersion	No	The Kubernetes version that this helm chart supports; should be in a SemVer range.
keywords	No	A set of keywords that describes the project.
home	No	A URL for the home page of the project, if there is one.
sources	No	A set of URLs for the source code of the project.
maintainers	No	Has three fields beneath it for name/email/url, so one knows who to notify of issues.
engine	No	Name of the template engine; defaults to gotpl.
icon	No	A Url to an icon for the project.
deprecated	No	A true/false boolean if this chart is deprecated; defaults to false.
tillerVersion	No	A SemVer range of the tiller version for the project.

In most cases, I wouldn't use both `appVersion` and `version`, but it can be useful if you are changing the deployed Kubernetes files while not actually changing the deployed application. We have used a subset of those options in the chart; many of those options are more useful when creating charts that are to be publicly exposed vs. a project that is for internal consumption, and this book is targeted more toward an internal application. These values we can use later in our templates.

Templates

Our templates are simply going to be our Kubernetes files that we created earlier, kind of. In that, they will have the structure of Kubernetes but will be able to contain dynamic values inside of it. We will use these dynamic values to be able to easily alter our builds between local, dev, qa, and prod without having to change any of the core features. Our templates can not only contain hard-coded values but can contain objects that can be sourced in three different ways:

1. Release metadata

2. Chart data

3. Values.yaml

Release Metadata

Every time you deploy your helm charts, this is considered a release. You are able to use the metadata of the release to populate the chart; this can be especially useful when creating the name since a name has to be unique across deployed environments and you can tie them to a release. But there is more than just name; there are many other attributes. In Table 7-5, there is a list of those attributes.

Table 7-5. *Release attributes*

Name	Description
Release.Name	The name of the release; this can be a hard-coded value or dynamically generated.
Release.Time	The release time.
Release.Namespace	The namespace for the release to be deployed to.
Release.Service	The name of the service performing the release; in all cases, this is `Tiller`.
Release.Revision	The revision number of the release; this is incremented for each release.
Release.IsUpgrade	Is set to true if the operation is an upgrade or rollback.
Release.IsInstall	Is set to true if it is an initial install.

Items like the `Release.Revision` are set automatically by the system; most of the others you will configure when creating your actual deployment of the chart. We will show how to change those later; for now, realize we can use these as values in our charts to create a unique set.

Chart Data

The items we set earlier in Table 7-5 for the chart, we also can reference those in our templates as well.

Values.yaml

Finally, this truly is the big one, the `values.yaml`; we discussed this briefly when we mentioned it existed in the file structure. This will be our heart and soul for configuration. This will allow us to not only create a configuration but also to be able to dynamically create changes by environment. What kind of changes do you make per environment? Let's think of a few:

- Image repository – While the repository usually stays the same between dev, qa, and prod, you will have a different repository for local vs. deployed.

- Image tag – This is one that will change as you go between environments. Often dev will be latest, whereas your staging and production should be tagged numbers that you know are deployed.

- Resources – How we configure the vertical scaling of memory, cpu, and so on will change between environments depending on the need and the configuration of the cluster.

- Replica sets – How we configure the horizontal scaling. I often recommend at least 2–3 pods for development regardless of need, if you plan to scale. This way, you have an idea if your application works OK with multiple service endpoints or if there is in memory data that may cause issues.

And whatever else you need to configure, these are just a few obvious examples.

Mapping Our Deployments

We mentioned earlier we will have a number of applications to deploy outside of our core applications to the system; we will also use helm charts to deploy those as well. These will all be used either directly or indirectly to support the complete system. We will start with deploying the built-in systems and then move on to our custom systems that we started to work on in the previous sections. We will be deploying our application as one helm chart, but we have a few other things we need to deploy first before we start; in Table 7-6, we have a list of them.

Table 7-6. *Extra helm deployments*

App	Custom Chart	Local Only	Description
Sealed Secrets	No	No	Used to have a mechanism to decrypt secrets that we store into git.
EMQTT	No	No	Used for our EMQTT deployment with secrets.

Dependency Helm Charts

In helm, you can specify dependencies within the helm chart and have those helm charts installed independent. This can be good for development purposes or if you are publishing a framework for consumption (i.e., you are deploying a helm with microservices that use a specific database only for it). However, for our own applications, I prefer to keep them separate. The major reason is that I want to keep my data layers more intact and workable against helm deletes/redeploys. Take our MQTT for example. This interacts also with the Raspberry Pi; we would want to keep it up and running at all times. We wouldn't want its uptime dependent on other deployments. In fact, in a full production system, you could even put the MQTT in its own cluster. But this also depends on the size of your system to weigh the necessity.

Deploy the Extra Charts

We will start off with deploying the dependency charts. These tend to be a bit easier, and we will deploy these here and on the server manually.

EventStore

We used the eventstore earlier to hold our CQRS events that we created dynamically. This needs to be persistable to work through pod and helm redeployments of the main application. We are going to use the helm chart created at `https://github.com/grigorov/eventstore-helm`.

Many of the features we don't need since we specifically do not want this accessible outside of our network. To deploy our helm chart, we will override only a few of the values, specifically disabling the ingress. In Listing 7-43, we have the values we will deploy for the helm chart.

Listing 7-43. The values to override, located in eventstore_values.yaml

```
# This is only used internally
ingress:
  enabled: false
# we don't need a host cause we will use the cluster route

persistence:
  enabled: true
```

In order to use this helm chart, we will have to add it to our helm repo and then install. In Listing 7-44, we add the chart to our home repo.

Listing 7-44. Adding the eventstore home chart to our home repo

➜ helm repo add eventstore https://eventstore.github.io/EventStore.Charts
"eventstore" has been added to your repositories

➜ helm repo update

Now in Listing 7-45 we can install the eventstore into our Kubernetes instance.

Listing 7-45. Installing the eventstore

```
helm upgrade --install --namespace iot cqrs-es -f eventstore_values.yaml
eventstore
```

Eventstore is now installed in our Kubernetes cluster.

EMQX

Next in Listing 7-46, we are going to do something similar for EMQT, by installing the EMQX chart from https://github.com/emqx/emqx-chart. Let's first go over the variables we are overriding. The main set is to turn on the SSL secrets and set the location of the EMQTT certs.

Listing 7-46. The values to override, located in emqtt_values.yaml

```
namespace: iot

image: devrealm/emqtt

persistence:
  enabled: true

emqxConfig:
  EMQ_LISTENER__SSL__EXTERNAL__KEYFILE: "\/etc\/ssl\/certs\/EmqttIot.key"
  EMQ_LISTENER__SSL__EXTERNAL__CERTFILE: "\/etc\/ssl\/certs\/EmqttIot.pem"
  EMQ_LISTENER__SSL__EXTERNAL__CACERTFILE: "\/etc\/ssl\/certs\/RustIOTRootCA.pem"
  EMQ_LISTENER__SSL__EXTERNAL__VERIFY: verify_peer
  EMQ_LISTENER__SSL__EXTERNAL__FAIL_IF_NO_PEER_CERT: true
  EMQ_LOG_LEVEL: debug
  EMQ_ADMIN_PASSWORD: your_password
```

Now in Listing 7-47 let's add the emqx repo, update it, and deploy it using the values for the chart.

Listing 7-47. Installing EMQTT

```
~ ➜ helm repo add emqx https://repos.emqx.io/charts
"emqx" has been added to your repositories

➜ helm repo update

➜ helm install --namespace iot --name my-emqx emqx/emqx
```

Sealed Secrets

We will allow you do the sealed secrets in your time. The point of sealed secrets is to create a secret-based system using public and private keys; that allows us to then check in a secret file that has the encrypted file here. You can also perform this with ejson as well. For information on Sealed Secrets and how to use it, you can go here: `https://github.com/bitnami-labs/sealed-secrets`; the Helm chart is located at `https://github.com/bitnami-labs/sealed-secrets`.

Deploying Our Chart

Deploying our charts is fairly easy once we put them in the right configuration; let's set up the directory structure to mimic what we have earlier. Since we are deploying all our microservices together, let's set up our directory structure with that in mind. Under the `deploy` directory in the root, we are going to create an `iot` directory which will have the typical helm structure, like in Listing 7-48.

Listing 7-48. The directory structure for our IoT deployment

```
/deploy
    /iot
    Chart.yaml
    values.yaml
    /templates
        _helpers.tpl
```

This is a typical, repeatable structure that you will replicate for any other helm charts you want to create. The values.yaml file will be empty for now, until we start adding to the templates. For the Chart.yaml, I have it defined in Listing 7-49.

Listing 7-49. Our Chart.yaml file for the iot project

```
apiVersion: v1
appVersion: "1.0"
description: Helm charts for our collectioThn of rust IOT microservices.
name: rust-iot
version: 0.1.0
```

This is typical structure and only filled out a few fields, but enough for us to get going. The templates directory is empty for now. Let's populate it with some templates that we will fill in later. The following empty template files will be needed to correspond to our services we want to deploy:

- ingress.yaml – The Kubernetes yaml for our ingress controller that will allow our routing into the system

- mqtt_deployment.yaml – The Kubernetes yaml for our MQTT service

- retrieval_deployment.yaml – The Kubernetes yaml for retrieval service that exposes the HTTP port for GraphQL and RESTful endpoints

- retrieval_rpc_deployment.yaml – The Kubernetes yaml for the retrieval service that exposes the RPC that our MQTT interacts with to save to the database

- upload_ss.yaml – The Kubernetes yaml for our StatefulSet upload service

- service.yaml – The Kubernetes service that will expose each of our pods internally

- secret.yaml – The secret file that will contain our certs for the MQTT as well as our database URL for our database passwords

We aren't going to step through all the files; I will have them all in the source documentation, but we will step through most of it though.

Helper File

The helper template is used to create functions that we can use for the rest of our templates. By default, any file that starts with an underscore will be considered a template, but the default is having the _helpers.tpl. We are going to use the helpers for now to create names dynamically that append the chart name to it as well as others that truncate the full name. In Listing 7-50, we have an example of creating a function mqtt.name that takes mqtt and adds the chart name to it. This helps in keeping our services unique across multiple help chart deployments in the same namespace.

Listing 7-50. Portion of the _helpers.tpl outputting the mqtt name

```
{{- define "mqtt.name" -}}
{{- default .Chart.Name "mqtt" | trunc 63 | trimSuffix "-" -}}
{{- end -}}
```

In addition, we can add even more complex functioning inside our template helpers. Let's look at a few calls we can use inside our template:

- if – We will use the if template to designate what parts of the yaml file to display and what parts not to. This is great to activate features.

- printf – The printf outputs dynamic or static variables and text. We can also wrap the output in quotes or binary encoding.

We use these calls in to create a mqtt.fullname function that will output mqtt with the chart and release name and any overridden names in Listing 7-51.

Listing 7-51. Portion of the _helpers.tpl outputting the mqtt full name

```
{{- define "mqtt.fullname" -}}
{{- if .Values.fullnameOverride -}}
{{- .Values.fullnameOverride | trunc 63 | trimSuffix "-" -}}
{{- else -}}
{{- $name := default .Chart.Name "mqtt" .Values.nameOverride -}}
{{- if contains $name .Release.Name -}}
{{- .Release.Name | trunc 63 | trimSuffix "-" -}}
{{- else -}}
{{- printf "%s-%s" .Release.Name $name | trunc 63 | trimSuffix "-" -}}
```

```
{{- end -}}
{{- end -}}
{{- end -}}
```

We will use these templates throughout our Kubernetes templates. You can reference these within the yaml with the call `{{ template <function_name> . }}`. We will use this same pattern for the rest of the microservice names and will use them later on in the following sections.

Secret

Let's move on with the secret service since you will need the secrets in place for our other services to work. We can use the Sealed Secrets to create this file, but for development purposes, we are going to create the secrets ourselves. There are four variables we need to store in the secrets:

- client.crt: – The public cert for our client

- client.key: – The private cert for our client

- root.ca: – The public Root CA

- databaseUrl – The database URL contains the url for the database referenced by the upload service

We are going to create a skeleton for testing with this, which we will only use for dry run testing. The dry run testing refers to running our helm charts to display what the translated Kubernetes code will look like; this is great for testing.

Listing 7-52 has the output of our `secret.yaml` file.

Listing 7-52. The secret.yaml file

```
{{- if .Values.useSecret -}} ①

apiVersion: v1
kind: Secret ②
metadata:
  name: {{ template "iot.fullname" . }} ③
type: Opaque
```

```
data:
  client.crt: {{ printf "DevStuff" | b64enc }} ④
  client.key: {{ printf "DevStuff" | b64enc }}
  root.ca: {{ printf "DevStuff" | b64enc }}
  databaseUrl: {{ printf "DevStuff" | b64enc }}
{{- end -}}
```

① In our values.yaml file, we have the definition of useSecret set initially to true.

② Defines this kind as a Kubernetes Secret.

③ References the function iot.fullname defined in the _helpers.tpl.

④ Prints out "DevStuff" in base64 since that is the opaque type we use for secrets.

This will create a good starting point for testing and for referencing. However, you don't want to check in a secret file with your actual data in it since that would be exposing certificates, URLs, and so on forever in your git repo or history.

For now, what we are going to do is just deploy the secrets ourselves outside of helm. This lets us manage it our own, and these shouldn't change that often or through another process (like using sealed secrets). To deploy it, there is a command line until that allows us to deploy our secrets directly to our Kubernetes system. In Listing 7-53, we create a secret that contains all our secrets needed, three from the file and one from a URL.

Listing 7-53. The command line to create a secret

```
ki create secret generic iot \
--from-literal=databaseUrl=postgres://user:password@localhost:5432/rust-
iot-db \
--from-file=PiDevice.pem=client.crt
--from-file=PiDevice.key=client.key
--from-file=RustIOTRootCA.pem=root.ca
```

You can run this from the directory that contains your certs, and you will have deployed the secret; you can examine it in the Kubernetes by running ki describe secret iot.

Upload Service

We worked with the upload service in our Kubernetes section finally deciding on using and creating a statefulset. We will use this as our basis for our upload service going forward. But we need to add a few items to make it a good template and fully functional:

1. Convert a few of the names to dynamic names.

2. Add Kubernetes labels to our metadata.

3. Add liveness and readiness probes.

4. Add our environmental variables.

Let's convert our selectors to use the template name we created earlier. We are going to use the template we created earlier; in addition, we need to add to our match labels. Since potentially you could release other applications with an upload or if you wanted to release two versions of the same helm chart under different releases. In Listing 7-54, we have a subset of the `upload_ss.yaml` file for our selectors.

Listing 7-54. The selector area of the upload_ss.yaml file

```
selector:
  matchLabels:
    app: {{ template "upload.fullname" . }}
    release: {{ .Release.Name }}
```

Next let's add extra metadata for the labels. These can be used for monitoring and allow more information to know what pod you are using when debugging the pod. In addition, the `app.kubernetes.io` labels are Kubernetes recommended labels.[1] These labels are also used by applications to interact with Kubernetes. In Listing 7-55, we have the labels defined.

Listing 7-55. The metadata label upload_ss.yaml file

```
kind: StatefulSet
metadata:
  name: {{ template "upload.fullname" . }}
  namespace: {{ .Release.Namespace }}
```

---

[1]https://kubernetes.io/docs/concepts/overview/working-with-objects/common-labels/

```
labels:
  app.kubernetes.io/name: {{ include "upload.name" . }}
  app.kubernetes.io/instance: {{ .Release.Name }}
  app.kubernetes.io/version: {{ .Chart.Version | replace "+" "_" }}
  app.kubernetes.io/component: iot
  app.kubernetes.io/part-of: {{ template "upload.name" . }}
  app.kubernetes.io/managed-by: tiller
  helm.sh/chart: {{ .Chart.Name }}-{{ .Chart.Version | replace "+" "_" }}
```

These two sections we will be using in the rest of the templates yaml files; we won't explicitly point it out in the book but will be in the code.

Next let's focus on the container section. In Listing 7-56, we are going to convert our image and policy names to dynamic values, add our liveness and readiness probes, and add env variables we had missing.

Listing 7-56. The container section of the upload_ss.yaml file

```
containers:
- name: upload-service
  image: "{{ .Values.services.upload.image.repository }}:{{ .Values.
  services.upload.image.tag }}" ①
  imagePullPolicy: {{ .Values.services.upload.image.pullPolicy }}
  ports:
  - containerPort: {{ .Values.services.upload.port }} ②
    name: web
  volumeMounts:
  - name: upload
    mountPath: /tmp/iot/download
  env:
  - name: SERVER_ADDR
    value: "{{ .Values.services.upload.host }}" ③
  - name: PORT
    value: "{{ .Values.services.upload.host }}"
  - name: RETRIEVAL_URL
    value: "http://{{ template "retrieval.name" }}.{{ .Release.Name
    space }}.svc.cluster.local:{{ .Values.services.retrieval.port }}" ④
```

```
    livenessProbe: ⑤
      tcpSocket:
        port: web
      initialDelaySeconds: 3
      readinessProbe:
        tcpSocket:
          port: web
        initialDelaySeconds: 3
    resources: ⑥
      {{- toYaml .Values.services.upload.resources | nindent 12 }}
```

① Set the image repository and tag from the `Values.yaml` since these values will be different in local vs. deployed and for environments.

② Use a dynamic container port that we can also use the same value in our services to make it easier to only need to change the port with one setting.

③ Dynamic values for our SERVER_ADDR and PORT.

④ Use the `kube-dns` dns entry that will match the retrieval service.

⑤ Add the liveness and readiness probes that connect to the web container port.

⑥ Dynamically adding resource entries.

The liveness and readiness probes are critical for use for mutual TLS site meshing and monitoring and are another section we will add to all our deployments by default. In this section, I've referenced quite a few different `Values.yaml` references. In Listing 7-57, I have the values we are using for that section.

Listing 7-57. The upload services section of the Values.yaml

```
services:
  upload:
    image:
      repository: local/upload_svc
      tag: latest
      pullPolicy: Never
    replicaCount: 2
```

```
type: ClusterIP
port: 3001
host: 0.0.0.0
resources: {}
```

All of these reference the values we used earlier in the upload_ss.yaml code. Before we move on, let's look at that resources again. In our upload_ss.yaml, you notice we had that as a placeholder. The resources contain our memory, cpu, and so on; this will use our default settings. In the yaml, we listed it as an empty {} block; thus, we aren't adding anything to it. However, if we did want to add to it, we could add to the block mimicking what you'd put in from the standard Kubernetes resources documentation. I've defined in Listing 7-58 an example of what that could look like.

Listing 7-58. The resources section defined with cpu and memories

```
resources:
    limits:
        cpu: 100m
        memory: 100Mi
```

Much of what we have done can be reused and are reused in the retrieval and MQTT service. We will only focus on the differences for the next sections.

Retrieval Service

The retrieval service is a bit unique in our deployments. With the retrieval service, we are deploying the application twice, first for the http endpoint and second for the rpc endpoint. Part of the reason to do this is the ease in scalability. To define two different areas, we will have the HTTP command associated with one port and the RPC associated with another. In Listing 7-59, we have our associations for the HTTP port.

Listing 7-59. The HTTP associations for retrieval service retrieval_deployment.yaml

```
command: ["./retrieval_svc"]
ports:
- name: http
  containerPort: {{ .Values.services.retrieval.port }}
  protocol: TCP
```

Http is the default service that gets ran for our http service; the rpc service was actually created as a subcommand of our service. In Listing 7-60, we have the rpc subcommand onto the RPC service.

Listing 7-60. The RPC associations for retrieval service in `retrieval_rpc_ deployment.yaml`

```
command: ["./retrieval_svc", "--", "rpc"]
ports:
- name: rpc
  containerPort: {{ .Values.services.retrieval.rpc }}
  protocol: TCP
```

In addition, both of these need to have access to the database and will need that `DATABASE_URL` we created in the secrets. In Listing 7-61, we use the `secretKeyRef` to reference that secret and inject it into the environmental variable.

Listing 7-61. The env database reference for `retrieval_rpc_deployment.yaml`

```
- name: DATABASE_URL
  valueFrom:
    secretKeyRef:
      name: {{ template "iot.fullname" . }}
      key: databaseUrl
```

Database Migrations

Database migrations can occur in two ways; one is manually running against the database itself. This is often how DBAs prefer, but it also requires coordination between deployments, and there is no guarantee that the service you deployed is for the database you created.

There is another way, and that is using the diesel migrations we created earlier. If you recall when we ran diesel migrations earlier, we used a `diesel` cli to run the migrations. This poses a few problems for us:

1. The compiled binary we create does not contain the `diesel` cli.

2. The compiled binary also doesn't contain the migration files themselves.

We could solve this by adding both of these things, but then we'd no longer have a small from scratch container. Instead, we will use a diesel_migrations plug-in that will wrap the migration files into our binary and allow us to use a subcommand to run the migration. In Listing 7-62, we have the additional create file that we defined in Cargo.toml.

Listing 7-62. The diesel_migrations in our Cargo.toml

```
# Needed to run diesel migrations
diesel_migrations = "1.4.0"
```

Now let's add the subcommand to the main.rs in Listing 7-63 that will commit those migrations.

Listing 7-63. The diesel migration subcommand in the main.rs

```
#[macro_use] extern crate diesel_migrations;
embed_migrations!("./migrations"); ①

fn subcommand_migrate(database_url: &str) -> MyResult<()> {
    use diesel::pg::PgConnection;
    use diesel::Connection;

    let conn = PgConnection::establish(&database_url)
        .expect(&format!("Error connecting to {}", database_url));

    info!("Running migrations");

    embedded_migrations::run_with_output(&conn, &mut std::io::stdout()) ②
        .chain_err(|| "Error running migrations")?;

    info!("Finished migrations");

    Ok(())
}
```

①   Adds the migrations folder to be included into our binary.

②   Runs the db migrations printing the output for the results; there is also a run(conn) that will run without the output.

Now we have a `retrieval_svc` that can be deployed to our servers and be able to run the migrations; where do we put the migrations before the service starts? We are going to use what is called `initContainers`. The init containers are containers that can run before the main container service starts. We will create one in Listing 7-64 that has an initialization container that runs before the main application that starts up performing the database migrations.

Listing 7-64. The diesel migration subcommand in the `main.rs`

```
initContainers:
- name: retrieval-migration
  image: "{{ .Values.services.retrieval.image.repository }}:{{ .Values.
  services.retrieval.image.tag }}" ①
  imagePullPolicy: {{ .Values.imagePullPolicy }}
  command: ②
  - "retrieval_svc"
  - "--"
  - "migration"
  env:
  - name: DATABASE_URL
    valueFrom:
      secretKeyRef:
        name: {{ template "iot.fullname" . }}
        key: databaseUrl
```

①   Uses the same container that we use for the retrieval service.

②   Runs our subcommand for the migration.

While initContainers do run for each of your pods, database migrations should be written that if they are run twice, you won't have destructive results. You may have an error (i.e., a create for a column that already exists) and that will be fine. But what will mostly likely happen is one container will run it, and the next will notice it's already run (the migration) and won't run it again.

Now we have a complete retrieval service that references the secret `DATABASE_URL`, performs the migrations, and runs for the RPC and HTTP service. Also note we only run this for the HTTP and not the RPC. You could have copied it there, but there is no reason it's fine to have it in just one, since we always deploy these services together because they are in the same chart.

MQTT Service

MQTT is our last microservice we need to configure. This microservice for the most part is like the retrieval service in configuration; the difference this time is the certs – the certs we have stored in the secrets and we need to mount a drive to the application that can referenced the secrets. To mount the secrets, we will define a volume for it, but then define a secret for the volume. Note since this is not an actual mount to a real volume but to the already allocated secrets, we do not have to create a PVC and can keep this as a deployment. Listing 7-65 has the `container` portion of our service with the secrets and referenced items.

Listing 7-65. The container portion of the `mqtt_deployment.yaml`

```
containers:
- name: {{ .Chart.Name }}
  image: "{{ .Values.services.mqtt.image.repository }}:{{ .Values.services.
  mqtt.image.tag }}"
  imagePullPolicy: {{ .Values.services.mqtt.image.imagePullPolicy }}
  command: ["./mqtt_service"]
  ports:
  - name: http
    containerPort: {{ .Values.services.mqtt.port }}
    protocol: TCP
  livenessProbe:
    tcpSocket:
      port: http
    initialDelaySeconds: 3
  readinessProbe:
    tcpSocket:
      port: http
    initialDelaySeconds: 3
  env:
  - name: HTTP_SERVER_ADDR
    value: "{{ .Values.services.mqtt.host }}"
  - name: HTTP_PORT
    value: "{{ .Values.services.mqtt.port }}"
  - name: CLIENT_CRT
```

```
      value: "/etc/secrets/client.crt" ①
    - name: CLIENT_KEY
      value: "/etc/secrets/client.key"
    - name: ROOT_CA
      value: "/etc/secrets/root.ca"
    - name: SERVER_ADDR
      value: "{{ .Values.services.mqtt.host }}"
    - name: PORT
      value: "{{ .Values.services.mqtt.ssl }}"
    - name: RPC_SERVER
      value: "{{ template "retrieval_rpc.name" }}.{{ .Release.Namespace }}.
      svc.cluster.local:{{ .Values.services.retrieval.rpc }}"
    - name: RPC_PORT
      value: "{{ .Values.services.retrieval.rpc }}"
  volumeMounts:
    - mountPath: "/etc/secrets" ②
      name: certs
      readOnly: true
  resources:
    {{- toYaml .Values.services.mqtt.resources | nindent 12 }}
volumes:
- name: certs ③
  secret:
    secretName: {{ template "iot.fullname" . }}
```

① Setting CLIENT_CRT like it was a normally mounted volume using the
   name of the secret as the filename.

② Mounting the certs to a path that we used in our environmental
   variable.

③ The actual mount of the secret we create to cert, which we can then
   reference a volumeMount.

Service

We have all our deployable pods configured; now we need to configure the services that expose each of them. We will have four services exposed. Because the definition of the services is small, we can keep them all in the same file, separating each definition with a --- which will tell the deployer that it's a new kind. All of the services have endpoints that reach the outside world, so we all need to have them accessible. In Listing 7-66, we have the listing for the MQTT service.

Listing 7-66. The MQTT service for the HTTP port on the `service.yaml`

```yaml
apiVersion: v1
kind: Service
metadata:
  name: {{ template "mqtt.fullname" . }}
  labels:
    app.kubernetes.io/name: {{ include "mqtt.name" . }}
    app.kubernetes.io/instance: {{ .Release.Name }}
    app.kubernetes.io/version: {{ .Chart.Version | replace "+" "_" }}
    app.kubernetes.io/component: iot
    app.kubernetes.io/part-of: {{ template "mqtt.name" . }}
    app.kubernetes.io/managed-by: tiller
    helm.sh/chart: {{ .Chart.Name }}-{{ .Chart.Version | replace "+" "_" }}
spec:
  type: {{ .Values.services.mqtt.type }}
  ports:
  - port: {{ .Values.services.mqtt.port }}
    targetPort: http
    protocol: TCP
    name: http
  selector:
    app: {{ template "mqtt.fullname" . }}
    release: {{ .Release.Name }}
```

There is not a large amount of customizations for this; about the only thing you could want to customize is if you wanted to use a NodePort for development vs. a ClusterIP, then you would have added if statements there.

Ingress

Finally, the last part of our equation is the ingress controller. For our ingress, we are forwarding to three endpoints:

- Retrieval service GraphQL endpoint

- MQTT HTTP endpoint

- Upload service endpoint

Remember the RPC endpoint is only routed internally so we don't need to define that in the ingress. Our ingress controller with the endpoint definitions is in Listing 7-67.

Listing 7-67. The MQTT service for the HTTP port on the `service.yaml`

```yaml
{{- if .Values.ingress.enabled -}}

apiVersion: extensions/v1beta1
kind: Ingress
metadata:
  name: {{ template "iot.name" . }}
  namespace: {{ .Release.Namespace }}
  labels:
    app.kubernetes.io/name: {{ template "iot.name" . }}
    app.kubernetes.io/instance: {{ .Release.Name }}
    app.kubernetes.io/version: {{ .Chart.Version | replace "+" "_" }}
    app.kubernetes.io/component: iot
    app.kubernetes.io/part-of: {{ template "iot.name" . }}
    helm.sh/chart: {{ .Chart.Name }}-{{ .Chart.Version | replace "+" "_" }}
    app.kubernetes.io/managed-by: tiller
spec:
  rules:
  - host: {{ .Values.ingress.host }}
    http:
      paths:
      - path: /apim ①
        backend:
          serviceName: {{ template "mqtt.fullname" . }}
          servicePort: {{ .Values.services.mqtt.port }}
```

```
  - path: /api ②
    backend:
      serviceName: {{ template "upload.fullname" . }}
      servicePort: {{ .Values.services.upload.port }}
  - path: /graph ③
    backend:
      serviceName: {{ template "retrieval.fullname" . }}
      servicePort: {{ .Values.services.retrieval.port }}
{{- end -}}
```

① MQTT endpoint that is exposed so our IoT devices can access the MQ.

② The API endpoint for creating API calls like uploading files.

③ The GraphQL exposed endpoint for querying comments and videos and updating them.

Some final tips when using Kubernetes and Helm before we move on, when you are confused whether to add or not have quotes – rule of thumb, you don't quote integers, but you ALWAYS should quote strings. With helm, you can always pipe through the quote function to quote them (i.e., `{{ .Values.SomeName | quote`).

Deploying Your Helm Chart

Finally, now that we have our Helm chart created, we can move on with deploying the chart. The charts use the `tiller` application on the server we created earlier to deploy the charts. Deploying the charts with helm will allow us to deploy multiple services at one time and also allow us to roll back the services.

Starting in the `deploy` directory, let's run through a couple commands and options. The first is how to install the chart; there are two options – one is to treat it as a new install and the other is to treat it as an upgrade to an existing install:

- `helm -n iot install iot` – Tells helm to install the `iot` application to the Kubernetes server

- `helm -n iot upgrade --install iot` – Tells helm to upgrade the `iot` application, installing it if it doesn't exist

Let's not run those commands quite yet though; let's first add an option to make it a dry run. You do not want to make such drastic changes without first seeing what your Kubernetes files are going to look like. For that, there is the --dry-run command. When applied, this option will tell us of any error with our helm templates with the creation. (Note: This won't tell us if the Kubernetes file is OK, just that the yaml is properly formatted.) But we can combine that with --debug and get the entire picture of what is going to be deployed. In Listing 7-68, we run the debug and dry run and print out a partial output of the results; the full one would be pages long.

Listing 7-68. The dry run/debug run for our IOT application

```
➜ helm install iot --dry-run --debug ①

[debug] Created tunnel using local port: '52896'

[debug] SERVER: "127.0.0.1:52896"

[debug] Original chart version: ""
[debug] CHART PATH: /~joseph/work/rust-iot/code/full_example_app/deploy/iot

NAME:   tan-joey ②
REVISION: 1
RELEASED: Mon Sep 16 12:12:54 2019
CHART: rust-iot-0.1.0
USER-SUPPLIED VALUES:
{}

COMPUTED VALUES: ③
ingress:
  enabled: true
  host: www.rust.iot
services:
  mqtt:
    host: 0.0.0.0

...


---
# Source: rust_iot/templates/secret.yaml ④
```

```
apiVersion: v1
kind: Secret
metadata:
  name: tan-joey-rust-iot ⑤
type: Opaque
```

① Runs the debug/dry run over the helm charts.

② When the release name is not supplied, creates a dynamic release name.

③ Outputs the values from the Values.yaml.

④ The Kubernetes template file that is being processed.

⑤ One of the values that was computed.

The release name that is created is somewhat interesting and funny; this is created as a combination of an [adjective]-[animal]; the joey here is in reference to the animal, not a nickname for me. Every time you run it, you will get a new unique name; for example, running it again, I got flailing-quetzal.

In Table 7-7, we run through a few more command-line options for helm runs.

Table 7-7. *Helm run options*

Option	Description
--recreate-pods	Instead of just updating the pods, this will recreate the pods. I generally prefer this in development mode. In production, you wouldn't want this as it would cause greater downtime.
--set name=value	If you want to override any of the settings that we defined in the Values. yaml at creation time, you can add multiple of these setters as command-line options.
--namespace [ns]	This will set the namespace to deploy our chart to.

Now we can deploy the application; when you deploy it, you will also see the names of all the pods, services, and so on that are created for it. In Listing 7-69, we deploy the application to docker-for-desktop.

Listing 7-69. Deploy the helm cart to docker-for-desktop

```
→ helm install iot
NAME:   harping-mandrill
LAST DEPLOYED: Mon Sep 16 12:50:15 2019
NAMESPACE: default
STATUS: DEPLOYED

RESOURCES:
==> v1/Deployment
NAME                                READY UP-TO-DATE AVAILABLE AGE
harping-mandrill--retrieval         0/1   1          0         2s
harping-mandrill--retrieval-rpc     0/1   1          0         2s
harping-mandrill-mqtt               0/1   1          0         2s

==> v1/Pod(related)
NAME                                                READY STATUS           RESTARTS  AGE
harping-mandrill--retrieval-6bfff44846-f8qf8        0/1   Init:0/1         0         2s
harping-mandrill--retrieval-rpc-64b9c65f68-dq8fx    0/1   ContainerCreating 0        2s
harping-mandrill--upload-0                          0/1   Pending          0         2s
harping-mandrill-mqtt-58c86c4c55-5zhhn              0/1   ContainerCreating 0        2s

==> v1/Secret
NAME                         TYPE     DATA  AGE
harping-mandrill-rust-iot    Opaque   4     2s

==> v1/Service
NAME                              TYPE       CLUSTER-IP        EXTERNAL-IP  PORT(S)   AGE
harping-mandrill--retrieval       ClusterIP  10.101.89.29      <none>       3000/TCP  2s
harping-mandrill--retrieval-rpc   ClusterIP  10.104.175.80     <none>       5555/TCP  2s
harping-mandrill--upload          ClusterIP  10.101.136.241    <none>       3001/TCP  2s
harping-mandrill-mqtt             ClusterIP  10.106.211.64     <none>       3010/TCP  2s
```

```
==> v1/StatefulSet
NAME                        READY  AGE
harping-mandrill--upload   0/2    2s

==> v1beta1/Ingress
NAME     HOSTS          ADDRESS  PORTS  AGE
rust-iot  www.rust.iot   80       2s
```

You will notice the release name is changed again. If you want to deploy the application with your own release name, you put the name before the directory that contains the charts like `helm install CustomReleaseName iot`.

And finally, you can check on the charts with `helm list`, which gives you the version and the status of the deployment. Note this only tells you if the deployment worked, but not the status of the deployed pods themselves. In Listing 7-70, we list the charts installed.

Listing 7-70. List all the charts installed

```
➜ helm list
NAME                REVISION    UPDATED                   STATUS     CHART
APP VERSION  NAMESPACE
harping-mandrill        1     Mon Sep 16 12:50:15 2019   DEPLOYED   rust-iot-0.1.0
1.0              default
```

Now if you want to delete this chart, you can do so by typing `helm delete harping-mandrill --purge`; the purge in my experience is almost always necessary or the chart won't get fully deleted.

At this point, we now have all our Kubernetes charts made; you can run through and test these locally. Now we just need to deploy this to the managed container system, not on our local computers.

Standing Up the System

We have all the scripts ready and have deployed to our local Kubernetes resources, but this only helps us when running against the localhost. This provides us a great way to test our Kubernetes scripts are working, but once that is verified, we want to deploy externally with Kubernetes using helm charts to a container provider.

For most big and even smaller companies, the standard is to use AWS, Azure, or GCP. All of these services offer a Kubernetes managed service, which will mean that your Kubernetes instance will be up and running once you pay with little to no work from you. And if you are doing this for your company or even small business, this is the obvious option. The prices start at $50/month, and of course, the sky is the limit. But they do allow ease to replicate across regions and areas.

Another option is to still use one of the big three, but set up your own Kubernetes system on a smaller instance. The reason behind this is simply cost; you can get a micro instance for about $10/month on AWS so the savings for the cloud-managed system is great. However, this means you will have to set up your own control plane as well as the replica nodes and also your own etcd and load balancers. Kubeadm is one of the most common tools to use for it, and you can find instructions for it on the Kubernetes site (`https://kubernetes.io/docs/setup/production-environment/tools/kubeadm/install-kubeadm/`). You can even use this to run Kubernetes off a Raspberry Pi or other mini server in your house and is not a bad option for learning how Kubernetes works and not thinking of it just as a black box. However, this is a Kubernetes section in a book and not a Kubernetes book, so we aren't going to do that.

What we want is managed Kubernetes like with the big companies, but not pay for the big companies. One option you have is to sign up for a trial account with GCP; they will give you a nice credit, but that won't last. Now we are going to use a smaller provider that still provides 99.99% uptimes. There are many smaller companies that provide a managed Kubernetes at a lower cost; the one I'm picking for the book is DigitalOcean (`www.digitalocean.com`). You can of course use whichever one you choose, but the examples on how to set up and deploy to will be via DigitalOcean.

We will actually go back to using AWS later in this book for our lambda deployments of Alexa services, but that's later. In that case, I would have liked to have stayed with AWS, but let's be economical here.

DigitalOcean

The #1 reason we are using DigitalOcean for our examples is price. At the time of the writing, the price to use DigitalOcean is $10 for one CPU with 2 GB of memory and 50 GB of disk. Minimal configuration is one node, but having at least two is much more preferred. In addition, if we want a managed Postgres database, that's $15/month for 1 GB Ram, one CPU, and 10 GB of disk. A managed database is always preferred for reliability and scalability. For development purposes, you can always skip that part and deploy a Postgres instance directly to your cluster.

In this section, we are going to take the Kubernetes and helm scripts we created early, set up the cluster in DigitalOcean, and deploy the cluster to Kubernetes.

This was created in the Fall of 2019, so the page could change when you actually read this book. But it should be similar.

The first step is simple; go to `www.digitalocean.com` and log in. You can log in with your Google account or your own account, but log in. Once you log in, you will be promoted with a screen like in Figure 7-11. Click the Kubernetes link on the left.

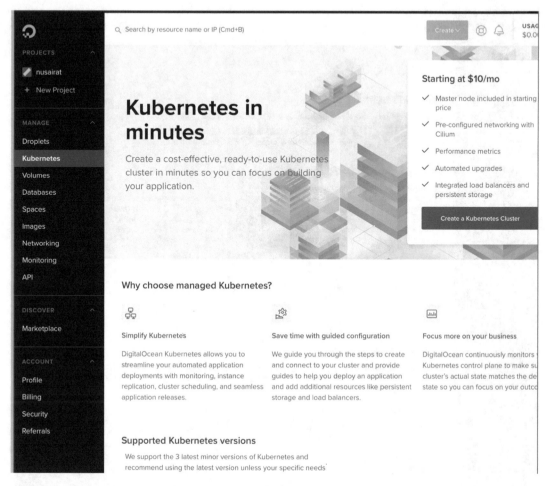

Figure 7-11. *DigitalOcean initial setup page*

Once on this page, click the `Create` link at the top; this will start our Kubernetes node creation. Once you have done that, you will see Figure 7-12.

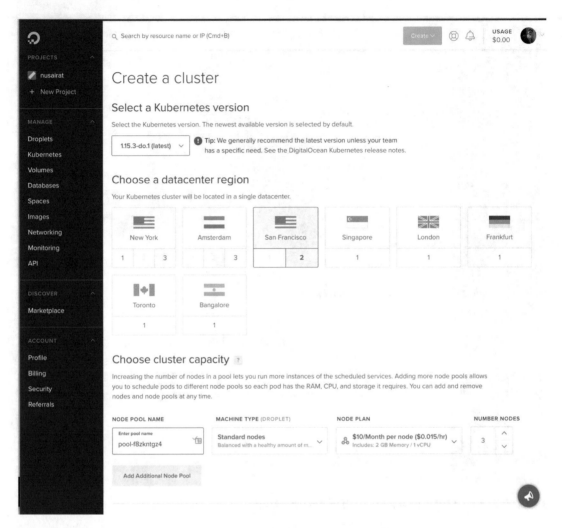

Figure 7-12. *DigitalOcean selecting data center and pools*

In here we will select the latest Kubernetes version, followed by selecting your region. This region should be where you are targeting your application, or for me, I just picked closest to where I lived, San Francisco. For now, you can select the cheapest plan and select 1 or 2 nodes. Enter a `NODE POOL NAME`; this should be something specific for our application; I choose `rust-iot-cluster` and hit Create Cluster. You will then be taken to a page that is in Figure 7-13.

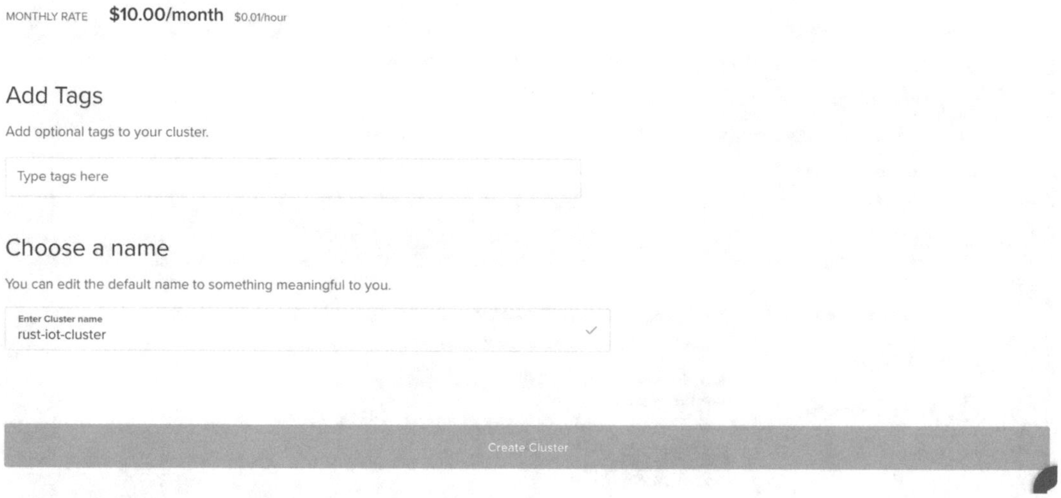

MONTHLY RATE   **$10.00/month** $0.01/hour

Add Tags

Add optional tags to your cluster.

Type tags here

Choose a name

You can edit the default name to something meaningful to you.

Enter Cluster name
rust-iot-cluster

Create Cluster

Figure 7-13. *Setting the name for your cluster*

You can verify your name and hit Continue; this will then take a bit as it spins up a virtual machine; creates the Kubernetes control plane, kube-proxy, and so on; and spins up the cluster. In Figure 7-14, you keep clicking the Continue.

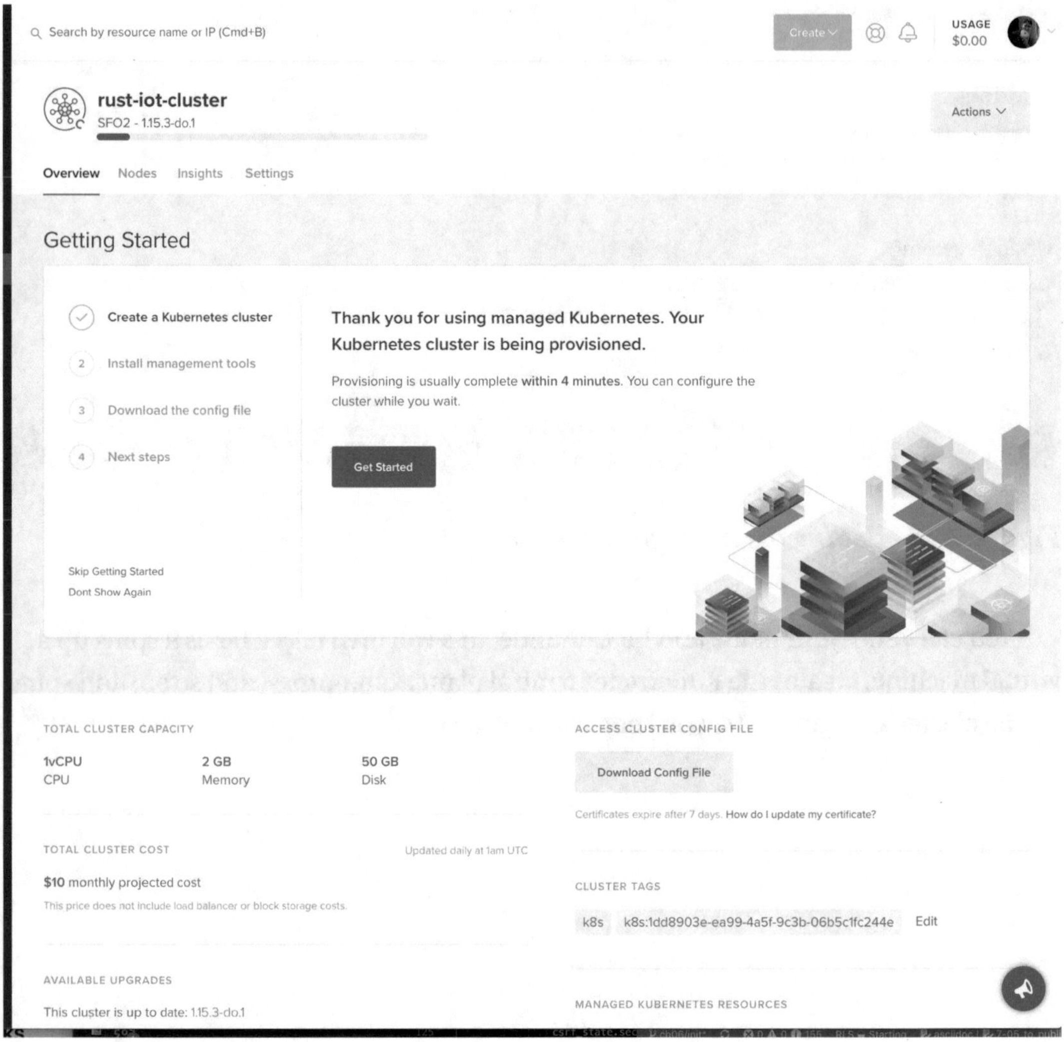

Figure 7-14. *Cluster initially created*

Eventually, you will get to step 3 that is reflected in Figure 7-15. This is an important page as it will give us our Kubernetes config file that we need to download and install to deploy Kubernetes and to use it in our CI/CD pipelines. Hit Continue and retrieve the file. This config expires in a month, so it will need to be rotated. You can always log back onto your application later to retrieve it if necessary.

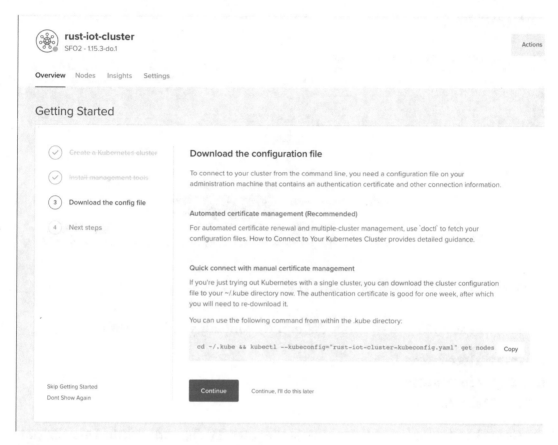

Figure 7-15. *Download the Kubernetes configuration file*

Register Your Domain

Finally, we need to tie a domain to our application. You can use whatever site including digitalocean to register your domain; I tend to keep all my domains on dnsimple.com; my instructions thus will be based on using it. For our application, I am registering rustfortheiot.xyz; the reason I picked xyz was because it was fairly inexpensive.

Inside of the DigitalOcean application, you need to add the domain; in Figure 7-16, it shows clicking the Domains tab and adding our new domain to the existing project.

Networking

Domains   Floating IPs   Load Balancers   Firewalls   PTR records

Figure 7-16. *Add the domain to the system*

From there, it will give you three dns entries to modify your setup with:

```
ns1.digitalocean.com
ns2.digitalocean.com
ns3.digitalocean.com
```

Go back to `dnsimple` or whatever other site you are using and click the Domain; you should see a page like in Figure 7-17.

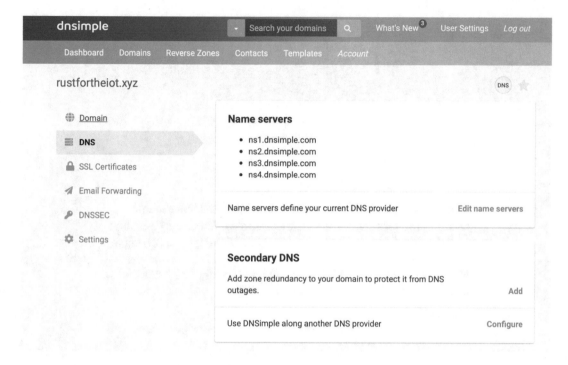

Figure 7-17. *Edit the dns entry for your server*

Click `Edit name servers`, and update the names to reflect the DNS names that digital ocean provided in Figure 7-18.

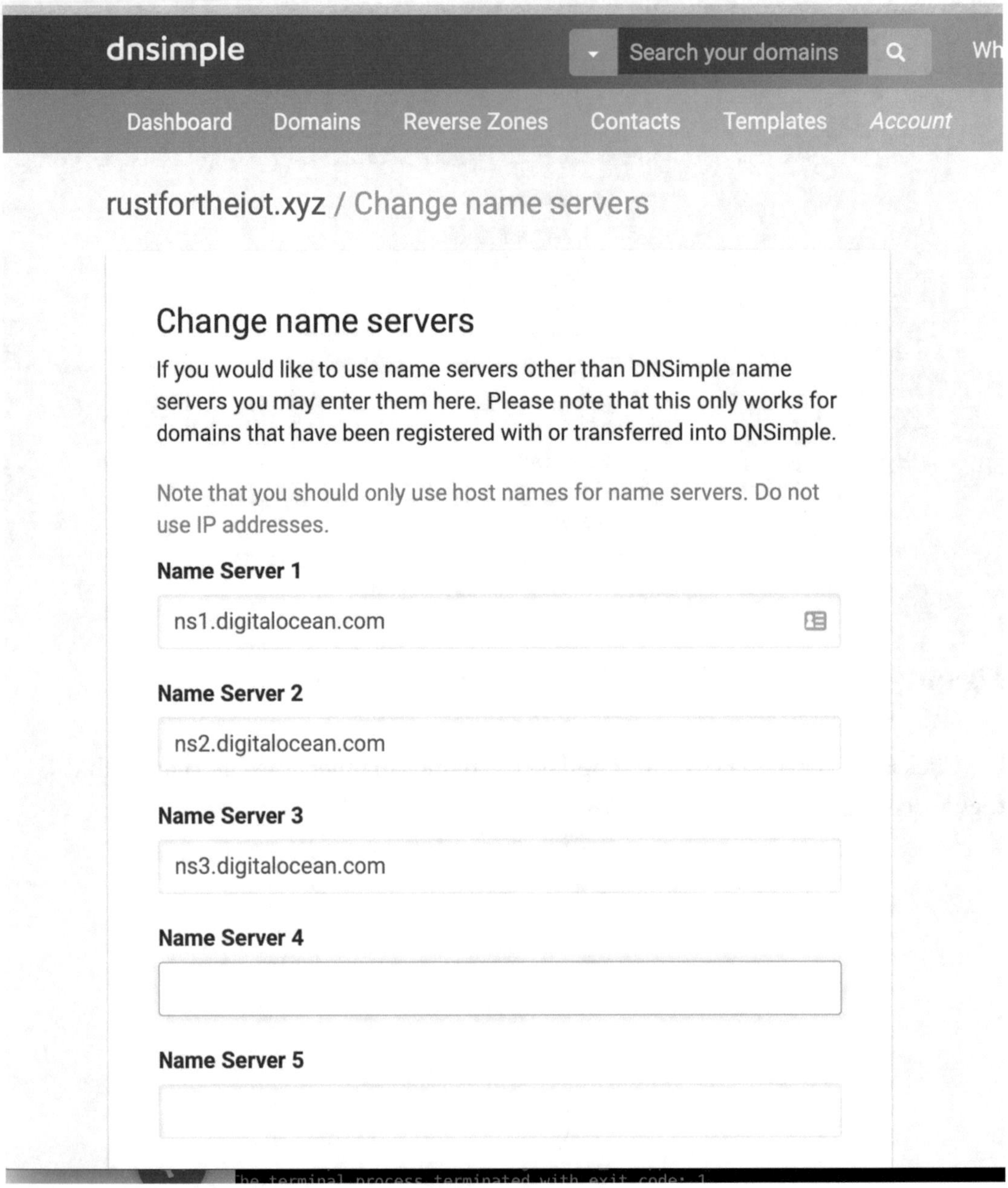

Figure 7-18. *Set the dns entries to digital ocean*

This will now allow our site to be routed to the Kubernetes application we set up. Now you have everything set up and are ready to start deploying to DigitalOcean servers.

Attaching to DigitalOcean Kubernetes

Before we set up and automate the process via Gitlab, we should test locally; in addition, we are going to need to locally check the Kubernetes instance, read log files, and respond to errors caused by outages. The CI/CD pipeline helps us but isn't everything either.

To start, let's take that kubeconfig you downloaded earlier; for me, the name was `rust-iot-cluster-kubeconfig.yaml`; the following data will assume you have that file in your home directory and are in it. The first step is let's make sure the config file works and you have a connection; in Listing 7-71, we make a connection to the cluster to retrieve the pods.

Listing 7-71. Retrieve the pods for our DigitalOcean cluster

```
➙ k get pods --kubeconfig=rust-iot-cluster-kubeconfig.yaml ①
No resources found.
```

    ①   Calling get pods passing in the kubeconfig for our downloaded file.

This results in `No Resources found`, which is expected since we haven't deployed anything to it yet. If instead you get an error like `Unable to connect to the server: x509: cannot validate certificate...`, this indicates either you can't reach the server or invalid certificate. If this happens, make sure you have the right file or try and download it again. Without passing in a namespace, this defaults to the `default` namespace; try that command again with `k get pods -n kube-system`; you will receive results like in Listing 7-72.

Listing 7-72. Retrieve the pods for our kube-system in DigitalOcean cluster

```
➙ k get pods --kubeconfig=rust-iot-cluster-kubeconfig.yaml -n kube-system
```

NAME	READY	STATUS	RESTARTS	AGE
cilium-operator-b8c856758-8lv6m	1/1	Running	2	15d
cilium-zl6zk	1/1	Running	0	15d
coredns-9d6bf9876-2lnzg	1/1	Running	0	15d
coredns-9d6bf9876-gn5ts	1/1	Running	0	15d
csi-do-node-k2mdn	2/2	Running	0	15d
do-node-agent-rczpw	1/1	Running	0	15d
kube-proxy-ltmjz	1/1	Running	0	15d

These are all our kube-system files that were automatically generated. Now we don't want to add kubeconfig every time we call the app we want to be able to simply switch contexts when need be. Let's add to our existing config. The kubectl will look at the environmental variable KUBECONFIG for the location of the config files by default; if that's not populated, it will look at ~/.kube/config. What we need to do is overwrite that config. This is actually pretty simple. We can configure the KUBECONFIG like you would a PATH variable by putting multiple files on it. We can put the current config as well as our new config on there. Then we run a kubectl command that will view the files, merge them, and flatten them into one output. This is what combines the two configs into one config. In Listing 7-73, we do all that and store the results into a new file.

Listing 7-73. Combine our configs and put the result into a new file

```
export KUBECONFIG=~/.kube/config:~/rust-iot-cluster-kubeconfig.yaml
kubectl config view --merge --flatten > ~/.kube/merged_kubeconfig
```

Open up and view the merged_kubeconfig file; it should contain your new cluster from digital ocean as well as the existing docker-for-desktop one. If the file looks right, you can replace your old config with the new one like we do in Listing 7-74.

Listing 7-74. Combine our configs and put the result into a new file

```
mv ~/.kube/config ~/.kube/config.bak ①
mv ~/.kube/merged_kubeconfig ~/.kube/config ②
```

① Always good to back up your existing config.

② Move your merged one into the new one.

Open a new window and you are good to go with testing.

ZSH and other bash shells can modify the prompt to include your git branch, rust version, and even Kubernetes cluster you are using. While the Rust version is not that necessary, I always find it supercritical to have the git branch and the cluster there always. It becomes very useful in preventing you to do something on the wrong cluster and killing something you shouldn't.

We can list out the various contexts and switch between them via the `kubectl` command line. In Listing 7-75, I view the various contexts and switch to our new digital ocean one.

Listing 7-75. Viewing the various contexts and switching to the digital ocean context

```
➜ k config get-contexts ①
CURRENT NAME                     CLUSTER                   AUTHINFO NAMESPACE
        do-sfo2-rust-iot-cluster do-sfo2-rust-iot-cluster  do-sfo2-rust-iot-
                                                           cluster-admin
*       docker-desktop           docker-desktop            docker-desktop

➜ k config use-context do-sfo2-rust-iot-cluster ②
Switched to context "do-sfo2-rust-iot-cluster".

➜ k config get-contexts ③
CURRENT NAME                     CLUSTER                   AUTHINFO NAMESPACE
*       do-sfo2-rust-iot-cluster do-sfo2-rust-iot-cluster  o-sfo2-rust-iot-
                                                           cluster-admin
        docker-desktop           docker-desktop            docker-desktop
```

① Retrieve all the current contexts for the Kubernetes cluster. Note: The current context is our docker-desktop.

② Set the current context to our DigitalOcean cluster.

③ Now the current context is moved to the digital ocean.

Now we will be able to work against our DigitalOcean cluster.

Note   If you have had Kubernetes installed previously and issue running or connecting against the server, you could have different versions of client and server Kubernetes. You can check your version with `kubectl version`. Make sure the major and minor are within one to two versions of age difference.

Deploying to DigitalOcean

At this point, we have options how we deploy. The first is through the local command line like we did for our `docker-for-desktop`, or you can start using the Gitlab CI/CD pipeline. Obviously, the choice is we start using the helm locally and then deploy to Gitlab CI/CD.

In addition, we aren't going attach our Eventstore, mqtt, and postgres to the Gitlab CI/CD.

Setting Up Gitlab CI/CD Pipeline

In the end, there are many ways to deploy your application, with helm chart and docker files though much of the hard part we've already done. This is really the easier part and the one that's most custom based on the user. I will take you through one example of how to do it. This should be seen more as a guide than gospel since it will depend on what you are using.

Deploying our applications is going to involve a two-step process:

1. Create docker images for all our applications.

2. Deploy your helm chart that references those images.

Fairly easy in theory. To run the Gitlab CI/CD pipeline, all you need to start is a `.gitlab-ci.yaml` file located in the root directory of your Gitlab project. In your CI/CD, you will need to define the various stages for the pipeline. For our application, we will have four stages:

- Build MQTT docker image.

- Build upload docker image.

- Build retrieval docker image.

- Deploy helm chart to Kubernetes.

Let's build the skeleton code in Listing 7-76 for the `.gitlab-ci.yaml` that we will add to.

Listing 7-76. Skeleton code for .gitlab-ci.yml

```
stages:
- build-upload
- build-mqtt
- build-retrieval
- deploy

build-mqtt:

build-retrieval:

build-upload:

deploy:
```

Build Docker Images

Let's start with creating the docker images. We need docker to build our docker images, but the Gitlab runners are running in docker, and Gitlab CI are docker containers themselves. Luckily, there is an image we can use called Docker in Docker. Now our stages will be able to have access to docker to build our docker images. To do this, you have to add the docker:dind service; in Listing 7-77, we add the services.

Listing 7-77. Adding the docker in docker to .gitlab-ci.yml

```
# should be docker:latest but can't because of GITLAB reseasons
image: docker:18-git
services:
- docker:18-dind
# - docker:dind
```

This takes care of running docker, but the next question is where to tag and where to push the images to. You have two options. The first is that your Gitlab repo itself has a built-in registry provided by gitlab. This can be useful as an intermediary depot. The second is most managed Kubernetes instances have a repository you can access as well. You can push the image there. The trick is if you push the image to gitlab, it requires no extra security to do because you by default have permissions, but then your DigitalOcean VM will need to have access to the repo, whereas if you push to DigitalOcean repo, you will have to make sure it has permission to push to that repository. In Listing 7-78, we are going to build for MQTT pushing to the gitlab repository.

Listing 7-78. Adding the "build-mqtt" to our .gitlab-ci.yml file

```
build-mqtt:
  stage: build-mqtt
  before_script:
  - cd code/full_example_app/mqtt_service
  - docker login -u $CI_REGISTRY_USER -p $CI_JOB_TOKEN $CI_REGISTRY
  script:
  - docker build -t registry.gitlab.com/nusairat/rust-cookbook/mqtt_service .
  - docker push registry.gitlab.com/nusairat/rust-cookbook/mqtt_service
  tags:
  - docker
```

Here you see build the service and then push the image to the repository; you can repeat this for the other two services till they are complete. If you want to see where the images are located, you can open your Gitlab project and on the side navigation go Packages ➤ Container Registry. For the free accounts, there is a 10 GB limit to the size of the repository. But with scratch images, even if you save quite a few versions, you will be fine.

Deploying the Helm Chart

Finally, we get around to deploying our application via the helm chart. Much how when accessing your Kubernetes instance from your local you need a kube config, you will also need the same for Gitlab. You also (in case of hacking) do not want to deploy your master config file that you downloaded. Instead, we will create a service account that can access the cluster and have `cluster-admin` privileges; at the same time, it also needs to be able to interact with the tiller service. (please note tiller is only required with Helm 2.x and below, if you are using the latest Helm 3.x and above this is not necessary) In Listing 7-79, we will create our service account.

Listing 7-79. Adding a service account to our Kubernetes instance on digital ocean

```
➜ kubectl create serviceaccount --namespace kube-system tiller ①
serviceaccount/tiller created
➜ kubectl create clusterrolebinding tiller-cluster-rule \ ②
        --clusterrole=cluster-admin --serviceaccount=kube-system:tiller
clusterrolebinding.rbac.authorization.k8s.io/tiller-cluster-rule created
➜ helm init --upgrade --service-account tiller ③
```

① Creates the tiller account in the kube-system namespace.

② Defines a role that allows tiller to have access to all the necessary permissions.

③ Installs tiller into that namespace.

Afterward, you can access that service account and retrieve the kubeconfig for it. You will take the contents of that file and store it in our Gitlab. On your menu, if you go to Settings ➤ CI/CD and then expand on variable, you will have an option set like in Figure 7-19.

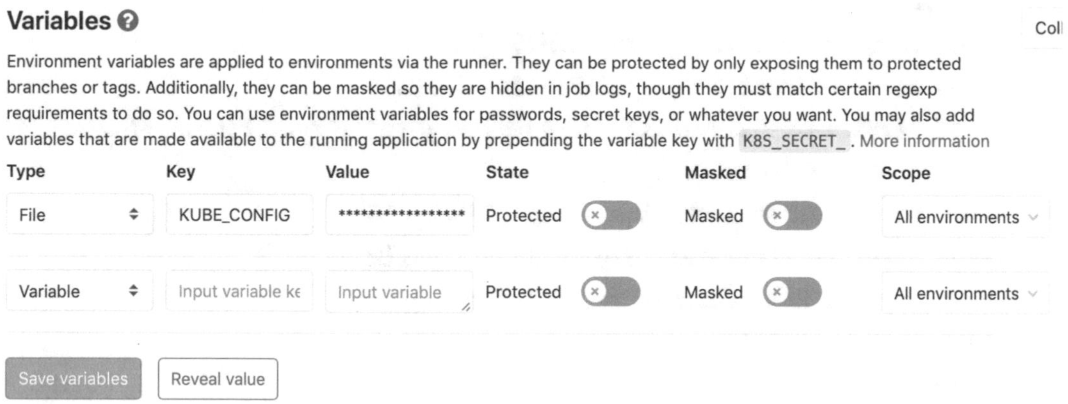

Figure 7-19. *Where to add the kube config*

Here you can add the kubeconfig file; make sure it is not stored in Opaque or you won't be able to view it. With the kube config, we will be able to call helm from our Gitlab instance and deploy the application like we were on our local. In Listing 7-80, we grab the config as an environmental variable, save it to the .kubeconfig, and deploy our application.

Listing 7-80. Adding the "deploy" to our .gitlab-ci.yml file

```
deploy:
  stage: deploy
  before_script:
  - apk add --update curl jq && rm -rf /var/cache/apk/*
  - "echo $KUBE_CONFIG > .kubeconfig"
  - alias helm="docker run -i --rm -v $(pwd):/apps -v $(pwd)/.kubeconfig:/
  root/.kube/config alpine/helm:2.12.3"
```

```
    - helm init --client-only
    script:
    - >-
      helm upgrade --install --recreate-pods
      --set services.upload.image.repository=registry.gitlab.com/nusairat/
        rust-cookbook/upload_svc
      --set services.upload.image.tag=$IMAGE_TAG
      --set services.upload.image.pullPolicy=Always
      --set services.mqtt.image.repository=registry.gitlab.com/nusairat/rust-
        cookbook/mqtt_svc
      --set services.mqtt.image.tag=$IMAGE_TAG
      --set services.mqtt.image.pullPolicy=Always
      --set services.retrieval.image.repository=registry.gitlab.com/nusairat/
        rust-cookbook/retrieval_svc
      --set services.retrieval.image.tag=$IMAGE_TAG
      --set services.retrieval.image.pullPolicy=Always
      --set ingress.host=dev.rustfortheiot.xyz
      --set useSecret=false
      --namespace iot
      backend
      deploy/iot
    environment:
      name: dev
```

You will notice we overwrote many of the variables for our dev instance. The image registry is probably the most obvious since we want to pull it from where our docker builds were pushing it to. In addition, we set the pull policy to Always since we always want to force a pull; this will be good for us in dev mode where our tag is always latest and need to make sure we are always getting the latest one. You can now check in this code, and Gitlab will start running the CI/CD automatically.

And there you have it, our fully functional deployed backend system. We will now use this system going forward to interact with the Raspberry Pi we will start to create in the next chapter.

Summary

This chapter was a very long and encompassing chapter. We covered quite a few topics that often are covered with a few books. However, deployment is a major piece of any application, and I wanted to give you the basis to at least be able to go out and understand more what you read. The Docker + Kubernetes + Helm is heavily used throughout the industry to deploy applications, and Kubernetes support is only growing among cloud providers. This is also our last chapter with a heavy backend focus. Starting next chapter, we will move on to the Raspberry Pi device which will communicate with the cloud. A note about this chapter, much of this was to help you deploying to a cloud for production and other purposes. When completing the next chapters, it is probably easier to just run the three microservices on your laptop/desktop and then have the Pi communicate with them. This makes debugging much easier.

CHAPTER 8

Raspberry Pi

Now that we have all the deployments of our code for the backend cloud services, it's time to dive into the Raspberry Pi (Pi) device itself. This next set of the book will all revolve around coding to the Raspberry Pi device. We will perform a variety of coding tasks on the Raspberry Pi mostly using libraries, some going bare metal. Much of this is to give a glimpse of how we can create a connected environment between device, cloud, and user.

For this first chapter, our major goal is to just get your Pi up and running. Much of the code will be reused from samples from previous chapters. But we will go over enough to make you feel sure-footed and able to run a basic application on the Pi. In this first chapter, we are going to set up the Raspberry Pi in one of the faster ways possible, get it up and running, and then start coding on it. In the last chapter, we will actually optimize this process using buildroot.

Goals

After completing this chapter, we will have the following ready and available:

1. Install Ubuntu Server on our Raspberry Pi and have it working with the local Wi-Fi.

2. A Hello World application that is built targeting the Raspberry Pi and runs on there.

3. The start of the creation of our client application running on the Pi, which we will build up on throughout the rest of the book.

© Joseph Faisal Nusairat 2020
J. F. Nusairat, *Rust for the IoT*, https://doi.org/10.1007/978-1-4842-5860-6_8

Raspberry Pi

Let's start with discussing Raspberry Pi itself and what it is. Raspberry Pis are small single-board devices originally developed in the United Kingdom by the Raspberry Pi Foundation. They first came onto the stage in 2012 and were pretty much an instant hit.

Raspberry Pis filled a void for many different groups. For hobbyist, it was the perfect device due to its small cost but powerful enough you could still easily use it as a small server, serving up microservices or other small stand-alone applications. In fact, when we first started writing this book, we thought of targeting a Raspberry Pi device for the deployment server as opposed to the cloud. There are some secure advantages doing this, since you are inside our own network, which would make it harder to hack. You could do more of your own certificate creations. Then of course, there is the cost you would have the one upfront cost of the Pi and not a monthly cost. In addition to the low cost of the Pis, they can easily be put around the house to perform various functions, often to do with either monitoring or voice interaction, which incidentally are the two items we will be using it for as well.

In addition, they can often serve as prototyping for eventual larger more complex projects. At the car startup I worked, they did just that. When you think about it not only from a cost perspective but time perspective, it makes sense. If you have to prototype, you are going to want the results as fast as possible. In addition, while your hardware team is designing and creating the hardware revisions, you will want to start coding some of the higher-level features as soon as possible. Low-level features may not be compatible depending on what you are doing and the devices you are targeting. But giving you quite a bit of a leg up and in a startup-minded development world, minimizing cost till you get investment is always a good thing.

Let's dive into creating our Raspberry Pi application.

Create Raspberry Pi Image

In the first chapter, we laid out what you needed to purchase to follow along with this book, until this point we haven't used any of the parts. That all changes, so get your Raspberry Pi kit out. In this section, we are going to unbox it, power it up, and install a base software image on it that will connect to the Internet. This should give us the first step in running our applications on the Pi.

Unbox the Raspberry Pi

Assuming you purchased the Raspberry Pi and accessories we linked to in the first chapter or an equivalent, we will now start to unbox and use it. Let's start by reviewing everything we need and will be using throughout the chapter.

Raspberry Pi Kit

The first is the Raspberry Pi kit itself; for this book, we are targeting the Raspberry Pi 4 with built-in Wi-Fi. The processor should be 64-bit architecture, and the speed and and ram of it will vary depending on when you purchased it. But for the examples in the book, I ran it off of a 1.4 GHz processor purchased in 2018. You should be fine along any variant of that. The kit will most likely contain the following:

- The Raspberry Pi board
- Heat sinks + glue (or sticky tape on the sink)
- Power adapter
- Case

Some specifics may vary depending on the actual Amazon kit you buy, and even though I've supplied the URL, the manufacturer may change the specifics. The basics of what was listed earlier will be in all of them though.

As a reminder, the kit can be purchased at `https://amzn.com/B07V5JTMV9` or any equivalent by searching for "Raspberry Pi 4 kit". This will be the board that we run much of the IoT software.

SD Card

A 32 GB SD card comes with the preceding kit. This will be where we store the operating system and the software for running the IoT device as well as storing any data before it reaches the cloud. Raspberry Pis use a microSD card, meaning it won't directly fit into your computer even if it has an SD card slot. But the kit contains a USB adapter to read the card. If you have an SD card slot reader on your computer, it may be easier to use a microSD to SD adapter that you can purchase fairly inexpensively here: `https://amzn.com/B0047WZO0O`.

Debug Cable

Lastly is the debugging cable; this is going to be necessary when we set up the server in the beginning, and it's just a useful tool to have for any debugging later on that is needed. As a reminder, you can purchase this cable at `https://amzn.com/B00QT7LQ88`.

Assembling Raspberry Pi

The Raspberry Pi itself is fairly easy to assemble; take the two heat sinks and they will either have a sticky back tape to pull off or glue in the kit. If there is a sticky back tape, take it off and put it on the two silver chips. If there is glue, you first place the glue on the heat sink and then apply the heat sinks directly to the chips.

Once the heat sinks are attached, we can then put the board in the case and snap the top. This gives us a nice little case without anything exposed and will also minimize our risk of touching the board directly and having a static discharge.

In Figure 8-1, we have the finished product of the Pi 4 board with heat sinks attached.

Figure 8-1. *Shows the board with the heat sinks attached*

Let's take another look at the board; in Figure 8-2, I have an overview picture of the board with various parts on the board labeled. Let's go over what some of those parts are.

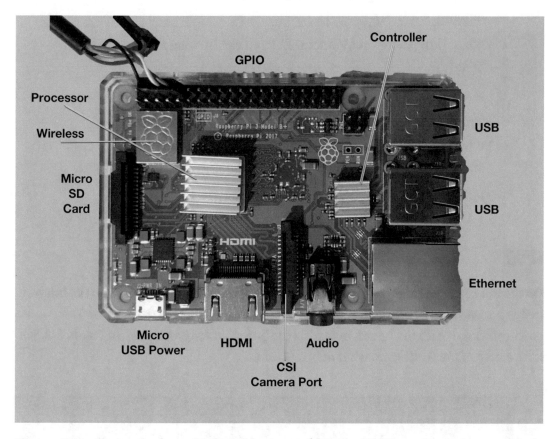

***Figure 8-2.** Shows the board labeled by items (this is a Pi 3 board but close to the 4)*

Let's start on the top and work our way around the board:

- GPIO – Is an 85 mm general-purpose input/output set of integrated circuits that we will use to integrate with the board. These are unused by default, but we can use them to perform interactions with our board.

- Controller – The controller for the USB and Ethernet LAN ports.

- USB – On the side, we have two sets of two USB ports.

- Ethernet – The bottom is our 10/100 Ethernet LAN port.

- Audio – Is a 3.5 mm four-pole video and audio socket.

- CSI camera port – A port we can attach our camera to.

- HDMI – An HDMI port that will allow us to attach the board to a monitor or TV.

- Micro USB power – A 5V micro USB that can be used to power the board.

- MicroSD card – On the underside of the board is where we put the card that we will create in a bit.

- Wireless – The wireless controller for the board. This runs the 2.4 GHz and 5 GHz 802.11 Wireless LAN and Bluetooth-supported controller.

- Processor – The Broadcom BCM283780 Cortex-A57 64-bit SoC 1.4 GHz 1 GB Ram chip.

GPIO

On the top of the board is the GPIO pins, which we will use to interface with the board in this and later chapters. Each of those represents different pins that are used for communication with the board, powering the board, or for grounding. In Figure 8-3, we have a map of the GPIOs and what they represent.

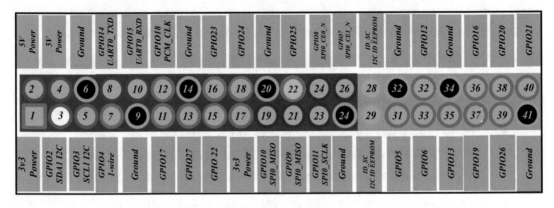

Figure 8-3. *Shows the GPIO layout of the board*

You will notice the number 2 and 4 slots are 5V leads. These can be used to power the peripherals on top or be used to actually power the board from an external source like a USB. Another two interesting slots are the 8 and 10. These are the UART slots. UART stands for Universal Asynchronous Receiver/Transmitter and is used to transmit data between devices. The one lead transmits and the other receives serial data. The data is transmitted asynchronously, so that means there is no clock signal to synchronize with. We don't use these much anymore for modern computers, but they used to be used for mice, printers, and modems before we had USB.

We will use these though for our initial communication with the board before we have our shell ready. At this point, you can attach your USB debug cable to the board. Attach the cables to the following parts:

- Black cable – Is our ground cable and should be plugged into the 6 pin

- White cable – Is our transmitter cable and should be plugged into the 8 pin

- Green cable – Is our receiver cable and should be plugged into the 10 pin

The end result is your cables should look like Figure 8-4.

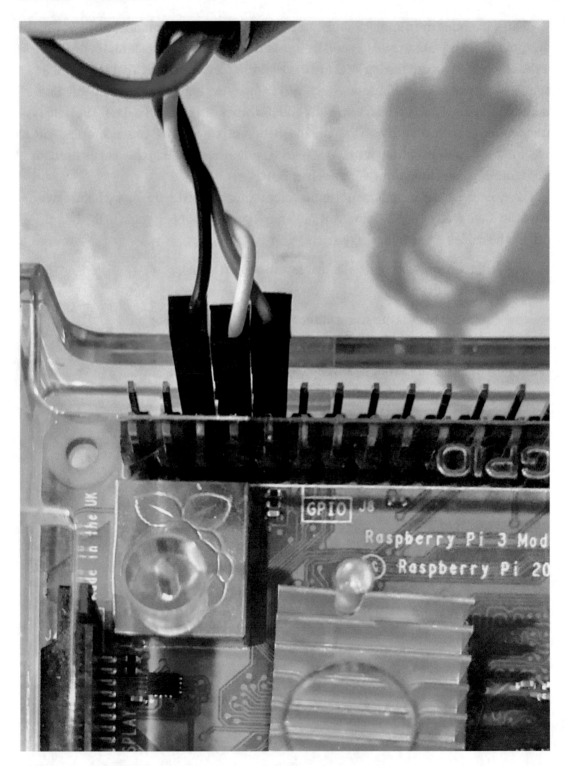

Figure 8-4. Our debug cable attached

You could in addition attach the red cable to the 2 pin, but we are going to just plug the board in since once we get it configured, we won't need to directly attach again, but in theory we could power the board from our computer.

We now have our board all set up and ready to be used; of course, nothing is on it right now, so let's take the microSD card format it and put an operating system on top of it.

OS Software

Let's now get into the nuts and bolts in setting up our Raspberry Pi, getting the operating system software installed. Much like buying your standard desktop computer, there are many variants of operating systems to install. There is the standard Raspbian which is the official operating system for all Raspberry Pis. There is also Mozilla OS, and even Windows has a specialty Windows 10 IoT core dashboard; as you can imagine since you are reading this book, Raspberry Pis are great for IoT devices. We are going to stick with the standard out-of-the-box Raspbian for this application. Performing builds in future chapters is a bit easier using Raspbian as well.

You can view all the possible operating systems you can install at `www.raspberrypi.org/downloads/`. The top of the page has the Raspbian link we are going to select; the output of that page looks like Figure 8-5.

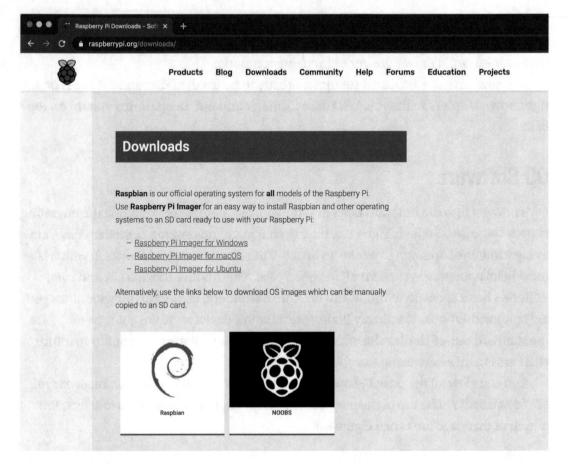

Figure 8-5. *The Raspberry Pi operating system list page*

Go ahead and click "Raspbian" link and scroll down a bit; you will see a screen that looks like Figure 8-6 showing the three different Raspbian versions to select from.

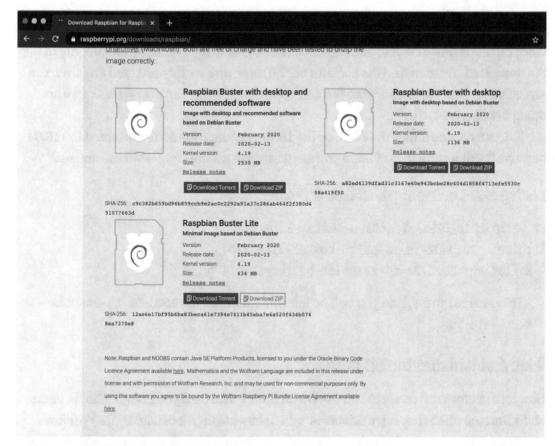

Figure 8-6. *The various Raspbian installs*

Our Pi won't be designed to hook up to a monitor; this is going to run code that we customize for it. For that case, all we need is the "Raspbian Buster Lite" version. Click the Download like for the ZIP version and you should have downloaded a file that looks like `2020-02-13-raspbian-buster-lite.zip`; the exact version may differ based on when you have reached this page. Raspbian is a derivation of the 32-bit Debian operating system, so many of the tools we use on Debian, we will use on Raspbian.

Installing the Software

Once the file is downloaded, we will take it through a few steps:

1. Unzip the compressed image.

2. Wipe our microSD card.

3. Install the image onto our microSD card.

Unpack the File

Once the file is downloaded, you can check the sha256sum to ensure the integrity of the download. You can find the shasum on the same link we downloaded and then run `sha256sum` on the file to verify the file. But assuming it is fine, let's unzip it like we are doing in Listing 8-1.

You can choose either the 18.04 or the 19.10 version; I would recommend the 18.04 because it will ensure the software you are writing to will be supported the longest.

Listing 8-1. Unzipping the Raspbian server

```
→ unzip 2020-02-13-raspbian-buster-lite.zip
Archive:  2020-02-13-raspbian-buster-lite.zip
  inflating: 2020-02-13-raspbian-buster-lite.img
```

This unzips the file, and you will be left with an image file 2020-02-13-raspbian-buster-lite.img.

Wipe and Initialize the SD Card

Now let's get the card ready to run the OS on our Pi. The card you bought should come blank, but too often they have drivers or other software on them usually for Windows computers. We want to blank them out and start fresh. The following code will initialize the disk but is specific for macOS using `diskutil`; the equivalent in Linux will be `fdisk` (with some slightly different options).

Plug in your adapter and your SD card in the adapter. In Listing 8-2, we are going to find where the device is attached to. Now your exact structure may look different than mine, so we will try to find the similarities.

Listing 8-2. Getting the list of disks attached to the computer

```
→ diskutil list
/dev/disk0 (internal, physical):
   #:                     TYPE NAME                  SIZE           IDENTIFIER
   0:     GUID_partition_scheme               *500.3 GB         disk0 ①
   1:               EFI EFI                     314.6 MB         disk0s1
   2:      Apple_APFS Container disk1           500.0 GB         disk0s2
```

```
/dev/disk1 (synthesized):
   #:      TYPE NAME                         SIZE              IDENTIFIER
   0:      APFS Container Scheme -          +500.0 GB            disk1
           Physical Store disk0s2
   1:      APFS Volume Macintosh HD - Data  465.2 GB            disk1s1 ②
   2:      APFS Volume Preboot              104.2 MB            disk1s2
   3:      APFS Volume Recovery             1.0 GB             disk1s3
   4:      APFS Volume VM                   8.6 GB             disk1s4
   5:      APFS Volume Macintosh HD         10.9 GB            disk1s5

/dev/disk2 (disk image):
   #:      TYPE NAME                         SIZE              IDENTIFIER
   0:      GUID_partition_scheme           +2.8 TB              disk2 ③
   1:      EFI EFI                          209.7 MB            disk2s1
   2:      Apple_HFS Time Machine Backups   2.8 TB             disk2s2

/dev/disk4 (external, physical):
   #:      TYPE NAME                         SIZE              IDENTIFIER
   0:      FDisk_partition_scheme          *32.0 GB             disk4 ④
   1:      Windows_FAT_32 system-boot       268.4 MB            disk4s1
   2:      Linux                            31.8 GB            disk4s2
```

① Our main internal disk.

② The disk that contains your hard drive OS and so on.

③ Time Machine drive if you had it attached.

④ The SD card attached.

The contents of the SD card you have will depend on the exact layout of your disk and what's default software is on there. Some come completely blank, and others have initialization software. The most important thing is to identify which disk you have; the last thing you want to do is erase another disk. During this process, I recommend also disconnecting any other external drive so as not to confuse yourself since the next few steps are destructive.

It's somewhat easy to spot the SD card on here by the size; you notice the 128.0 GB which is the size of the SD card I purchased for this. The SD card is on /dev/disk4; you will need this for the rest of the calls we are going to make.

Next, let's erase the SD card and put a FAT32 filesystem on top of it instead. In Listing 8-3, we erase the disk targeting /dev/disk4, installing FAT32 as the file system. Remember this phase permanently erases the data, proceed at caution, and make sure you have the right disk.

Listing 8-3. Erasing the SD card with FAT32 on top

```
➜ diskutil eraseDisk FAT32 EMPTY /dev/disk4
Started erase on disk4
Unmounting disk
Creating the partition map
Waiting for partitions to activate
Formatting disk4s2 as MS-DOS (FAT32) with name EMPTY
512 bytes per physical sector
/dev/rdisk4s2: 249610688 sectors in 3900167 FAT32 clusters (32768 bytes/cluster)
bps=512 spc=64 res=32 nft=2 mid=0xf8 spt=32 hds=255 hid=411648 drv=0x80
bsec=249671680 bspf=30471 rdcl=2 infs=1 bkbs=6
Mounting disk
Finished erase on disk4
```

At this point, the disk is erased and formatted to a FAT32 file system, but the disk is still mounted to our directory structure. We will need to unmount it before we install the image. In Listing 8-4, we unmount the disk.

Listing 8-4. Unmount the disk

```
➜ diskutil unmountDisk /dev/disk4
Unmount of all volumes on disk4 was successful
```

Instructions on Erasing on Linux

The preceding data shows how to perform this operation on the Mac, and the following data will present how to perform this same series but on a Linux box:

- In order to list the disk contents, you will use "fdisk -l" which will list all your disks (we will assume "/dev/disk4" is the location).

- Enter `fdisk /dev/disk4"` to put the console in an interactive mode, selecting "d" to select the partition. You will then be given a list of partitions to delete; if just one, select "1". Keep going through the rest of the partitions till they are all deleted.

- Now we want to create a new partition, type "n" for new and then "p" to create the primary partition. You will have to enter "1" to make this the first partition and hit Enter. After that, it will ask you to set the first and last cylinder; just click Enter to select the defaults. When you are finally done, you will enter "w" to write the new partition to the SD card. At this point, your partition should be ready.

- Type "`unmount /dev/disk4`" to unmount the disk and prepare it for FAT32 creation.

- We will use "`mkfs.vfat`" to make a FAT32 partition. Enter "`mkfs.vfat -F 32 /dev/disk4`" and that will put a FAT32 on your SD card.

Install Image

Finally, let's put the image on our application. In Listing 8-5, we will use the dd command to install the image onto our SD card.

Listing 8-5. Installing the RasPi image onto the card

```
➔ sudo dd bs=4m if=./2020-02-13-raspbian-buster-lite.img of=/dev/disk4
conv=sync
739+1 records in
739+1 records out
3102821376 bytes transferred in 967.374066 secs (3207468 bytes/sec)
```

This will take a little bit of time, so be patient once you hit Enter. Also, depending on if you are using Linux or OSX, there are a few errors you may get; these instructions are for OSX, but a few errors and the resolutions you may find:

- `dd: bs: illegal numeric value` – Adjust your 4m to a smaller value; conversely, one could have a larger value if you get no error. But 4 seemed to be fine for my needs.

- `dd: unknown operand status` – On the 4m, change it to capital M; on Linux it usually wants a capital M and on OSX a lowercase m.

The "conv=sync" at the end is to make sure the writing is absolutely complete and all the buffers flushed. This way, we don't inject the SD card with some writing still occurring. At this point, our card should have the base Pi image on it.

If you look at your list of volumes, you should have one that is called `boot` now. This is where the files the Raspberry Pi will boot from. One that will be of importance to us later is the `config.txt`. We will update it for certain configuration changes later. For now, just put a blank file into the root of the boot volume called `ssh` (`touch /Volumes/boot/ssh` if on a Mac). This file being there will allow us later to be able to ssh into the Pi.

Final Setup Steps

Now that we have our SD card ready, it's time to remove it and insert it into the Pi. The SD card in your computer won't fit, but the microSD card will. Remove it from the SD card, and put it into the slot on the underside of the Pi. Once that's inserted, plug in the power cable to the USB power slot, and you can plug the power cable into the wall at this point too, which is what we have in Figure 8-7.

Figure 8-7. *The microSD card installed into our Raspberry Pi*

We now have our Pi up and running, and if you plugged in an Ethernet cable, it would be attached to the Internet. We could actually log into it that way as well. However, we want it to work on Wi-Fi so we can use it anywhere in the house. Let's take that USB debug cable that's already attached to your Pi and connect it to your computer. This will allow us serial access onto the board. We will need to do a few things to get this serial connector work since by default most apps don't speak serially anymore. We will need a serial terminal app.

1. Determine the serial name for the USB plugged in.

2. Install an application that will allow us virtual terminal access.

Plug the USB cable into your computer; the Pi can be on or off at this point. You will be able to look for all the devices both virtual and connected under the /dev directory, but this one will be tagged as usbserial. We will need to know the device name so that we can tell our application which serial connection to connect to. In Listing 8-6, we do a listing of our directory to find the name of all usbserials.

Listing 8-6. Find the USB serial connector

```
➜ ls -al /dev | grep cu.usbserial
crw-rw-rw-  1 root     wheel        18,  13 Nov  2 18:46 cu.usbserial-14340
```

Assuming you only have one connected, you will only have one entry to contend with. If you get more, disconnect other USB serial devices. Now let's install an application that will let us perform the serial connections. There are two different applications we can install, screen or minicom; for our purposes, let's install screen; you can do this by these:

*   On OSX – brew install screen

*   On Linux – sudo apt-get install screen

We will now connect to the port (you can do this while the Pi is off, just nothing will show). The screen command takes two parameters: the connection and a baud rate; the baud rate for our Pi is 115200. Call the command screen /dev/cu.usbserial-14340 115200 from a terminal window (at this point, make sure you are plugged in; if not, you will just see a blank screen). Now you will see a terminal screen like in Figure 8-8. Since this is our first time with the new OS, you may see quite a bit of verbose messages before we get to a prompt.

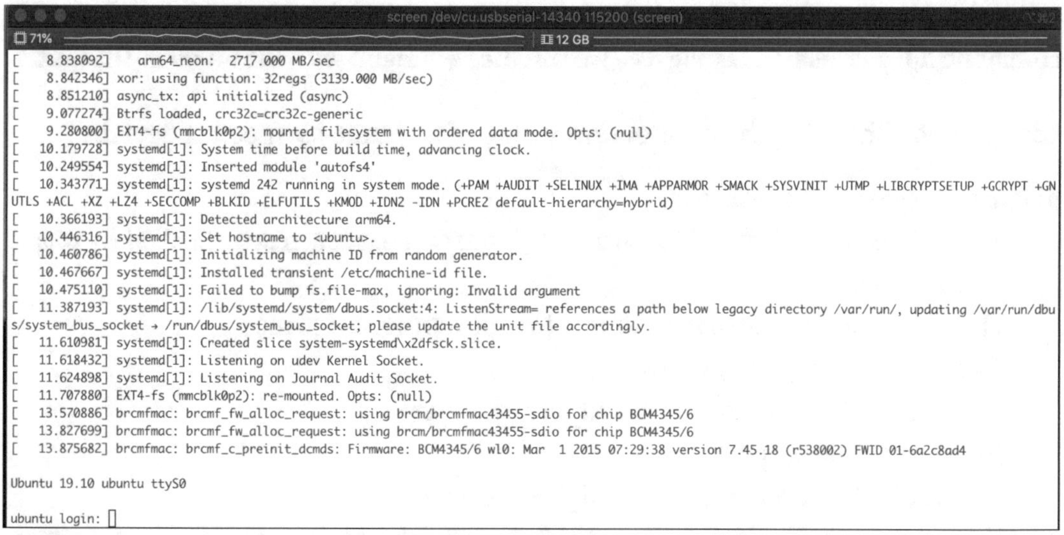

Figure 8-8. *Screen capture from USB cable debug login*

In order to log in, you will use the default username pi and the password `raspberry`; after your first login, you should change your password. That initial login screen should look like Listing 8-7.

Make sure the terminal screen is on your primary screen; I had issues with the password accepting when not on the primary screen.

Listing 8-7. Login screen on your initial logging to the Raspberry Pi

```
Raspbian GNU/Linux 10 raspberrypi tty1

raspberypi login: pi
Password:

Linux raspberry pi 4

pi@raspberrypi:~ $ passwd
Changing password for pi.
Current password:
New password:
Retype new password:
passwd: password updated successfully
pi@raspberrypi:~$
```

At this point, we can quickly check the status of our Internet connection with the command ip address; in Listing 8-8, we run the command with the following output.

Listing 8-8. Checking the connection status of Internet-connected devices

```
pi@raspberrypi:~$ ip address
1: lo: <LOOPBACK,UP,LOWER_UP> mtu 65536 qdisc noqueue state UNKNOWN group
   default qlen 1000
     link/loopback 00:00:00:00:00:00 brd 00:00:00:00:00:00
     inet 127.0.0.1/8 scope host lo
        valid_lft forever preferred_lft forever
     inet6 ::1/128 scope host
        valid_lft forever preferred_lft forever
2: eth0: <NO-CARRIER,BROADCAST,MULTICAST,UP> mtu 1500 qdisc fq_codel state
   DOWN group default qlen 1000
     link/ether b8:27:eb:5b:1e:80 brd ff:ff:ff:ff:ff:ff
3: wlan0: <BROADCAST,MULTICAST> mtu 1500 qdisc noop state DOWN group
   default qlen 1000
     link/ether b8:27:eb:0e:4b:d5 brd ff:ff:ff:ff:ff:ff
pi@raspberrypi:~$
Meta-Z for help | 115200 8N1 |
```

You will notice that while we have a wireless connection with wlan0, we have no actual IP address; that is because we have not configured it to log into your Wi-Fi router.

Set Up Wi-Fi

Let's set up the wireless router; now these set of instructions will assume you have a password protection on your home router. This will be a two-step process; the first step will be to add a file that contains our wireless SSID and the password. The second step will be to then reboot the Pi to have everything take effect.

First things first – we are going to update the cloud initialization file /etc/wpa_supplicant/wpa_supplicant.conf to store our wireless connection information. The file may have a few lines of details in it; we are going to add network configurations to it for our wireless Ethernet settings; you will have to log in as sudo (sudo su - is a good way to get into super user mode) and update the file so it looks like Listing 8-9.

Listing 8-9. Creating our wireless connection file

```
pi@raspberrypi:~$ sudo su -
pi@raspberrypi:~$ vi /etc/wpa_supplicant/wpa_supplicant.conf

network={
    ssid="Nusairat Wireless" ①
    psk="testingPassword" ②
}
```

    ①   Is the name of your wireless SSID?

    ②   Is the password for your wireless SSID (mine isn't really just a password; it's 1-2-3-4)?

At this point, you can reboot the Pi with the command `reboot` and then log back in. Now when you do `ip address`, you should see an actual ip address; try performing a `ping google.com` to verify you are reaching the Internet. Also make note of your IP address; we will use that later.

Now if that doesn't work, it could be because you have a block on your wireless connection. Log in as sudo and run `rfkill -list`; if you see anything marked "yes" under the `Wireless LAN`, we are going to need to unblock it. On the version I had, there was a soft block on the `Wireless LAN`; thus, we couldn't start up the wireless connection. In order to remove that block, run `rfkill unblock 0` to unblock it, and now let's start up the Wireless LAN with `ifconfig wlan0 up`. I've put these commands into Listing 8-10 to make it easier to follow along and try. Now if you reboot, your wireless connection should be up and ready to use.

Listing 8-10. Contents of wpa-wlan0.conf

```
root@ubuntu:~# sudo su -
pi@raspberrypi:~ $ rfkill list
0: phy0: Wireless LAN
    Soft blocked: yes
    Hard blocked: no
1: hci0: Bluetooth
    Soft blocked: no
    Hard blocked: no
```

```
pi@raspberrypi:~ $ rfkill unblock 0
pi@raspberrypi:~ $ ifconfig wlan0 up
pi@raspberrypi:~ $ reboot
```

OK, so now we have a Pi that has Internet access and importantly local access. Now we will be able to ditch the USB serial cable and log directly onto the board. (Note: The debugging cable can still come in handy, and you don't have to worry about SSH timeouts either.)

Setup SSH Access

You can now try to SSH into the box on your own; simply type `ssh ubuntu@<the ip you wrote down earlier>`. We can obviously do this by using the IP address and using the password each time, but this can get quite tedious over time.

Let's do a few things to make our life easier. First off, the IP address (the one I asked you to remember) that's hard to remember every time, let's give ourselves a shortcut for it in. In your `/etc/hosts` file, you can add host names to map to IP addresses. In Listing 8-11, I map `pi` to the ip address and add that entry to `/etc/hosts` file. (Note: You will have to do `sudo vi /etc/hosts` to edit it.)

Listing 8-11. Add pi to your /ets/hosts

```
pi 192.168.7.70
```

Now in order to ssh to the box, all we have to do is `ssh ubuntu@pi`; you can go ahead and try it, but unfortunately, we still have to enter our password, and that can be annoying itself. This will become even more annoying as we make builds and send them to the Pi for testing. Let's fix this by telling our Pi that the public key from our computer has access to the Ubuntu account on the Pi always. If you use Gitlab or any git instance, you probably have your public key created already. If you have, just skip to "Update Authorized Keys"; if you don't, read on and we will set up the public key. If you aren't sure if you have a public key, perform `ls ~/.ssh`, and if you get no files returned, then you don't, and we will need to set it up.

Generating a public key on a Linux/OSX is fairly simple and identical; there are luckily built-in commands to create the keys. You can use the command `ssh-keygen` to generate the key; I would save it in the default location; if not, the rest of the instructions won't work. But now, you can run `cat ~/.ssh/id_rsa.pub` and should have your keys installed.

Update Authorized Keys

Now that we have a key, we are going to copy this over to the Pi and store it in the `~/.ssh/authorized_keys` location. This will tell the server that any request with that key as its SSH key will be authorized without requiring login. In Listing 8-12, get the contents of our local `id_rsa.pub` and copy it over to the Pi.

Listing 8-12. Run this command from your computer to the Pi

```
~ ➜ ssh-copy-id -i ~/.ssh/id_rsa.pub pi@pi
The authenticity of host 'pi (192.168.7.70)' can't be established.
ECDSA key fingerprint is SHA256:UnLvF5X/5yFzGgGFkMOi7DK4lOR3aU3SH+okDAySf4c.
Are you sure you want to continue connecting (yes/no)? yes
Warning: Permanently added 'pi' (ECDSA) to the list of known hosts.
pi@pi's password:

Number of key(s) added:         1

Now try logging into the machine, with:   "ssh 'pi@pi'"
and check to make sure that only the key(s) you wanted were added.
```

You will have to enter the password one last time in there. But after this is done from your computer, run `ssh ubuntu@pi`, and you will be able to access your Pi without any password or remembering the IP address each time. Do remember though if the Pi's IP ever changes, you will have to update your `/etc/hosts`. Now that we have the Pi ready, let's start installing software.

Client Application

Now that we have the Pi all set up and we can log onto it, let's start to get code written to go on the Raspberry Pi device. We are going to write two applications for this section. The first one is a simple hello world, just to see how a simple application works on the Pi. The second will be the start of our full-fledged application.

Hello World Application

Let's start with the simple hello world application. It's our basic hello world that gets created when we run `cargo new hello-world`. Go ahead and create one right now; our issues are going to be in deploying, not creating the application. In Listing 8-13, we will build the application and copy it the Raspberry Pi.

Listing 8-13. Build Hello World and copy it to the Pi

```
➜ cargo build ①
   Finished dev [unoptimized + debuginfo] target(s) in 0.06s
➜ scp target/debug/hello-world ubuntu@pi:/home/ubuntu/hello-world ②
```

① Build our hello world application.

② Copy the created target to the Raspberry Pi home directory for Ubuntu.

Now that the file is there, open up another terminal window, ssh into the box, and run the application. In Listing 8-14, you will see the result of that action.

Listing 8-14. SSH and run the Hello World on the Pi

```
➜ ssh ubuntu@pi
Welcome to Ubuntu 19.10 (GNU/Linux 5.3.0-1007-raspi2 aarch64)
ubuntu@ubuntu:~$ ./hello-world
-bash: ./hello-world: cannot execute binary file: Exec format error
```

Well that didn't work, did it? This should not seem like too much of a surprise if you understand Rust; like most compiled languages, they are targeted to a platform. We will need to target this for Raspberry Pi.

Cross Compiling

With `rustup`, we can cross compile our applications to work on other systems, and in this case, we are going to target the Raspberry Pi Ubuntu system. In Listing 8-15, we are going to add and target `armv7-unknown-linux-musleabihf`.

Listing 8-15. Installing the `armv7-unknown-linux-musleabihf` target

```
→ rustup target add armv7-unknown-linux-musleabihf
info: downloading component 'rust-std' for 'armv7-unknown-linux-musleabihf'
 12.6 MiB /  12.6 MiB (100 %)   6.7 MiB/s in  2s ETA:  0s
info: installing component 'rust-std' for 'armv7-unknown-linux-musleabihf'
```

If you are using a Windows computer, run `rustup target add armv7-unknown-linux-gnueabihf`. Now that the target is installed, we need to define it as a possible target to use for the application that will also define the linker to use. You can define the targets to build in `~/.cargo/config`. In Listing 8-16, we define the linker to use.

Listing 8-16. Defining the linker in .cargo/config

```
[target.armv7-unknown-linux-musleabihf]
linker = "arm-linux-gnueabihf-ld"
```

Now what does all this mean? The names? The linker? What we are defining is the cross compiler we are going to use to create a secondary target to build the application. Let's take a look at the name of the linker we added. This name isn't random; it's actually a specific name that makes up four different attributes that are put together in a format of {arch}-{vendor}-{sys}-{abi}[1]:

- arm – The architecture we are targeting. Raspberry Pis use an ARMv7 development board.

- vendor – The vendor, in many cases, is optional; in those cases, it is marked as unknown.

- sys – The system we are compiling to, since we are deploying it to an Ubuntu Linux system, "linux".

- abi – The system that indicates the C library we are using for the cross compiling. In our case, it is the Musl GCC cross compiler; if you want more information on this library, you can read about it here: `https://wiki.musl-libc.org/getting-started.html`.

---

[1]`https://github.com/japaric/rust-cross#terminology`

We can build this against that target by adding the flag `--target armv7-unknown-linux-musleabihf` to our `cargo build`. If we did this, we would get the error in Listing 8-17.

Listing 8-17. Defining the linker in .cargo/config

```
➜ cargo build --release --target armv7-unknown-linux-musleabihf
   Compiling hello v0.1.0 (/Users/jnusairat/temp/hello)
error: linker `arm-linux-gnueabihf-ld` not found
  |
  = note: No such file or directory (os error 2)

error: aborting due to previous error

error: Could not compile `hello`.

To learn more, run the command again with --verbose.
```

This error is because of our indirect use of the `ring` crate; the `ring` crate is used for cryptographic operations and is fairly a common library to use for any type of certificate use or other crypto functions. This software uses a mixture of Rust and C code, which means in order to compile, you will need a C cross compiler. To that end, we will have to add `musl-gcc`. Let's install the cross compilers. In Table 8-1, we list the commands for installing on Linux, OSX, and Windows (please note I only have a Mac so that's what I tried it on).

Table 8-1. *GCC cross compilers for arm*

System	Command
OSX	brew install arm-linux-gnueabihf-binutils
Linux	sudo apt-get install gcc-arm-linux-gnueabi
Windows	Will need to install the Raspberry Pi tool chain from `https://gnutoolchains.com/raspberry/`.

Run the command based on the computer you are on. Now that you have the tools installed, let's try to rebuild the application. In Listing 8-18, we rerun the builder.

Listing 8-18. Defining the linker in .cargo/config

```
→ cargo build --release --target armv7-unknown-linux-musleabihf
    Compiling hello-world v0.1.0 (/Users/joseph/Library/Mobile Documents/
    com~apple~CloudDocs/work/rust-iot/code/ch08/hello-world)
    Finished release [optimized] target(s) in 4.57s
→ ls -al target/armv7-unknown-linux-musleabihf/release/hello-world
-rwxr-xr-x  2 joseph  staff  2774584 Nov  4 19:02 target/armv7-unknown-
linux-musleabihf/release/hello-world
```

Success! You will also notice I compiled for a release profile; I do this because I wanted an optimized build, and also we haven't defined anything yet for a dev profile (but you could have just as easily removed the --release tag). You will notice this file is located at target/armv7-unknown-linux-musleabihf/release/hello-world vs. our usual target/debug; we can build to multiple targets, and they would each reside in their corresponding directories.

Now in Listing 8-19, let's copy this to our Raspberry Pi and run the hello world, just to make sure we've done everything correct.

Listing 8-19. Copying over our Hello World to the Raspberry Pi

```
→ scp target/armv7-unknown-linux-musleabihf/release/hello-world ubuntu
    @pi:/home/ubuntu/hello-world ①

hello-world
100% 2710KB          4.0MB/s          00:00

→ ssh ubuntu@pi ②

ubuntu@ubuntu:~$ ./hello-world ③
Hello, world!
```

  ①   Copy over the release to the home directory.

  ②   SSH to the Pi.

  ③   Run the Hello World app successfully.

Success again, we have the Hello World application working on a Pi that was compiled from our OS. There is one final set of installs we need to do before we can continue though, and while it wasn't necessary for the Hello World application, it will be necessary when we compile our bigger application. This is basically further musl files for cross compilation (mostly due to our MQTT crates). In Table 8-2, I have the instructions for OSX and Linux.

Table 8-2. *Further MUSL libraries that need to be installed*

System	Command
OSX	brew install MarioSchwalbe/gcc-musl-cross/gcc-musl-cross
Linux	sudo apt install musl:i386=1.1.19-1

Please note the installation will take some time, so be patient during the download and install process. For OSX, you may add the `--verbose` flag if you want to make sure your installer is working.

Developing the Client Application

Now that we have our hello world deploying, let's get to something more complex, the start of our MQ client application. We will be creating two applications on the Raspberry Pi that will learn how to communicate with each other. The first client application will be the `rasp-pi-mq`, and as the name sounds, this will deal with our MQTT server. We broke these two applications up for a few reasons: one is the resilience we wanted of the MQ application since it has to handle most of the communication with the outside world. And the other reason is for practice of having two applications communicate on the same device together (the techniques here are different than having two microservices communicate with each other). Much of the code we are going to use in this chapter has been created before, so we will only repeat what is necessary (but all of the source code is available for the book on the accompanying site). For our first application, we are going to create an application that runs continuously and sends a heartbeat back to the server at a predefined interval. While this is a simple case, it will give us much of what we need to go with on future chapters.

To make it easier to figure out what we are doing, let's define the requirements:

1. Have the Pi look up a UUID of the device that we will create later at provisioning but will use this for determining uniqueness of a device.

2. Upload all our certificates necessary to communicate to the server.

3. Create a heartbeat to run at interval.

4. Set up to run from the command line.

Much of this will be from code we have used before; others will be new code; I will go into the necessary details when necessary. Obviously though the big difference is before we were writing code to receive data, and here we are sending data for the heartbeat. Start by setting up your basic application with the standard loggers we have used before. This is going to require using a few standard crates that we've used in other pages; these are in Listing 8-20.

Listing 8-20. Create a UUID in /var/uuid

```
log = "0.4.5"
pretty_env_logger = "0.4.0"
error-chain = "0.12.2"
clap = "2.32.0"
# To find relative directory
shellexpand = "1.1.1"
```

In addition, you can set up your main method with the loggers we used before like in Listing 8-21. Most of these seem familiar; I'm just repeating it here to make sure we are all on the same page.

Listing 8-21. The start of our main method

```
fn main() {
    env::set_var("RUST_LOG", env::var_os("RUST_LOG").unwrap_or_else(||
    "info".into())));
    pretty_env_logger::init();
    info!("Starting Up MQTT Manager on Pi ...");
}
```

Creating UUID

The initial application is set up, but we are going to need to have a few files exist on the board. If you recall earlier, we need to have each device have its own unique UUID; in theory, these won't change even as the software changes. For now, we just need to hard-code a value to a specific location; that location for us will be /var/uuuid. Let's first get a UUID; the easiest way to do that is to go to the command line and type uuidgen. This will create a new UUID for you; store that into the file /var/uuid on your Pi (if you do not have `uuidgen installed, you can also generate a number at www.uuidgenerator.net/). In Listing 8-22, I've copied my value into it on the Pi.

Listing 8-22. Create a UUID in /var/uuid

```
pi@raspberrypi:~ $ sudo apt-get update
pi@raspberrypi:~ $ sudo apt-get install uuid-runtime
Reading package lists... Done
Building dependency tree
...
pi@raspberrypi:~ $ sudo touch /var/uuid
pi@raspberrypi:~ $ sudo chmod 666 /var/uuid
pi@raspberrypi:~ $ uuidgen > /var/uuid
root@ubuntu:~# cat /var/uuid
93c1dfd9-cc07-4f14-aa3c-07f17b850039
```

Now that we have the UUID on the board, let's retrieve it from the device on startup so we can use the UUID to send over the MQ. In order to do that, we will read the file from the Pi and then parse the string into a UUID object. In Listing 8-23, we parse this object wrapping it in a result return.

Listing 8-23. Retrieving the UUID from the device

```
const UUID_LOCATION: &str = "/var/uuid";

fn read_device_id() -> MyResult<Uuid> {
    use std::fs;

    let uuid_str = fs::read_to_string(UUID_LOCATION.to_string())?; ①

    let uuid = Uuid::parse_str(uuid_str.trim()).unwrap(); ②
```

```
    debug!("Device UUID :: {:?}", uuid);
    Ok(uuid)
}
```

① Reads the contents of the file into a String.

② Parses the string into a Uuid struct.

With the method in our `main.rs`, we can use the following code to our main() function to capture the UUID:

```
let uuid = read_device_id().chain_err(|| "No device id file found").unwrap();
```

Transferring Certificates

Next, we need to get all those device certificates we created in the previous chapter and store them to the device. If you recall, there are three files we need for the MQ to work with an SSL connection:

- Client certificate

- Client key

- Root certificate

In Listing 8-24, we copy those files from ~/book_certs to the /home/pi directory to use for our application.

Listing 8-24. SCP the certificate files to the Pi

```
➜ scp ~/book_certs/PiDevice.pem pi@pi:/home/pi/PiDevice.pem
PiDevice.pem                                100% 1135    47.6KB/s    00:00
➜ scp ~/book_certs/PiDevice.key pi@pi:/home/pi/PiDevice.key
PiDevice.key                                100% 1675   136.2KB/s    00:00
➜ scp ~/book_certs/RustIOTRootCA.pem pi@pi:/home/pi/RustIOTRootCA.pem
RustIOTRootCA.pem                           100% 1168    68.2KB/s    00:00
```

Setting Up Arguments

Now that we have our files on board, let's think about what arguments we are going to need for this application to make it work both now and in the future. We are going to have the server do two things: one contact our endpoints via MQTT for sending and receiving heartbeats and requests. In addition, we will need https endpoints to perform direct queries and to upload and download files.

It's good to remember the MQ and the HTTPS endpoints work hand in hand; the MQ provides us a way to receive commands from the Web, but to also transmit data when needed too, while the HTTPS is for more immediate queries or pushes of data.

To that end, we will need seven arguments passed to this application:

1. MQ client certificate

2. MQ client key

3. Root certificate

4. MQ server address

5. MQ server port

6. HTTPS server

7. HTTPS port

The final two we won't use in this chapter, but we will use later on. We've gone over creating arguments a few times so we don't need to cover how to do each one; the two things I do want to show is the actual call to set up the argument matchers and the short name to variable; that way, you have a reference for what I'm using when I reference them in examples later in the chapter. In Listing 8-25, we have the `command_line_args` method to get all the command-line arguments.

Listing 8-25. Parsing all the command-line arguments in src/main.rs

```rust
fn command_line_args() -> ArgMatches<'static> {
    App::new(APP_TITLE)
        .version(env!("CARGO_PKG_VERSION"))
        .author(env!("CARGO_PKG_AUTHORS"))
        .about(APP_DESCRIPTION)
        .setting(AppSettings::ColoredHelp)
        .arg(args::client_crt::declare_arg())
        .arg(args::client_key::declare_arg())
        .arg(args::rootca::declare_arg())
        .arg(args::server::declare_arg())
        .arg(args::port::declare_arg())
        .get_matches()
}
```

And in Table 8-3, we list the command-line values to names that we are creating.

Table 8-3. *Command-line arguments for the Rasp Pi MQ app*

Name	Short Value
Client cert	-c
Client key	-k
Root CA	-r
Server	-s
Port	-p
Http server	-e
Http port	-h

Creating the Heartbeat

OK, now that we have the basics out of the way, let's get into something fun, creating the heartbeat. Calling the heartbeat isn't too hard, but it does require us to remember Rust's borrowing model. To do so, let's start with the call from the main method using the arguments we created before. In the `main()` method, we are going to make the call in Listing 8-26.

Listing 8-26. Calls the `start_heartbeat` function in src/main.rs

```
start_hearbeat(&matches, &uuid);
```

In here, we are passing a reference to the `matches` because we will need the `matches` when we expose other calls. In addition, we clone the Uuid; we are going to have to clone it a few times to use it around, but it's small so it won't add much to the stack.

Now let's take a look at the `start_heartbeat` in Listing 8-27 which will get all the objects we need from the `matches`.

Listing 8-27. The `start_heartbeat` function in src/main.rs

```
fn start_hearbeat(matches: &ArgMatches, uuid: &Uuid,) {
    let server = matches.value_of(args::server::NAME).unwrap().to_string();
    let port = matches.value_of(args::port::NAME).unwrap().parse::<u16>().unwrap();

    let client_crt = matches.value_of(args::client_crt::NAME).unwrap().to_string();
    let client_key = matches.value_of(args::client_key::NAME).unwrap().to_string();
    let rootca = matches.value_of(args::rootca::NAME).unwrap().to_string();

    heartbeat::start(uuid.clone(), server, port, client_crt, client_key, rootca);
}
```

Here we will retrieve all the values from the `matches` and set them to local variables that we can then pass in to the `heartbeat::run` function. So far, it's pretty normal. We are going to create some methods in the `heartbeat` module. Before we dive into it too much, what we have to remember is we are going to be setting up multiple threads to occur because we are looping infinitely. We will need to wrap the variables in the `std::sync::Arc` to keep them using the heap memory instead. In addition, we will also be making use of `tokio` timers to do the interval looping, to set the application to send heartbeats every hour. Let's take a look at this code in Listing 8-28 and then dissect it more after.

Listing 8-28. The `heartbeat::run` function in src/heartbeat.rs

```
use tokio::time::{interval_at, Duration, Instant}; ①

use uuid::Uuid;
use crate::mqtt::{App, MqttClientConfig};
use crate::mqtt::client::send as client_send; ②
use log::info;

use std::sync::Arc;

const INTERVAL_IN_SECONDS: u64 = 60 * 60; ③

#[tokio::main] ④
pub async fn start(uuid: Uuid, server: String, port: u16,
            crt: String, key: String, ca: String) -> Result<(), Box<dyn
            std::error::Error>> {
```

```
    info!("Setup and start our MQ ...");

    run(uuid, server, port, crt, key, ca);

    Ok(())
}

fn run( uuid: Uuid, server: String, port: u16,
            crt: String, key: String, ca: String) {
    let config = MqttClientConfig { ⑤
        ca_crt:  ca,
        server_crt: crt,
        server_key: key,
        mqtt_server: server,
        mqtt_port: port,
        uuid: uuid.to_string()
    };
    let record_config = config.clone();

    let mut interval = interval_at(Instant::now(), ⑥
                                Duration::from_secs(INTERVAL_IN_SECONDS)); ⑦

    tokio::spawn(async move {
        loop {
            interval.tick().await;
            send(&config, &uuid); ⑧
        }
    });

    crate::actions::recording::monitor(&record_config, &uuid);
}

fn send(config: &MqttClientConfig, uuid: &Uuid) { ⑨
    info!("Send Heartbeat for {}", uuid);
    let app = App { uuid: uuid,  status: 0, msg: "Everything is great ..",
    peripherals: vec!["Camera", "Sense HAT"]};
    client_send(config, app);
}
```

① Uses the tokio timer.

② Uses the MQTT application and Config client we created before.

③ Sets our interval in seconds; this will set up the interval for one hour.

④ Starts up our Async via tokio.

⑤ Creates our MqttClientConfig object for referencing the data.

⑥ Creates an interval that will start immediately.

⑦ And will fire every hour.

⑧ The task that will be run each hour is sending a message to the heartbeat.

⑨ Sends data to the MQ.

Two parts here are interesting; the tokio threading allows for all sorts of options for creating threads. In our case, we are using tokio to run an interval thread that will send every 60 seconds. Remember that the tokio::run is nonblocking; it simply creates a new thread, so this method will return immediately, which is the main reason we need to put the configuration data on the heap so it's not lost or reborrowed by subsequent calling code.

The other thing is the send method itself. Right now, it's pretty simple; it just sends an everything is great. And everything is great; from a server perspective, we will assume everything is not so great if we don't hear back from it every hour. This method will get more interesting as we add on peripherals later in the book, but right now, we have about everything needed to run this application.

Keep Alive

One final thing, like I said, the timer is nonblocking. As of now, we'd run this, and it may run the timer once and then exit the application immediately. To solve this, we will add an infinite loop to the end of the main() function; an easy-to-use infinite loop is in Listing 8-29.

Listing 8-29. The infinite loop at the end of our main function in src/main.rs

```
loop {
    std::thread::sleep(std::time::Duration::new(10, 0));
}
```

Run from the Command Line

Now that we have this all together, let's build it and run it. You will be able to build with the same command we used in the hello world app; you can then transfer it over and run it passing in the command-line arguments we had before.

Listing 8-30. Starts up the Raspberry Pi MQ application specifying our generated certificates

```
./rasp-pi-mq -c /home/ubuntu/PiDevice.pem -k /home/ubuntu/PiDevice.key -r /
home/ubuntu/RustIOTRootCA.pem -s 192.168.7.31
```

If you see any errors connecting to your server, it's probably because you don't have your application running on your desktop or a firewall blocking it. But assuming everything works, we now have our first IoT use case complete. A backend server is running with your device communicating with it.

Summary

This chapter was our first chapter with the Raspberry Pi, and hopefully yours is now running and communicating with the backend servers. Walking through I wanted to get you comfortable with the Pi, the installation of the components, installing the image, and copying over code for execution. In the next chapter, we will create another application that will also run on the Pi. And we will perform more tasks and installation on the Pi; some of it will include removing the SD card and updating the boot partition again.

CHAPTER 9

Sense HAT

In the last chapter, we started to have the Pi communicate with our backend servers and running a more advanced version of "Hello World". In this chapter, we are going to build up on this existing application by adding and using a set of hardware components. After all, one of the things that makes the Pi so great is its hardware extensibility. That is one of the biggest selling points of the Raspberry Pi, being able to add on sensors, cameras, or even custom components that communicate with the board and the GPIO specifically. We will be using a few of these components, but to start with, I want us to use a component that gives us an all-in-one board to use, the Sense HAT. We will be interacting with this board throughout the chapter, gathering the temperature for the board as well as using it as the basis for our future command interaction with the board. In addition, we will integrate it with our login authorization flow.

Goals

For this chapter, we are not going to go over every feature; we are only going to use three of those features for interacting with our application. We will use the LED for textual and warning displays. The textual displays will be used for the temperature and login as well as any warning lights for connectivity or other problems.

Our goals when finished will be to have a functional board with Sense HAT that has the following capabilities:

- Able to calculate the temperature.

- Display the temperature when the user clicks the center of the joystick.

- Use the display to show the device code to log in with.

- Display a question mark when we have MQTT connectivity issues.

- Display a holiday image for Christmas and Halloween.

© Joseph Faisal Nusairat 2020
J. F. Nusairat, *Rust for the IoT*, https://doi.org/10.1007/978-1-4842-5860-6_9

Hardware

In the previous chapter, we added a basic running heartbeat to the application. This was fairly simple, and much of our time was spent making sure it could compile and deploy to the Pi. What our advanced Hello World would do was the Pi app started and would periodically send a heartbeat. In this chapter, we plan to complicate things quite a bit more, and that will require us to use new peripheral, the Sense HAT, and to add some more complicated code. This chapter will be a new application for the Raspberry Pi. We are going to keep the heartbeat separate in its own process, and this will be an entirely new application. Both running on the Raspberry Pi though. In Chapter 11, we will discuss how to have the heartbeat and this application communicate with each other.

The Sense HAT is an all-in-one board that can be affixed to the top of of your Pi taking up all 40 of the GPIO pins, which will provide the complete interface to the board and the power to the board. The board is unique, in that it has quite a few chips on it to allow us quite a bit of different features to detect the world around us. The chipsets can determine these:

- Air pressure

- Humidity

- Temperature (collocated on the air pressure and humidity sensors)

- Gyroscope – The orientation of the Pi and if it is changing

- Magnetometer – To measure magnetic forces

- Accelerometer – To measure the movement and speed of the Pi

All these combined can provide quite a bit of interactivity to measure your outside world. In fact, Raspberry Pis with Sense HAT were used aboard the International Space Station to conduct experiments. Also the board allows us some interaction and communication with the user; to that end we have an

- 8x8 LED matrix display

- Five-button joystick

The device is easy to install and somewhat easy to use in isolation; however, we want to use it as a system which requires simultaneous use and multiple interactions between components. The goal for this section is to attach the Sense HAT and using a few crates control the temperature, LED, and joystick. We will make more use of the joystick in the following chapters, but for now, we will keep it basic. One of the big challenges for this chapter is to run multiple background processes while still allowing input from the joystick:

- Daily displays of the temperature

- Display of holiday lighting

For this chapter, many of the crates I have tweaked the functionality. Quite a few of them have not been updated in years, but that is mostly because the underlying code to interact with the sensors has not changed either. I do hope to merge some of my changes back to their parent and will modify the code online when I do.

All of this needs to happen while still allowing for joystick control. Remember that Rust is a very memory-safe language, so we won't be simply passing in the LED and Atmospheric `structs` in multiple threads run by different modules that simply wouldn't work. We will be using instead multi-producer, single-consumer channels to run all of our logic. This will give us our multi-threaded capabilities without worrying about multi-threads trying to own the same memory. But that part is down the road a bit; let's start with installing the Sense HAT.

Install

The SenseHAT is a somewhat brilliant all-in-one board, designed specifically for the Raspberry Pi. It's a board that gives us many features in one compact inexpensive board. Before we dive into the board features, let's start with getting this unboxed and installed. In Chapter 1, I gave you a link to a Sense HAT you can purchase from Amazon; if you've forgotten it, the URL for the board to purchase is `http://amzn.com/B014HDG74S` (and is the board I used for this chapter).

Once you have it, let's open it up; in Figure 9-1, we have a picture of the unboxing and all the parts.

Figure 9-1. *Shows the unboxing of our Sense HAT*

This contains a manual, the board itself, and the spacers used to attach it to the main board. The Sense HAT is going to attach to your GPIO board; however, it can't attach to it directly due to space limitations of the chips and sensors already on the board. That is why the kit contains spacers with it both for the GPIO and the board. Start by attaching the GPIO extender to your board like in Figure 9-2.

Figure 9-2. *Board with the GPIO extender*

Now we will install the SenseHAT on top of the board, but first let's attach the spacers to the board; if we don't, the board will be unstable and you risk bending the pins or worse. Screw the spacers in to the SenseHat, then attach the spacers to the four corners, and attach the board on to the top. In Figure 9-3, we have the complete board assembled and powered on.

Figure 9-3. *The board attached and started up*

One **final thing before powering it up, take out your SD card you had in before
and go back to the config.txt. You will have to uncomment the line**

```
# uncomment if hdmi display is not detected and composite is being output
hdmi_force_hotplug=1
```

With the line uncommented, it will allow you to turn on the Pi without a display
attached to it. Now you can attach the board and turn it on; it will light up all the LEDs
each time and then turn off. If you haven't altered the preceding config, you will need
to attach an HDMI monitor or the lights will just stay on and it won't finish the booting
process. Once the LED goes off, it will be ready to log onto the board.

Sensors

The sensors on the board are run by an Atmel chip that operates on a i2c (pronounced eye-squared-cee) protocol which require us to code against that protocol to work correctly. Thus, all our sensors we have will be communicating on the same protocol. This will help us in the debugging of it because this will allow us to run commands against the board directly from the shell to check its status. This is a standard protocol on a bus that Raspberry Pi uses to speak to other embedded devices, and the same logic can be applied to other attached sensors as well. The i2c is a two-wire bus that has serial data (SDA) and a serial clock (SCL). Your Pi can contain multiple i2c buses and will contain one or more primaries and secondaries. Because the lines are shared between multiple secondaries, each device attached to it will have a specific address that it communicates on.[1] Those addresses can vary by the type of device we attach; in Table 9-1, I list the addresses for all of the sensors on the Sense HAT.

Table 9-1. *Sensors and chipsets on the board*

Name	Sensor	Address
Accelerometer	LSM9DS1	0x1c(0x1e)
Magnetometer	LSM9DS1	0x6a(0x6b)
Pressure	LPS25H	0x5c
Humidity	HTS221	0x5f
LED matrix	LED2472G	0x46

The addresses are all documented on the Sense HAT found at https://pinout.xyz/pinout/sense_hat. It's a good overview if you want details of what the circuits are doing and where I got some of my information from.

Since we are using the Raspbian Buster Lite OS, we will need to install drivers for the Sense HAT; these normally are preinstalled with the image if you used the full Buster OS. We also need to install some tools that allow us to make sure the Pi and the HAT are communicating properly. It's also good for debugging purposes. One of the easiest ways to perform debugging is to examine the i2c bus. In Listing 9-1, after logging on to the

---

[1]http://raspberrypi-aa.github.io/session3/i2c-temp-pressure.html

board, we will install the Sense HAT libraries needed as well as a tool that will help us communicate via the i2c protocol. (Note: The install is very verbose, and I've shortened it down for brevity.)

Listing 9-1. Install i2c tools on the board

```
pi@raspberrypi:~ $ sudo apt-get update ①
Get:1 http://archive.raspberrypi.org/debian buster InRelease [25.1 kB]
Get:2 http://raspbian.raspberrypi.org/raspbian buster InRelease [15.0 kB]
...
pi@raspberrypi:~ $  sudo apt-get install -y sense-hat ②
Reading package lists... Done
Building dependency tree
Reading state information... Done
The following additional packages will be installed:
...
pi@raspberrypi:~ $ sudo apt install -y i2c-tools ③
Reading package lists... Done
Building dependency tree
Reading state information... Done
The following additional packages will be installed:
  libi2c0 read-edid
  ...
Processing triggers for man-db (2.8.5-2) ...
Processing triggers for libc-bin (2.28-10+rpi1) ...
```

① Downloads package information for all configured sources needed or the next two steps may fail.

② Installs necessary libraries for communication with the Pi.

③ Installs tools to debug communication between the Pi and the HAT.

Now that we have it installed, go ahead and run the command i2cdetect -y 1. The -y indicates we want non-interactive mode, and the 1 tells it which i2c bus to use. The Raspberry Pi board only has two i2c buses: one of them is the GPIO and the other is on the P5 header where you'd have to solder into that header to use. Since we attached the Sense HAT to the GPIO, we are using i2c-1. In Listing 9-2, we run the command on the Raspberry Pi.

Listing 9-2. Running i2cdetect on the board

```
ubuntu@ubuntu:~$ sudo i2cdetect -y 1
     0  1  2  3  4  5  6  7  8  9  a  b  c  d  e  f
00:          -- -- -- -- -- -- -- -- -- -- -- -- --
10: -- -- -- -- -- -- -- -- -- -- -- -- 1c -- -- --
20: -- -- -- -- -- -- -- -- -- -- -- -- -- -- -- --
30: -- -- -- -- -- -- -- -- -- -- -- -- -- -- -- --
40: -- -- -- -- -- -- UU -- -- -- -- -- -- -- -- --
50: -- -- -- -- -- -- -- -- -- -- -- -- 5c -- -- 5f
60: -- -- -- -- -- -- -- -- -- -- 6a -- -- -- -- --
70: -- -- -- -- -- -- -- --
```

You might notice a few things pop out if you remember the addresses we just
went over. Notice the 6a and 5f; those are our magnetometer and humidity sensor,
respectively. What we should also have is a 5c, but where 50 and c meet, you may have
UU (I tried with three boards, and my Pi 3 was inconsistent and showing it). The UU
indicates a busy used state. Just be aware, if you do see a UU, then you won't be able to
use that sensor for the temperature reading; that will become important when we do the
temperature calculations to know which sensors we have available.

Note   There are other debugging tools that help visualize your bus. "lsmod |
grep i2c" will give you an output:

```
st_pressure_i2c         16384  0
st_magn_i2c             16384  0
st_magn                 20480  2 st_magn_i2c,st_magn_spi
st_pressure             20480  2 st_pressure_i2c,st_pressure_spi
st_sensors_i2c          16384  2 st_pressure_i2c,st_magn_i2c
st_sensors              28672  6 st_pressure,st_pressure_i2c,st_magn_i2c,st_
                               pressure_spi,st_magn,st_magn_spi
industrialio            90112  9 st_pressure,industrialio_triggered_
buffer,st_sensors,st_pressure_i2c,kfifo_buf,st_magn_i2c,st_pressure_spi,st_
magn,st_magn_spi
```

This tells you all the sensors there are available; in addition, you can run "`sudo i2cdump 1 [address]`" to query the state of individual settings on your device.

If you want more details on how the Sense HAT and Pi systems work, there are quite a bit of documentations out there; I just wanted you to get enough of an overview that the coding going forward you would know where certain features come from. For now though, we are going to move on to setting up interactions with the LED and the temperature sensors. The way we are going to perform these operations is by using a variety of crates to control the sensors and display and then writing small wrappers to them for our individual functions we need.

LED Display

First up on our list is the LED screen. The LED screen is the big 8x8 multi-colored LEDs we saw light up when we started the Pi. Since we aren't using a standard screen for our application, this LED display is going to become very important to display our interactions with the user, since for this particular device, this is the one we are using. Also I wanted to use the device to have a bit of fun with by displaying different emblems for Christmas and Halloween. Let's start by going over everything I want our display to show, and then we can talk about how to do it. In Table 9-2, I have a listing of our different type of displays we are going to code to and the corresponding function that will encapsulate the logic.

Table 9-2. *Displays we will create on the Sense HAT*

Name	Function	Description
Blank	blank	Blank out the screen to clear it out after we have displayed any symbols or sequences.
Question mark	question	A question mark to display in case of an error.
Processing	processing	Run through a progress screen that shows sequential blocks, to be used while waiting for a response from another system.
Symbols	display_symbol	Used to display an 8x8 LED "image" to the screen; this will be a predefined multi-color output.
Text display	display	Will output a different set of text, one letter at a time with a predefined wait of 800 ms.
Text scrolling	scroll_text	Also displays a set of text, but instead of shifting a whole letter at a time, this will scroll the text through.

These are quite a bit of functions we want to implement, but each will solve for us all our use cases; we need to display a variety of text and anything else to the screen. To start with, we will be making use of the sensehat-screen crate (https://github. com/saibatizoku/sensehat-screen-rs). We will also incorporate the features that are necessary for allowing us to perform various textual displays to the screen. In Listing 9-3, I add the crate as well as applied the features for displaying and scrolling our text.

Listing 9-3. Adding sensehat-screen to our Pi application

```
[dependencies]
sensehat-screen = { version = "0.2", default-features = false, features =
["fonts", "linux-framebuffer", "scroll"] }
```

We are also adding in the features for controlling the fonts and scrolling; these are both needed for our application in order to display static and scrolling text; in addition, the linux-framebuffer is how we are going to write to the LED. There are other features like rotate and clip that we aren't using so I didn't include them, but you can go to the site and add extra features to your individual application.

The screen crate is a self-contained module via the `sensehat_screen::Screen` struct. We will be wrapping this and implementing the methods we mentioned earlier to interact with the screen. The `Screen` itself is a high-level API that interacts with the `linux-framebuffer`. `Screen` will open to the framebuffer's file descriptor in order to connect and write to the LED matrix. From there, it will just be writing our input. Input comes in the form of the `FrameLine` struct that contains raw bytes needed for the buffer. From there, the `Screen` will take the `FrameLine` information and write it to the LED matrix. We will be converting Unicode to bytes directly when we create our holiday pictures; in other situations, we will use wrappers provided by the crate that allow us to convert the text to raw bytes without us having to create our own font catalog.

Frames

The 8x8 LED display will display colors on each matrix in a 16-bit RGB565 color representation; this basically gives you the color pallet you had in your old Atari Lynx (yes, very old school reference) but obviously not as a tight of a pattern. We are going to send to the framebuffers an 8x8 set of RGB colors. How this translates though is not an actual dual array but as a u8 single array that divides the RGB color in half for each LED. Thus, you will have a 128-sized array of u8 types (`[u8: 128]`), which is 8 x 8 x 2. This gives you two bytes for each color and then defines each LED matrix possible. For our "images" like the pumpkin and Christmas tree and any other static display, we will set up the constants in a multi-line format, so visualizing it can be easier.

We are going to feed to the framebuffers an 8x8 array of colors that converts the hexadecimal representation of the color into bytes. The individual pixels are 16-bit RGB color representation. One challenge is to come up with the colors to use; most online sites that have color pickers use RGB888, the standard for websites CSS. However, the LED matrix uses RGB56 instead; there are a few sites that make it easy to come up with the colors; the following two URLs are what I used to pick colors:

- `https://chrishewett.com/blog/true-rgb565-colour-picker/` –
  Allows you to adjust the red green and blue to get the color and the RGB56 code

- `https://trolsoft.ru/en/articles/rgb565-color-picker` –
  Reverses it and allows you to input the RGB56 code and see the color for it

In Listing 9-4, I have a 128 u8 representation of a Christmas tree that we will use to display during the month of December preceding boxing day.

Listing 9-4. A constant for a Christmas tree, file is in led/mod.rs

```
// Christmas Tree
pub const CHRISTMAS_TREE: [u8; 128] = [
    0x00, 0x00, 0x00, 0x00, 0x00, 0x00, 0xFF, 0xFF, 0xFF, 0xFF, 0x00, 0x00,
    0x00, 0x00, 0x00, 0x00,
    0x00, 0x00, 0x00, 0x00, 0x00, 0x00, 0xE0, 0x07, 0xE0, 0x07, 0x00, 0x00,
    0x00, 0x00, 0x00, 0x00,
    0x00, 0x00, 0x00, 0x00, 0xE0, 0x07, 0xE0, 0x07, 0xE0, 0x07, 0xE0, 0x07,
    0x00, 0x00, 0x00, 0x00,
    0x00, 0x00, 0xE0, 0x07, 0xE0, 0x07, 0xE0, 0x07, 0xE0, 0x07, 0xE0, 0x07,
    0xE0, 0x07, 0x00, 0x00,
    0xE0, 0x07, 0xE0, 0x07, 0xE0, 0x07, 0xE0, 0x07, 0xE0, 0x07, 0xE0, 0x07,
    0xE0, 0x07, 0xE0, 0x07,
    0xE0, 0x07, 0xE0, 0x07, 0xE0, 0x07, 0xE0, 0x07, 0xE0, 0x07, 0xE0, 0x07,
    0xE0, 0x07, 0xE0, 0x07,
    0x00, 0x00, 0x00, 0x00, 0x00, 0x00, 0x61, 0x80, 0x61, 0x80, 0x00, 0x00,
    0x00, 0x00, 0x00, 0x00,
    0x00, 0x00, 0x00, 0x00, 0x00, 0x00, 0x61, 0x80, 0x61, 0x80, 0x00, 0x00,
    0x00, 0x00, 0x00, 0x00,
];
```

This will produce a tree with a light at the top and then green throughout. You will notice in the second line we have 0xE0, 0x07, 0xE0, 0x07; this represents two LED lights of RGB565 color 07E0 and 07E0 which is a green color. You may be taking a double take on the input and the color and noticed the pairing is reversed from the input. That is not a typo; that is how you have to input the set. So keep that in mind when adding colors. In Figure 9-4, you can see the output that this will create.

Figure 9-4. *A Christmas tree being displayed on the Sense HAT*

This is a black and white book, so the color variants may not show up here, but once you run the code on the board, it will. In addition, I've also added some yellow boxes we will use for concentric box display (for a processing image) and a pumpkin that we can use for the month of October. The code is in the repository; I have not included it here as I doubt any of you are going to line by line copy it.

But now that we have the understanding of it, let's go back to adding code for it. As I said text is easy, and images aren't. We are going to add a `struct FrameProcessor` that will share as an easy cheat to display a few items:

- Our set of yellow concentric squares

- A question mark

- An off frame which will be translated as a buffer of [0x00; 128] for our blank display

The easiest way to create a FrameLine from a set of RGB colors is to create the 128 slice. From there, we can use the call FrameLine::from_slice passing in the slice to create the FrameLine struct. Let's look at this code in Listing 9-5.

Listing 9-5. The code from the FrameProcessor; file is in led/screen.rs

```
struct FrameProcessor {
    off_frame: FrameLine,
    yellow_squares: [FrameLine; 4],
    question_mark: FrameLine,
}

impl FrameProcessor {
    fn new() -> FrameProcessor {
        let ys = [ ①
            FrameLine::from_slice(&super::YELLOW_SMALL),
            FrameLine::from_slice(&super::YELLOW_MED),
            FrameLine::from_slice(&super::YELLOW_LARGE),
            FrameLine::from_slice(&super::YELLOW_XL),
        ];

        // Question Mark
        let white_50_pct = PixelColor::WHITE.dim(0.5); ②
        let q_mark = FONT_COLLECTION.get('?').unwrap();

        FrameProcessor {
            off_frame: FrameLine::from_slice(&super::OFF), ③
            yellow_squares: ys,
            question_mark: font_to_frame(&q_mark.byte_array(), white_50_pct), ④
        }
    }
}
```

① Creates an array containing all the individual yellow squares.

② For use with the question mark, we want the display of it to be only 50% brightness.

③   Initializes our new frame starting with the OFF frame from the slice
we defined in led/mod.rs.

④   The question mark uses font_to_frame from the sensehat_screen to
convert the font to a FrameLine.

You will notice that this struct is not public, and it's intended to be used only by
the LedControls struct that we are creating next which will use these to send to the LED
matrix.

LED Controls

Now that we have the processing for a few of our image use cases and understand how
we display with framebuffers, let's turn our attention to implementing the code to display
to the LED. We are going to create a LedControls structure that will wrap all our calls
to the Screen and FrameProcessor. This will drive all the interactions from the outside
modules to the LED display. In Listing 9-6, we are creating that struct.

Listing 9-6. Creating the struct for LedControls; file is in led/screen.rs

```
use sensehat_screen::{font_to_frame, PixelColor, Screen, FrameLine, FONT_
COLLECTION, Scroll}; ①

use std::thread;
use std::time::Duration;

const LED_DEV_PATH: &str = "/dev/fb1"; ②

pub struct LedControls {
    screen: Screen, ③
    frame: FrameProcessor
}

// Clone is needed because ::  pub trait FlowDelegate: Clone {
// so its constituent parts have to be Clone
// This is needed for our Authenticator
impl Clone for LedControls { ④
    fn clone(&self) -> Self {
        LedControls {
```

```
        screen: Screen::open(LED_DEV_PATH).unwrap(),
        frame: FrameProcessor::new()
    }
}
}
}

impl LedControls {
    pub fn new() -> LedControls { ⑤
        LedControls {
            screen: Screen::open(LED_DEV_PATH).unwrap(),
            frame: FrameProcessor::new()
        }
    }
}
```

① Use all the structs from the crate that are needed by our application.

② The LED Path; this is the default path to talk to the file descriptor; this should be the same on your boards as well.

③ Our struct has two properties that we need to instantiate before using.

④ The Clone will be used later when having to pass through to our authentication modules.

⑤ The implementation and creating of our LedControls.

Note using creating new FrameProcessor::new() on cloning is probably not the best idea since you could potentially have two different parts of an application writing to the screen at the same time and lead to a corrupted screen. However, on startup, the authentication is a blocking process and won't allow any further functions till you log in, so this shouldn't occur.

Two things really of note here: on bullet 5, if there is an error accessing the file descriptor, this will cause a panic. I haven't wrapped it because if it does, then the rest of our app has a difficult time working since we will never be able to display the authentication or anything else to the screen. In addition, you will notice here we are implementing the Clone in bullet 4 as opposed to deriving it. The reason for this is Screen does not derive Clone so we would not be able to use the self-deriving macro. For our code, we are just going to open another connection to the file descriptor.

Next, we are going to add the individual functions that will produce output to the screen. I won't be adding the code to test those here, as we are going to wait till we integrate it with the rest of the system, but feel free to run through testing each as we go along on your own Pi. We will be able to use the FrameLine instances we created earlier to pass to the screen to write them out. We use the call screen.write_frame passing in the FrameLine to it, which will write those frames to the LED. Let's take a look at each method we are implementing; you will note they all follow the same general pattern.

Blank Screen

First up in Listing 9-7 is blanking the screen. This will use the off_frame from the FrameProcessor we just created.

Listing 9-7. Blanks the screen; file is in led/screen.rs

```
pub fn blank(&mut self) {
    self.screen.write_frame(&self.frame.off_frame);
}
}
```

Question Mark

In addition, we can combine multiple write_frame together with delays in order to change what is displayed. In Listing 9-8, we display a question mark first, wait 3 seconds, and then blank the screen since we no longer want the question mark at that point.

Listing 9-8. Displays a question mark for 3 seconds; file is in led/screen.rs

```
pub fn question(&mut self) {
    self.screen.write_frame(&self.frame.question_mark);
    thread::sleep(Duration::from_secs(3));
    self.screen.write_frame(&self.frame.off_frame);
}
}
```

Displaying an Image

Here we make use of the Christmas tree and pumpkin images we created earlier to display them to the screen for a given time and then blank them out after. Now in Listing 9-9, since the images we used before are in a format of [u8: 128], we will have to convert that to a FrameLine before processing. We could have put these two displays in our FrameProcessor, but I didn't want to tie this method to only be able to display those two images.

Listing 9-9. Displays an array image for a given set of time before blanking out the screen; file is in led/screen.rs

```
pub fn display_symbol(&mut self, frame: &[u8; 128], length: u64) {
    let frame_line = FrameLine::from_slice(frame);
    self.screen.write_frame(&frame_line);
    thread::sleep(Duration::from_secs(length));
    self.screen.write_frame(&self.frame.off_frame);
}
}
```

Processing Screen

The processing screen function in Listing 9-10 will use the yellow concentric arrays we created earlier and run it through three times to make it appear like there is a "busy" state on the board. Ideally, you could make this fancier with interrupts or checks if it needs to keep going, but this is something simple one can build up on to later.

Listing 9-10. Processing display; file is in led/screen.rs

```
pub fn processing(&mut self) {
    let sleep_time = 500;
    let yellow_squares = self.frame.yellow_squares;

    for x in 0..2 {
        for ys in &yellow_squares {
                self.screen.write_frame(ys);
            thread::sleep(Duration::from_millis(sleep_time));
        }
    }
}
}
```

Display Text

Finally, we get to actually displaying text that is passed in. Here we need to pick the color, pick the font, and then convert that text into a FrameLine. In Listing 9-11, we display text before blanking the screen after 800 ms.

Listing 9-11. Display a text string; file is in led/screen.rs

```rust
pub fn display(&mut self, word: &str) {
    // get the screen text
    // uses a macro to get the font string
    let screen_text = FONT_COLLECTION.sanitize_str(word).unwrap(); ①
    let white_50_pct = PixelColor::WHITE.dim(0.5);

    // Display the items
    for unicode in screen_text.chars() {
        if let Some(symbol) = FONT_COLLECTION.get(unicode) { ②
            let frame = font_to_frame(&symbol.byte_array(), white_50_pct); ③
            self.screen.write_frame(&frame); ④
        }
        thread::sleep(Duration::from_millis(800));
    }
    // now turn the display back off
    self.screen.write_frame(&self.frame.off_frame);
}
}
```

① Will take the text passed in and convert the set to a vector of
FontUnicode.

② Now converts the Unicode to a byte array representation.

③ Converts that byte array to a FrameLine that can be used to write to
the LED.

Scroll Text

The preceding listing just displays the text one by one with a delay between each letter,
but a somewhat fancier method is to scroll the text across the LED display. The code in
Listing 9-12 will scroll text across the screen.

Listing 9-12. Function to scroll text across the screen; file is in led/screen.rs

```rust
pub fn scroll_text(&mut self, word: &str) {
    let sanitized = FONT_COLLECTION.sanitize_str(word).unwrap();

    // Render the `FontString` as a vector of pixel frames, with
    // a stroke color of Blue and a BLACK background.
```

```
let pixel_frames = sanitized.pixel_frames(PixelColor::BLUE,
PixelColor::BLACK); ①

// Create a `Scroll` from the pixel frame vector.
// this will create some arrows to scroll over
let scroll = Scroll::new(&pixel_frames); ②

// Consume the `FrameSequence` returned by the `left_to_right`
method.
scroll.left_to_right().for_each(|frame| { ③
    self.screen.write_frame(&frame.frame_line());
    thread::sleep(::std::time::Duration::from_millis(250));
});
    }
}
```

① Create a vector of PixelFrame for each inner font of the text passed in with the colors for the font color and background image (black will be blank).

② Create the Scroll structure that will store the pixel frames for display.

③ Finally display the text, scrolling in from left to right with a 250 ms delay between each.

You can scroll any direction from left to right, right to left, top to bottom, or bottom to top. Each has an appropriately named method.

All of these functions will provide us all our tools needed to interact with the screen in the rest of the application. I would suggest trying a few just to get the hang of it.

Temperature Display

For now, let's move on to our sensor inputs. There are actually quite a few sensors on the board, and the crate we are using for this section has access to all the sensors. The gyroscope and accelerometer though didn't really fit into a use case for the book, but you can investigate this crate later to learn how to gain access and use them. For this book, we are going to focus on getting a temperature reading. There are two temperature sensors on the board: one collocated with the pressure sensor and the other with the humidity sensor. You can use either sensor or you can use both and take the average between the two. We are just going to use the humidity sensor (I actually had issues with one of my SenseHats on the pressure sensor).

Before we actually show the full set of code, let's build up on getting the temperature. First off, we are going to import our crates, and once again this will require some minor modifications. The branch I created adds more feature flags in order to turn off sensors we aren't going to use without the code panicking if it has an issue accessing a sensor. If you recall earlier, there was an issue accessing the pressure sensor; if it was in a UU state, the code would panic; I decided this isn't really a good thing if you aren't going to use that sensor anyways. And feature flags seemed to be the least intrusive way to fix this. The import of crates in Listing 9-13 will then not try to use or initialize the pressure sensor.

Listing 9-13. Adding `sensehat-screen` to our Pi application, in Cargo.toml

```
[dependencies]
sensehat = { version = "1.1.1", default-features = false, features =
["humidity"], git = "https://github.com/nusairat/sensehat-rs.git", branch =
"chore/fix-retrieve-error"}
```

You will notice one of the feature flags is for `humidity`; I also added one for `pressure` that is available but not being used. Now earlier we talked about how we need to talk to the sensors in the `i2c` bus at specific addresses. This crate uses the `i2cdev` crate to do all the communication for us and get all the information needed from those sensors and wrap it in a nice usable `struct`. If you get curious, there is a `htss221.rs` module in the crate that has all the code and information on how to communicate with the `i2cdev` crate and how to read the bytes that the device is transmitting. The `i2cdev` crate is an easy-to-use crate to interact with if you know how you are trying to communicate. For example, if you wanted to interact with the humidity chip, we know from before that we are communicating to the `/dev/i2c-1`; since this is attached to the GPIO board, we also know from the documentation that it is on the address `0x5f`; in order to instantiate the `LinuxI2CDevice` to communicate specifically with that chip, all you'd have to do is this:

```
i2cdev::linux::LinuxI2CDevice::new('/dev/i2c-1', 0x5f)
```

And if you searched the `sensehat-rs` crate we are using, you'd find a line similar to that in order to initialize access to the board. If you run into a new `i2c` bus device that there is no current support for, one cheat is to find a corresponding Python library. Python has a very rich community that creates Pi applications. You can use that as a basis to know what kind of data is needed to be read and written to the i2c. But let's take a look at what we want; we want access to the temperature reading; this is pretty easy; in Listing 9-14, we initialize the SenseHat and retrieve the temperature reading in celsius.

Listing 9-14. Determining the temperature from the humidity sensor

```
let hat = SenseHat::new().unwrap()
let temp = hat.get_temperature_from_humidity().unwrap().as_celsius();
println!("Temp : {:?} C", temp);
```

This will print out the temperature right now. You can go ahead and try it locally.

If you actually did it, you will notice the temperature seems a bit hotter than you expected. The reason for this is those sensors are RIGHT next to the board and other chips that are heating the air around our HAT sensors. This is picking up the heat dissipated by our Pi giving us a spurious reading. Now if you only care about registering drastic changes in temperature, then this is probably fine, and you can continue. However, if you want to try and get a more accurate temperature, there are a few things we can do.

First thing we can do is get a ribbon cable and move the SenseHat further away from the board; this will help produce a more accurate reading because it won't be picking up any heat from the Pi's CPU. However, this will look bad, and I don't particularly like that solution.

The other solution is going to require us do two things:

1. Get the temperature of the CPU which we can use to know how much the temperature of the sensor is being offset by.

2. Apply a factor to it to try and determine the calibrated difference.

Essentially, we are going to have this equation to determine the real temperature:
```
temp_calibrated = temp - ((cpu_temp - temp)/FACTOR)
```
This will take the difference of the CPU minus the sensors' temperature and divide it by a factor that will give us the amount to subtract. This factor is the tricky part; this is a calculated value based on the Pi's reading and and actual thermometer's reading. If you have the time and a real thermometer in the house, I'd take six or so readings during the day and apply them to that equation and average it to get the most accurate factor for your area. If instead you want a more average of a factor, the Weather Underground Pi project has done this already. We can use the factor they determined and generalize it to

all. It won't be as accurate since location and other factors are involved, but the number they came up with was 5.466 as the factor. Now this factor made it more accurate for me but was still not 100% accurate. But you at least get the idea of what we are trying to accomplish. If you want, run this and create your own factor to use.[2]

The one question you may be asking yourself after reading that is how do I get the CPU temperature? It's actually easier than you may think; the temperature is set in celsius in the file /sys/class/thermal/thermal_zone0/temp. Now we have all the details we need. Let's begin our code; what we are going to do is similar to our LED and create an Atmospheric wrapper struct to get a formatted version of the temperature back. This structure will wrap that connection to the SenseHat. In Listing 9-15, we create our Atmospheric struct with one public method get_temperature() that will return the temperature in fahrenheit.

Listing 9-15. Creating our Atmospheric interactions; file is in sensors/ atmospheric.rs

```
use sensehat::SenseHat;
use std::fs;
use log::{debug, info};

const THERMAL_TEMP: &str = "/sys/class/thermal/thermal_zone0/temp"; ①

const WUNDERGROUND_ADJUSTMENT_FACTOR: f64 = 5.466;

pub struct Atmospheric {
    hat: SenseHat<'static> ②
}

impl Atmospheric {
    pub fn new() -> Atmospheric {
        Atmospheric {
            hat: SenseHat::new().unwrap() ③
        }
    }
```

---

[2]https://github.com/initialstate/wunderground-sensehat/wiki/Part-3.-Sense-HAT-Temperature-Correction

```rust
pub fn get_temperature(&mut self) -> String {
    // Get the temperature from the humidity
    // we could also do pressure
    let temp = self.hat.get_temperature_from_humidity().unwrap().as_
celsius(); ④
    let thermal_tmp = fs::read_to_string(THERMAL_TEMP.to_string()).
unwrap(); ⑤
    let thermal_tmp_str = thermal_tmp.as_str().trim();

    // CPU temp needs to be divided by a 1000 to get the actual Celsius
    // temperature,
    // It supplies it like : 55991
    let cpu_temp: f64 = thermal_tmp_str.parse().unwrap(); ⑥
    let calculated_temp = temp - (((cpu_temp * 0.001)- temp)/
5.466) - 6.0; ⑦
    let calc_temp_f = calculated_temp * 1.8 + 32.0; ⑧

    debug!("Calculated Temp: {:?} C", calculated_temp);
    info!("Calculated Temp: {:?} F", calc_temp_f);

    format!("{:.1} F", calc_temp_f) ⑨
}

pub fn get_temperature_in_c(&mut self) -> f32 {
    // Get the temperature from the humidity
    // we could also do pressure
    let temp = self.hat.get_temperature_from_humidity().unwrap().as_
celsius();
    let thermal_tmp = fs::read_to_string(THERMAL_TEMP.to_string()).
unwrap();
    let thermal_tmp_str = thermal_tmp.as_str().trim();

    // acquire CPU temp
    let cpu_temp: f64 = thermal_tmp_str.parse::<f64>().unwrap() * 0.001;
    let calculated_temp = temp - ((cpu_temp - temp) / WUNDERGROUND_
ADJUSTMENT_FACTOR );
```

```
        // F32 is the type needed by hap current_temperature
        calculated_temp as f32
    }
  }
}
```

①   Set as a constant the location of the file containing the CPU temperature.

②   Our only property is the `SenseHat struct` from the crate.

③   Instantiate the `struct`; please note if you've added any features that sensor is marked as UU in our `i2cdetect`, this will fail.

④   Retrieve the temperature from the humidity sensor in celsius.

⑤   Retrieve the thermal temperature from the file.

⑥   Convert the string temperature to a float.

⑦   Apply our equation we went over earlier using the temperatures we just retrieved.

⑧   Convert the temperature to fahrenheit because while I have two science degrees, I live in the United States.

⑨   Format the value back to only have one digit, since the computed value has many decimal values.

If your sensors all work and want an even more accurate reading, you can take an average of the humidity and pressure sensors for the temperature as well. One thing to note is that the `std::fs::read_to_string` read is relatively fast and cheap, especially given the file is only one line, so we don't need to worry about constant reads from the application. Also we are only going to be pulling the temperature sporadically. We will be using this code later for part of our daily schedule and with our joystick interactions.

Joystick Control

You may have not noticed it, but there is a little button on the top of the Sense HAT, closest to the Ethernet port; this is our joystick. The joystick can be moved left, right, top, or bottom, and there is even a center switch as well. Using the `sensehat-stick` crate (`https://github.com/saibatizoku/sensehat-stick-rs`) will allow us an easy interaction with the joystick. This crate allows us to detect the direction and the action performed on the joystick. We will only be doing some basic things with this crate for this chapter, but in later chapters, we are going to expand on this module.

For now, let's start by adding the crate to our dependencies. In Listing 9-16, we add the stick.

Listing 9-16. Adding `sensehat-stick-rs` to our Pi application in our Cargo.toml

```
[dependencies]
sensehat-stick = { version = "0.1", default-features = false, features =
["linux-evdev"], git = "https://github.com/nusairat/sensehat-stick-rs.git"
}
```

Once again, I had to update the crates for this; there was an issue that while the crate allowed you to see all the actions, it didn't let you do any comparisons or equal comparisons to the actions. Interacting with the joystick requires one just to perform an infinite loop processing the events as they come in. In Listing 9-17, we have a simple example where we get the event and print out the results.

Listing 9-17. Simple example of interacting with the joystick

```
use sensehat_stick::{JoyStick, JoyStickEvent, Action, Direction};
let stick = JoyStick::open().unwrap();
loop {
    for ev in &stick.events().unwrap() {
        info!("Stick -- {:?}", ev);
    }
}
```

For each event, there is an `action` and a `direction`; the various directions are Enter-Up-Down-Left-Right.

And the various actions are Release-Press-Hold.

I think it's fairly self-explanatory what each of these means. Go ahead and run the code in your application placing it as the last thing you do in the `main` and you can see some variety of the output it creates as you move the joystick around. We will be creating a `joystick` module later that will help with our interactions.

Creating Interactions

At this point, you should be able to interact with the various sensors on the Raspberry Pi, and hopefully you've run through a couple quick tests. This was the easy part, because running everything one time as a single call in Rust is straightforward. But now, we want to take everything we've done and combine it into a few interactions.

As I mentioned when we started this section, we will be using channels via `tokio` crate. The channels will allow us to create multiple producers and a single consumer. The question of course begs what we are producing and what we are consuming. For our applications, the producers will produce a single command at a time. Commands will be enums that we can easily expand to in the future. Right now, our command enums are as follows in Listing 9-18.

Listing 9-18. The commands we will be using for our first iteration of the pattern; file is in manager.rs

```
#[cfg(feature = "ch09")]
#[derive(Debug)]
pub enum Action {
    ShowTemperature,
    Print(Display)
}

#[derive(Debug)]
pub enum Display {
    Halloween,
    Christmas,
    QuestionMark,
    Text(String)
}
```

These commands will handle the two main use cases of displaying the temperature and printing out text or images to the screen. In the end, our consumer will receive the commands from the channel and perform actions on the `LedControls` and `Atmospheric` structs that we created earlier.

To start off, we are going to create two main set of modules producing the following commands: the `daily` and `joystick` modules.

- Daily – A module that runs at intervals to display the temperature at 8
  a.m. and will display either a Christmas tree or a pumpkin at noon if
  it's the Christmas or Halloween season.

- Joystick – A module that will perform actions when we click in
  different directions. For this chapter, when you depress the center, it
  will display the temperature.

When all of this is put together, we will have a Pi board that can respond to
commands happening in real time by the user and also be allowed to perform
background routine operations all against the same modules. Giving us in essence multi-
threaded multi-module access to singular components without violating any borrow
checking or constantly creating new inputs to the sensors potentially causing deadlocks.

Tokio Async Run

We've used tokio in previous chapters mostly with the Rumqtt crate, but let's dive into a
bit more detail. The asynchronous processing has changed quite a bit with Rust in 2019,
and tokio packages have been updated accordingly. If you used tokio in version 0.1,
you had to do quite a bit of instantiating your runners directly and had to handle your
process through promises and futures. Now with the async feature in the 1.39 version of
Rust, we will be using polling instead of the promise/future route. Tokio 0.2 takes full use
of the new async/await methods.

The async/await allows a developer to create a function asynchronously and then
to await the return of the data and the finish of processing it. We will be using this to run
our scheduler.

First up, let's set up our dependencies in Listing 9-19 to include the latest tokio
and futures crate. This crate is heavily contributed and added to so don't let the 0.3
version scare you, they have a solid road map to 1.0 and heavily respond to questions on
Discord.

Listing 9-19. The tokio and futures crate dependencies, code in file Cargo.toml

```
[dependencies]
tokio = { version = "0.2.4", features =["full"] }
tokio-timer = "0.2.12"
futures = "0.3"
```

Now at the end of our `main` method, we are going to call an asynchronous method that will launch all of our background threads. In here, we create a channel that will allow us to send values between. This channel is similar in operation to channels you may have used in languages like Golang. The channel itself is initialized with a buffer, which we are keeping low since most of the communication will be performed by someone interacting with the Raspberry Pi and thus should never get too high. The channels return two objects: a transmitter and a receiver. The transmitters are used to transmit the data to the channel, and the receiver receives it. In Listing 9-20, we create the function that will be run in our main; afterward, we will implement each of the functions it calls.

Listing 9-20. Implementation of the tokio async code, code in file main.rs

```rust
#[tokio::main] ①
async fn run(matches: &ArgMatches, uuid: &Uuid) -> Result<(), Box<dyn
std::error::Error>> {
    use tokio::sync::mpsc;

    info!("Setup and start our channel runners ...");

    // defines the buffer to send in
    let (tx, rx) = mpsc::channel(100); ②
    let joy_tx: Tx = tx.clone(); ③
    let daily_tx: Tx = tx.clone();

    // Start our timer matcher
    // we want to do this after the authentication so we don't have any
    interruption from the
    // login; this will also run Asynchronously
    daily::run(daily_tx); ④

    // Setup and run the Joystick now; ⑤
    joystick::run(joy_tx);

    // Ready our receivers
    let led_controls = Arc::new(Mutex::new(LedControls::new())); ⑥
    let atmospheric = Arc::new(Mutex::new(Atmospheric::new()));
```

```
manager::run(rx, &led_controls, &atmospheric).await; ⑦

debug!("Complete");
Ok(())
}
```

① Uses the macro definition shortcuts creating a `Builder::new` with the default of a `threaded_scheduler` to start up our async processing.

② Creates the channel with an initialization of a 100 in the buffer.

③ Since we cannot pass the transmitter to multiple modules, we need to clone it for each module we want to pass it to.

④ Runs our daily background scripts transmitting commands when it hits a daily input.

⑤ Awaits our joystick input, sending commands back based on the input.

⑥ We wrap the `LedControls` and `Atmospheric` since they will be run asynchronously in the manager.

⑦ Calls our manager that will await forever waiting for transmissions.

In that function, you have three calls we have not defined yet; let's go ahead and define them.

Daily Runs

Our first stop is to set up the daily module. The daily module is a module that will run every hour on the hour firing off an event checker, as well as firing when we first boot up the application. In this module, we will spawn a thread that loops infinitely. We will then fire off our events inside the loop. Now we wouldn't want an infinite loop that constantly checks, since that would be a waste of resources. Instead, we will make use of `tokio::time` module to control an interval and duration to fire. Having this duration will allow us to only fire the event checker when it's on the hour. We will use our loop in conjunction with an interval check. We first will create the interval, given the time we want it to start at and the duration; from there, we can let the interval `tick`, pausing till the time has passed. This gives us in Listing 9-21 the ability to run code once an hour.

Listing 9-21. The main daily runner that will loop and run our special printouts, code in file daily.rs

```
const INTERVAL_IN_SECONDS: u64 = 60 * 60;

 pub fn run(mut tx: Tx) {
    use std::ops::Add;

    let local: DateTime<Local> = Local::now(); ①
    let min = local.minute();

    // Determine the time till the top of the hour
    let time_from_hour = 60 - min; ②
    debug!("Min from hour : {:?}", time_from_hour);
    let time_at_hour = Instant::now();
    time_at_hour.add(Duration::from_secs((60 * time_from_hour).into())); ③

    // Compute the interval
    let mut interval = interval_at(time_at_hour, Duration::from_
    secs(INTERVAL_IN_SECONDS)); ④
    tokio::spawn(async move { ⑤
        // run on initial start-up then timers after
        run_initial(&mut tx).await; ⑥

        loop {
            interval.tick().await; ⑦
            info!("Fire the Timer Checker; ");
            display_special(&mut tx); ⑧
        }
    });
 }

async fn send(tx: &mut Tx, action: Action) { ⑨
    if let Err(_) = tx.send(action).await {
        info!("receiver dropped");
        return;
    }
}
```

① Get the local time; this is going to be used as a basis to know how long we are from the hour.

② Determine the amount of minutes till the top of the hour since we want to fire this at the top of the hour.

③ Add that difference so now that `time_at_hour` will be the time of the next hour (i.e., if it's 3:37, now this variable will be 4:00).

④ Create our interval; the first parameter is the start, and the second is the interval; in this case, we check it every 60 minutes.

⑤ Spawn a new thread for our asynchronous call.

⑥ Run our initial call to print either a Christmas tree or pumpkin.

⑦ This is the start of the infinite loop; this will await the first tick which occurs at the top of the hour.

⑧ On the hour, it now runs the display.

⑨ The send method used by other calling functions to send our `Action` to the receiver.

Few things to note here, the `tx.send` can only be called in an `async` functions which also means its parent has to be in an `async` function as well and so forth. This is why you are going to see a layer upon layer of `async` until you get to the `tokio::spawn`; from that point, the `async` addition to the function is no longer necessary. Also this `send` method will be in the other modules, but we aren't going to print it out each time in the book.

We should also handle errors from the receiver better, but this code was already complicated enough as it is, but something for the reader to think about when using in a real-world application.

Next let's look at that `run_inital` function that gets ran when the Pi app first starts up; in Listing 9-22, we have that function which will check if it's Christmas or Halloween.

Listing 9-22. Checks if it's Christmas or Halloween, code in file daily.rs

```
async fn run_initial(tx: &mut Tx) {
    let local: DateTime<Local> = Local::now();
    if is_christmas(&local) {
        send(tx, Action::Print(Display::Christmas)).await;
    }
```

```
    else if is_halloween(&local) {
        send(tx, Action::Print(Display::Halloween)).await;
    }
}
```

And then in Listing 9-23, we run the `daily_special` that gets ran hourly, which will send an action to show the temperature at 8 a.m. or at noon if it's Christmas or Halloween to display the tree and pumpkin, respectively.

Listing 9-23. Our daily checker that gets ran hourly, code in file daily.rs

```
async fn display_special(tx: &mut Tx) {
    let local: DateTime<Local> = Local::now();

    // now switch based on the variable to display
    // we will only call this on the hour so we don't need to check the
    minute
    // also could be a delay so better to not be that precise
    if local.hour() == 8 {
        //display_weather(tx);
        send(tx, Action::ShowTemperature).await;
    }
    else if local.hour() == 12 {
        if is_christmas(&local) {
            send(tx, Action::Print(Display::Christmas)).await;
        }
        else if is_halloween(&local) {
            send(tx, Action::Print(Display::Halloween)).await;
        }
    }
}
```

Finally, we should take a look at the functions that check if it's the month of October (Halloween) or December (Christmas) in Listing 9-24.

Listing 9-24. Checks if it's October or if it's December before the 26th, code in file daily.rs

```
fn is_halloween(local: &DateTime<Local>) -> bool {
    local.month() == 10 && local.day() == 31
}

fn is_christmas(local: &DateTime<Local>) -> bool {
    // Any day in Christmas before the 25th
    local.month() == 12 && local.day() <= 25
}
```

This section shows us how to loop through a spawned function as well as how to create an interval and duration.

Joystick

We discussed the joystick code before but didn't write any code specifically for the application; let's loop back and write some code. This code will be a combination of what you saw earlier with the `tokio` async processing and the joystick code we did earlier. We will create a new module `joystick` with an entry point of `run(__)` to the module. Once again, we need to create a spawned thread and loop through it, except this time in Listing 9-25, we are checking for event input and responding to the event accordingly.

Listing 9-25. Joystick responses, code in file joystick.rs

```
pub fn run(mut tx: Tx) {
    let stick = JoyStick::open().unwrap();
    run_on_loop(stick, tx);
}

fn run_on_loop( mut stick: JoyStick,
                mut tx: Tx) {
    use tokio::task;

    info!("Run Async Calls on the joystick");
    // Use Spawn Blocking since Stick Events is a blocking call, otherwise
    we risk blocking
    // the current thread
```

```
task::spawn_blocking(move || { ①
    loop {
        // TODO : Add some logic to break up the time if not you hold
        the button down
        // And you may get it displaying 5 times
        for ev in &stick.events().unwrap() {
            info!("Stick -- {:?}", ev);
            // Create a response based on events
            // can be blank since the processing is inside
            if check_temp_event(&ev) { ②
                info!("Check Temperature Event");
                send(&mut tx, DisplayAction::ShowTemperature)
            }
            // TODO we will add more complexity later to this
            else {
                // let's just display a question mark
                warn!("Not Supported Event");
            }
        }
    }
});
}
```

①   Iterates through any events received.

②   Checks for a temperature event; we will build this out more in
    future chapters.

Lastly in Listing 9-26, we are going to implement the check_temp_event that will
check if the user entered and held down the button, the trigger for displaying the
temperature to the screen.

Listing 9-26. Checks if the user wanted the temperature, code in file joystick.rs

```
fn check_temp_event(ev: &JoyStickEvent) -> bool {
    // When the button is held down.
    if ev.action == Action::Hold
```

```
                && ev.direction == Direction::Enter {
                return true;
        }
        return false;
}
```

We now have all the producers we are creating for this chapter; you have potentially three sets of producers sending data to the receiver to use.

Receiver

As you can see clearly in all of this code, each time we are sending back the enums we defined earlier. In some cases, we pass in dynamic values like the text; in others, they are singular commands, ShowTemperature, but each one sends this through the transmitter. Now we will create the receiver for those commands. In Listing 9-27, we have our receiver that awaits an event, the rx.recv().await; this will await events and continuously run and wait for the next event. Incidentally, this forever await is also why we don't have to add a loop{} in the main.rs, because this await is going to be waiting indefinitely for the next command to appear.

Listing 9-27. Our receiver await processing, code in file manager.rs

```
pub type Tx = mpsc::Sender<Action>; ①
pub type Rx = mpsc::Receiver<Action>;

#[cfg(feature = "ch09")]
pub async fn run(    mut rx: Rx,
                     led_controls: &Arc<Mutex<LedControls>>,
                     atmospheric: &Arc<Mutex<Atmospheric>>) {
    // Receives the information
    while let Some(action) = rx.recv().await { ②
        info!("Received :: {:?}", action);
        // now let's parse out what should happen.Action
        match action { ③
            Action::ShowTemperature => {
                display_weather(&atmospheric, &led_controls);
            },
```

```
            Action::Print(display) => {  ④
                match display {
                    Display::Halloween => {
                        display_halloween(&led_controls);
                    },
                    Display::Christmas => {
                        display_christmas(&led_controls);
                    },
                    Display::Text(text) => {
                        display_text(text, &led_controls);
                    },
                    Display::QuestionMark => {
                        question_mark(&led_controls);
                    }
                }
            },
        }
    }
}
```

① Defines transmitter and receiver types of Action; this is used as a type
    shortcut in the other modules to know the type of transmitter being
    sent; it could be any struct or enum, but they have to be the same
    struct/enum for each channel.

② Awaits the receiver for transmitted data.

③ Matches our Actions.

④ Matches our Displays.

Finally in Listing 9-28, everything we have been working on in this section comes
together. The sensor struct you created is now called by the various commands we
passed through. For each command we add, we will have to create a corresponding
function that processes and handles. Your logic should mostly still occur in producers;
this is merely to handle the interactions the board provides.

Listing 9-28. Processes each of the messages, code in file manager.rs

```rust
fn question_mark(led_controls: &Arc<Mutex<LedControls>>) {
    //let mut led = Arc::get_mut(&mut led_controls).unwrap();
    let mut led = led_controls.lock().unwrap();
    led.question();
}

// Display Christmas tree for 30 seconds
fn display_christmas(led_controls: &Arc<Mutex<LedControls>>) {
    let mut led = led_controls.lock().unwrap();
    led.display_symbol(&CHRISTMAS_TREE, 30);
}

 // Display pumpkin tree for 30 seconds
fn display_halloween(led_controls: &Arc<Mutex<LedControls>>) {
    let mut led = led_controls.lock().unwrap();
    led.display_symbol(&HALLOWEEN, 30);
}

fn display_weather(atmospheric: &Arc<Mutex<Atmospheric>>, led_controls:
&Arc<Mutex<LedControls>>) {
    let mut atmo = atmospheric.lock().unwrap();
    let temp: String = atmo.get_temperature();
    let mut led = led_controls.lock().unwrap();
    led.display(&temp);
}

// Display any text
fn display_text(text: String, led_controls: &Arc<Mutex<LedControls>>) {
    let mut led = led_controls.lock().unwrap();
    led.scroll_text(&text);
}
```

This section gives us the start to being able to expand functionality to the board as well as expand background processing that will be necessary when we add other modules to the Pi. Pis are powerful computers, so don't be afraid to create a multi-threaded device so long as you keep all the memory and borrowing safeguards in place.

Logging In

We can now interact with the board devices, but we need to be able to interact more with all those endpoints we created in the first half that require a user. In order to interact with the services, we are going to have an authenticated user. The authenticated user will allow us to send a request token to the server to verify our users and verify they have access to box.

In Chapter 6, we went over the device authentication flow. In that chapter, we showed via curl commands and the web UI interactions how to perform a device flow authentication with Auth0. In this chapter, we are going to use those interactions into our code and integrate it into our Raspberry Pi application.

Yup OAuth 2

There are quite a few different authentication crates for Rust out there, and I looked through a few different ones. The yup-oauth2 is one of the more popular and has a solid diverse set of functionality in it. My main choice for picking it however is that none of the other crates had the necessary level of interaction that yup-oauth2 did for device flows. Remember, a device authentication flow calls to the server to get a code, returns that to the user, and then keeps checking back to the server to make sure the user has been authenticated. This was not the code I wanted to customize myself.

The only downside to yup-oauth2 is it seemed very much geared to the Google OAuth 2 Device Flow, which probably makes sense in terms of percentage of usage; however, that meant out of the box it did not work for our needs. Mainly there was one critical thing that needed to be customized, the name of the device_code sent; this field is not configurable, and we needed to configure them because Auth0 expects it to be device_code and Google just expects it to be code, different for Auth0. The code is hard-coded throughout yup-oauth2, so the only way to make this work was to branch this off. Once again, we will have to use a modified version; you can find that version at https://github.com/nusairat/yup-oauth2/. They are doing quite a few changes; in fact, from the time I started to write this chapter to finishing this book, the code changed drastically, and they are constantly improving the crate.

Let's talk about the flow we are going to code to our device:

- On startup of our application, the application will check for a valid JSON Web Token stored in the filesystem; if it exists and is valid, you will just proceed as normal and be considered logged in.

- If the token does not exist, then call out to Auth0 to get a device code to use for authentication.

- Display the device code on the LCD so that the end user knows what the device code they need to use is.

- In the background, periodically check to see if the user has been authenticated.

- Once authenticated, proceed to the next steps.

Luckily, most of this comes out of the box for us to use and will only require us configuring the application. For the authentication functionality we will create its own library. This will allow us greater reuse in terms of writing other apps that need authentication as well.

Since the authentication has to communicate directly with the LedControls and it's now in its own library, this presents another problem but gives us a new learning experience; how do we have the LedControls we created in the previous section interact with the library? The solution is we will use traits that will configure how to display the logic, which in reality really is a better way since apps may want to write the output differently.

Let's get this app started though. Since this application will not be part of the main Pi application, but instead will be a library referenced by it, let's start by creating a library. We still use the cargo new like we normally do, but now we pass in a --lib flag which generates a lib.rs instead of a main.rs. In Listing 9-29, we generate this application.

I'd put this in the same level that your other applications are in; it will be useful later when we have to reference it.

Listing 9-29. Creating a rasp-auth library package

```
➜ cargo new rasp-auth --lib
     Created library `rasp-auth` package

➜ ls -al rasp-auth/src
total 8
drwxr-xr-x  3 joseph  staff   96 Dec 15 16:28 .
```

```
drwxr-xr-x  6 joseph  staff   192 Dec 15 16:28 ..
-rw-r--r--  1 joseph  staff    95 Dec 15 16:28 lib.rs
```

We have created the library; now let's update the `Cargo.toml` file to the contents in Listing 9-30.

Listing 9-30. Creating a `rasp-auth` library package

```
[package]
name = "authentication"
version = "0.1.0"
authors = ["Joseph Nusairat <joseph@nusairat.com>"]
edition = "2018"

[dependencies]
yup-oauth2 = {git = "https://github.com/nusairat/yup-oauth2.git", branch =
"chore/fix-merge-errors"}

tokio = { version = "0.2", features = ["fs", "macros", "io-std", "time"] }
chrono = "0.4"

log = "0.4"
```

This will include all the dependencies we need for this section; you will notice for the yup-auth2 I am referencing the git directory for my fork that has the necessary changes to support Auth0.

For our library, all the code we will be writing next will be contained in the `lib.rs` file. The code is not that long and it's all performing a singular operation, so it did not make sense to add multiple modules.

Authentication Library

This library is going to have to do essentially three things:

1. Be a wrapper to run the authentication system so that we can minimize our code in the Pi app.

2. Create a flow specifically to be used for Auth0 and a device flow procedure.

3. Implement the use of a generic wrapper for display.

Before we start coding, let's discuss a bit how yup-auth0 works. The yup-auth0 crate requires you populate a few structs before you run the authorization:

- ApplicationSecret – This contains the endpoint for the authorization and auth orization URIs as well as any SSL certs and client IDs and secrets.

- FlowDelegate – One of the traits we will be customizing. There is a more specific trait for our use, DeviceFlowDelegate. The delegate is used to help the OAuth system to determine what to do at each phase of the authentication flow. It controls the flow for the following events:

- When user code is presented

- Request code is expired

- Pending

- Denied

- DeviceFlowAuthenticator – Builds our authenticator that will take in the DeviceFLowDelegate and also set where we plan to store the persisted token to.

Each of these builds up on one another until we have our authorization ready to be executed. The JSON token being persisted allows us to have an easy way to access the token between restarts and software failures without forcing the user to constantly re-authorize. And bonus with this crate is that it will check for an existing token, and if valid, it will not ask the user to have to go through the authorization flow again. Once executed, we will execute the future in tokio, awaiting retrieving the final token. In Listing 9-31, we have the authentication method that will implement this.

Listing 9-31. The authentication method

```
pub async fn authenticate(&self) -> bool
    where VD: VisualDisplay + Send + Sync { ①
    // Trait needed for the futures use

    info!("Authenticate");
    // Create our application secret
    let application_secret = ApplicationSecret { ②
        client_id: self.client_id.clone(),
```

```rust
            client_secret: self.client_secret.clone(),
            token_uri: format!("https://{}/oauth/token", self.url),
            auth_uri: format!("https://{}/authorize", self.url),
            redirect_uris: vec![],
            project_id: Some(PROJECT_ID.to_string()),   // projectId
            client_email: None,    // clientEmail
            auth_provider_x509_cert_url: None,    // X509 cert auth provider
            client_x509_cert_url: None,    // X509 cert provider
        };

        // Create the flow delegate
        let flow_delegate = AuthOFlowDelegate { ③
            output: self.output.clone()
        };

        let auth = DeviceFlowAuthenticator::builder(application_secret) ④
            .flow_delegate(Box::new(flow_delegate))
            .device_code_url(format!("https://{}/oauth/device/code",
            self.url))
            .persist_tokens_to_disk(JSON_SECRET_LOCATION)
            .grant_type("urn:ietf:params:oauth:grant-type:device_code")
            .build()
            .await
            .expect("authenticator");

        // Set our scopes of data we want to obtain
        let scopes = &["offline_access", "openid", "profile", "email"]; ⑤

        match auth.token(scopes).await { ⑥
            Err(e) => warn!("error: {:?}", e),
            Ok(t) => info!("token: {:?}", t),
        }
        // Unblocked now, let's blank out before we return
        let mut output_ctrls = self.output.lock().unwrap(); ⑦
        output_ctrls.clear();
        true
    }
```

①   Used to define the VisualDisplay we are passing through (we will get to this more in a bit).

②   Defines the `ApplicationSecret` as well as setting our URIs that are Auth0 specific.

③   The `FlowDelegate`; here we are using a custom struct so that we can display the pin to the Sense HAT.

④   Creates the `authenticator` which takes the flow delegate as well as the JSON location to persist to disk on a successful authentication and to be reused on refresh. This also takes in our `grant_type` that is specific to Auth0.

⑤   The scopes we need to add to get all the tokens we need in the response; you may recall these are the same scopes we used in Chapter 6.

⑥   Runs authentication of a user for the given scopes and with the configurations we created in step 4.

⑦   Clears out our LCD display which may have had the device code displayed.

This method will run the basic authentication; as you can see, this has quite a few moving parts that we need to go over:

- `VisualDisplay` – Will be our trait that defines the `input`

- `Access` – Will be the struct that this function will be an implementation on.

VisualDisplay

As stated, we need to make the display become generic, specifically because of our application needing to display to an LED output, but this also makes the authentication a more reusable library for different front-end devices that want to display the user data. In the future, you could reuse this module and change from our LED display to an LCD display or an Android display, without having to change the authentication module. In Listing 9-32, we are defining three functions for a trait needed to display.

Listing 9-32. The VisualDisplay trait

```
use yup_oauth2::{self, ApplicationSecret, DeviceFlowAuthenticator}; ①
use yup_oauth2::authenticator_delegate::{DeviceAuthResponse,
DeviceFlowDelegate};
use log::{info, warn};
// Used to pin that data to a point in memory, makes sure it's a stable
memory location
use std::pin::Pin;
use std::future::Future;

// Always store to this location
const JSON_SECRET_LOCATION: &str = "tokenstorage.json"; ②
// Probably should be a command line parameter
const PROJECT_ID: &str = "rustfortheiot"; ③

pub trait VisualDisplay { ④
    fn clear(&mut self);
    fn display_text(&mut self, text: &str);
    fn display_processing(&mut self);
}
```

① Imports needed for this crate.

② JSON secret storage location; you can share this location between the apps running to be able to send authentication requests.

③ The name of our project id that we defined in Auth0.

④ Visual Display trait.

We define three methods on that trait:

- clear – To clear out the display, blanking the screen so that whatever output we have doesn't stick around.

- display_text – Displays any output text that we want to display. This can be the user code or an error response.

- display_processing – Used to display an output saying the input is processing right now.

All of these cover all the use cases for displaying to the user the status via the LED display; this methodology of using a trait also allows us to add on to it as need be.

Entry Point Struct

Next, we are going to go over a struct that will be created in order to instantiate our access into this application. This will be an Access struct; it will contain information specific to your individual authentication application. In Listing 9-33, we have that initial structure.

Listing 9-33. The Access struct that is our public input into the application

```
pub struct Access<VD> {
    client_id: String,
    client_secret: String,
    url: String,
    output: Arc<Mutex<VD>>
}
```

The first three items are directly related to your individual Auth0 accounts, and you will need to plug in your own values when we instantiate the Access. The fourth, the output, is what is driving our input to the display device. Since we are performing multi-threaded access, we are also wrapping it in an Arc<Mutex<T>> call.

Now in Listing 9-34, we are going to define the implementation to this. You've actually already seen one of the methods we will put into the impl, it's the authenticate function we defined earlier. But now, let's define the where clause for the impl as well as a method to instantiate it. The where clause is necessary so that the compiler knows certain traits are on the VisualDisplay and are needed by subsequent calls in these functions (I generally prefer using new whenever the function is being accessed outside of the immediate module).

Listing 9-34. Defining the impl for the Access struct

```
impl<VD> Access<VD>
    where
        VD: VisualDisplay + Send + Clone + 'static ①
{
```

```
pub fn new(client_id: String, client_secret: String, url: String,
output: Arc<Mutex<VD>>) -> Access<VD> { ②
    // retrieve the access tokens if they exist
    Access {
        client_id: client_id,
        client_secret: client_secret,
        url: url,
        output: output
    }
}
```

①   Defining the conditions the VisualDisplay will have to implement to
     be used in our application.

②   The new function to create an Access struct.

The Send, Clone, and 'static are needed because the VisualDisplay is going to be used in various phases of the Auth life cycle, and they are required to by the future call, making use of the Send trait, and the flow delegate, which requires the Clone trait. This is a pretty standard procedure for Rust and allows us to enforce traits that need to be on the property that is being passed. In addition, the method we defined in Listing 9-31 will be part of this implementation.

At this point, you have almost all that is needed for authentication, one final set of code to implement for here, and that is to create our own flow delegate.

Auth0 FlowDelegate

The final set of code is our implementation of the FlowDelegate; there are really two reasons we need to create our own flow delegate:

1.   We need to overwrite the default settings to use Auth0-specific properties instead of Google-specific properties on the JSON authorization request.

2.   We want to customize the output of the device code to the LED display instead of just to the console log which is the default.

In order to output to the LED display, we are going to have to pass in our VisualDisplay in order for the code to have access. In Listing 9-35, we set up the struct that we instantiated in the authentication method.

Listing 9-35. Defining the AuthOFlowDelegate

```
use std::sync::{Arc, Mutex};

// Flow Delegate requires a Clone
#[derive(Clone)]
pub struct AuthOFlowDelegate<VD> {
    output: Arc<Mutex<VD>>
}
```

The struct is now set up; we now need to implement the FlowDelegate trait which will make this application work. In Listing 9-36, we start the implementation of the FlowDelegate.

Listing 9-36. The implementation for AuthOFlowDelegate

```
impl<VD> DeviceFlowDelegate for AuthOFlowDelegate<VD> ①
    where
        VD: VisualDisplay + Send + Sync ②
{
    /// Display to the user the instructions to use the user code
    fn present_user_code<'a>( ③
        &'a self,
        resp: &'a DeviceAuthResponse,
    ) -> Pin<Box<dyn Future<Output = ()> + Send + 'a>> {
        Box::pin(present_user_code(&self.output, resp))
    }
}
```

① Defines that we are implementing AuthOFlowDelegate for the FlowDelegate trait.

② The clone is needed for any properties used in the FlowDelegate and that is why we need to add it to our VisualDisplay.

③ Sends a call to display our user code to the LED display.

The last thing we need to do is output the device code. Since our Pi only has an LED display, we are going to need to output to the LED the device code in order for the end user to know what to do. We will output it with the format " > [DEVICE CODE]"; ideally, you would tell the user in an instruction manual that they have to authenticate when they see dashes come across the screen. In Listing 9-37, we implement the present_ user_code to perform that functionality.

Listing 9-37. The present_user_code function on the AuthOFlowDelegate implementation

```
async fn present_user_code<VD>(output: &Arc<Mutex<VD>>, resp:
&DeviceAuthResponse)
    where
        VD: VisualDisplay {
    use chrono::Local;

    info!("Please enter {} at {} and grant access to this application",
    resp.user_code, resp.verification_uri); ①
    info!("You have time until {}.", resp.expires_at.with_timezone(&Local));
    // Push to the ED Display
    let mut output_unwrap = output.lock().unwrap(); ②
    let text = format!("> {}  ", resp.user_code);

    // Bit of a fake since it will stop processing after this function
    output_unwrap.display_text(text.as_str()); ③
    output_unwrap.display_processing(); ④
}
```

① Print out to the logger the user code and verification URL; this is to make easier for our debugging purposes.

② Get the output VisualDisplay that we passed in to the authorization. Here we unwrap and lock which is needed to get the object from Arc<Mutex<T>>.

③ Output the device code to our LED display. This will give the user a visual representation of the device code they need to log in.

④ Change the UI to display a "is processing" image that is repetitive.

In a perfect world, you'd probably repeat the code or add other queues or a way to repeat if necessary. I didn't want to overly complicate the code so I will leave it to the reader to do that part. Our library is now complete; we can switch back to integrating this code into the Raspberry Pi application.

Raspberry Pi App Integration

The final step is to integrate with the Raspberry Pi application itself. Luckily, with the way we designed our library file, this is a pretty easy task. The first thing you need to do is set up a few more argument matchers to store our client id, secret, and auth URI. I am not going to implement them here (we've done it plenty of times), but the names for what we are creating are in Table 9-3.

Table 9-3. *Arguments used for the Authentication*

Name	Short	Description
auth_client_id	-i	Will store the client id for the Auth0 device flow we set up early.
auth_client_secret	-t	Will store the client secret for Auth0.
auth	-a	The URL for our Auth0 account; for my application, I set the default to rustfortheiot.auth0.com.

Ideally, you can check in all the property values but the client_secret, this you should set dynamically on start. Even more, you'd probably want to have it in something like a vault repository. Next, we need to implement a struct that implements the VisualDisplay since the library has no knowledge that we have an LED matrix to display to. In Listing 9-38, we implement the trait for the LedVisualDisplay.

Listing 9-38. Implement the LedVisualDisplay that is for our authentication; code is in main.rs

```
impl authentication::VisualDisplay for LedControls {
    fn clear(&mut self) {
        // let mut led_control_unwrap = self.led.lock().unwrap();
        // led_control_unwrap.blank();
        self.blank();
    }
```

```rust
    fn display_text(&mut self, text: &str) {
        // let mut led_control_unwrap = self.led.lock().unwrap();
        // led_control_unwrap.scroll_text(text);
        self.scroll_text(text);
    }

    fn display_processing(&mut self) {
        // let mut led_control_unwrap = self.led.lock().unwrap();
        // led_control_unwrap.processing();
        self.processing();
    }
}
```

You will notice we are able to just apply the VisualDisplay trait onto the LedControls; this adds the extra functionality and allows us to simply pass in the LedControls to the authentication module. In Listing 9-39, I have the final set of code that will call the authentication library using those parameters passing in the LedControls.

Listing 9-39. The run_authentication function that is in our main.rs of our Pi application

```rust
#[tokio::main]
async fn run_authentication(matches: &ArgMatches) {
    use authentication::Access;

    info!("Run Authentication ...");

    // Initialize the LED controls
    let led_controls = Arc::new(Mutex::new(LedControls::new()));

    let client_id = matches.value_of(args::auth_client_id::NAME).unwrap().
    to_string();
    let client_secret = matches.value_of(args::auth_client_secret::NAME).
    unwrap().to_string();
    let url = matches.value_of(args::auth0::NAME).unwrap().to_string();

    let access = Access::new(client_id, client_secret, url, led_controls);
```

```
    // Authenticate
    if access.authenticate().await == false {
        error!("Not Logged In:");
    }
}
```

Summary

In this chapter, we greatly expanded the ability of our Pi device with the added Sense HAT hardware. We now have a device that can communicate securely with the backend as well as perform various local interactions. As we continue, we will make use of the authentication module to transmit and receive data.

## CHAPTER 10

Camera

In the previous chapter, we added our SenseHat which contains six types of sensors, and we made use of the humidity, barometric, and joystick sensors. This allowed us to have a more intelligent Pi. In this section, we are going to add an additional peripheral, the camera. The camera is probably the most important peripheral when writing an application whose main feature is video and still capture.

But what we want to capture is still a question; when dealing with most aftermarket solutions, they tend to focus on a few approaches of the type of video content to capture:

1. Capture all the video. Everything the camera sees is captured to video and then stored locally, in the cloud, or on a network file system. This allows the user to have maximum set of video. Oftentimes, the video stored locally will get rotated out; in addition, cloud service providers also rotate the video content out. Although if you are storing video to S3, the cost for storage these days is not too pricey; however, you will be paying quite a bit in the data transfer of uncompressed video files. And sometimes that isn't worth it; it often depends on what you want to capture. Oftentimes, this cost can be too much and you just want to capture stills. Your standard camera will capture 24–30 frames per second (FPS). This makes for nice smooth motion, but we don't always need that and are OK just capturing 1 frame per second. This won't look smooth; nothing you'd necessarily want to post as a live video, but if your camera is there to just record someone breaking in or monitoring access, it will give you everything you need. This saves on processing time as well as on upload and storage cost.

© Joseph Faisal Nusairat 2020
J. F. Nusairat, *Rust for the IoT*, https://doi.org/10.1007/978-1-4842-5860-6_10

2. Capture video when there is motion. Another solution that is popular is to capture motion only. This solution is used to not only minimize storage and transport cost but also to minimize the time someone is needing to review video for. With this solution for a monitoring system, you will only have to review when there was motion. In addition, one can also capture stills on a slower frame rate to preserve space even more.

Both methods can be used in conjunction with facial recognition to enhance the videos – to know when there is a person at the location as well as to perhaps know who the person is. These two methods or combinations of those (like capture stills unless there is active movement and then start capturing full frames) can create quite a dynamic set of use for video in our application. In addition, you can combine Pis, each with cameras to get more complete pictures of an area.

Goals

There is a plethora of use cases that can be applied to using camera capture and OpenCV in particular. If I covered all the cases the code and the chapter could go on forever, and alas we still have some other topics to cover. But I wanted to make sure the reader had all the tools needed to create as dynamic as an application as they want when writing on their own. To that end the goals for this chapter is to add the camera to our Raspberry Pi that will capture all video and apply facial detection to pictures. In addition it will capture a jpeg image if a face is detected at a rate of once every 5 minutes. In detail our goals are :

1. Installing the Raspberry Pi Camera

2. Turning on the camera and capturing video

3. Running face detection on the video

4. Saving the video to a new file and intervals

5. Saving an image file on facial detection

Facial Recognition

Facial recognition has become extremely popular in day-to-day basis, from unlocking your phones to tracking who comes to your door with a Nest/Ring camera. Facial detection can even help you track your employees' whereabouts. In addition, it can simply be used by your camera to determine whether the motion detected was a car going by or a person walking. This latter part generally being more useful.

Facial detection in modern days is usually done two different ways. The first way is through machine learning. The machine learning can either use trained or pre-trained networks to detect user faces. These use neural networks to learn how to detect ones face and require the images fed into the network. TensorFlow is the most standard library used for network training and running, and the tensor team does have rust crate for use. However, that would at least need an entire chapter if not more dedicated to it as neural networks is a quite complex model to give any justice to.

Instead we will use an older concept that still uses some training, Open Computer Vision (OpenCV). OpenCV can actually work in conjunction with deep learning as well, but is also designed to interact with the camera directly and won't require us to have to use a different crates to read from the camera first. We can do it all in one. Thus for the book we are going to choose to use OpenCV for our camera capture, detection, and saving of video and images.

Installation

There are many different cameras for the Pi you can purchase, from the very basic to the ones that have night vision. And of course, they all range in price. The one we are using for the book and had you buy in Chapter 1 is a 5 megapixel very basic camera that should cost around $10 (`https://amzn.com/B07QNSJ32M`). Regardless of what you buy, as long as it has a 15-pin MIPI Camera Serial Interface (CSI) connector, you will be able to connect it to the board. Each board has one 15-pin connector specifically for cameras.

To start with, power down the Pi, and carefully detach your SenseHAT. Set it aside for now and let's find the connector for the camera. If you look at the board closest to the Ethernet ports, you will notice a cable attachment, as shown in Figure 10-1.

Figure 10-1. *Showing the board where the connector is and connected all the way*

You should be able to pull up on the connector; this will allow a separation that you can then fit the cable through. Now you can insert the ribbon cable, and it is very important to do this with the correct side; it only goes in one way. The ribbon without the prongs will face the Ethernet port (on mine, it's the blue side). You need to do this the correct way; if not, the camera will not work at all. The ribbon connected properly will look like Figure 10-2.

Figure 10-2. *Camera connected to the board*

The flip side with the connections will be toward the USB-C ports, and you can see that in Figure 10-3.

Figure 10-3. *Camera connected to the board*

Now you can complete it by putting the SenseHat back on top roping the cable through like in Figure 10-4.

Figure 10-4. *Connector pulled through with SenseHat on*

The camera is now fully connected, but one final step in order for the Pi to recognize the camera is we need to update the config.txt to tell it to turn on the camera. Remember, this file is on the SD card itself, and you will have to take the card out and plug in to your own computer to update config.txt on the card. You will add the line start_x=1 like in Listing 10-1 to your config.txt. You will have to take out the disk from your Pi in order to have access to the file when mounted to your other computer.

Listing 10-1. Enable the camera in the `/boot/config.txt` on the Raspberry Pi

```
start_x=1
```

If you want to quickly test to make sure the camera is working, you can log onto your Pi and run `raspistill -o testshot.jpg`; this will take an image and save the still to `testshot.jpg`, from their secure copy (via scp) it back to your computer, and you can check it out. Now that we have the camera installed on the Raspberry Pi, we can start coding against it. But before we actually dive into the code, we will need to prep our build system to be able to compile OpenCV libraries for the Raspberry Pi. In order to accomplish this, we are going to switch gears and use the cross crate to build the application.

Cross

In the previous chapters, we have been performing the cross compilation for the Pi creating a MUSL capable application. This tends to work well for testing or building applications where the underlying system is not under your control. MUSL gives the user greater compatibility and uses static linking of libraries to build and run the application. But there is another option in our cross compiling ways, and that is glibc which has been around for decades has tight controls into the x86 world. You do have to have a tighter control of the operating system to use glibc; however, since we are going to create an installable ISO in a few chapters that contains the OS and the application, we will have that tight control needed. Using the gnu compilers might also make sense if you are on a Linux system right now as well. You can perform this changing your target right now if you want to compile the application (of course currently, it might fail since all the necessary libraries aren't installed).

This notion of the library installation keeps coming back to haunt us. And in this chapter, we will be adding OpenCV libraries, which means we will need even more libraries installed to compile the application, and their musl/gnu equivalents to cross compile with – if only there was an easier way.

Luckily, there is. We are going to use a docker container that has all of our necessary libraries in it to be able to compile our application. Docker is a great solution, and we will use it later as well when creating our custom ISO image in the final chapter. In the previous chapters, we used a combination of installs and configurations to get the application to be cross compiled. This works, but also means if you are on a team of developers, you will have to make sure they all follow the same instructions; in addition, if they are on different computers, it adds to the confusion. Using the local builds worked well earlier on, but using docker to cross compile will help us create more easily reproducible builds and allow us to properly run the builds in a build system later on (we won't cover that in this book but is usually part of the process).

If we used docker on our own, it would pose a bit of a challenge. While we'd have to build the image with our code being copied and compiled. Once it's built, we'd then need to connect to a running container of that image to retrieve compiled artifact off and then stop the image being run. This is very messy; luckily, there is a crate that wraps all this logic into a nice neat crate to use, cross.

Rust Embedded – Cross Crate

The rust-embedded project on GitHub is a plethora of great libraries and tutorials for doing embedded application development. The cross crate is specifically designed to help us cross compile the application for multiple systems (https://github.com/rust-embedded/cross). Cross will allow us to cross compile in docker images with the output of the target being stored on the local file system. And while the first run of the cross compiler can be slow (in order to pull down docker images), subsequent runs are very fast. The beauty of cross is it gives us all the benefits of cross compiling and adding dependent libraries without the headache of having to add them explicitly to our local system and being also forced to include the cross compiler libraries.

Running cross is easy; you will need to have docker installed, but we already have it installed in previous chapters. And then in Listing 10-2, we will install the cross binary which is used for cross compiling.

Listing 10-2. Installing cross

```
→ cargo install cross
    Updating crates.io index
      Package `cross v0.1.16` installed,
```

Using Cross

Cross is almost too easy to use; it essentially uses the same commands as the Cargo CLI works with. In previous examples, we built with cargo build --target armv7-unknown-linux-musleabihf; using cross, we would simply build with cross build --target armv7-unknown-linux-musleabihf. The only exception will be when it starts up the first time, you will see the docker images getting downloaded. The same targets you have in your normal cargo build you will also have in cross. In addition, you have a new file, the Cross.toml, for more configurations. Cross.toml can be used to specify environmental variables you want to pass in from your system to the underlying docker image. In Listing 10-3, we pass through the RUST_BACKTRACE and a custom POSTGRES_URL to the image. (Note: This is an example, and we don't need this for our application.)

Listing 10-3. Environmental variables being passed in via the Cross.toml file

```
[build.env]
passthrough = [
    "RUST_BACKTRACE",
    "POSTGRES_URL",
]
```

Under the covers, it has a docker image for each target defined and thus a corresponding Dockerfile for each image. We aren't going to review the contents of those files, but if you want to, here are two locations to look at:

https://hub.docker.com/r/rustembedded/cross/tags – This is the actual docker hub location, with all the available image tags to use.

https://github.com/rust-embedded/cross/tree/master/docker – This is the directory that contains the source files for those docker images. If you dive into a few of them, you will see the base image they use (often Ubuntu) and what libraries they are adding. There is often quite a bit of overlap between the images, and are often bringing in the same libraries but for different targets.

The tag directory is important to pay attention to, because that will be the image that is used when targeting the build.

Customizing

However, all of this wouldn't be very helpful if we couldn't add our own library dependencies. And we can do exactly that with the application. Inside the Cross.toml we defined earlier, you can overwrite the docker image for a custom docker image to target your application. You will add a target.{TARGET_NAME} field along with the image inside the toml file. In Listing 10-4, we overwrite the target for armv7-unknown-linux-gnueabihf with a custom image that we will build shortly that will include the OpenCV libraries.

Listing 10-4. Overwrites the target for `armv7-unknown-linux-gnueabihf`, in `Cross.toml` file

```
# Custom Library with Authenticator in it
[target.armv7-unknown-linux-gnueabihf]
image = "opencvs-auth:musl"
```

This creates our custom image. Now there is no need to create your own docker file with Rust and cargo installed. The easiest is to pick an image we already want to use and use that as our base image. Since this chapter is about the camera and using OpenCV, those are the library files we need to compile with the application. For us, our base image will be a variant of `rustembedded/armv7-unknown-linux-gnueabihf`. The out-of-the-box Gnu library uses Ubuntu as the base image, but I wanted to use Debian instead so I took the base image, slightly tweaked it, and pushed it to docker hub. The docker hub location of this image is at `https://hub.docker.com/repository/docker/nusairat/images/general`.

We will use this as our base image; just remember it's just a branch of the armv7 gnu build. Let's go through and start building our image for the Raspberry Pi master app. Our goal is to have this work on a 32-bit Arm7 operating system; to that end, you will notice we pull the arm hard float `armhf` version of libraries as opposed to the `arm64`. I would advise not to be tempted to use the 64 bit since 64-bit support on Raspberry Pis is not full featured or that good. Also much of the following set of Docker code we are creating is based off of the work done on Paul's blog that can be found here: `https://solarianprogrammer.com/2018/12/18/cross-compile-opencv-raspberry-pi-raspbian/`. He also has instructions how to cross compile OpenCV for a Pi Zero. I wanted to make sure to give the proper credit; there were a few nuances (like some re-namings) and some of the extra library installs that I would have spent far too long figuring out without it.

The entire file is located in the `rasp-pi-app-master` folder, but let's dive into the individual parts. In Listing 10-5, we have our FROM tag from the custom GNU Debian image I mentioned earlier. This is how we start every `Dockerfile`.

Listing 10-5. From for our application, in the Dockerfile

```
FROM nusairat/cross:arm7-gnu-debian
# FROM nusairat/cross:arm7-musl-debian
```

From there in Listing 10-6, we install the ArmHf architecture needed to compile and use against an ArmHf OS and device. This will be needed because the libraries we pull in will need to be compiled to ArmHf since that is our target.

Listing 10-6. Install the binaries to compile the ArmHf architecture, in the Dockerfile

```
RUN dpkg --add-architecture armhf
RUN apt-get update && apt-get install -y qemu-user-static
```

We then install the necessary Python libraries in Listing 10-7 to compile the application. While we won't be using Python directly, it was needed by the underlying OpenCV crate to interface with the OpenCV libraries.

Listing 10-7. Install the python binaries, in the Dockerfile

```
RUN apt-get install -y  python3-dev
RUN apt-get install -y python3-numpy
RUN apt-get install -y  python-dev
RUN apt-get install -y  python-numpy

#We'll also need libpython for the armhf architecture:
RUN apt-get install -y libpython2-dev:armhf
RUN apt-get install -y libpython3-dev:armhf
```

In addition, there are also misc libraries used for image manipulations and codecs that OpenCV calls in order to do perform its processing on videos; we will install those next in Listing 10-8.

Listing 10-8. Necessary image manipulations and codecs, in the Dockerfile

```
RUN apt-get install -y libtiff-dev:armhf zlib1g-dev:armhf
RUN apt-get install -y libjpeg-dev:armhf libpng-dev:armhf
RUN apt-get install -y libavcodec-dev:armhf libavformat-dev:armhf
libswscale-dev:armhf libv4l-dev:armhf
RUN apt-get install -y libxvidcore-dev:armhf libx264-dev:armhf

# install the default cross compilers from Debian which can be used to
create armhf binaries for Raspberry Pi:
```

```
RUN apt-get install -y crossbuild-essential-armhf
RUN apt-get install -y gfortran-arm-linux-gnueabihf

# Install CMAKe etc
RUN apt-get install -y cmake git pkg-config wget
```

Finally, we get to downloading the OpenCV source code and preparing it for compilation. We use CMAKE to set the options we want for the OpenCV. I have included mostly default options as well as installing the necessary libraries. The OPENCV_ GENERATE_PKGCONFIG is necessary to work with the OpenCV crate. There are quite a few steps in this process, so in Listing 10-9, I break down the various steps.

Listing 10-9. The download and OpenCV install, in the Dockerfile

```
WORKDIR /root

①
RUN mkdir opencv_all && cd opencv_all \
    && wget -O opencv.tar.gz https://github.com/opencv/opencv/
archive/4.1.0.tar.gz \
    && tar xf opencv.tar.gz \
    && wget -O opencv_contrib.tar.gz https://github.com/opencv/opencv_
contrib/archive/4.1.0.tar.gz \
    && tar xf opencv_contrib.tar.gz \
    && rm *.tar.gz

②
# variables required to successfully build GTK+
ENV PKG_CONFIG_PATH /usr/lib/arm-linux-gnueabihf/pkgconfig:/usr/share/
pkgconfig
ENV PKG_CONFIG_LIBDIR /usr/lib/arm-linux-gnueabihf/pkgconfig:/usr/share/
pkgconfig

# At this point, we can use Cmake to generate the OpenCV build scripts:
RUN cd /root/opencv_all/opencv-4.1.0 \
    && mkdir build && cd build

③
WORKDIR /root/opencv_all/opencv-4.1.0/build
RUN cmake -D CMAKE_BUILD_TYPE=RELEASE \
        -D CMAKE_INSTALL_PREFIX=/opt/opencv-4.1.0 \
```

```
    -D CMAKE_TOOLCHAIN_FILE=../platforms/linux/arm-gnueabi.toolchain.
    cmake \
    -D OPENCV_EXTRA_MODULES_PATH=~/opencv_all/opencv_contrib-4.1.0/
    modules \
    -D OPENCV_ENABLE_NONFREE=ON \
    -D ENABLE_NEON=ON \
    -D ENABLE_VFPV3=ON \
    -D BUILD_TESTS=OFF \
    -D BUILD_DOCS=OFF \
    -D PYTHON3_INCLUDE_PATH=/usr/include/python3.7m \
    -D PYTHON3_LIBRARIES=/usr/lib/arm-linux-gnueabihf/libpython3.7m.so \
    -D PYTHON3_NUMPY_INCLUDE_DIRS=/usr/lib/python3/dist-packages/numpy/
    core/include \
    -D BUILD_OPENCV_PYTHON2=OFF \
    -D BUILD_OPENCV_PYTHON3=ON \
    -D BUILD_EXAMPLES=OFF \
    # Needed for the rust app
    -D OPENCV_GENERATE_PKGCONFIG=ON ..

④
#Make the application
RUN make -j16
RUN make install/strip
```

① Download the OpenCV 4.1.0 archive and untar the file.

② Create necessary environmental variables for build and directories.

③ Run cmake based on our configurations that include python and the necessary libraries.

④ Compile the OpenCV library (this will take a bit of time).

Lastly, in Listing 10-10, we do some final copying of files to the right location as well as copying in the OpenCV package config file. This just defines the library directories and lib startup flags for the application. This is custom created and based partially on the libraries we installed earlier. I haven't included it here only because the one line is 814 characters long and is just listing out the libraries.

Listing 10-10. Defining the finally copying of the files, in the Dockerfile

```
# Change the name since it was mislabeled by the installer

①
RUN cd /opt/opencv-4.1.0/lib/python3.7/dist-packages/cv2/python-3.7/ \
    && cp cv2.cpython-37m-x86_64-linux-gnu.so cv2.so

②
## Copy opencv-4.1.0-armhf.tar.bz2 and opencv.pc from your home folder to
your Raspberry Pi.
RUN cd /opt \
    && tar -cjvf ~/opencv-4.1.0-armhf.tar.bz2 opencv-4.1.0

③
## Creates a Pkg-config settings file
WORKDIR /root
# Copy in the OPENCV from our file system
COPY opencv.pc opencv.pc

# Move the opencv.pc we copied in
RUN mv ~/opencv.pc /usr/lib/arm-linux-gnueabihf/pkgconfig

④
# This is where our gnuebihf config will be
ENV PKG_CONFIG_PATH /usr/lib/arm-linux-gnueabihf/pkgconfig/
ENV OPENCV_PACKAGE_NAME /usr/lib/arm-linux-gnueabihf/pkgconfig/opencv.pc
ENV LD_LIBRARY_PATH /opt/opencv-4.1.0/lib
ENV PKG_CONFIG_ALLOW_CROSS 1
```

① Renamed since the installer doesn't give it the correct name.

② Copies the built OpenCV to the /opt directory.

③ Copies our local version of the package config.

④ Sets the environmental variables needed for the Rust build.

This will finish up our Dockerfile and includes everything needed to compile OpenCV as well as allows us to cross compile from our PC/Mac to a 32-bit Raspberry Pi system. However, before we can use it with cross, we need to build the docker image. In Listing 10-11, we build the docker image, tagging it as opencvs-auth:musl (the same tag we referenced earlier in the Cross.toml).

Listing 10-11. Docker build for our custom image used to create an environment to build our application

```
➜ docker build -t opencvs-auth:musl .
Sending build context to Docker daemon  1.741GB
Step 1/36 : FROM armv7-unknown-linux-musleabihf:debian
 ---> 33af951b181a
Step 2/36 : RUN dpkg --add-architecture armhf
 ---> Using cache
 ---> 661ffd2fde76
...
Step 36/36 : ENV PKG_CONFIG_ALLOW_CROSS 1
 ---> Running in f7b7742b4571
Removing intermediate container f7b7742b4571
 ---> 58e0118e604e
Successfully built 58e0118e604e
Successfully tagged opencvs-auth:musl
```

Now we are able to use the image in our cross build. In Listing 10-12, we run cross targeting the armv7-unknown-linux-gnueabihf and assuming you did everything right it should cross compile.

Listing 10-12. Cross compiling build using the image we created previously

```
➜ cross build --target=armv7-unknown-linux-gnueabihf
   Compiling libc v0.2.66
   Compiling autocfg v1.0.0
   Compiling proc-macro2 v1.0.8
   ...
   Compiling rasp-app v0.1.0 (/project)

    Finished dev [unoptimized + debuginfo] target(s) in 7m 19s
```

The result of the cross compile outputs to the local directory structure just like if you used a standard cargo build. You can view the directory structure of the result in Listing 10-13.

Listing 10-13. View the output of our build

```
➜ ls -al target/armv7-unknown-linux-gnueabihf/debug
total 246576
drwxr-xr-x    10 jnusairat  334330370          320 Feb 11 21:50 .
drwxr-xr-x     3 jnusairat  334330370           96 Feb 11 21:42 ..
-rw-r--r--     1 jnusairat  334330370            0 Feb 11 21:42 .cargo-lock
drwxr-xr-x   161 jnusairat  334330370         5152 Feb 11 21:42 .fingerprint
drwxr-xr-x    27 jnusairat  334330370          864 Feb 11 21:42 build
drwxr-xr-x   403 jnusairat  334330370        12896 Feb 11 21:50 deps
drwxr-xr-x     2 jnusairat  334330370           64 Feb 11 21:42 examples
drwxr-xr-x     3 jnusairat  334330370           96 Feb 11 21:48 incremental
-rwxr-xr-x     2 jnusairat  334330370    113688176 Feb 11 21:50 rasp-app
-rw-r--r--     1 jnusairat  334330370          553 Feb 11 21:50 rasp-app.d
```

The final result produces a file that is 113 MB (if you have the OpenCV crate configured in your application). We don't have that quite yet, but I wanted us to have the compiling of the application ready, so when we start building in the next section, you can also start testing. Since we are ready, let's not waste time and let's start building the application.

Open Computer Vision

Before we dive into coding, let's expand on our conversation about what OpenCV is. OpenCV was originally designed by Intel in the 1990s, released in 1999, to help with real-time computer vision. Computer vision is more than just grabbing computer frames from a computer and recording to file or displaying them on another screen. The purpose is to allow the processing and analyzing of the video the camera records. In the beginning, this was mainly used to analyze objects and extract edges, lines, and 3D modelling from the video. In essence, the computer would be able to analyze and tell the user what it saw. The computer could describe the shapes, colors, and so on. The application of this is useful for monitoring, for assisting the visually impaired, and even for defense. Over the decades, CV has grown to make use of deep learning and other advanced algorithms to detect faces and the world around you. Cameras have become a very powerful tool because they are now relatively cheap, meaning you can easily have multiple and can tell quite a bit about the world around you. For example, Tesla uses only cameras around the car to run its self-driving system.

While we won't be creating anything near as advance as that, the potential applications for an OpenCV system on your Raspberry Pi are endless with the right amount of coding, processing, and storage. This gives us the gateway to create a powerful application with less than $100 worth of hardware.

Installing OpenCV

We previously installed OpenCV for our Docker build but not for our local. While we won't need this to compile the application for the Pi, it's useful for testing purposes, and since OpenCV isn't platform dependent, we can use this code locally and on our Pi. When running locally, it will use your computers' built-in camera (assuming you have one). The easiest installation for OSX is to use brew; you can perform that install with `brew install opencv`. There are quite a bit of various instructions on how to install OpenCV on other platforms; you can search the `https://docs.opencv.org/` site to find the instructions for whichever platform you are using.

Now let's add OpenCV to our application's `Cargo.toml`. The Rust crate can be used for any version of OpenCV above 3.2; we will be targeting the most recent, OpenCV 4.x; as such in Listing 10-14, we include that feature into our build.

Listing 10-14. The OpenCV crate with additional features, in Cargo.toml

```
# For writing out EXIF data
#rexiv2 = "0.9.0"

[dependencies.opencv]
version = "0.29"
default-features = false
features = [
    "opencv-4",
    "buildtime-bindgen",
]
```

In addition to the OpenCV 4 crate, we are including the `buildtime-bindgen` feature. This module is only needed for development when building on Windows or OSX; once you are ready to deploy the Pi, it can be removed or at least commented out (although it won't hurt anything if it's kept in).

Running the Application

Let's review what we are planning to build with the OpenCV system; our application won't be too advanced, but it's also not the most basic either. This application will do the following things:

- Capture the video from an attached camera.

- Display to a local screen (for development).

- Run facial recognition on the screen.

- Record the video in chunks.

- Save an image when a face is detected at a given interval.

- Show the current date and time on the recorded video.

All of these will give a breath of information on how to create your one camera capturing application. The code is going to be mostly in one function, but we will break off the discussion into usable chunks; you can always refer to the source code to see the entire listing.

Most of the code we are going to be writing will be in one file, the src/camera/video.rs file. In Listing 10-15, we have the imports, mostly importing from the opencv crate.

Listing 10-15. Imports for our video capturing, in src/camera/video.rs

```rust
use std::{thread, time::Duration};
use opencv::{
    core,
    highgui,
    imgproc,
    objdetect,
    prelude::*,
    types,
    videoio,
};
```

```rust
use opencv::videoio::{VideoCapture, VideoWriter};
use opencv::objdetect::CascadeClassifier;
use opencv::calib3d::UndistortTypes;
```

Much of the application will be in the run_face_detect function where we will pass in a boolean which is used to decide whether we should open up a window to see what we are recording. This is useful for debugging locally, but we do not want it running on the Raspberry Pi since we have no attached devices to view. In Listing 10-16, we have this outline.

Listing 10-16. The skeleton outline of our function, in src/camera/video.rs

```rust
const MINUTES_BETWEEN_IMAGES: i64 = 1;
const MINUTES_BETWEEN_NEW_VIDEO: f64 = 0.5;
const FPS_FACTOR: f64 = 0.5;

// can run a Haar Cascade on the image
pub fn run_face_detect(show_window: bool) -> opencv::Result<()> {
    info!("Start face detection ...");
  loop { }
}
```

The loop will be where we continuously run the video capture and processing; before we do that, we need to get into some setup that occurs before the loop. We will have to initialize a few things:

- The window to display the output to

- The camera to capture from

- Initialization of our writers to capture the video to

- Initialization of our face detection

We will tackle each of these in the following sections so part of the code will reside before the loop and the others inside the loop; I'll call it out where the code goes when need be.

Capturing the Video

Let's start with capturing the content of the video camera; this will require us having OpenCV connect to the camera and reading content from it. In Listing 10-17, we capture the content from the index of the capture devices. The default is 0, and since we only have one camera we are capturing from, we can set it there. The next parameter is the reader implementation; this can be DSHOW, MSFMF, or V4L, but again the default that we are using is ANY.

Listing 10-17. The camera initialization, in src/camera/video.rs

```
let mut cam =  videoio::VideoCapture::new_with_backend(0, videoio::CAP_ANY)?;
// 0 is the default camera
// Open the camera
let opened = cam.is_opened()?;
if !opened {
    panic!("Unable to open default camera!");
}
```

Then inside the loop, we will capture the video frame by frame. After you capture each frame, you could write it back to a file, or you could do post processing on it; it's really up to the user at that point (we will do both in a bit). In Listing 10-18, we capture from the camera frame by frame.

Listing 10-18. Capturing the video content onto a frame, in src/camera/video.rs

```
let mut frame = Mat::default()?;
cam.read(&mut frame)?;

// Sleeps in case there is no screen coming
if frame.empty().unwrap() {
    debug!("frame empty? camera not initialized?");
    thread::sleep(Duration::from_secs(50));
    continue;
}
```

You will notice we check if that frame has any width; if there is none, we wait for 50 seconds and retry. The reason is if there was no width, that would be because the camera hasn't started up or some IO operation is temporally blocking it, giving it that delay gives the system time to have the camera ready. We will manipulate this frame in a bit.

Displaying to the Camera

Next up, let's add in the camera monitor. This is not necessary to have unless we want to watch the output of the video recording during debugging; hence, why we will wrap all these calls in an `if` flag? Ideally, you would turn this on via command-line arguments defaulting to false. The display is all driven by the `opencv::highgui` libraries. In Listing 10-19, we initialize the call to that library.

Listing 10-19. Initializing our call to open a window to capture the video, in src/camera/video.rs

```
let window = "video capture";
if show_window {
    highgui::named_window(window, 1)?;
}
```

And then inside the loop we pass the frame to the window that was created in Listing 10-20.

Listing 10-20. Show the window of the video captured, in src/camera/video.rs

```
if show_window {
    highgui::imshow(window, &frame)?;
    // can be used for a bit of a delay
    if highgui::wait_key(10)? > 0 {
        break;
    }
}
```

At this point, we have the camera capturing out video and then returning it to our monitor; however, we still have not performed any processing of the video.

Capturing the Facial Recognition

Let's change that now and apply some processing to the video frames that we are receiving so that we can detect the people's faces. We will use OpenCV and Haar Cascades to not only detect whether or not the display on the screen is a face but also where those faces are and to put a rectangle around them. This is often also done with deep learning; with deep learning, you have to perform the learning part of it as well, and this actually requires quite a bit of work in not only determining what you are looking for but the tolerance of differences in the patterns. We don't really have time for it in this book to cover training, but we do have time to cover how to use a pre-trained cascade algorithm. And to that extent, we are going to use pre-trained face detection algorithms to apply to our frames in order to detect faces.

While the science of face detection is relatively new, the math we use behind it is over a century old. Neural networks were first proposed in 1873 and 1890 by Alexander Bain and William James, respectively. They produced the theoretical basis on how neurons fired together and much of the basis for neural networks today. There are a variety of neural networks from temporal neural networks to convolution networks. Convolution neural networks use mathematical operations to produce the output of the neural network. For our facial detection, we will be using something similar; we will be using what is called Haar feature to perform the facial detection. The Haar feature is just like a kernel in convolution neural networks, except a Haar feature is manually trained and calculated.

Haar sequences were first theorized by the Hungarian mathematician Alfred Haar in 1909. He created an orthonormal system for the space between square functions. These concepts were then brought together by Paul Viola and Michael Jones in there 2001 paper "Rapid Object Detection Using a Boosted Cascade of Simple Features". The basis of the Haar features is to use the black and white (or gray-scale) differences between horizontal and vertical lines to calculate patterns.

If you think about your face and the shading of it, we have natural horizontal and vertical lines in it. You essentially have three different types of features. Your edge features are where one side is dark and the other is light; you can think of your eyebrows or nose as one. You also have line features where you have one side light, middle dark, and next light; your lips closed would be an example. All of these features work vertically or horizontally. And you can even have four rectangle features as well. What this reduction does is it reduces all our calculations to looking at most four pixels (edges have 2, lines 3, rectangles 4). Take our beautiful model in Figure 10-5 also known as my wife. This is a gray-scaled image of her.

Figure 10-5. *Shows the original picture*

Now let's apply some lines drawn to quite a few pixels based on edge and line features; the white will be the lighter and the black will represent the darker area in Figure 10-6.

Figure 10-6. *Shows the original picture with the edge/line features*

Now in a pure black and white image, these would be simply zeroes or ones. However, people's faces aren't generally distinguishable black and white so we use a gray scale. In a 24x24 pixel window, we can receive over 160,000 features; this is quite a bit to process and wouldn't be usable in real time. But with the Viola-Jones algorithm, we can break it down to 6000 features; you can even have 200 features for 95% accuracy. This is because most videos you take the face is not the major component that is coming into play; much of it is external noise that can be eliminated. The way they went about making this optimization is by running the 6000+ features over 38 stages. At each stage, if nothing is detected, then the classifier moves on to another part of the image. So to find a face in the preceding image, you may see it go through various parts of the frame without finding a face. Interestingly to note, the first five stages look through 111 features, broken up as 1-10-25-25-50 features at each stage. The idea is to fail fast on the majority of the areas where there would be blank space. This optimization is what makes the classifiers very fast and able to run in real time. And this is the basis for the code we will be writing next to create the facial detection.[1]

Using Trained Cascades

Using this logic, you can create not only facial recognition but even emotion recognition or even determine if someone is smiling or not. Now all of these are based on the calculation of patterns. Like we stated earlier, these are manually trained algorithms, and many of these algorithms have been published for general public consumption. OpenCV publishes a list of Haar Cascades that we we can use for our applications; they are published at https://github.com/opencv/opencv/tree/master/data/haarcascades. For our application, we will be using the haarcascade_frontalface_alt.xml; you should download this to our local file system. In Listing 10-21, we load up this classifier in order to apply it to our face.

Listing 10-21. Loading up the Haar Cascade into our application, in src/camera/video.rs

```
if !std::path::Path::new(&haar_cascade_file).exists() { panic!("Haar
Cascade is needed!"); }
let mut face = objdetect::CascadeClassifier::new(&haar_cascade_file)?;
```

Running the Cascade

Now that we have the cascade, we just need to apply it to our classifier. Remember even the inexpensive camera we installed is in color, and as we just went over, the classifier uses gray scale for its variant calculations. So before we run the classifier on the frame, we are going to need to convert the frame to gray scale. In addition, high-resolution cameras will have more pixels, and while there is potentially greater accuracy, this will take the face detector longer to process each image. Therefore, in addition to converting the image to gray scale, we are going to reduce the size of the frame we process on. In Listing 10-22, we convert to gray scale and then resize the image passing in the gray-scale color.

---

[1]https://docs.opencv.org/3.4/db/d28/tutorial_cascade_classifier.html

Listing 10-22. Converting the frame to gray scale and resizing the frame, in src/
camera/video.rs

```rust
let mut gray_frame = Mat::default()?; ①
imgproc::cvt_color(
    &frame,
    &mut gray_frame,
    imgproc::COLOR_BGR2GRAY,
    0
)?;

// Resizes an image.
// The function resize resizes the image src down to or up to the
    specified size.
let mut reduced = Mat::default()?; ②
imgproc::resize(
    &gray_frame,
    &mut reduced,
    core::Size {
        width: 0,
        height: 0
    },
    0.25f64, ③
    0.25f64,
    imgproc::INTER_LINEAR
)?;
```

① Converts the frame to a gray scale.

② Reduces the gray frame to smaller more manageable size.

③ The scale factor to use; here we pass in .25 so we reduce the image
   by 3/4.

The reduced variable will now contain our reduced gray-scale image. We can now
take the face object we created based on the Haar Cascade and run the face detection
matcher on it. If a match is found, it will return a set of rectangle boxes for each face
it matches in the frame. The set will not only tell us if there is a face on the frame but
will also tell us where the face is. This will allow us to dynamically create a rectangle

bounding box that will be visible on the application. In Listing 10-23, we apply the bounding box onto the original full-size color frame using the coordinates found.

Listing 10-23. Bounding box of the face applied to the frame, in src/camera/video.rs

```
let mut faces = types::VectorOfRect::new();
face.detect_multi_scale( ①
    &reduced,
    &mut faces,
    1.1,
    2,
    objdetect::CASCADE_SCALE_IMAGE,
    core::Size {
        width: 30,
        height: 30
    },
    core::Size {
        width: 0,
        height: 0
    }
)?;
```

- Run the face detection on the frame detecting faces of different sizes returning a list of rectangles for it.

- Calculate the squared coordinates multiplying the coordinates by a factor of 4 since we reduced the previous by a 1/4.

- Draw a rectangle on the original frame.

We now have a working face detector, and in fact, if you run this with the show_ window enabled, you will see the face bounding box dynamically appear and will follow your face around the camera. You can go ahead and move the face around to see the limits of the Haar Cascade (it's not very good at side face detection).

Saving the Video Content

We have the camera now capturing and running facial recognition software on the image, but beyond that, it doesn't do much with the video but just allows us to watch it in real time. In addition, we created an entire backend whose main purpose is to capture video. So let's give the backend video something to capture. In this section, we will save the video. This part can get a bit tricky to get the capture right. You need to make sure the frames you are capturing are getting output to the same rate you are writing. There is also a delay because you aren't just getting the video you capture and immediately dumping it into the new file. We will do our best to make this smooth, although I've noticed some delay in using it as well. However, OpenCV comes with all the libraries to create a new video, so we won't have to rely on anything else to save the captured video. In order to do so, we need to know a few things about the video we want to create:

- Height

- Width

- Frames per second

- Codec

The first three are fairly easy; since we aren't applying any lasting resize to the frame, we will just use the height and width of the video that we are receiving. The frames per second we also will retrieve from the video we are reading from, but then apply a factor to it to make the timing appear smoother. You may have to set that factor yourself. In Listing 10-24, we use these three factors to create the `size` and `fps` variables.

Listing 10-24. Calculate the size and FPS of the video, in src/camera/video.rs

```
let width = cam.get(videoio::CAP_PROP_FRAME_WIDTH).unwrap();
let height = cam.get(videoio::CAP_PROP_FRAME_HEIGHT).unwrap();
let fps = cam.get(videoio::CAP_PROP_FPS).unwrap() * FPS_FACTOR;
info!("Camera Settings : {:?} x {:?}, with {:?} fps", width, height, fps);

// Size for the output
let size = core::Size {
    width: width as i32,
    height: height as i32
};
```

For the codec, there are a variety of codecs we can use; however, we will have to pick one that works best for the system you are working on; for ours, I'm using the H264 codec, since that codec is widely supported by web browsers, and in the future, you may want to review the videos from the Web. There is a huge variety of codecs you can use; a complete listing is on the `fourcc` page at www.fourcc.org/codecs.php. I've created a helper method in Listing 10-25 to create the four-CC code for our application.

Listing 10-25. The fourcc code, in src/camera/video.rs

```
fn fourcc() -> i32 {
    videoio::VideoWriter::fourcc('m' as i8, 'p' as i8,'4' as i8,'v' as i8).
unwrap()
}
```

In addition, for the name of the file, we will use a dynamic name based on the date/time in Listing 10-26. We could have used a UUID, but in these cases, I prefer a more readable name when debugging.

Listing 10-26. Dynamically creating the video filename, in src/camera/video.rs

```
fn create_file_name() ->  String {
    let now: DateTime<Utc> = Utc::now();

    let date = now.format("%d.%m.%Y_%H.%M.%S");

    format!("{}/video-{}.mp4", media_dir, date)
}
```

Before we start the loop, initialize the writer. The writer will start up a file that will encode for the size, fps, and codec we supplied. Additionally, we don't want to send out huge files to the servers, so we are going to chunk the files in dynamic increments set as constant variables. I would recommend 15–30-min chunks; it all depends on you, although for testing 30 seconds to one minute is easier. In Listing 10-27, we set the initialized start of the video writer; these fields then get passed to the `handle_video` function.

Listing 10-27. Initialize the video writer, in src/camera/video.rs

```
let mut writer = videoio::VideoWriter::new(create_file_name().as_str(),
fourcc(), fps, size, true)?;
// Frames per second, for a minute, times how many minutes
let frames_per_file = fps * ONE_MIN_IN_SECONDS * MINUTES_BETWEEN_NEW_VIDEO;
info!("Will create {:?} frames per a file", frames_per_file);
```

Inside of the handle_video function in Listing 10-28, we use i to start counting the frames detected so we know when to save the video and create another video to start instead.

Listing 10-28. Starts the loop for the video capture, in src/camera/video.rs

```
let mut i : f64 = 0f64;
let mut start_time: DateTime<Utc> = Utc::now();
let mut file_name = "none".to_string();

loop {
```

And finally, when the frames_per_file variable we set equals the amount of frames we processed (i), we will close the video file writer (via release) which will trigger all the contents to be saved to that filename and then start a new writer (Listing 10-29).

Listing 10-29. Save video to a file and start a new file, in src/camera/video.rs

```
writer.write(&mut frame)?;

fn record(writer: &mut VideoWriter, frames_per_file: f64, size: core::Size,
fps: f64,
          i: &mut f64, start_time: &mut DateTime<Utc>,
          mut frame: &mut Mat, file_name: &mut String) ->
          opencv::Result<()> {
    // Write it locally with the file
    writer.write(frame)?; ①

    if *i == frames_per_file {
        info!("Created File : from {:?} to {:?}", start_time, Utc::now());
        writer.release()?; ②
        *file_name = create_file_name();
        *writer = videoio::VideoWriter::new(&file_name.as_str(), fourcc(),
        fps, size, true)?; ③
        *start_time = Utc::now();
        *i = 1f64;
    }
}
```

```
    else {
        *i = 1f64 + *i; ④
    }

    Ok(())
}
```

①   Writes the frame to the video writer.

②   Releases the video lock flushing the contents to the file system.

③   Creates a new video writer with a new filename that should be unique.

④   Each frame that gets run gets incremented.

This code exists at the end of our loop we created, but now we save to the file system a video of us with rectangles around the face.

Apply Text to the Video

When looking at the videos later, it may be nice to know the date/time the video was taken. In addition to a bounding box, we will also write to the screen the date/time (if you want to get real adventurous, you could also add the temperature). We use the put_text command in Listing 10-30 to apply the text to the screen. There are quite a few options you can pass in including the font, location, and color of the text. We will do mostly defaults for this in Listing 10-30.

Listing 10-30. Drawing the date/time onto the frame, in src/camera/video.rs

```
let now: DateTime<Utc> = Utc::now();
let date = format!("TS: {}", now.format("%d/%m/%Y %H:%M.%S")); ①

// scalar is the color / true : for bottom left origin
let point = core::Point::new(10, 20); ②
imgproc::put_text(&mut frame,
                  date.as_str(),
                  point,
                  highgui::QT_FONT_NORMAL, ③
```

```
0.8,
// BGR .. reverse of RGB
core::Scalar::new(0., 0., 255., 0.), ④
2,
imgproc::LINE_8,
false)?; ⑤
```

① The date time formatting.

② The location where to put it on the screen; these are the x/y coordinates to start the display.

③ The font to choose from; we are choosing the standard normal QT font.

④ The RGB color to pick, but the field is set in reverse byte order so BGR. In this case, it will be red.

⑤ Whether to reverse the image.

In Figure 10-7, you can get an idea of the display you will be recording when a face is detected on the screen, with the date and timestamp appearing as well.

Figure 10-7. *Shows the picture with the facial bounded box and the date timestamp*

Saving the Image Content

Finally, let's see an example of saving just one frame to an image. Most of this work is to simply give us an example of saving an image. I don't want an image saved every second or even hour; we will save the image every time there is a face detected. The code here is a bit opinionated in when to save. The rules for saving an image in Listing 10-31 will be that if a face has been detected in the frame, and we have not seen a face for a prescribed length defined by the MINUTES_BETWEEN_IMAGES variable, we will save the image and then reset the last_face_detect_time.

Listing 10-31. Saving the image and restarting the image writer, in src/camera/video.rs

```
if !faces.is_empty() { ①
    // Send that the face was detected
    send(&mut face_tx, true);

    // is this our first face in a minute, save an image as well.
    // this part is only needed for start up
    debug!("IMAGE: Check for a face every {:?} minutes", MINUTES_BETWEEN_
    IMAGES);
    match last_face_detect_time {
        Some(last_face_time) => {
            let next_image_time = last_face_time + chrono::Duration::
            minutes(MINUTES_BETWEEN_IMAGES); ②
            info!("IMAGE: Last Time: {:?} / Next Detect Time: {:?}",
            last_face_time, next_image_time);
            if Utc::now() > next_image_time { ③
                info!("IMAGE: Save image");
                if save_image(&frame).is_err() { ④
                    warn!("Error saving the image to the file system");
                }
                // reset the time
                last_face_detect_time = Some(Utc::now());
            }
        },
```

```
        None => {  ⑤
            // first time detected save it off
            info!("IMAGE: Save first image");
            if save_image(&frame).is_err() {
                warn!("Error saving the image to the file system");
            }
            last_face_detect_time = Some(Utc::now());
        }
    };
}
```

①   Checks if a face was found in the frame.

②   Gets the time for the next image time; this is calculated by the last time it was detected plus our duration.

③   Checks if we should save off by seeing if that next image time has passed.

④   Creating a dynamic filename much like we did with the video and saving it.

⑤   The else is for the use case of the first time the Pi starts/restarts and image is saved.

While the OpenCV will successfully create us a JPEG image, it does not add any EXIF data on creation; in order to do so, we will need to make use of the rexiv2 crate. The rexiv2 crate wraps around two external libraries gexiv2 and exiv2; those will need to be installed on the cross compiler and also on your Pi itself. We won't cover that here, but I wanted to go over the code to make this work. With this, you will set multiple tags for the images and then the crate will write that information to the image. In Listing 10-32, we are only writing the "Make", but you could supply as much information as you'd like.

Listing 10-32. Calls the run_face_detect we've been coding, in src/camera/video.rs

```
use crate::errors::MyResult;

fn save_image(frame: &Mat) -> MyResult<bool> {
    use rexiv2::Metadata;
```

```rust
info!("IMAGE: Save image");
let image_name = create_image_name(); ①
let mut params = opencv::types::VectorOfint::new();
params.push(opencv::imgcodecs::IMWRITE_JPEG_OPTIMIZE); ②
// Need gexiv installed on the computer for this to work
opencv::imgcodecs::imwrite(image_name.as_str(), &frame, &params).
unwrap(); ③
match opencv::imgcodecs::imwrite(image_name.as_str(), &frame, &params) {
    Ok(_) => {
        // now save the meta data
        if let Ok(meta) = Metadata::new_from_path(image_name.as_str()) {
            // defined in main.rs
            meta.set_tag_string("Exif.Image.Make", crate::APP_NAME); ④
            meta.save_to_file(image_name).unwrap(); ⑤
        }
    },
    Err(e) => {
        error!("Error writing the file out :: {:?}", e);
        return Ok(false);
    }
};

Ok(true)
}
```

① Create a unique name for the image; this is based on the timestamp.

② Parameters for the image creation are set.

③ OpenCV writes the frame to an image file.

④ Set the Make portion of the Exif metadata.

⑤ Save the file.

We could set more on there, but I will leave this up to you to implement. In addition, you notice GPS is sadly missing. There are a number of options we could do here to make it work. There are servers that will give you your location based on IP address; some cost money and some are rate limited. There is also an ability to use the Wi-Fi locations around you to get your GPS coordinates, but I could never get this to work so I didn't include the code. Finally and your best option is you can buy a GPS HAT for your Pi.

Calling the Video Processing

The last step is calling this from the main application; we will use tokio again to spawn the processes; we will create inside the mod.rs for the camera library to call the function we were just working. That way, you will be able to place the actual call as a single-line call in main::run function. In Listing 10-33, we will spawn an async process to run the face detector.

Listing 10-33. Calls the run_face_detect we've been coding, in src/camera/video.rs

```
use crate::manager::{FaceTx};

const VIDEO_DIR: &str = ".";

pub fn run_video_capture(mut face_tx: FaceTx) {
    use tokio::task;

    debug!("Start spawn process ..");

    task::spawn_blocking(move || {
        // I want to see me
        debug!("Spawning ...");
        match video::run_face_detect(face_tx, false) {
            Err(err) => {
                error!("Error processing the face :: {:?}", err);
            },
            Ok(_) => {}
        }
    });
}
```

You will notice I am doing an error capture here; this is somewhat important since there are OpenCV errors that can occur for a variety of reasons. Most of the reasons relate to being able to open the camera or the monitor window. You can put some retry logic in there, but that will be left to you.

Deploying to the Pi

After you have finished coding the camera addition to the Pi application, we will want to deploy and run it. If you try to do that right now, you will be disappointed; it will fail with an error like in Listing 10-34.

Listing 10-34. Running the application on the Raspberry Pi

```
./rasp-app: error while loading shared libraries: libopencv_calib3d.so.4.1:
cannot open shared object file: No such file or directory
```

This error is because we do not have OpenCV 4 installed on the Raspberry Pi, and it will be another library we need to install. This library and procedure to install will be a bit more time-consuming than our other installs (all said a little over an hour).[2] For this to work, we are going to install a few libraries to support the OpenCV and then install and configure OpenCV from source.

To start with, let's increase the swap size for the ram; normally, it's set at 100, but to build the OpenCV, it will make our lives easier if we increase it to 2048. In Listing 10-35, we will `sudo vi /etc/dphys-swapfile` and increase the size to 2048.

Listing 10-35. Increase the size of the Swap

```
pi@raspberrypi:~ $ sudo vi /etc/dphys-swapfile

...
# set size to absolute value, leaving empty (default) then uses computed
value
#   you most likely don't want this, unless you have a special disk
    situation
CONF_SWAPSIZE=2048 ①
...
```

    ①   This is the line to search for to adjust the size.

---

[2]`www.pyimagesearch.com/2019/09/16/install-opencv-4-on-raspberry-pi-4-and-raspbian-buster/`

Next, we are going to have to add some libraries to make OpenCV work for us; most of these libraries help us in creation of the videos, images, and so on. There are additional files that will help for display that we will not be installing since we aren't attaching a display to the Pi. In Listing 10-36, we install the extra libraries needed.

Listing 10-36. Installing the necessary libraries; this will take about 5 minutes

```
pi@raspberrypi:~ $ sudo apt-get install -y build-essential cmake pkg-config ①
pi@raspberrypi:~ $ sudo apt-get install -y libjpeg-dev libtiff5-dev
libjasper-dev libpng12-dev ②
pi@raspberrypi:~ $ sudo apt-get install -y libavcodec-dev libavformat-dev
libswscale-dev libv4l-dev ③
pi@raspberrypi:~ $ sudo apt-get install -y libxvidcore-dev libx264-dev
pi@raspberrypi:~ $ sudo apt-get install -y libatlas-base-dev gfortran ④
```

① Standard libraries used for building and packaging compiled applications.

② Libraries used for using and saving JPEG files.

③ Libraries needed for the video IO packages and video streams.

④ Libraries for operations in OpenCV, mostly matrix operations.

Now in Listing 10-37, let's install the python libraries that we will reference later in the build.

Listing 10-37. Installing the python libraries; this will take about 2 minutes

```
pi@raspberrypi:~ $ sudo apt-get install -y python3-dev
pi@raspberrypi:~ $ sudo apt-get install -y python3-numpy
```

OpenCV Install

Now we have everything we need to actually download and install OpenCV. The version we will install needs to be the same version we used in the previous section when creating the docker image via cross build tool. For this book, we are using 4.1.0. In order to build OpenCV, we need to download and install opencv and opencv_contrib; we will download them both and unpackage them in Listing 10-38.

Listing 10-38. Downloading OpenCV and OpenCV Contrib and unpackaging the contents; this will take about 2 minutes

```
pi@raspberrypi:~ $ mkdir opencv_all && cd opencv_all \
        && wget -O opencv.tar.gz https://github.com/opencv/opencv/
        archive/4.1.0.tar.gz \
        && tar xf opencv.tar.gz \
        && wget -O opencv_contrib.tar.gz https://github.com/opencv/opencv_
        contrib/archive/4.1.0.tar.gz \
        && tar xf opencv_contrib.tar.gz \
        && rm *.tar.gz
```

To install the application, we are going to create a build directory, configure it, and then compile and install the application. To do this, in Listing 10-39, we'll start by creating a build directory and switch to that directory.

Listing 10-39. Create the directory and change to that directory

```
pi@raspberrypi:~ $ cd opencv-4.1.0 && mkdir build && cd build
```

Now we will use cmake that we installed earlier to create our makefile and configurations. The environmental arguments will mimic what we did earlier in cross; the only major difference is that we will install it to /usr/local. In Listing 10-40, I've included this configuration.

Listing 10-40. This configures the makefile to build OpenCV; this will take about 3 minutes

```
pi@raspberrypi:~ $ cmake   -D CMAKE_BUILD_TYPE=RELEASE \
        -D CMAKE_INSTALL_PREFIX=/usr/local \
        -D OPENCV_EXTRA_MODULES_PATH=~/opencv_all/opencv_contrib-4.1.0/
        modules \
        -D OPENCV_ENABLE_NONFREE=ON \
        -D ENABLE_NEON=ON \
        -D ENABLE_VFPV3=ON \
        -D BUILD_TESTS=OFF \
        -D BUILD_DOCS=OFF \
        -D INSTALL_PYTHON_EXAMPLES=OFF \
```

```
-D BUILD_EXAMPLES=OFF \
-D PYTHON3_INCLUDE_PATH=/usr/include/python3.7m \
-D PYTHON3_LIBRARIES=/usr/lib/arm-linux-gnueabihf/libpython3.7m.so \
-D PYTHON3_NUMPY_INCLUDE_DIRS=/usr/lib/python3/dist-packages/numpy/
core/include \
-D BUILD_OPENCV_PYTHON2=OFF \
-D BUILD_OPENCV_PYTHON3=ON \
-D OPENCV_GENERATE_PKGCONFIG=ON ..
```

If you are trying to build this on a Raspberry Pi Zero instead of a 4, it will take longer; in addition, you will have to disable NEON and VFPV3 since they are not supported by the Pi software. In addition, most of the timings I've estimated will be much longer on a Zero or Pi 3.

Now the part that will take the most time is making the binaries. This will take roughly an hour, so go grab some food, a tea, and so on before starting. We will pass in -j4 to make four threads to make use of the four cores on the Pi. In Listing 10-41, we will make the binaries and install it.

Listing 10-41. This makes the binaries and installs it to the Pi; this will take about 60 minutes

```
pi@raspberrypi:~ $ make -j4
pi@raspberrypi:~ $ sudo make install && sudo ldconfig
```

Now that OpenCV is installed, you will be able to run the application on the Raspberry Pi.

Summary

This chapter brought us all our interactions with the camera. This was not a terribly long chapter but very important for the purpose of this book. We covered how to use OpenCV to allow us to more easily develop an application that interacts with a camera. This saved us quite a bit of custom development and makes that code more easily portable between local development and the Pi. The final result was saving off video and images to our local directory complete with timestamps and face detection on the videos. However, we did not cover what to do with those images once saved. Right now, we are simply saving them locally. In the next chapter, we will cover the processing of these images, and for that, we will switch back to the MQTT module which will push the files to the cloud.

CHAPTER 11

Integration

In this chapter, we will be going over everything to do with finishing the integration. We are not adding any new sensors to the Pi or any drastic functionality. What we are adding is the ability to interact with these components as a unit. This chapter becomes very important, because without it, we have many random one-off applications. This will tie all these pieces into a more cohesive unit.

What pieces are we talking about? The core pieces of the Pi, the temperature sensor, and the video camera which also can double as a motion sensor. We are going to tie functionality between the Pi, the cloud, and an iPhone. This will be accomplished in three ways:

1. Uploading saved videos to the cloud; we need to upload the videos to the cloud in a way that can withstand loss of backend connectivity.

2. Calling commands from the cloud. For recording, we want to be able to control from the backend our ability to start and stop recordings.

3. Integrating our device with HomeKit to monitor the temperature and to act as a motion sensor.

First is saving recordings; if you recall in Chapter 3, we wrote code for our cloud backend that is used to accept video and image data, analyze the metadata, and save the file. In the last chapter, we set up the code to write to the Pi's hardware itself; it's time we send that data to the cloud to be stored in our `upload_svc` backend.

Next in Chapter 4, we had the MQ on the backend send recording commands to the `mqtt_service`. To tell the system when to stop recording, start recording, since by default, we are recording always. However, there are times you may not want to have your cameras record. There are many reasons from privacy to space. In addition, we will create the ability to have resilient solutions for sending to the cloud to handle cloud downtimes or no Internet services on the Pi.

© Joseph Faisal Nusairat 2020
J. F. Nusairat, *Rust for the IoT*, https://doi.org/10.1007/978-1-4842-5860-6_11

And finally, one last tie in; we are going to integrate the application with Homekit. We will allow the device to communicate back the temperature as well as use the face recognition as motion sensor to inform the Homekit user when there is motion.

This will all be done by some code and techniques you've seen before and by some new frameworks and techniques. Let's begin.

Uploading Video

We have the video stored on the Pi and ready for upload; all we need to do is upload it now, which in itself is a relatively simple task as long as the videos are small enough, but there are other factors we have to worry about. For the most part, IoT applications can communicate like most other backend applications would. However, one of the biggest issues is the resilience of the Internet connectivity. While two backend servers (at least network wise) have very high uptime availability, the service-level agreement (SLA) for a home network is nowhere near the same. In addition, you are also dealing with home hardware for the modems and routers. And finally, you can have power outages which disrupt connections. Bottom line, we don't want to lose video uploads.

The way we are going to solve this is the same way many IoT devices solve the issue of wanting to send data over but have intermittent networks. This is very often the case for vehicles that send driver and other data back to servers, since vehicles often move into areas of no connectivity like garages or tunnels. And that is to use SQLite database.

Be aware there are other issues that in a bigger book we could tackle like the size of the video. You could send each file in asynchronous chunks and then put them back together again on the upload_svc. Also there are other ways to solve this without using SQLite; however, SQLite is a commonly used database on micro hardware, and I wanted to make sure we at least discussed its use in the book.

SQLite

SQLite was originally designed to work as a database with damage control systems aboard missile destroyer. It is a RDBS/ACID-compliant database system written in C that it is designed to be used by embedded system, as opposed to your standard client-server that most database you are used to. This means it's designed to be accessed by applications on the same system as the database as opposed to remote applications. SQLite has been in use since 2000, and while it does perform quite a bit of the same functions of a database, the database does not guarantee domain integrity. In addition, there is no user/password access since it's not designed to be accessed remotely; instead, access is based on file system permissions.

The SQLite system implements most of the standard SQL-92 features; the big difference comes in assigning and adding column values. It is not strongly typed; therefore, you can insert integers into strings and strings into integers. This of course can cause unexpected behavior if you do it incorrectly. So take care when you are designing your application; luckily, our needs are relatively basic.

We are going to use it to store all videos and images that we have created and are ready for upload, in addition, an indicator flag on whether the video has been uploaded or not. The SQLite database will have many of the same SQL calls that you are used to; of course, for our needs it's very basic of one table that is easily updatable and insertable.

Another use case that is often used in conjunction with the SQL databases is in use with the message queues, so that whenever a message fails to send for whatever reason, it gets stored in the SQLite database for sending later.

After it's inserted, we will run a background job to upload it to our servers at a set interval. If this fails, we can then try again later. The retry count will be stored in that database, and we can add code later to notify the user for quick uploading. This will make the video availability not in real time, but that is OK for our needs.

Design

With SQLite, we will create our database on initialization of the application. This will store all the necessary information as well as a bit of metadata about the entry. We are going to create two modules to handle the uploading: a db module that will handle all the querying of data and updating on failures and then the send module that will upload the file to the server. In order to code this, we are going to make use of SQLite crates as well as crates for uploading the file to the server. In Listing 11-1, we have the four crates needed.

Listing 11-1. Defining the SQLite and reqwest crates, in Cargo.toml file

```
# Database Items
rusqlite = "0.21.0"
# this version is needed to work for rusqlite
time = "0.1.38"
```

```
# Used for sending the file to our server
reqwest = { version = "0.10.4", features = ["blocking"] }
## Needed for linux bindings
openssl-sys = "0.9.54"
```

The final crate, `openssl-sys`, is needed in order to create secure connections to the upload application. In addition, we will need to install SQLite and OpenSSL to our docker container in order to cross compile the application. In Listing 11-2, we have the additional apt-get needed for the application.

Listing 11-2. Defining the SQLite and OpenSSL, in Dockerfile

```
RUN apt-get install -y libsqlite3-dev:armhf

# Install Open SSL needed for communication back to the UploadService
RUN apt-get install -y libssl-dev:armhf
```

This will give us the necessary libraries to create the application interfaces needed.

To run this on the Pi, you will need to install SQLite on there; you can do that with `sudo apt-get install -y sqlite3` command. In addition, in our `db.rs` file, we have defined a constant location of `/var/database` for our database.

We won't be creating a complex database system for keeping record of our videos; instead, we will have one table that will store the metadata for our recordings. In Table 11-1, I've listed out the fields that we will have in the database table.

Table 11-1. *Database fields for our video entries*

Name	Description
file_name	The name of the file that was stored by the video recorder.
uploaded	Saved as an integer, but a boolean value of whether it's updated.
retry_count	The amount of times we've attempted to upload the video.
upload_time	The time of successful upload.
recording_start	Passed by the video module of the time the video recording started.
recording_end	Passed by the video module of the time when the video recording ended.

Creating the Interactions with the Database

Let's start by creating the code to initialize the database. In Listing 11-3, this code will create the initialization for the database, and we will also set up the struct to match the database out.

Listing 11-3. Creating the struct and initializing the database, in src/camera/db.rs

```rust
use rusqlite::{params, Connection, OpenFlags, Result, MappedRows};
use time::Timespec;
use chrono::{DateTime,Utc};
use crate::errors::{DbResult, MyResult};
use log::{warn, error, info};

#[derive(Debug)]
pub(super) struct VideoEntry {
    file_name: String,
    uploaded: bool,
    retry_count: i32,
    upload_time: Option<Timespec>,
    recording_start: Timespec,
    recording_end: Timespec,
}

const PATH : &str = "rust-iot.db";

pub(super) fn initialize() -> bool {
    let conn = create_conn(OpenFlags::SQLITE_OPEN_READ_WRITE |
OpenFlags::SQLITE_OPEN_CREATE).unwrap();

    let size = conn.execute(
        "CREATE TABLE IF NOT EXISTS video_entry (
                file_name           TEXT PRIMARY KEY,
                uploaded            INTEGER,
                retry_count         INTEGER NOT NULL,
                upload_time         TEXT NULL,
                recording_start     TEXT NOT NULL,
```

```
                    recording_end      TEXT NOT NULL
                    )",
        params![],
    ).unwrap();

    if size == 1 {
        true
    }
    else {
        false
    }
}

fn create_conn(flags: OpenFlags) -> Result<Connection> {
    Connection::open_with_flags(
        PATH,
        flags
    )
}
```

We will run this each time the application is restarted and should be resilient to failures. While it returns true/false, we will not do anything with the result. Next, let's go on a few application pieces that we will need to be able to make the app work. There are really a few functions we need to code for:

- Adding an entry to the database; this is called from the video module.

- Uploading the video file.

- Marking an entry when successfully uploaded.

- Incrementing a counter when not successfully uploaded.

Adding Entry to the Database

The first step is to add entries to the database; whenever we run the writer.release() on the video module, we want to record an entry to the database to have the application upload. In Listing 11-4, we code the database addition in the video module.

Listing 11-4. Add a video entry to the database when a file descriptor is released, in src/camera/video.rs

```
writer.release()?;
db::add(&file_name, *start_time, Utc::now());
```

Now let's code the method in Listing 11-5. The method will insert into video_entry a reference to the file and defaulting upload to false and retry count to zero.

Listing 11-5. Add the video entry to the database, in src/camera/db.rs

```rust
pub fn add(name: &str, start: DateTime<Utc>, end: DateTime<Utc>)  {
    let conn = create_conn(OpenFlags::SQLITE_OPEN_READ_WRITE).unwrap();

    let start_ts = Timespec {
        sec: start.timestamp_millis(),
        nsec: start.timestamp_subsec_nanos() as i32,
    };

    let end_ts = Timespec {
        sec: end.timestamp_millis(),
        nsec: end.timestamp_subsec_nanos() as i32,
    };

    let result = conn.execute(
        "INSERT INTO video_entry (file_name, recording_start, recording_
        end, uploaded, retry_count)
                VALUES (?1, ?2, ?3, 0, 0)",
        params![name, start_ts, end_ts],
    );

    match result {
        Ok(_) => {
            info!("Added {:?} to database", name);
        },
        Err(e) => {
            error!("Error Trying to insert into database :: {:?}", e);
        }
    }
}
```

Uploading the Video File

Now that we have entries in the database, we will have to upload the files. We will write code to upload the files on an hourly basis. On each hour, it will try to upload all the files in the database, which includes files that failed previously. Once uploaded, the files will then be available in the cloud.

In case of continuous failures or extremely slow uploads, there could be an issue where the file system runs out of space, or those uploads due to slowness are trying two at the same time. I have no program for these edge cases but should be thought of.

Let's start with the code for the hourly upload; the code in Listing 11-6 will be called from the main::run and will spawn a thread that hourly will call a function that sends non-uploaded files to the server.

Listing 11-6. Code to upload hourly to the server, in src/camera/mod.rs

```
use uuid::Uuid;

const HOURLY: u64 = 60 * 60;
const BI_MINUTE: u64 = 60 * 2;

// Send our videos hourly to the cloud
pub fn hourly_upload(device_id: String, url: String) {
    use tokio::time::{Duration, interval_at, Instant};

    db::initialize();
    tokio::spawn(async move {
        // every other minute duration
        let mut interval = interval_at(Instant::now(), Duration::from_
        secs(BI_MINUTE));
        loop {
            interval.tick().await;
            info!("Upload to the Server");
            let entries = db::retrieve_entries(device_id.as_str(),
            url.as_str(), VIDEO_DIR);
            info!("Received entries : {:?}", entries);
            match db::send_to_server(entries.unwrap(), device_id.as_str(),
            url.as_str(), VIDEO_DIR).await {
                Ok(_) => {},
                Err(e) => {
```

```
                    error!("Error Sending to the Server {:?}", e);
                }
            }
        }
    });
}
```

You will notice why there is an interval delay; we start the timer now; that is because we do not need it to upload on the hour, just want to space out the file upload. This function calls send_to_server which is the main workhorse for the application; this will query the database for entries and attempt to upload them. In Listing 11-7, we have the code to query all the non-uploaded files and attempt to upload them to the backend server.

Listing 11-7. Code to send to the server, resetting the entries when not uploaded, in src/camera/db.rs

```
pub(super) fn retrieve_entries(device_id: &str, url: &str, dir: &str) ->
DbResult> {
    use std::fs::remove_file;
    use futures::executor::block_on;

    let conn = create_conn(OpenFlags::SQLITE_OPEN_READ_ONLY)?;

    // Get the non-uploaded ones
    let mut stmt = conn.prepare("SELECT file_name, recording_start,
    recording_end, uploaded, retry_count From video_entry Where
    uploaded = 0")?; ①

    let entries = stmt.query_map(params![], |row| { ②
        // No upload time since it's not uploaded yet
        Ok(VideoEntry {
            file_name: row.get(0)?,
            recording_start: row.get(1)?,
            recording_end: row.get(2)?,
            uploaded: row.get(3)?,
            upload_time: None,
            retry_count: row.get(4)?,
        })
    })?;
```

```rust
    for row in rows {
        entries.push(row.unwrap());
    }

    Ok(entries)
}

pub(super) async fn send_to_server(entries: Vec, device_id: &str, url:
&str, dir: &str) -> DbResult<()> {
    use std::fs::remove_file;
    // Entries
    for video_entry in entries {
        info!("Upload : Video Entry : {:?}", video_entry);

        let full_path = format!("{}/{}", dir, &video_entry.file_name);
        let file_name = video_entry.file_name.clone();

        // Send to the backend
        match super::send::send_to_backend_async(device_id, url,
        &file_name, &full_path).await { ③
            Ok(value) => {
                if value == true {
                    mark_uploaded(video_entry.file_name); ④
                    // There is a chance this wasn't marked correctly
                    remove_file(&full_path).unwrap() ⑤
                } else {
                    increment(video_entry.file_name, video_entry.
                    retry_count); ⑥
                }
            },
            Err(e) => {
                warn!("Error sending the video {:?}", e);
                increment(video_entry.file_name, video_entry.retry_count); ⑦
            }
        };;
    }
    Ok(())
}
```

① Selects from the database all the file metadata that has not been uploaded.

② Reads the data from the database and stores into a Result<MappedRows> of VideoEntry structs.

③ Calls the method to send the entry to the upload_svc for storage.

④ Called on successful upload will mark in the database this entry is uploaded.

⑤ Removes the underlying video file from the Pi to conserve space.

⑥ If the file is not uploaded successfully, it will increment our counter in the database. This occurs if the server status was anything but 200.

⑦ This will also increment, but this will be triggered if there are any other errors unassociated with the status returned by upload_svc.

Currently, the counter just keeps getting incremented on failures with nothing happening. If you were going to implement this, you may want to break the file up or simply send an error to the server so the user is aware that a video file exists on the Pi but is having upload issues. Without manual intervention, you will only have a few options.

Sending to the Server

Sending the file to the servers uses the same reqwest crate that we used in Chapter 3 to receive the uploaded file. The reqwest crate does have the ability to do asynchronous processing, but for the multipart crate, we are going to run it synchronously. The crate will upload with the device_id as a URL parameter and the file sent. The device_id is used to store into the database the correct file referencing the correct device so that we later will be able to tie the right video to the right device from the backend databases. In Listing 11-8, we have the send_to_backend.

Listing 11-8. Implementation of send_to_backend to send the file to the backend, in src/camera/send.rs

```
use crate::errors::HttpResult;

use log::info;
use reqwest::blocking::{multipart, Client};
use std::fs::File;
```

```
use std::io::Read;

const PATH : &str = "api/upload"; ①

pub(super) async fn send_to_backend_async(device_id: &str, url: &str, file_
name: &String, full_path: &String) -> Result> {
    use futures_util::{future, stream};

    let name = get_filename(file_name);
    println!("full_path :: {:?}", full_path);
    println!("file_name :: {:?}", file_name);
    println!("name :: {:?}", name);

    // Get the file and send over as bytes
    let file = std::fs::read(full_path);

    // Check if we have the file, if we dont its gone for some reason
    // just delete it from the database then, in actuality you could do
    // some error state messaging instead
    match file {
      Ok(f) => {
        // need to set the mime type
        let part = reqwest::multipart::Part::bytes(f) ②
          // TODO alter although only file exension matters
          .file_name(name)
          .mime_str("video/mp4")?;

        let form = reqwest::multipart::Form::new() ③
          .part("file", part);

        let client = reqwest::Client::new();

        info!("Sending >>> {:?}", format!("{}/{}/{}", url, PATH,
        device_id).as_str());

        let res = client
          .post(format!("{}/{}/{}", url, PATH, device_id).as_str()) ④
          .multipart(form)
          .send() ⑤
          .await?;
```

```
        if res.status() == 200 { ⑥
            Ok(true)
        } else {
            warn!("Status: {}", res.status());
            Ok(false)
        }
    },
    Err(e) => {
      warn!("Error Getting the File {:?}", e);
      Ok(true)
    }
  }
}

fn get_filename(filename: &String) -> String {
    if filename.contains("/") {
        let x: Vec<&str> = filename.split("/").collect();
        x.last().unwrap().to_string()
    } else {
        filename.to_string()
    }
}
```

① The path on the server to upload; it's the URI we referenced in Chapter 3.

② Start of our multipart form request.

③ Attaching the absolute file to the multiple part form.

④ Creating the URL with the format of api/url/<device_id>.

⑤ Sending the multipart form synchronously.

⑥ Returning true on a successful status.

On bullet 6, you saw that we return true or false depending on whether the file is successfully uploaded. Whether it was successful or not depends on the next course of action.

Marking Entry Successfully Uploaded

If a video is successfully uploaded, we will mark it uploaded in the database, so it doesn't get uploaded again, and we will delete the file. In Listing 11-9, we mark the file as uploaded.

Listing 11-9. Marks the file as uploaded, in src/camera/db.rs

```
fn mark_uploaded(name: String) -> bool {
    let conn = create_conn(OpenFlags::SQLITE_OPEN_READ_WRITE).unwrap();

    let size_result = conn.execute(
        "UPDATE video_entry
         Set uploaded = 1
         Where name = ?1",
        params![name]
    );

    // Determine the result
    match size_result {
        Ok(size) => {
            if size > 0 {
                info!("Marked {:?} as uploaded", name);
                true
            }
            else {
                false
            }
        },
        Err(_) => {
            false
        }
    }
}
```

In there, we just set the uploaded to 1 to mark that it has been uploaded.

Marking Entry when Not Successful

For entries that aren't successful, in Listing 11-10, we increment the current retry_count by one.

Listing 11-10. Increments upload attempt, in src/camera/db.rs

```
fn increment(name: String, current_count: i32) -> bool {
    let conn = create_conn(OpenFlags::SQLITE_OPEN_READ_WRITE).unwrap();

    let size_result = conn.execute(
        "UPDATE video_entry
         Set uploaded = 0,
         retry_count = ?1
         Where name = ?2",
        params![current_count + 1, name]
    );

    // Determine the result, of course not much one can do with it
    match size_result {
        Ok(size) => {
            if size > 0 {
                true
            }
            else {
                false
            }
        },
        Err(_) => {
            false
        }
    }
}
```

While we are not doing anything with the code, you can add extra logic later based on the retry_count; this could be dividing the file into smaller chunks or to even give up trying to upload file and notify the user. The options are up to the reader.

Sending Commands

One of the keys of any IoT application is to push commands from the server via a UI or mobile to the device. There are a few ways this can be accomplished. Depending on the proximity of the device to the mobile, they may use Bluetooth or Wi-Fi; this allows a speedier uptake. However, many devices, since they are designed to work when you are on the network and outside the network, have to go through a backend that then routes the communication to the device. We have already set up the infrastructure in previous chapters on both the backend and the Pi to use the MQTT.

In Chapter 4, we went over how to publish to a recording topic; that topic pushed to the message queue a command to tell a device whether to start or stop the recording. In addition, if you recall, the MQ application on our Pi is a separate application from our master application which communicates with the camera. In addition to connecting our MQ to retrieve the commands from the MQ, we will need to set up communication between the applications; we will be using inter-process communication (IPC) to perform it. In Figure 11-1, I have diagramed the interaction between all these parts.

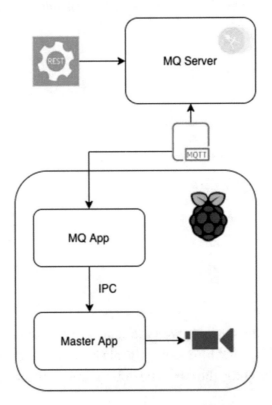

Figure 11-1. *Diagram of the interaction of our application*

IPC

Our applications on the Pi each have their own processes, and often we need to share data between the two. There are a number of ways of how to do this in an operating system; IPC is the way we are going to implement those communications for this book. Inter-process communication is a technique by operating systems to allow communication of shared data between processes. With IPC, each application is either a client or a server, and you can send as many or as little communication over each of those channels. In general with IPCs, you can have multiple clients and one server, although in the crate we are using, this is limited to the server accepting only one client at a time.

One of the features of IPC is that the applications can communicate asynchronously if they choose to, allowing you to not have the communication active at the time. Your operating system depends on how the IPC channel will communicate; in addition, this also depends on your IPC implementation. IPC can talk over sockets, file descriptors, message queues, shared memory, memory-mapped files, or more. The precise implementation may affect performance but won't affect the underlying concept.

Packet IPC

The crate we are using for our implementation is `packet-ipc` (`https://github.com/dbcfd/packet-ipc`). Packet IPC wraps `crossbean-channel` and `ipc-channel` to create easy-to-use code code to create our IPC channel. The use of both of these underlying crates was my driving force into using packet IPC. The `ipc-channel` is a Rust native implementation of communicating sequential processes; it is a multi-process drop in replacement for Rust channels. This uses file descriptors for Unix and Mach ports for Mac as its underlying implementation of the channels. (Note: There is no Windows support right now.) Using this wrapper will make our application a bit easier to write.

Application

Let's dive into writing the code for this section. I have divided it up into essentially four areas:

- Receiving – Recording commands from the MQ

- MQ app – Setting up IPC server

- Main app – Setting up IPC client

- Communicating IPC client with camera module

Once all of these four are wired up, we will be able to control the cameras recording from the backend servers. In order to use the IPC channel, we will add the crate definition in both our applications. In Listing 11-11, we have the import defined.

Listing 11-11. Defining the crate to use, in Cargo.toml file

```
packet-ipc = "0.9.0"
```

Subscribing to the Message Queue

Much of the code we wrote to subscribe to publish on the MQ is the same set of code we wrote for our microservices. The code that is the same we won't duplicate here, but the newer code we will write. We've added the publishing code when we wrote the heartbeat, but not the subscribing code. For the monitor_notifications and subscribe function we wrote in Chapter 4, we can cut and paste them into our necessary modules.

What's left is to create a recording module that subscribes to the topic and allows us to retrieve the recording and then send it to the IPC server. In Listing 11-12, we will copy and paste to reuse the struct we decomposed from.

Listing 11-12. Defining the struct for our Recording, in src/actions/recording.rs file

```
#[derive(Serialize, Deserialize, Debug)]
pub enum RecordingType {
    Start,
    Stop
}

#[derive(Serialize, Deserialize, Debug)]
struct Recording {
    uuid: Uuid,
    rtype: RecordingType
}
```

In here, we will have a recording type, which tells the device whether to start or stop the application. In Listing 11-13, we will subscribe to the topic recording/<uuid>; the UUID is the device id. This is the differentiator that allows the device to ONLY receive communication for that particular device and not every device there is. The JSON is brought back decoded, and the Start/Stop recording type is sent to the IPC.

While we are not going to do it here, in a real application, you should apply quite a bit more authentication at the cert level that makes sure that ONLY that cert can access that device id. This is because you don't want a user to pop the Pi and then use the certs to subscribe to every recording command there is. That could be quite the privacy issue.

Listing 11-13. Defining the subscription to the recording, in src/actions/recording.rs file

```
const MOD_NAME: &str = "recording";

pub fn monitor(config: &MqttClientConfig, device_id: &Uuid) {
    let (mut mqtt_client, notifications) = create_client(&config, MOD_
    NAME).unwrap(); ①
    info!("Subscribe to recording monitor ...");
    let topic = format!("recording/{:?}", device_id); ②
    subscribe(&mut mqtt_client, topic.as_str(), QoS::AtMostOnce); ③
    debug!("Monitor the notifications ... ");
    monitor_notifications(notifications, process); ④
}
/**
 * Submit the recording to the other application
 */
pub fn process(topic: String, pl: Vec<u8>) { ⑤
    use serde_json::{Value};
    info!("Process Recording :: {}", topic);

    let pl = String::from_utf8(pl); ⑥
    match pl {
        Ok(payload) => {
            let mut recording: Recording = serde_json::from_str(payload.
            as_str()).unwrap(); ⑦
            crate::ipc::send(recording.rtype) ⑧
        },
        Err(error) => {
            error!("Error sending the payload: {:?}", error)
        },
    };
}
```

①   The instantiation of the client with the unique module name.

②   The topic name to subscribe to which is `recording` plus the device id.

③   Subscribing to the topic.

④   Using the return of the notifications to monitor and pass to the `process` function to handle the notifications response.

⑤   The function that will be called when a message is sent to the topic.

⑥   Decomposing the messages into a string.

⑦   Translating the string into our `Recording` struct.

⑧   Calling the yet-to-be-built `ipc` handler sending in just the command to `Start` or `Stop`.

You will notice that we are handling JSON here instead of Protobuf; the reason for this is we only converted the heartbeat code to Protobuffers and not the recording. But as you can see, copying the message is cleaner than copying the struct. Realize here that we are only dealing with two commands; if we wanted to expand or have an entire command module, we could have placed that here.

We are decomposing the string here; as you will see in a bit, we send a string over on the IPC, and thus if the command was a more complex JSON, we could have decomposed the message on the client side of the IPC.

IPC Server Side

The IPC server creates a server but cannot send any data till a client connects to it. We will have on the MQ side set up the server and then send our data as a packet. When the client creates a server connection, it creates a unique file descriptor; this file descriptor is what the client needs to know in order to retrieve the packet. This allows us to have multiple client/server architecture on the same system (even though we are using just one). In order to determine this architecture, we will write the file location to a file descriptor that our client can then retrieve later and use to subscribe to the client.

In Listing 11-14, we create our server connection, convert the string to byte array, and send the packet on the server, awaiting the client to connect and retrieve it.

Listing 11-14. Defining the IPC server, in src/ipc.rs file

```
const file_location: &str = "/tmp/pi_upc_server_name_file"; ①

pub fn send(recording: RecordingType) {
    // lock server and use
    let mut server_tx = init().expect("Failed to accept connection"); ②

    let payload = format!("{:?}", recording); ③
    let x = payload.as_bytes();

    server_tx
        .send(&vec![Packet::new(std::time::SystemTime::now(), x.to_vec())]) ④
        .expect("Failed to send");
}

/**
 * Initialize the server connection to be used.
 */
pub fn init<'a>() -> Result<ConnectedIpc<'a>, Error> {
    // Start up the server
    let server = Server::new().expect("Failed to create server"); ⑤
    let server_name = server.name().clone();
    file::write(file_location.to_string(), &server_name);

    info!("Server Name :: {:?}", server_name);

    return server.accept()
}
```

① Define the location of the file that has our file descriptor.

② Create the connection to the server.

③ Convert the string to array bytes to be used for the payload.

④ Send the packet from the server, setting the timestamp to the current time.

⑤ Create a new server connection.

In bullet 4 where we send the packets, we could send multiple packets here. This can work well in a scenario where you are stacking commands to be sent to the client or need to parse into individual strings to send. Now that we have the Pi MQ working, we will turn our attention to the client side.

Client Side

On the client side, we are going to need to update the video module in order to monitor the ipc channel to know how to update the recording. Let's go over what we need to do and how to make this work. We already have created the code to do a continuous loop over the video. This video records and saves the file. Here are the steps then to integrate the concept of starting and stopping the video:

1. Create a variable that tells whether we are recording.

2. Create another variable that tells whether we should be recording (i.e., a message from the IPC saying to stop recording).

3. Spawn a loop to monitor that IPC client.

4. Act on the recording variables in the loop.

The dual variables will become apparent later, but using them allows us to infinitely write out the video to file in case of a stop command, since if we didn't, the video may get lost due to a reboot or may never get uploaded.

Let's start with the public-facing function we created in the previous chapter, run_face_detect. Right before we start our video loop that we made, we will create two variables. The first will be wrapped in an Arc<Mutex<String>>. This will allow us to create a thread-safe wrapper around a string. Now we are going to need to have multiple threads access it, and in addition, we will need to update that outside of the main recording loop. In order to do so, we will clone the Arc<Mutex<String>>; cloning it allows us to preserve a reference to the underlying String but cloning the Arc wrapper. In Listing 11-15, we have an excerpt from the run_face_detect.

Listing 11-15. Update to run_fac_detect for our video monitoring, in src/camera/video.rs file

```
let recording_execute: Arc<Mutex<String>> = Arc::new(Mutex::new
(START.to_string())); ①
let recording_monitor = recording_execute.clone(); ②

monitor_controls(recording_monitor); ③

match handle_video(face, show_window, ④
            writer, frames_per_file, last_face_detect_time,
```

```
            face_tx, size, window, fps,
            cam, &recording_execute) {
    // Only returns if there is an error
    Ok(_) => {},
    Err(e) => {
        error!("Error handling the video :: {:?}", e);
    }
};
```

① Create the Arc<Mutex<String> wrapper around the string variable defaulting to starting the video recording.

② Clone that variable, which we can use when we want to monitor the IPC server and update with.

③ Call out to a function that will create the IPC client to connect to the server.

④ The function that handles the recording passing a reference to the recording_execute that we can use to test if we've recorded.

Now we just need to code the monitor_controls and update a section in handle_video that checks if it's recorded.

IPC Client

Let's start with coding the IPC client. The client will spawn a thread that will continuously attempt to connect to the server and receive the packets from the server. If a packet is retrieved, we set the contents of the package to the recording_monitor variable we just discussed. Oftentimes, we won't have anything to connect to, so the client connection will fail; this is a normal thing to happen, and we will let the error fall out gracefully. Since we want this to happen in virtual real time, we will be checking the thread every second; we could increase this based on performance, and in reality, we could put the length even longer and just trim the video on the Pi before storing.

Connecting to the client and receiving packets is a two-step process:

1. We connect our client to the server and receive the packets from it, pushing each packet onto a stack and then returning that stack.

2. We join all the packets together to have a vector of results and then process the packets.

The first part deals with the client connection and retrieval, and the second deals with performing actions on the packets. For us, the actions are simply returning the value stored since we are only expecting and allowing one packet per one message from the MQ. We mentioned that the server can send multiple packets; thus, in the client code, we could expect to receive multiple packets at a time and push all those packets to the awaiting asynchronous processor. In Listing 11-16, we define the monitor_controls function as well as connect and process the packets.

Listing 11-16. Defining the IPC client, in src/camera/video.rs file

```rust
fn monitor_controls(recording_monitor: Arc<Mutex<String>>) {
    use std::{str,fs};
    use packet_ipc::{AsIpcPacket, Client, Error, IpcPacket, Packet, Server};
    use std::{thread, time};

    let one_second = time::Duration::from_secs(1);

    thread::spawn(move || { ①
        loop {
            thread::sleep(one_second); ②

            let server_name = fs::read_to_string(file_location.to_
            string()).unwrap(); ③

            let client_res = Client::new(server_name.clone()).map(|mut cli| { ④
                let mut packets = vec![];
                // Pushes a packet
                // This contains the information received from the client
                let val = cli.recv(1); ⑤
                info!("Push a packet! :: {:?}", val);
                // can keep receiving till you get No packets back
                packets.push(val); ⑥
                packets
            });

            match client_res {
                Ok(res) => {
                    info!("Await ...");
```

```
        let res: Result<Vec<_>, Error> = res.into_iter().collect(); ⑦
        let res = res.expect("Failed to get packets");

        let packets = res[0].as_ref().expect("No message"); ⑧
        let data = packets[0].data();
        info!(">> {:?}", str::from_utf8(data).unwrap());
        let value = str::from_utf8(data).unwrap();

        let mut guard = recording_monitor.lock().unwrap(); ⑨
        *guard = value.to_string(); ⑩
      },
      Err(e) => {}
    }
  }
});
}
```

① Spawns a continuous thread to loop creating a client to connect to a server to check if there have been any packets pushed.

② Sleeps the thread for one second so that we are not trying to kill the process.

③ Retrieves the server file descriptor to know what to connect to.

④ Creates the client connection based on the server file descriptor name.

⑤ Receives the packet from the client that is connected.

⑥ Uses the value from the received connection and pushes the returning string on to our packet.

⑦ Iterates over the packets that are received by the client.

⑧ Retrieves the first packet and will be subsequently the only packet we have.

⑨ On the `Arc<Mutex<String>>` will lock the value so we can write to it.

⑩ Writes the value from the packet to the dereferenced location.

Writing the packet to the dereferenced location will then allow the recording_ execute the ability to retrieve that value and process. This thread will run continuously and only update the command to start or stop when a new value is received.

Integrating on the Video Loop

Finally, we will integrate the use of the recording_execute into the video loop to determine when to start and stop recording. There are a few different scenarios we need to code against. While this loop is running, you have the current state on whether we are recording and then you have a state on whether we should be recording, and we need to reconcile these two situations in multiple scenarios; these scenarios are these:

1. Application is currently recording and application should be recording. This is a normal recording state; don't change anything from what we coded before. In here, you should only check if the frames_per_file has been reached and if it has started a new recording. If not, continue.

2. Application is currently recording and application should NOT be recording. In this situation, you need to stop the loop from recording, and release the file so it writes the file out to the Pi.

3. Application is NOT recording and the application should be recording. In this case, start the recording and set the recording state to true.

In Listing 11-17, we implement these rules wrapping around the existing video write code.

Listing 11-17. Updating the record function with the recording_exercise variable, in src/camera/video.rs file

```
fn is_record(command: &Arc>) -> bool{
    let c = &*command.lock().unwrap();
    let cmd = c.as_str();
    match cmd {
      START => true,
      STOP => false,
```

```
          _ => false
      }
}

fn dont_record(command: &Arc<Mutex<String>>) -> bool {
    let c = &*command.lock().unwrap();
    let cmd = c.as_str();
    match cmd {
      START => false,
      STOP => true,
      _ => true
    }
}

fn record(writer: &mut VideoWriter, frames_per_file: f64, size: core::Size,
fps: f64,
          recording_execute: &Arc<Mutex<String>>, i: &mut f64, start_time:
          &mut DateTime<Utc>,
          is_recording: &mut bool, mut frame: &mut Mat, file_name: &mut
          String) -> opencv::Result<()> {
    // Currently recording, and no stop command
    if *is_recording
        && is_record(&recording_execute) { ①
        // Release and restart the file
        // Write it locally with the file
        writer.write(frame)?;

        if *i == frames_per_file {
            info!("Created File : from {:?} to {:?}", start_time, Utc::now());
            writer.release()?;
            *file_name = create_file_name();
            *writer = videoio::VideoWriter::new(&file_name.as_str(),
            fourcc(), fps, size, true)?;
            db::add(&file_name, *start_time, Utc::now());
            *start_time = Utc::now();
            *i = 1f64;
        }
```

```
    else {
        *i = 1f64 + *i;
    }
}
// is recording but received a stop command
// so set the is_recording to false and write a release file
else if *is_recording
    && dont_record(&recording_execute) { ②
    // Stop the recording and save to the file
    *is_recording = false;
    writer.release()?;
    db::add(&file_name, *start_time, Utc::now());
}
// not currently recording, but needs to start again
else if !*is_recording
    && is_record(&recording_execute) { ③
    *is_recording = true;
    *start_time = Utc::now();
    *file_name = create_file_name();
    *writer = videoio::VideoWriter::new(&file_name.as_str(), fourcc(),
    fps, size, true)?;
    *i = 1f64;
}
else {
    warn!("Not supported.");
}

Ok(())
}
```

① Handles the first use case of application recording and should be recording.

② Second use case of application is recording and should not be recording.

③ Third use case of application is not recording but should be.

Now at this point, the backend servers can communicate with our Pi and start and stop the camera recording.

HomeKit

If you aren't familiar with HomeKit, it's probably because you don't have an iPhone. HomeKit is Apple's software to connect smart home appliances. HomeKit was started as an impressive and ambitious project to connect devices all in a secure way. When the project was first released, any hardware device would require an encryption co-processor in order for it to connect and be used. This guaranteed secure communication between devices and allowed for greater privacy. We obviously don't have an encryption co-processor, but in iOS 11, this was changed to allow for so encrypted software authentication instead. Homekit works by connecting between devices and a hub via Bluetooth or Wi-Fi. The hub is what consolidates all the information about the devices and allows you to not only control them but create scenarios to activate or deactivate them all via timers, rules, and so on.

What makes the Apple HomeKit unique compared to its competitors, Google and Amazon, is the hub to device interaction. While other systems have a hub, they often serve as a passthrough back to backend servers. All your data and recordings then get sent to those servers, and all your actions are recorded; thus, other providers are able to track you. This is also why they can build and learn your interactions, when your comings and goings are, and so on much easier. With HomeKit, it's an entirely secure world. For the privacy minded, this is appealing in that it still gives you solid good UI and ecosystem, without giving up your security.

Generally, to create a fully stable commercially sellable system, you will have to go through more Apple hoops. However, they do allow for testing and individual use of their own set of tools. And we will make use of this to add HomeKit to our Raspberry Pi.

As we touched on earlier, we will be using HomeKit to add temperature and motion sensor readings. The temperature comes from our Pi, the same temperature that we display on the LED screen. The motion sensor is a bit trickier. While we could have added some code to determine changes in the frames from frame to frame or even from frame to the fifth frame, we are going to use the motion sensor indicator to indicate when there is face detection. This provides an interesting use case, but also allows us an easier intercept in code that is already written.

HomeKit Accessory Protocol (hap-rs)

The hap-rs is mostly a pure rust-built project that is used to communicate Rust code with a HomeKit device over Wi-Fi (via IP). The Bluetooth protocol is not supported currently. I say mostly a pure Rust application because while the crate is written in Rust, it does use ring as a dependency to perform all the encryption/decryption necessary to communicate between the code and the HomeKit hub. And ring uses a hybrid of Rust, C, and assembly language under the covers. The current version of the crate (`https://github.com/ewilken/hap-rs`) does use ring 14.x; I have since forked the repo and updated the code to ring 16.x so we can use the code inside our existing Pi application. We can use the dependency via Listing 11-18.

Listing 11-18. Defining the hap-rs, in Cargo.toml file

```
hap = "0.0.10"
```

The code uses a combination of custom code and auto-generated code. Much of the custom code is for the configuration and communication, while the auto-generated code deals with defining the accessories and characteristics for them. In the `hap-rs` code base, there are currently 31 accessories that are supported via that code generation. All but four of them are fully supported with their full characteristics. The accessories that are defined but not currently supported are these:

- IP camera

- Light sensor

- Thermostat

- Video doorbell

The main reason these aren't fully supported is because their implementation would require more than auto-generated code can provide. If you are curious, there is an issue to track this at `https://github.com/ewilken/hap-rs/issues/11`, or you can even submit your own patches to it. You will notice IP camera is one, which is why we are using a motion sensor as a device instead of IP camera for our Pi interaction.

Accessories

I've mentioned accessories a few times here; it's good for us to talk about how HAP works and the interface points we have to communicate with it. In the documentation, each accessory is composed of multiple services which in turn are composed of multiple characteristics. This can get a bit confusing, in that what we call an accessory in abstract is manually defined in the code, and what we call a service here is called an accessory in the code. Let's take a look at an example of a thermostat like the Ecobee. The Ecobee thermostat is composed of two accessories: a thermostat and a motion accessory, each of which will show up as a separate device on the Homekit. Each of these accessories will be composed of multiple characteristics themselves. These characteristics are used for display and control of the device. In Table 11-2, we have the characteristics for thermostat.

Table 11-2. *Characteristics for a thermostat*

Name
current_temperature
cooling_threshold_temperature
current_relative_humidity
heating_threshold_temperature
target_heating_cooling_state
target_relative_humidity
target_temperature
temperature_display_units

All of these units will be accessible; in addition, the characteristics of motion sensors are in Table 11-3.

Table 11-3.   *Characteristics for a motion sensor*

Name
motion_detected
status_active
status_fault
status_low_battery
status_tampered

These characteristics each interact with the HomeKit application and are the rust crates' way of interacting with the application. Each one can have two methods defined: an on_read and an on_update. The on_read is used whenever the Homekit needs to read the current state from the code. An example would be the temperature; when it needs to read the temperature, the on_read on the Homekit will access the method and return the value. The on_update is used whenever the Homekit needs to send a value to the rust code. For example, on a thermostat, you want to set the temperature; the temperature you set from the Homekit will be sent to the rust code. The use of these in conjunction allows us to create a complete loop of interactions with the rust code and the Homekit.

Creating Our HomeKit

For our Homekit Pi device, we are going to implement the motion sensor and temperature sensor in a new homekit module. In order to create the homekit integration, in Listing 11-19, we will need to define each of the accessories and then a configuration file to define the Pi.

Listing 11-19.   Defining the Pi configuration, in src/homekit.rs file

```
let config = Config { ①
    name: "Rasp Pi".into(),
    category: Category::Thermostat,
    ..Default::default()
};
```

```
debug!("What's the pin :: {:?}", config.pin);

// Adds our transport layer to start
let mut ip_transport = IpTransport::new(config).unwrap(); ②
ip_transport.add_accessory(thermo).unwrap(); ③
ip_transport.add_accessory(motion).unwrap(); ④

// Spawn the start of the homekit monitor
tokio::spawn(async move {
    debug!("IP Transport started");
    ip_transport.start().unwrap(); ⑤
});
```

① Create the overall config defining the name that the device will show up when adding on Homekit.

② Create an IP transport layer with that configuration.

③ Add the thermostat accessory.

④ Add the motion accessory.

We will define those two accessories in a bit, but the first part of the config is interesting; there is also a field for the pin that is used when connecting to the device. When not set, the default is 11122333. We haven't set it here because it doesn't work (it's mentioned briefly at https://github.com/ewilken/hap-rs/issues/15). So just use the default for now.

Implement Generic Temperature Sensor

We haven't normally done this throughout the book; normally, we jump into the code for the section, but this time we are going to break it up a bit due to the complexity of the moving parts. Let's take a look how a temperature sensor functionality works. All of your available accessories will be in hap::accessory.

We can start in Listing 11-20 by instantiating a temperature sensor struct from that accessory.

Listing 11-20. Defines the temperature sensor

```
let mut thermo = temperature_sensor::new(Information {
    name: "Thermostat".into(),
    ..Default::default()
}).unwrap();
```

This creates the thermostat sensor, and with the code in the previous listing, it gets wired up to show in the Homekit. But that's all; there are no values being set or transmitted. In order to interact with the Homekit, you will need to implement one of two traits:

- `hap::characteristic::Readable` – For any events that are read from Homekit

- `hap::characteristic::Updatable` – For any events that are updated by Homekit

In Listing 11-21, we are going to create a struct that holds the temperature reading and allows it to be set and updated by the two traits we mentioned.

Listing 11-21. Defines the temperature structure

```
#[derive(Clone)]
pub struct Temperature {
    temp: f32, ①
}

impl Readable<f32> for Temperature { ②
    fn on_read(&mut self, _: HapType) -> Option<f32> { ③
        println!("On read temp.");
        Some(self.temp)
    }
}

impl Updatable<f32> for Temperature { ④
    fn on_update(&mut self, old_val: &f32, new_val: &f32, _: HapType) { ⑤
        println!("On updated temp from {} to {}.", old_val, new_val);
        if new_val != old_val { self.temp = *new_val; } ⑥
    }
}
```

① Sets a struct to hold a temperature value as float 32.

② Implements the Readable trait using f32 type value.

③ Implements the one function that reads the temperature and reads the structs value.

④ Implements the Updatable trait using f32 type value.

⑤ Implements the one function that reads the temperature and updates the structs value.

⑥ The function only updates the value if it's been altered and changes the self.temp to the new value.

The one thing of note is the f32; why f32? This is all dependent on the type of object we are going to apply the trait to. Temperatures are used for f32; if this had been a motion sensor, we would have used a boolean. The final step is to wire this up with the configuration we initially created. In Listing 11-22, we wire up the application.

Listing 11-22. Integrates our temperature struct with the homekit

```
let thermometer = Temperature { temp : 22.2 };

// there is also a status_active
thermo.inner.temperature_sensor.inner.current_temperature.set_
readable(thermometer.clone()).unwrap();
thermo.inner.temperature_sensor.inner.current_temperature.set_
updatable(thermometer.clone()).unwrap();
```

We instantiate the struct with a default value. The set_readable and set_updatable each take as a parameter a struct that implements the Readable and Updatable trait, respectively, which in our case, the Temperature struct we created satisfies both.

With this, we would have a temperature gauge that updates and displays a default value. If you look deeper into this code, there is one question you may be asking yourself: how are we going to set it? The motion detection is based off the face detection in our video code, and the temperature is based off of the atmospheric sensor that we apply to our manager module. In order to accomplish that, we are going to make use of more tokio channels to create interactions with, so that basically we can create sending and receiving commands.

Implementing Temperature Sensor

Let's start with the temperature accessory and implement that code first. In order to make the accessory work, we are going to in the on_read call out to the manager to request it find the data for us. For this, we are going to make use of the existing channels and add an additional command. But we are also going to create a new set of channels that will allow the manager to broadcast data back to the homekit (when it's been requested). I've diagramed this interaction in Figure 11-2.

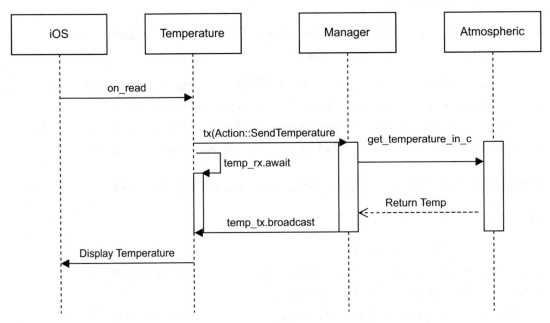

Figure 11-2. *Diagram of the interaction of the homekit with the atmospheric temperature*

We will send to the manager its own transmitter specifically for the temperature and send its corresponding receiver to the homekit so those two channels can communicate. Since this is a one-off communication channel, we don't need anything as heavy as the mpsc; instead, we will use a different channel, the toko::sync::watch; this single-producer, multi-consumer channel only retains the last value sent, which is fine for us since we only care about the most recent temperature reading. In your main.rs, you will add to the run function the code in Listing 11-23.

Listing 11-23. New channel with a default value of 25, in file src/main.rs

```
let (temp_tx, mut temp_rx) = watch::channel(25f32);
```

You will then need to pass the temp_rx to the homekit module and the temp_tx to the manager module. Inside of homekit, we won't need the on_update, since updates do not get driven from the homekit device; instead, we will just need an on_read, and in addition, the struct will not retain any value state of the temperature since we do not need to receive that information. What the struct will need to maintain is the rx and tx values that allow the cross communication. In Listing 11-24, we create the struct and our on_read call.

Listing 11-24. The Temperature struct and the Readable implementation, in file src/homekit.rs

```
pub struct Temperature {
    rx: TempRx,
    tx: Tx,
}

impl Temperature {
    fn new(mut tx: Tx, rx: TempRx) -> Temperature {
        Temperature { ①
            tx,
            rx
        }
    }
}

impl Readable<f32> for Temperature {
    fn on_read(&mut self, _: HapType) -> Option<f32> {
        debug!("On read temp.");

        //let value = get_temperature(self.tx, &mut self.rx);
        let val : f32 = get_temperature(&mut self.tx, &mut self.rx); ②

        Some(val)
    }
}
```

```
#[tokio::main]
async fn get_temperature(tx: &mut Tx, rx: &mut TempRx) -> f32 {
    send(tx, Action::SendTemperature).await; ③

    let val = rx.recv().await; ④
    val.unwrap()
}
```

① Instantiate the struct with the sender and receiver.

② Call out to our method to receive the temperature.

③ Send to the manager our request of sending the temperature.

④ Receive the value back, unwrapping and returning.

The send is the same send we used in previous sections which sends an action command. This allows us to have cross-thread communication without violating any borrowing rules and thus preserving thread and memory safety. In addition, we will need to insatiate the struct in our `initialize` in Listing 11-25.

Listing 11-25. Instantiating the temperature struct, in file src/homekit.rs

```
let thermometer = Temperature::new(temp_cmd_tx, temp_rx);
thermo.inner.temperature_sensor.inner.current_temperature.set_
readable(thermometer).unwrap();
```

Recall in a previous listing, we had already used thermo to add the accessory. The last thing to finish would be to implement the manager. This will require two updates, one creating the send_temperature method in Listing 11-26.

Listing 11-26. Creation of send_temperature function, in file src/homekit.rs

```
fn send_temperature(atmospheric: &Arc<Mutex<Atmospheric>>, temp_tx:
&TempTx) {
    let mut atmo = atmospheric.lock().unwrap();
    let temp = atmo.get_temperature_in_c();
    temp_tx.broadcast(temp);
}
```

And now in our matcher we created before, create a catch for the SendTemperature action calling the function we just created in Listing 11-27.

Listing 11-27. Creation of send_temperature function, in file src/homekit.rs

```
Action::SendTemperature => {
    send_temperature(&atmospheric, &temp_tx)
},
```

With this, your homekit will be able to get the temperature from the Pi and return it to the homekit app on your iOS device.

Implementing Motion Sensor

Let's move on to the motion sensor; the motion sensor will detect any face motion that the camera picks up. So when it detects motion, it is because you are looking at the camera, and when it doesn't, you aren't. This code will look much like the temperature code, and as you can see in Figure 11-3, it has the same basic skeleton for the call.

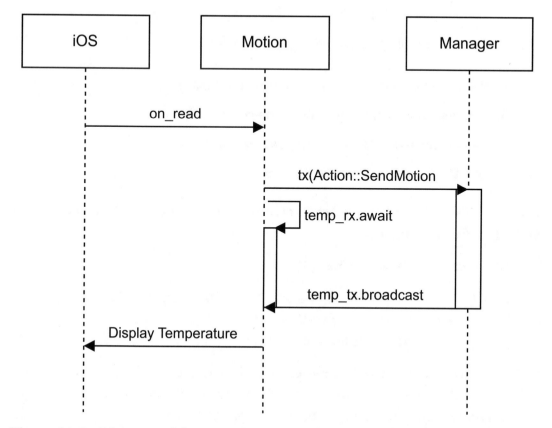

Figure 11-3. Diagram of the interaction of the homekit with motion detection

The bigger difference comes in the manager itself. The manager does not have access to other modules that it can query if there is face detection. Instead, face detection is handled in the video loop. To solve this in the video loop, we will add another channel that allows communication from the sensor back to the manager to tell the manager if a face is currently detected. In Figure 11-4, we have this loop displayed.

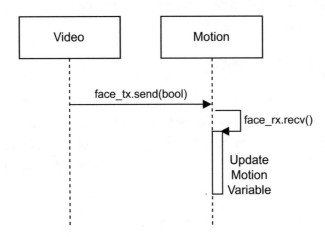

Figure 11-4. *Diagram of the signalling of a face detection*

This will require us in the main to define two more channels:

1. For notifying the manager a face is detected

2. For homekit to request knowing if a face is detected

In Listing 11-28, we add these two channels.

Listing 11-28. Adding two additional channels to communicate face and motion, in file src/homekit.rs

```
let motion_cmd_tx: Tx = tx.clone();

// basically like a watcher but we needed features that watcher didn't provide
// Single producer/ consumer for this setup
let (face_tx, face_rx) = mpsc::channel(1);

// Face detector, for single producer single consumer
// One shot cannot be used in loops it's designed for one shot
// let (motion_tx, motion_rx) = oneshot::channel::<bool>();
let (motion_tx, motion_rx) = watch::channel(false);
```

You will notice we do use the `mpsc::channel` for the face detection; this had to do with certain traits that were needed for it to work that weren't in the `watch::channel`; we did keep it as only a channel with a count of one since we only care about the most recent request. With this, we will also pass the variables to the these:

- `face_tx` – Face sender to the video module so we can send face detection updates.

- `face_rx` – Face receiver to the manager module to receive face detection status from the video.

- `motion_tx` – Motion transmitter to the manager to send back to homekit the motion status.

- `motion_rx` – Motion receiver to the homekit module to receive motion information from the manager.

Video Module

Starting with the video module, we will on every loop send an asynchronous request back to the manager on whether a face is detected. In Listing 11-29, we have a partial of the `handle_video` function.

Listing 11-29. Adding two additional channels to communicate face and motion, in file src/camera/video.rs

```
face.detect_multi_scale(
...

        // If any faces are detected send the face detection here
        if faces.len() == 0 { ①
            send(&mut face_tx, false);
        } else {
            send(&mut face_tx, true);
        }
```

①   If we do not detect faces, send false, and if we do, send true.

Manager Module

This code will feed directly into the manager module, but not within the same loop as our action. We will instead take a page out of how we used the command object by setting a variable to be used in two loops. Before we run our normal manager receiver, we will in the run function span a thread that waits for the face sender and updates the motion variable accordingly. In Listing 11-30, we have that set of code that will go at the top of run.

Listing 11-30. In the manager checking for movement, in file src/manager.rs

```rust
let motion = Arc::new(Mutex::new(false)); ①
let motion_set = motion.clone();

// Receives the motion
// Spawn a task to manage the counter
tokio::spawn(async move {
    while let Some(movement) = face_rx.recv().await {
        let mut m = motion_set.lock().unwrap(); ②
        *m = movement;
    }
});
```

  ① Sets the two variables: one to be used by the face receiver and the other for motion detection.

  ② Sets the motion variable to know if a face is detected or not.

  Now that we have the motion detected, let's go ahead while we are in the manager module and add the code similar to SendTemperature to return the motion detection. I won't go into much detail since we already covered it previously with the temperature. In Listing 11-31, we have the motion action as well as the send_motion function.

Listing 11-31. In the manager receiving the motion request and sending it, in file src/manager.rs

```rust
Action::SendMotion => {
    send_motion(&motion, &motion_tx);
}
```

...

```rust
fn send_motion(motion: &Arc<Mutex<bool>>, mut tx: &MotionTx) {
    let m = motion.lock().unwrap();
    tx.broadcast(*m);
}
```

Homekit Module

Now onto the final piece is the homekit module update. In here, we will have to implement the Readable trait for our struct and receive the motion detection back. This code is virtually identical to the temperature one except for slightly different names, and we are using a boolean instead a float 32. In Listing 11-32, we have the motion code.

Listing 11-32. The implementation of motion for the homekit, in file src/homekit.rs

```rust
pub struct Motion {
    rx: MotionRx,
    tx: Tx,
}

impl Motion {
    fn new(mut tx: Tx, rx: MotionRx) -> Motion {
        Motion {
            rx,
            tx
        }
    }
}

impl Readable<bool> for Motion {
    fn on_read(&mut self, _: HapType) -> Option<bool> {
        debug!("On read motion.");

        //let value = get_temperature(self.tx, &mut self.rx);
        let val : bool = get_motion(&mut self.tx, &mut self.rx);

        Some(val)
    }
}
```

```
#[tokio::main]
async fn get_motion(tx: &mut Tx, rx: &mut MotionRx) -> bool {
    send(tx, Action::SendMotion).await;

    let val = rx.recv().await;
    val.unwrap()
}

fn initialize(...) {
    ...
    let mut motion = motion_sensor::new(Information {
        name: "Motion".into(),
        ..Default::default()
    }).unwrap();
    let motion_detect = Motion::new(motion_cmd_tx, motion_rx);
    motion.inner.motion_sensor.inner.motion_detected.set_readable(motion_
    detect).unwrap();

    ...
}
```

That includes the motion code and the instantiation for the motion. At this point, we have all the code and pieces together to create our homekit environment; next up is to connect it to our homekit.

Adding to Homekit

Finally, let's incorporate this with Homekit; I will step you through some screenshots on how to do it. To start with, either start up your app locally or deploy to the Pi and start up from there.

Open homekit up, and on the top right-hand side, click the "+" button; you will receive options to "Add Accessory" or "Add Scene" like in Figure 11-5.

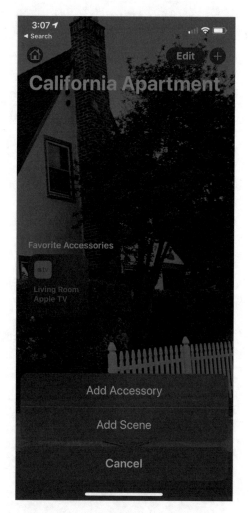

Figure 11-5. *Screenshot of the screen with add accessory*

Click "Add Accessory"; this will take you to a screen giving you multiple options. In our case, since this is a custom non-certified device, we don't have a code to scan; click "I Don't Have a Code or Cannot Scan" like in Figure 11-6.

Figure 11-6. *Screenshot to add your accessory*

Here you will display multiple options that are being broadcast from the local network. Make sure your iOS device is on the same network as the Pi, and it should show up. In Figure 11-7, you will see the "Rasp Pi".

Figure 11-7. *Available devices to add*

You will notice it has a thermostat symbol; this is decided by the category we choose in the config. Once you click it, you will get a warning that it is an "Uncertified Accessory", which is because it is a homegrown application.

Once added, you will see a message saying the Pi is being added in Figure 11-8; this is when the communication between our Pi and the Homekit starts to go up (if you run the app in debug mode, you will see messages for this).

Figure 11-8. *Adding Rasp Pi display message*

Once accepted, you will get two screens that prompt adding the sensors and to what room you want to add the sensors. In Figure 11-9, we are adding the thermostat sensor.

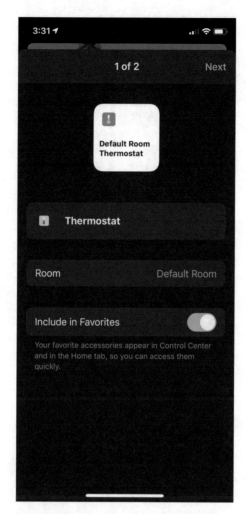

Figure 11-9. *Adding Rasp Pi thermostat sensor*

And in Figure 11-10, we are adding the motion sensor.

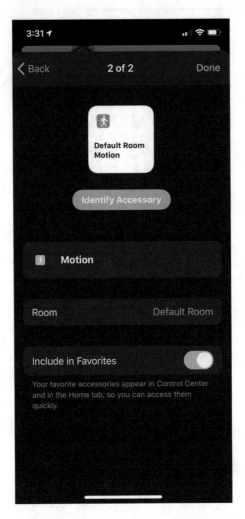

Figure 11-10. *Adding Rasp Pi motion sensor*

Finally, the sensors will now show up in Figure 11-11 showing the rest of your homekit application; this will now be interactive and talking to your Pi whenever returning.

Figure 11-11. *Our Rasp Pi sensors added the homekit application*

One note, at the time of this writing, some users have noticed on disconnect (i.e., the device is restarted) the communication between the homekit and the Pi will cease and you have to re-add it. This is a known bug that is being looked at; however, this project is a side project for the user, so I am sure they'd appreciate any help. While I wouldn't necessarily consider this production ready, for hobbyists, it works well enough and helps you extend the functionality of your Pi.

Summary

In this chapter, we mostly integrated the components we have created in the previous chapters with our cloud backend, both synchronously by sending files to an http endpoint in the upload_svc and asynchronously by processing commands for the Pi via our message queue. Using the MQ allows us to receive those commands even if the Pi is offline at the time. Finally, we provided a mechanism outside of the Pi to view our sensors for our Raspberry Pi via Homekit.

CHAPTER 12

Final Thoughts

We have touched on many topics in this book that have ranged the gauntlet in creating a full cycle IoT application in Rust. This application uses many crates, which are in various phases that I can't control and may not be compatible with future versions of Rust. My main goal for this book was to help put together a path to creating an IoT application and showing you how to make all the crates needed work together, since often I've found that the biggest challenge when creating a larger application is to get everything to play well together. Even our small application with a scope of video and a SenseHat still required quite a bit of work in the front and back to make it work. As we are at the end, I wanted to touch on one final topic. In Chapter 7, we covered deploying the application; I wanted to end with discussing how to deploy the binary.

If you are working on this for your own side project and your own Pis, you can simply deploy the application as we have been doing. For the most part, we are using a base software; we are not relying on any custom UI interfaces that have to be installed and configured. There are of course some extra libraries, and the following software have been installed:

- SenseHat library support
- OpenCV libraries
- SQLite database
- OpenSSL support

In addition, while we can reuse certificates, we do need to manually create and install the certificates for each Pi. But all of this really comes into play when dealing with a higher-scale building of IoT devices, and before we go, let's talk about that and some of the tools and techniques to install software on devices at scale.

© Joseph Faisal Nusairat 2020
J. F. Nusairat, *Rust for the IoT*, https://doi.org/10.1007/978-1-4842-5860-6_12

Custom Buildroot

First up is getting the operating system and necessary parts installed onto the device beyond a base out-of-the-box image. Buildroot uses a custom set of makefiles and configurations for creation of a Linux system intended for embedded system. We can use buildroot to custom make our Pi image complete with any customizations that we need. This allows us to start with a smaller size Linux OS and only add the libraries we want and not the one we don't. With this, we can create a final `sdcard.img` with the image we want. This image can contain all the necessary dependencies we mentioned earlier at the same versions. And if you are writing this for your own personal use, you can even embed your Wi-Fi SSID and password so that you won't have to manually add it when initializing your new Pi.

In order to use the buildroot system, you will need to download the zipped software. The software will contain all the necessary scripts to build and customize. The buildroot for Raspberry Pis can be found here: `https://buildroot.org/downloads/`; the code is updated often and you can lock yourself to an older version or use a newer version. But this gives you a baseline with the buildroot; it will build all the necessary binaries for your application.

The one trick of using the buildroot is where to build it at; if you are on a Linux computer, you can run all the commands locally and create your image from there; however, on a Mac or Windows, we will have to use a `Dockerfile` to build in a container, but be forewarned, this can be a very large container and may take some time. But the process of creating your image from the buildroot is fairly straightforward.

1. Download and uncompress the buildroot version you've chosen.

2. (Optional) Add any custom interfaces or setup.

3. (Optional) Set any flags for the makeconfig that you want to use in addition to the default ones.

4. (Optional) Update the post build script for anything that needs to be executed after the image is ready.

5. Compile the application into an image ready for being deployed to the Pi.

We will create a buildroot together that is good for running local Raspberry Pis. For our buildroot, I've done a few customizations that I will touch on, although I haven't added all the library support needed. The previous libraries will have to be added post build.

I mostly wrote this image so I would have Pi image readily available to just plug in and restart without having to hook up to the computer to manually run.

In Listing 12-1, this is the complete Docker file that will create an image with a few customizations for a good base image that allows SSH and Wi-Fi access.

Listing 12-1. Buildroot to build an image for a Raspberry Pi 4, in file Dockerfile. buildroot

```
# Set to allow us to run configuration as root
ENV FORCE_UNSAFE_CONFIGURE 1

# Get WGET and WPASupplicant we need both to setup the files
## wget is needed for the download, wpasupplicant is needed for creating
   the Root
## The rest are needed to build with the makefile

①
RUN apt-get update; \
    apt-get install -y --no-install-recommends \
    wget wpasupplicant \
    patch \
    cpio \
    python \
    ca-certificates \
    unzip rsync bc bzip2 ncurses-dev git make g++ file

# Working

②
ARG buildroot=buildroot-2019.05.3
#ARG buildroot=buildroot-2019.08.3
# not working most recent
#ARG buildroot=buildroot-2019.11.1

③
# Download the binary
RUN wget http://buildroot.org/downloads/$buildroot.tar.gz

# Uncompress it
RUN tar xvzf $buildroot.tar.gz
```

```
# Partial how to https://malware.news/t/enabling-wifi-and-converting-the-
  raspberry-pi-into-a-wifi-ap/20667

## And the Wireless Lan file
## To the interfaces directory.
RUN ls -al
RUN ls -al ./$buildroot/
RUN ls -a ./$buildroot/board/
RUN ls -a ./$buildroot/board/raspberrypi
```

④

```
COPY interfaces ./$buildroot/board/raspberrypi/interfaces

# WPA Supplicant
## https://askubuntu.com/questions/138472/how-do-i-connect-to-a-wpa-wifi-
   network-using-the-command-line
## install the wpa_passphrase and use it to create the file

## Add the Pass Phrase
## Need to make sure we have this app on the debian
## (all the other raspberrypi* are symlinks to this folder)
```

⑤

```
RUN wpa_passphrase "Nusairat Wireless" "password" >> ./$buildroot/board/
raspberrypi/wpa_supplicant.conf
RUN more ./$buildroot/board/raspberrypi/wpa_supplicant.conf

## Add items to the post build to enable the interfaces
```

⑥

```
COPY buildroot_add.txt .
RUN cat buildroot_add.txt >> ./$buildroot/board/raspberrypi/post-build.sh
RUN more ./$buildroot/board/raspberrypi/post-build.sh

# Need to enable certain options available for the WPA Supplicant
COPY added_options.txt .
RUN cat added_options.txt >> ./$buildroot/configs/raspberrypi4_defconfig
RUN echo "RasPi Config :: " && more ./$buildroot/configs/raspberrypi4_
defconfig
```

⑦

```
# Adjust base on using a Pi 3 or 4
RUN cd $buildroot && \
    make raspberrypi4_defconfig

# This is the big run
RUN cd $buildroot && \
    make
```

① Install necessary debian libraries that we will need to use to compile and build the image.

② Set the version of the buildroot we are planning to use.

③ Download and unzip the buildroot image.

④ Copy over custom interfaces for the Pi board.

⑤ Use the wpa_passphrase to generate the wpa_supplicant file needed to have the Wi-Fi SSID and password on the board by default.

⑥ Copy our custom buildroot which targets the interfaces and packages we need for the Pi.

⑦ Make config the Pi for Raspberry Pi 4 and build the image.

Note the last step will take quite a bit of time; it could even be over an hour depending on your computer's speed and the docker resources. You will notice that we did three customizations for this Dockerfile that brought in external files. Let's examine each of these files and the customizations.

First off are the interfaces in Listing 12-2; this will add in the wpa-supplicant we created in the docker file and allow us to have wireless connectivity. By default, with the buildroot only Ethernet connection is supported.

Listing 12-2. Wireless interfaces for the buildroot

```
# RustIOT :: Interfaces added
auto lo
iface lo inet loopback
    auto eth0
```

```
iface eth0 inet dhcp
    pre-up /etc/network/nfs_check
```

```
wait-delay 15
```

```
auto wlan0
iface wlan0 inet dhcp
    pre-up wpa_supplicant -B -Dnl80211 -iwlan0 -c/etc/wpa_supplicant.conf
    post-down killall -q wpa_supplicant
```

```
wait-delay 15
```

```
iface default inet dhcp
```

Next up, in Listing 12-3 is the buildroot medications; these will copy configurations and others from our local to the eventual image. By default, you don't necessarily need to do this, and there is a default configuration. But we need to also add our wpa supplication and interfaces.

Listing 12-3. Package copying for the buildroot

```
# RustIOT :: Buildroot add additions
cp package/busybox/S10mdev ${TARGET_DIR}/etc/init.d/S10mdev
chmod 755 ${TARGET_DIR}/etc/init.d/S10mdev
cp package/busybox/mdev.conf ${TARGET_DIR}/etc/mdev.conf
cp board/raspberrypi4/interfaces ${TARGET_DIR}/etc/network/interfaces
cp board/raspberrypi4/wpa_supplicant.conf ${TARGET_DIR}/etc/wpa_supplicant.conf
#
```

And last up, we are adding extra configurations for the makefile config. The additions in Listing 12-4 are used to add the wireless support, enable SSH root login access, and set the password. By default, root SSH access is not available, which would mean we would only be able to log in by an attached keyboard and monitor.

Listing 12-4. Makefile build options for the buildroot

```
BR2_ROOTFS_DEVICE_CREATION_DYNAMIC_MDEV=y
BR2_PACKAGE_RPI_WIFI_FIRMWARE=y
BR2_PACKAGE_WPA_SUPPLICANT=y
BR2_PACKAGE_WPA_SUPPLICANT=y
```

```
BR2_PACKAGE_WPA_SUPPLICANT_NL80211=y
BR2_PACKAGE_WPA_SUPPLICANT_PASSPHRASE=y
# Needed for the DHCP Clients
#BR2_PACKAGE_DHCP_CLIENT=y

# Add SSH
BR2_PACKAGE_OPENSSH=y
BR2_TARGET_ENABLE_ROOT_LOGIN=y
BR2_TARGET_GENERIC_ROOT_PASSWD="1234"

# Set the size of the ROOTFS
BR2_TARGET_ROOTFS_EXT2_SIZE="132G"
```

Once the build is complete, you will have on the docker image a usable SD card image in the Dockerfile. In order to pull the image created by the Dockerfile, you will have to attach a running container and copy the file locally. In Listing 12-5, we run through the command-line steps to copy the file from the running container to the local filesystem.

Listing 12-5. Retrieving the `sdcard.img` from the docker container

```
➜ docker build -t br_test -f Dockerfile.buildroot  .
➜ docker create -ti --name dummy br_test bash
    7e8846c0a1a4437c1b467d4ebec1c31746c344bc94ad3597dd43f9c9a81b7354
➜ docker cp
7e8846c0a1a4437c1b467d4ebec1c31746c344bc94ad3597dd43f9c9a81b7354:/
buildroot-2019.05.3/output/images/sdcard.img ~/buildroot/sdcard.img
docker rm -f dummy
```

The key is when you create the image, it will output a long id of the image; you use that as a reference to pull from the directory structure of the image we created on the dockerfile. And then remove the running container once finished. Ideally, this kind of automated process can be put inside CI build system, and obviously after this, you will have to write the image to put the image onto the SD cards like we did in Chapter 7.

Provisioning the Application

Finally, we need to put the application onto the board along with the certs and a device id. This is where it becomes a bit more variable. You wouldn't want to wrap custom certs into an image; that is just overly expensive. Ideally, the certificates should be created ahead of time, even batched up so you always have many to pick from. Then when you are ready to provision the board, you can push them directly on to either the card itself or onto a provisioned board. In general, you'd want to then start up the application and run through some scripts to make sure everything works. This burn in process is designed to test the board, makes sure the certificates work, and makes sure all the applications work as designed. Here, you'd assign the device id either via automated script or by calling out to backend servers to realize this board is active and legitimate. This burn in process also helps detect any defects in the hardware and allows you to remove that board before it's sold to a consumer or used by yourself.

Last Words

Books are a labor of love, and countless hours away from friends and family to write, this book was over a year in the making and I took quite a few pivots during the process based on what was available and ready. And I believed for good memory management, security, and beauty of code, Rust allows for amazing IoT projects to be created. Good luck.

Index

© Joseph Faisal Nusairat 2020
J. F. Nusairat, *Rust for the IoT*, https://doi.org/10.1007/978-1-4842-5860-6

Printed in the United States
By Bookmasters